This is the first intellectual biography of the eighteenth-century French composer and theorist Jean-Philippe Rameau. Rameau is widely recognized as the founder of tonal harmonic theory. Through his principle of the fundamental bass, Rameau was able to explicate the structure of tonal music with unprecedented concision and clarity, earning himself in his day the popular accolade "Newton of Harmony."

Ranging widely over the musical and intellectual thought of the eighteenth century, Thomas Christensen orients Rameau's accomplishments in light of contemporaneous traditions of music theory as well as many scientific ideas current in the French Enlightenment. Rameau is revealed to be an unsuspectedly syncretic and sophisticated thinker, betraying influences ranging from neo-platonic thought and Cartesian mechanistic metaphysics to Locke's empirical psychology and Newtonian experimental science. Additional primary documents (many revealed here for the first time) help clarify Rameau's fascinating and stormy relationship with the Encyclopedists: Diderot, Rousseau, and d'Alembert.

TITLES IN THIS SERIES

1 *Haydn's "Farewell" Symphony and the Idea of Classical Style*: James Webster
2 *Ernst Kurth: Selected Writings*: Lee A. Rothfarb
3 *The Musical Dilettante: A Treatise on Composition by J. F. Daube*: Susan P. Snook-Luther
4 *Rameau and Musical Thought in the Enlightenment*: Thomas Christensen

CAMBRIDGE STUDIES IN
MUSIC THEORY
AND ANALYSIS

GENERAL EDITOR: IAN BENT

RAMEAU AND MUSICAL THOUGHT
IN THE ENLIGHTENMENT

Portrait of Rameau engraved by J. J. Benoist after J. Restout, 1771

RAMEAU
AND MUSICAL THOUGHT
IN THE ENLIGHTENMENT

THOMAS CHRISTENSEN
Associate Professor of Music, University of Iowa

PUBLISHED BY THE PRESS SYNDICATE OF THE UNIVERSITY OF CAMBRIDGE
The Pitt Building, Trumpington Street, Cambridge, United Kingdom

CAMBRIDGE UNIVERSITY PRESS
The Edinburgh Building, Cambridge CB2 2RU, UK
40 West 20th Street, New York NY 10011–4211, USA
477 Williamstown Road, Port Melbourne, VIC 3207, Australia
Ruiz de Alarcón 13, 28014 Madrid, Spain
Dock House, The Waterfront, Cape Town 8001, South Africa

http://www.cambridge.org

© Cambridge University Press 1993

This book is in copyright. Subject to statutory exception
and to the provisions of relevant collective licensing agreements,
no reproduction of any part may take place without
the written permission of Cambridge University Press.

First published 1993
Reprinted 1995
First paperback edition 2004

A catalogue record for this book is available from the British Library

Library of Congress cataloguing in publication data

Christensen, Thomas Street.
Rameau and Musical Thought in the Enlightenment / Thomas Christensen.
p. cm. – (Cambridge studies in music theory and analysis: 4)
Includes bibliographical references and index.
ISBN 0 521 42040 7 (hardback)
1. Rameau, Jean-Philippe, 1683–1764 – Criticism and interpretation.
2. Music – France – 18th century – History and criticism. 3. Music –
theory – 18th century. 4. Enlightenment – France. I. title.
II. Series.
ML410.R2C5 1993
784.2' 092' –dc20   92–39886 CIP

ISBN 0 521 42040 7 hardback
ISBN 0 521 61709 X paperback

To the memory of my mother
Katharine McCarroll Christensen (1923–1967)

CONTENTS

	List of illustrations	*page* xi
	Foreword by Ian Bent	xiii
	Acknowledgments	xvii
	Introduction	1
1	Rameau and the Enlightenment	5
2	Rameau as music theorist	21
3	Precursors of harmonic theory	43
4	The generative fundamental	71
5	The fundamental bass	103
6	The *corps sonore*	133
7	Mode and modulation	169
8	Rameau and the philosophes	209
9	D'Alembert	252
10	The final years	291
	Appendix 1 A note on harmonic and arithmetic proportions	307
	Appendix 2 "L'Art de la basse fondamentale" and Gianotti's *Le Guide du compositeur*	309
	Select bibliography	313
	Index of subjects	321
	Index of proper names	323

ILLUSTRATIONS

PLATES

	Portrait of Rameau engraved by J. J. Benoist after J. Restout, 1771. Reproduced by permission of the Bibliothèque Nationale	*frontispiece*
1.1	"Le Triomphe de Rameau." Engraving by C. N. Cochin *fils*. Reproduced by permission of the Bibliothèque Nationale	*page* 10
2.1	Title page to the *Traité de l'harmonie*	27
3.1	Table and transposition of "scale triads"	48
3.2	Rameau's figured-bass notation for Corelli's sonata Op. 5 no. 3	59
4.1	Fludd's monochord	73
4.2	Zarlino's syntonic-diatonic division of the octave	75
4.3	*Traité*, 4. Rameau's string divisions	92
4.4	*Traité*, 36. Rameau's demonstration of the inversional equivalence of triads	97
5.1	*Nouveau système*, 80–81. Opening of Rameau's analysis of the monologue from Lully's *Armide*	121
6.1	An illustration of Newton's "experimentum crucis" demonstrating the refraction of light into a spectrum of seven colors. From Abbé Pluche, *Le Spectacle de la nature* (Paris, 1732), IV, 164	143
6.2	Voltaire's correlation between Newton's color spectrum and the seven notes of the diatonic scale	144
6.3	Illustration of some acoustical experiments from Abbé Nollet, *Leçons de physique experimentale* (Amsterdam, 1745), III, 438	147
7.1	*Génération harmonique*, Plate 6	183
7.2	*Génération harmonique*, 43	185
7.3	Voltaire and Rameau engraved by C. de Tersan. Reproduced by permission of the Bibliothèque Nationale	188
7.4	*Démonstration*, Plate C	196
7.5	*Démonstration*, Plate M	204
7.6	*Démonstration*, Plate N	205
8.1	Briseux's *Traité du beau*, Plate 32	234
9.1	An engraving of Jean Le Rond d'Alembert; engraver unknown	254
9.2	Title page to the first edition of d'Alembert's *Elémens de musique* (1752)	258
10.1	Frontispiece to the *Code de Musique* (1760)	293

FIGURES

4.1	Descartes's first monochord division	78
4.2	Descartes's second monochord division	79
4.3	Rameau's revised illustration of his monochord division	91
6.1	Taylor's formula for the fundamental frequency of a vibrating string	135
6.2	Modes of a string's movement when loaded by two or three weights	151
6.3	A vibrating string at time t and t'	153
7.1	Summary of Rameau's derivation from the *corps sonore*	208
10.1	The derivation of sevenths by interlocking harmonic and arithmetic proportions	300

FOREWORD BY IAN BENT

Theory and analysis are in one sense reciprocals: if analysis opens up a musical structure or style to inspection, inventorying its components, identifying its connective forces, providing a description adequate to some live experience, then theory generalizes from such data, predicting what the analyst will find in other cases within a given structural or stylistic orbit, devising systems by which other works – as yet unwritten – might be generated. Conversely, if theory intuits how musical systems operate, then analysis furnishes feedback to such imaginative intuitions, rendering them more insightful. In this sense, they are like two hemispheres that fit together to form a globe (or cerebrum!), functioning deductively as investigation and abstraction, inductively as hypothesis and verification, and in practice forming a chain of alternating activities.

Professionally, on the other hand, "theory" now denotes a whole subdiscipline of the general field of musicology. Analysis often appears to be a subordinate category within the larger activity of theory. After all, there is theory that does not require analysis. Theorists may engage in building systems or formulating strategies for use by composers; and these almost by definition have no use for analysis. Others may conduct experimental research into the sound-materials of music or the cognitive processes of the human mind, to which analysis may be wholly inappropriate. And on the other hand, historians habitually use analysis as a tool for understanding the classes of compositions – repertories, "outputs," works, versions, sketches, and so forth – that they study. Professionally, then, our ideal image of twin hemispheres is replaced by an intersection: an area that exists in common between two subdisciplines. Seen from this viewpoint, analysis reciprocates in two directions: with certain kinds of theoretical inquiry, and with certain kinds of historical inquiry. In the former case, analysis has tended to be used in rather orthodox modes, in the latter in a more eclectic fashion; but that does not mean that analysis in the service of theory is necessarily more exact, more "scientific," than analysis in the service of history.

The above epistemological excursion is by no means irrelevant to the present series. Cambridge Studies in Music Theory and Analysis is intended to present the work of theorists and of analysts. It has been designated to include "pure" theory – that is, theoretical formulation with a minimum of analytical exemplification; "pure" analysis – that is, practical analysis with a minimum of theoretical underpinning; and writings that fall at points along the spectrum between the two extremes. In these capacities, it aims to illuminate music, as work and as process.

However, theory and analysis are not the exclusive preserves of the present day. As subjects in their own right, they are diachronic. The former is coeval with the very study of music itself, and extends far beyond the confines of Western culture; the latter, defined broadly, has several centuries of past practice. Moreover, they have been dynamic, not static, fields throughout their histories. Consequently, studying earlier music through the eyes of its own contemporary theory helps us to escape (when we need to, not that we should make a dogma out of it) from the preconceptions of our own age. Studying earlier analyses does this too, and in a particularly sharply focused way; at the same time it gives us the opportunity to re-evaluate past analytical methods for present purposes, such as is happening currently, for example, with the long-despised methods of hermeneutic analysis of the late nineteenth century. The series thus includes editions and translations of major works of past theory, and also studies in the history of theory.

That Rameau is the most significant figure in the music theory of the modern (i.e. post-medieval) era is generally accepted today. His impact on musical thought since his time has been monumental. His ideas provided a battle ground over which theorists fought for a century and a half after his death. His insights into the nature of music, brilliant and sophisticated in their day, withstood the assaults of his opponents and retain their potency for us now. Every theorist and analyst of the twentieth century is influenced by his ideas, whether consciously or unconsciously, and is conditioned by his frame of reference.

Our view of Rameau's work is, however, a stereotype. His ideas have been purveyed in a succession of simplified forms, the first being those by d'Alembert in his *Elémens de musique* of 1752 and by Rousseau and d'Alembert in the first volumes of the *Encyclopédie* in 1751. Knowledge of his original writings is nowadays largely restricted to the first of his treatises, the *Traité de l'harmonie* of 1722. This is not surprising. For a start, the discourse of French eighteenth-century music theory is unreadable without highly specialized historical knowledge. Secondly, Rameau's own use of vocabulary is inconsistent, his syntax notoriously unclear, and his capacity for organization low. Thirdly, while the treatises subsequent to the *Traité* introduced important new observations, they did so amidst a welter of revisions, modifications and recantations that failed to yield at the end of his life a definitive "theory" or even a stable formulation.

Thomas Christensen's study is the first to present a picture of Rameau's theoretical work in its totality, including materials discovered only in recent years. It provides for the first time a lucid chronological unfolding of Rameau's ideas from before 1722 in notes now lost, through his treatises, letters, polemics and other writings, right to his death in 1764. It teases the meanings out of Rameau's intractable language, and carries us effortlessly along his laborious quest for ultimate theoretical codification. In the course of this journey, it builds up a fascinating picture of Rameau the man, and portrays vividly his contemporary proponents and antagonists. It completely rethinks Rameau's relationship to previous music theory, relates his work skillfully to music practice, and – perhaps above all – succeeds in setting Rameau's ideas and aspirations deep in the intellectual currents of his day, not only interpreting them as the product of a tension between Newtonian empiricism and Cartesian systematization, but also subtly showing how many different modes of thought and methodologies went to make up Rameau's complex world of ideas.

ACKNOWLEDGMENTS

This book is one I almost never wrote. While for many years I have been reading and publishing articles on the music theory of Rameau, when I began to pen a draft of this book in the summer of 1989 I had a quite different plan in mind. Specifically, I wished to write a "reception history" of Rameau's theory in Germany during the eighteenth century. It had always struck me as paradoxical that German theorists like Kirnberger expressed such hostility toward Rameau, yet at the same time incorporated the basic tenets of his fundamental bass in their own theories. At the same time, ostensible disciples of Rameau like Marpurg proved upon closer examination to have distorted many of his most important ideas.

I was fortunate enough to receive generous support from the American Council of Learned Societies and the Fulbright Foundation to pursue research on this question in East Germany during the academic year 1989–90. Amidst the dizzying political and social turmoil of that exhilarating period of history, with its street demonstrations, transportation strikes, collapsing governments, and eventual tumbling walls, I somehow managed to find spare moments and energy to carry on research in various archives and libraries in East Berlin, Dresden, and Leipzig. In the course of trying to explicate the German theorists' complex interpretation of Rameau's ideas, I kept finding myself having to return to Rameau's own writings in order to analyze his thoughts on a given topic, and examine their connection to indigenous French intellectual currents of the eighteenth century. Little by little the prefatory and background material of my study assumed ever larger proportions. After my return to the States in 1990, it soon became clear to me that a separate study was demanded, one in which all of Rameau's theoretical arguments would be not only analyzed systematically but oriented historically within the rich contexts of the French Enlightenment. The present book will, I hope, satisfy this need. I look forward as a future project to fulfilling my original promise made to my funding sources and completing the *Rezeptionsgeschichte* of Rameau's theory I began in 1989.

In the course of writing this book, I have accrued many debts – both of a material and an intellectual nature. Again I must cite the catalyst of the fellowships offered me in 1989 by the ACLS and the Fulbright Foundation. Without their support, as well as that of the University of Pennsylvania in providing me leave support, I should not have found the time for beginning this project. Numerous librarians and archivists both here and abroad have also made my research much easier. For their collective help they have my sincere thanks.

While trying to sort out many of Rameau's most infuriatingly oblique theoretical ideas, I have had the benefit of many enlightening and good-humored conversations with Professor Joel Lester of the City University of New York. I owe another intellectual debt to Professor David Lewin of Harvard University, although he might be surprised to hear this. I was fortunate enough to write my doctoral dissertation under his guidance while a graduate student at Yale University. It was from David that I first discovered that Rameau still had a number of worthwhile things to say to music theorists today. His scholarship has continually been a model of inspiration and emulation for my own work with its judicious balance of analytic rigor and historical nuance. I am grateful to Jeanne Nickelsburg for her help in editing the final manuscript. Finally, I should like to thank the staff of Cambridge University Press for their help. Penny Souster has expertly supervised the arduous production of this book with patience and good cheer. Ian Bent, as series editor, has from the beginning been an enthusiastic supporter of this project. He has been ever willing to offer his sound counsel, and at the more difficult moments of production, his encouragement and consolation.

A few sections of this book, particularly Chapters 6, 7, and 9, have been extracted and revised from material contained in three earlier articles of mine: "Eighteenth-Century Science and the *corps sonore*: The Scientific Background to Rameau's Principle of Harmony," *Journal of Music Theory* 31/1 (1986): 23–50; "Rameau's 'L'Art de la basse fondamentale,'" *Music Theory Spectrum* 9 (1987): 18–41; and "Music Theory as Scientific Propaganda: The Case of D'Alembert's *Elémens de musique*," *Journal of the History of Ideas* 50 (1989): 409–27. My thanks to the editors of these journals for their permission to quote some of this material.

INTRODUCTION

If there is one music theorist whose writings are truly deserving of that overused cachet "revolutionary," it must surely' be Jean-Philippe Rameau. Since the appearance of his *Traité de l'harmonie* in 1722, both the conceptualization and the pedagogy of tonal music have been profoundly altered. With his system of the *basse fondamentale* (the "fundamental bass"), Rameau was able to clarify the harmonic practice of his contemporaries with unparalleled concision, and, in turn, radically simplify the pedagogy of the thorough bass and composition. Through Rameau's pioneering efforts, the study of harmonic coherence assumed a central position in the program of music theory, a position it has retained relatively unchallenged to this day.

Yet despite his acknowledged position as the founder of tonal harmonic theory, Rameau's accomplishments have proven resistant to any uniform historical assessment. In the past, many historians of music have depreciated Rameau's theoretical writings in comparison to his operatic compositions, evidently feeling that they lacked the import of his music, and at the very least, with their perceived scientific sterility and speculative abstractions, reflected badly upon the composer who possessed such an otherwise sublime artistic sensibility.[1]

But even for those historians who have been more sympathetic towards Rameau's theoretical work, pinning down just what this theory consisted of has been no simple task. Rameau never succinctly summarized his theory, or at least not without further revision in later writings. Over the course of some forty years and a dozen major publications, Rameau was constantly working out his system of harmony, seeking out and testing new and ever-changing theoretical arguments. Many of these theoretical arguments were inspired by contemporaneous science. In virtually all of his theoretical writings, Rameau attempted to apply the methods, evidence,

---

[1] Hence Cuthbert Girdlestone includes only a short and error-filled résumé of Rameau's theory at the end of his important biography, with the excuse that "Rameau lives for us through his music, and through his music only," adding, "if he had never 'speculated' at all, we should not feel impoverished and the history of music would not have been very different" (Cuthbert Girdlestone, *Jean-Philippe Rameau: His Life and Work*, 2nd edition [New York, 1969], 519). These are astonishing statements to make considering the relative neglect Rameau's operas have suffered (at least until very recently) in comparison to the widespread dissemination and influence his theory has enjoyed. I would hazard that far more musicians today are familiar with, say, the notion of the subdominant or the theory of chordal inversion than they are with the music of *Castor et Pollux* or *Le Temple de la Gloire*.

and language of science as he understood it – but with distinctly mixed results. For all of the composer's profound and sensitive insights into the nature of tonal harmony, his scientific arguments could be filled with embarrassing errors of empirical observation and flaws in reasoning. The mathematical "demonstrations" and acoustical "experiments" he offered to establish his principle of harmony can seem inept and naive to us today, and, indeed, were often condemned as just that by scientists of his own day. Compounding the problem is Rameau's turgid and repetitive prose, which is as uninviting in the original French as it is in any translation. The result is a difficult and unwieldy body of literature that has frustrated redaction by even the most sympathetic of Rameau's readers, both past and present.

Historians of music theory have thus found themselves facing an unhappy choice. On the one hand, they could try to wade intrepidly through the maze of Rameau's writings, chronicle the many twists and turns of his thought, and bear as patiently as possible his scientific pretensions. On the other hand, historians could attempt to extract an essential theoretical "core" from his writings, and do what the composer himself never seemed to be able to do: settle upon a single, consistent, and coherent doctrine, distilled of all extraneous scientific baggage.

The British music historian Matthew Shirlaw opted for the first approach in his 1917 history of harmonic theory.[2] In probably the most systematic and sympathetic reading Rameau has ever received, Shirlaw produced a comprehensive – and to this day unrivaled – analysis of the composer's theory. Shirlaw closely followed the most abstruse of Rameau's theoretical arguments down every by-way and cul-de-sac. At the same time, he tried to give a fair hearing to Rameau's scientific arguments, although he was often quick to note his displeasure with many of these. The result is a richly-detailed exposition that reveals much of the power and originality of Rameau's thought, as well as its obvious shortcomings.

But the result makes a frustrating read. However sympathetic Shirlaw tries to make his hero out to be, we are confronted with a fickle-minded theorist who cannot seem to make up his mind on any subject, and worse, muddled his theory with extraneous scientific arguments. Despite what he probably wished to convey, Shirlaw left us with a picture of a brilliant musician who unfortunately allowed himself to trespass intellectual territory where he manifestly appeared to have no business or competence.

These problems have prompted the second kind of historiography I referred to above, wherein Rameau's thought is reduced to an essential "core." This is actually the oldest approach taken by historians of theory, one that can be traced back to the earliest popularizations of Rameau's theory by d'Alembert and Rousseau. The historian begins by selecting a single text as canonic (often the *Traité de l'harmonie*), or by amalgamating diverse parts of different texts into one whole. At this point, the historian might then demarcate Rameau's theory into a "core" of fundamental propositions and arguments, and a secondary periphery of auxiliary hypotheses, evidence, and corollaries that are ultimately not essential to the heuristic value of

---

[2] Matthew Shirlaw, *The Theory of Harmony* (London, 1917).

the core.³ In other words, this historian operates on the assumption that there is a relatively stable set of primary empirical axioms that comprise the essence of Rameau's musical theory (normally consisting of the generation and behavior of the fundamental bass) that must be distinguished from the shifting scientific "rhetoric" he added on their behalf. Such rhetoric, the argument goes, is really a superficial addition irrelevant to the "pure" musical content of Rameau's theory, and can thus be parenthesized – if not eliminated – without any impairment to the theory.⁴

As the reader has probably gathered, I believe both these historiographical methods to be flawed. For in neither one is a really comfortable place found for Rameau's "science." At best, his scientific rhetoric is patronizingly seen as a capitulation to modish ideas clumsily applied by the untutored composer, but ultimately unrelated to his real musical thought. At worst, it is sinisterly viewed as a pernicious obfuscation that should be excised from any consideration of his theory; it is the deplorable product of the vain composer's desire to secure credibility and approbation from his peers through unnecessary and ultimately disingenuous intellectual posturing.

I would maintain, however, that far from being either fashion or obfuscation, Rameau's scientific arguments were critical to the conception and evolution of his theory, and consequently indispensable for our own understanding of it. As I hope to show in the following study, eighteenth-century science provided the essential epistemological models and language by which Rameau conceived and articulated his ideas. To pretend that this can be somehow separated from that theory without distortion is, I believe, deeply naive and misguided. I am convinced that we must take into serious and sympathetic consideration the various scientific rhetorics of Rameau's theoretical arguments, however strange or incongruous they may appear to us today, or however discordant they may seem to be with one another.

We can begin such a process by first situating the composer in that turbulent intellectual vortex known as the French Enlightenment, and then attempting to uncover the sources, motivations, and resonance of his theoretical enterprise. This I will try to do in Chapter 1 of the present study. Many of the "problems" he addressed, the myriad solutions at which he arrived, and the language by which he expressed these solutions will be much more intelligible when seen against the colorful and changing intellectual background of the eighteenth-century French Enlightenment. Above all, the constant recourse to scientific argumentation that runs through his writings will be seen as more than a clumsily applied patina. Rameau understood the science of his day far better than he is usually given credit for. In later chapters, I shall be identifying and analyzing the many differing scientific and philosophical ideas that influenced Rameau's rhetoric: Cartesianism

---

3 My description is an appropriation from one of Thomas Kuhn's many characterizations of an orthodox scientific paradigm. *The Structure of Scientific Revolutions*, 2nd edition (Chicago, 1970).
4 Typical of this approach are those nineteenth-century historians of theory most influenced by positivist ideologies like Fétis and Riemann. Other more recent attempts to provide a coherent synopsis of Rameau's theory are by Joan Ferris, "The Evolution of Rameau's Harmonic Theories," *Journal of Music Theory* 3/1 (1959), 231–55; and Hans Pischner, *Die Harmonielehre Jean-Philippe Rameaus* (Leipzig, 1963).

(Chapter 2), Mersenne's neoplatonism (Chapter 4), materialist mechanism (Chapter 5), experimental physics (Chapter 6), Newton's theory of gravity (Chapter 7), Locke's sensationalist epistemology (Chapter 8), and pantheistic and occasionalist doctrines (Chapter 10). In many respects, we will see how Rameau's theory is a surprisingly reliable intellectual barometer of Enlightenment thought. Many of the issues raised by Rameau's efforts to construct a fully scientific music theory will be brought together for final reconsideration in Chapter 9 when we look at the reception and critique of his theory by one of the most important scientists and philosophers of the eighteenth century, Jean Le Rond d'Alembert. Of course Rameau's theory was not simply a composite of contemporaneous intellectual ideas. Rameau was dealing with real musical problems – both empirical and pedagogical – that enjoyed a long pedigree in music theory. We will see in Chapters 3 and 4 how much the concept of the fundamental bass owed to traditional *musica theorica*, and how many of his specific harmonic formulations can be traced to a practice already codified in many seventeenth-century French thorough-bass and composition texts.

What makes Rameau's theory such a fascinating and rewarding subject for investigation, I believe, is the rich dialectical interplay it manifests between musical and cultural forces, between the "internal" problems of musical practice and pedagogy that he addressed, and the "external" ideas and language indigenous to the French Enlightenment by which he solved them. To reveal this dialectic, the historian must move back and forth in a kind of counterpoint between Rameau's texts and his social-cultural contexts. This is what I hope to have accomplished in the present study. While I have not been able to resolve all of the underlying tensions created by such a dialectical approach, I think the picture that emerges over the following pages better captures the richness of his theoretical thought. Finally, I hope it conveys to the reader the sheer magnitude of Rameau's accomplishments in his having identified and explicated the salient features of an emerging tonal language using intellectual models and languages that, while intrinsic to the culture of the French Enlightenment, have remained surprisingly resilient and resonant over some two and a half centuries.

1

RAMEAU AND THE ENLIGHTENMENT

La musique de Rameau est un des exemples de beautés neuves toujours regrettées par quelquesuns. C'est le Newtonisme de la musique, qui essuie les mêmes contradictions, et qui remportera peut-être la même victoire.

Terrasson

No musical personality has been more closely identified with the eighteenth-century French Enlightenment, nor thought to have epitomized more fully its intellectual character, than the composer-theorist Jean-Philippe Rameau (1683–1764). In an age when nature was widely believed to have a rational order and mechanical basis, Rameau's success in explaining the complex empirical practice of music by a single natural principle was seen as an outstanding achievement.

The principle Rameau discovered, first enunciated in his monumental *Traité de l'harmonie* of 1722, was the *basse fondamentale* – the fundamental bass.[1] Without yet involving ourselves in the technical details of his theory, we can let the following generalization suffice as a workable description:

Rameau argued that all music is foundationally harmonic in structure. Every harmony (or chord) is generated from a single fundamental (or what we call today a chord "root") in some consistent way. In the *Traité*, this way was monochord (string) divisions, while in later writings it was the acoustical phenomenon of harmonic upper partials generated by many vibrating systems (the *corps sonore*). By manipulating the various ratios and proportions of his monochord divisions and *corps sonore*, Rameau was able with more or less success to account for all of the harmonies commonly employed in French Baroque practice. Moreover, by reducing most chord-root motion to a simple cadential paradigm of a dissonant seventh chord resolving to a consonant triad, he was able to show how the succession of chord fundamentals imitated these same ratios and proportions. From this mechanistic basis, all other musical parameters – melody, counterpoint, mode, and even rhythm – could be seen as derivative. Thus, both the vocabulary and grammar of tonal music appeared to stem from the same natural numerical acoustical source.

---

[1] Jean-Philippe Rameau, *Traité de l'harmonie réduite à ses principes naturels* (Paris, 1722); reproduced in volume one of *The Complete Theoretical Writings of Jean-Philippe Rameau (1683–1764)*, ed. Erwin R. Jacobi, 6 vols. (American Institute of Musicology, 1967–72); hereafter cited as *CTW*.

Of course Rameau's theory was not quite as simple as all this. His system of the fundamental bass suffered from a number of problems, both logical and empirical. And over the forty remaining years of his life after the publication of the *Traité de l'harmonie*, Rameau strove energetically to resolve these problems. Nonetheless, the essential arguments of his theory proved persuasive. Musicians found Rameau's theory invaluable in simplifying the pedagogy of composition and thorough bass. Laurent Gervais, the author of an elementary treatise on thorough bass, marveled at the obstacles Rameau faced:

It was not very long ago that a means was found to reduce accompaniment to certain principles. Those that were previously followed proved to be so confusing and often unreliable that one's attention was perpetually shackled. It was necessary to recall all the rules by which a bass could form different progressions. The student was always struggling, and only after a number of years of work could he attain a modicum of confidence, more from the habits of the ear than from well-established principles. . . It was left for someone to simplify practice by reducing the large number of chords to a few that are easy and familiar from the first lessons. This is what M. Rameau did in his learned *Traité de l'harmonie* with the *basse fondamentale*.[2]

But Rameau's theory was not only important to music pedagogues; it also enjoyed an extraordinarily widespread and favorable reception among educated non-musicians of the time, particularly among that informal circle of *hommes des lettres* and cultural critics known as the "philosophes."[3] What impressed the philosophes about Rameau's theory had less to do with any putative musical value of the fundamental bass than the confirmation it gave to their collective epistemologies; Rameau's theory appeared to them to be a model of judicious philosophy, validating their conviction that nature was governed by a small number of quantifiable and interconnected mechanistic principles that could be discovered through careful analysis and calculation. Thus, the Abbé de Condillac, the leading critic of seventeenth-century rationalist philosophy, could praise Rameau's theory as an exemplar of the empirical *esprit systématique* "in which experience provides or confirms the principles. . .[Rameau's system] appears to me to be a model of this genre; order, clarity, and precision are its characteristics."[4]

The mathematician-philosophe Jean Le Rond d'Alembert agreed with Condillac. In his celebrated *Discours préliminaire* to the *Encyclopédie*, d'Alembert hailed Rameau the opera composer as a "génie, mâle, hardi, et fécond," adding:

But what more specifically distinguishes him is the fact that he has very successfully pondered on the theory of music; that he has been capable of finding the principle of harmony and of melody in the [fundamental bass], that by this method he has reduced to

---

2 Laurent Gervais, *Méthode pour l'accompagnement du clavecin* (Paris, 1733), Avertissement.
3 Following the lead of most recent Enlightenment historians, I will retain the richly connotative French designation *philosophe* without the cumbersome italics.
4 Approbation to Jean Le Rond d'Alembert, *Elémens de musique théorique et pratique* (Paris, 1752), 172.

more certain and more simple laws a science which was formerly given over to arbitrary rules, or rules dictated by blind experiment.[5]

The important music lexicographer and historian Jean Benjamin de Laborde concurred:

Rameau appeared and dispelled this chaos. He brought at once clarity and order, revealed the mysteries of the art, and reduced music to general principles. Finally, he offered a fecund system in which all the parts reciprocally clarified and fortified one another . . .[6]

THE "NEWTON OF MUSIC" . . .

As the enthusiastic commendations of Condillac, d'Alembert, and de Laborde all suggest, Rameau's theory of music was seen as a *scientific* system. In both method and structure, it was frequently compared to Newton's systematization of celestial mechanics and optics. Newton's great accomplishment, historians of science have frequently reminded us, was not so much one of discovery as synthesis. In his monumental *Philosophiae Naturalis Principia Mathematica* of 1687, Newton profoundly reinterpreted and reduced the received observations, hypotheses and laws of his scientific predecessors. By showing how Galileo's kinematics of free fall and inclined planes could be explained using the same fundamental principle of gravitational force as Kepler's three laws of planetary orbit, Newton offered an astonishing example of scientific unification that would stand as paradigmatic in the Enlightenment. Material bodies on earth were shown to behave according to the same laws that governed the motions of the planets.

In much this manner, Rameau was able to unify the many rules governing dissonance treatment with the empirical chordal formulations of seventeenth-century thorough-bass pedagogy, all subsumed within the mathematical framework of speculative canonist (monochord) theory. Consider, as an illustration, the following table of possible two-part dissonance resolutions compiled by the Italian theorist, Angelo Berardi, and reprinted in Brossard's famous *Dictionaire de musique* of 1703.[7]

"When the treble syncopates"	"When the bass syncopates"
The 2nd resolves to the unison	The 2nd resolves to the 3rd
The 4th resolves to the 3rd	The 4th resolves to the 5th
The 7th resolves to the 5th or 6th	The 7th resolves to the octave
The 9th resolves to the octave	The 9th resolves to the 10th
The 11th resolves to the 10th	The 11th resolves to the 12th
etc.	etc.

---

5 Jean Le Rond d'Alembert, *Preliminary Discourse to the Encyclopedia of Diderot*, trans. Richard N. Schwab (Indianapolis, 1963), 100–01. D'Alembert did not limit his admiration to this single encomium. Two years later he published a competent and highly influential résumé of Rameau's theory (see footnote 4 above). We will look at d'Alembert's complex and stormy relationship with Rameau in more detail in Chapter 9.
6 Jean Benjamin de Laborde, *Essai sur la musique ancienne et moderne*, 4 vols (Paris, 1780), III, 466–67.
7 Angelo Berardi, *Documenti armonici* (Bologna, 1687); M. de Brossard, *Dictionaire de musique* (Paris, 1703), s.v. "syncope."

Each of these interval progressions was considered to be distinct by Berardi and Brossard, since each concerned a different interval resolving in a unique way. Rameau disagreed. In referring to this table, Rameau wrote derisively about the "faults of authors in establishing rules of harmony" and "the different sources of these rules and on the mistakes for which they are responsible."[8] Such rules, he continued:

> do not make the progression of each part clear enough, when they affirm that the sixth should follow the fifth, that the seventh should be resolved by the third, the fifth, or the sixth, etc. Sometimes one of these parts should remain on the same degree, sometimes each of them should move; sometimes one should ascend, sometimes descend, etc.[9]

By invoking various axioms such as the generative fundamental, inversional identity, supposition and the like, Rameau was able to account for most of these dissonant progressions as instances of the same basic fundamental-bass progression of a dissonant seventh chord resolving by a perfect fifth to a consonant triad. (The only exception was the interval of the fourth, since Rameau did not accept that it was a dissonance to begin with.) He was thus able to subsume the rules of counterpoint within his theory of the fundamental bass. Admittedly, this reduction was not uniformly successful. As we will see over the following chapters, Rameau had to fudge a number of explanations in order to have his theory account for all possible intervallic progressions. Still, the breadth and elegance of Rameau's synthesis was stunning, and recognized as such by his contemporaries. Not surprisingly, Rameau was often granted the accolade "Newton of Music." The English historian of music John Hawkins reported in 1770 that Rameau was highly regarded by his countrymen, since:

> he has shown that the whole depends upon one single and clear principle, viz., the fundamental bass; and in this respect he is by them compared to Newton, who by the single principle of gravitation was able to assign reasons for some of the most remarkable phenomena in physics; for this reason they scruple not to style Rameau the Newton of Harmony.[10]

Meanwhile Jean-Paul Grandjean de Fouchy, the *secrétaire perpétuel* of the Académie Royale des Sciences, could report in the centennial survey of the Académie published in 1760 that "Monsieur Rameau, having explained the principle of harmony, has endowed his musical system with all the truth that Newton has provided for optics."[11] Jean-François Marmontel began a lengthy ode to Rameau with this stirring comparison:

> *Newton* des Sons, astre de l'Harmonie,
> Non, le concours des plus heureux hasards,
> Ne peut fixer la carrière des Arts:

---

8 *Traité*, 105; translated as the *Treatise on Harmony* by Philip Gossett (New York, 1971), 119. Unless otherwise noted, all English citations from the *Traité* are from Gossett's generally reliable translation. For the benefit of readers with access to the original text or one of its many facsimile editions, I will cite both sources in all subsequent references.
9 *Traité*, 109; Gossett, 123.
10 John Hawkins, *A General History of the Science and Practice of Music* (London, 1776).
11 *Histoire de l'académie royale des sciences: Centiéme ou dernier Volume de la première centurie* (Amsterdam, 1760), 337.

> Tu nous l'apprens: c'est aux mains du Génie,
> A déchirer le bandeau d'Uranie.
> La vérité sur les ailes du tems,
> Vers nous, dit-on, s'avançant d'âge en âge,
> De ses rayons perce enfin le nuage,
> Qui la dérobe à nos esprits flotans.
> Tu la préviens. C'est aux talens sublimes,
> De ses secrets ravisseurs orgueilleux,
> A la tirer du fond de ses abymes,
> A l'arracher du sein même des Dieux,

Paraphrasing Pope's famous epigram in homage to Newton ("Nature and Nature's laws lay hid in night; God said 'Let Newton be!' and all was light"), Marmontel enthusiastically continued:

> *Rameau* paroit, & la nuit se dissipe,
> Dans ses accords il surprend leur principe;
> Et des rayons qu'il en fait rejaillir,
> L'Art éclairé ne craint plus de faillir.[12]

Whether Rameau ever read Marmontel's poem we do not know. But he surely would have been delighted by the comparison. Rameau never concealed his ambition to elevate music theory to the stature of a fully scientific enterprise. Before he had come along, he would pointedly remind anyone who would listen, music theory had consisted of, on the one hand, desultory empirical rules of counterpoint and the thorough bass, and, on the other hand, abstract speculations concerning Pythagorean numerology and tuning systems.

> All those who have hitherto wished to prescribe rules of harmony have abandoned the source of these rules. As the first sound and the first chord revealed to them was given no sort of prerogative, everything was considered to be equal. When they spoke of the order of perfection of consonances, this was done only to determine which consonances were to be preferred when filling in chords. When they gave some reasons for a specific progression of thirds and sixths, this was done only by means of comparisons. When they finally reached dissonances, everything became confused: the second, the seventh, and the ninth. When they said that dissonances should always be prepared, they gave rules to the contrary; when they said that dissonances should all be prepared and resolved by a consonance, they contradicted this elsewhere. No one said why some dissonances wish to ascend and others to descend. The source was hidden and everyone, according to his own inclination, told us what experience had taught him.[13]

Only with his discovery of the fundamental bass, Rameau declared with characteristic immodesty, did this confusion begin to be cleared up. Only through his own efforts was music theory on the road to becoming a truly systematic science.

---

12   Jean-François Marmontel, "Epître à Rameau," contained in Pierre-Louis d'Aquin de Châteaulion, *Siècle littéraire de Louis XV* (Amsterdam, 1753), Part I, 83–86; *CTW* VI, 213–15.
13   *Traité*, 105–06; Gossett, 119.

Plate 1.1 "Le Triomphe de Rameau." Engraving by C. N. Cochin *fils*

Since about 150 years, that is, since Zarlino and many others who have added nothing new to his discoveries, I am the only one who has written scientifically, good or bad, on music except for a few sectarians of my ideas.[14]

Rameau, as may be gathered, was keen that his theory be understood as a *scientific* theory, possessing the same degrees of synthesis, clarity, and certainty as the most advanced scientific discoveries of his day. He continually asserted in his writings that his theory rested upon the firm bases of mathematical reasoning and empirical demonstration. When appropriate – and Rameau thought it was often appropriate – he also borrowed freely from the research of contemporaneous scientists, culling whatever ideas or bits of evidence he felt useful to his own music theory, and emulating their languages and methods. Above all, Rameau sought recognition and approbation for his theory from scientists. To this end he assiduously sought out contacts with contemporary scientists and scientific academies. In a letter to d'Alembert, Rameau confessed that "the most flattering reward to which I aspire is the approbation and the esteem of the learned."[15] Beginning with Rameau's initial collaboration with Louis-Bertrand Castel in the 1720s, and continuing right through his stormy relationship with d'Alembert in the 1750s, there was scarcely a moment when Rameau was not in close touch with at least one prominent scientist whose friendship and support he cultivated, and, as it turned out more often than not, ended up alienating.

Rameau was his own most ardent propagandist. Already in 1727 he had sent a copy of his second published treatise, the *Nouveau système de musique théorique*, to

---

14   *Réponse de M. Rameau à la lettre de M. d'Alembert* (1761), 35; *CTW* V, 384.
15   *Mercure de France* (May, 1752), 75; *CTW* VI, 238.

the British Royal Society (then the most prestigious scientific institution in Europe) soliciting its official approbation.[16] Closer to home, he dedicated his *Génération harmonique* of 1737 (a work that incorporated the acoustical theories of the scientist Dortous de Mairan) to the Parisian Académie Royale des Sciences, hoping also to receive its approval. Dissatisfied with its tepid endorsement, Rameau tried again with his next treatise, the *Démonstration du principe de l'harmonie* of 1750. Rameau read a draft of this treatise before a session of the Académie in 1749, and sent copies of his completed work to a number of additional scientists and academies around Europe with obsequious solicitations for their endorsement.

This time, Rameau's efforts were not in vain. His manuscript indeed received the Académie's official approbation. In a glowing tribute appended to its publication, d'Alembert praised on behalf of his colleagues the composer-scientist who

> successfully explains by means of this principle [the fundamental bass] the different facts of which we have spoken, and which no one before him had reduced to a system as consistent and extensive... Thus, harmony, previously guided by arbitrary laws or blind experience, has become through the efforts of M. Rameau a more geometric science, and one to which the principles of mathematics can be applied with a usefulness more real and sensible than had been until now.[17]

And as we have just noted, soon thereafter d'Alembert wrote his Preliminary Discourse to the *Encyclopédie* in which he paid glowing tribute to the music theorist.

Yet Rameau proved to be a precarious ally to the philosophes. There were many aspects to his theory that did not harmonize so easily with the favorable picture d'Alembert drew of the *musicien-philosophe,* undermining their (and our) attempts to elevate Rameau's accomplishment as paradigmatic of Enlightenment science. We can begin with Rameau's ostensible scientific method. Fouchy compared Rameau's system to the optics of Newton. Yet the sober empiricism and measured inductivism characteristic of that latter work are little in evidence in Rameau's *Traité*. The composer himself, after all, always saw his epistemology as far more Cartesian than Newtonian.

... OR THE "DESCARTES OF MUSIC"?

As every student of philosophy well knows, the seventeenth-century philosopher René Descartes sought in his *Discours de la méthode* to describe a method of reasoning by which one could arrive at the truth in any subject with absolute certainty. His method, simply put, is for one to begin with an open and objective mind, cleared of all prejudices and received opinions. One then examines the subject at hand, and arrives at primitive notions whose truths are immediately recognized by their clarity and self-evidence. These notions will be the principles

---

16 Leta E. Miller, "Rameau and the Royal Society of London: New Letters and Documents," *Music and Letters* 66/1 (1985), 19–33.
17 Jean-Philippe Rameau, *Démonstration du principe de l'harmonie* (Paris, 1750), xlv–xlvi.

of that particular science. For epistemology, Descartes's principle is the recognition of one's existence (the *cogito ergo sum*). For physics, it is the notions of extension, matter and impenetrability. From these principles, Descartes believed one could deduce secondary principles and consequences with the precision of geometry.

The logic and simplicity of Descartes's method seemed impeccable. An entire generation of European intellectuals was converted to Cartesianism (although not without resistance, to be sure). As d'Alembert gratefully acknowledged in his Preliminary Discourse to the *Encyclopédie*, by teaching mankind to reject received opinions and rely instead upon one's own reason, Descartes almost singlehandedly began the revolution in philosophy and science of which the eighteenth century perceived itself to be the culmination.[18]

Rameau always thought his fundamental bass to be a model of Cartesian rigor. In an oft-quoted passage from the Preface to the *Traité*, Rameau announced that "Music is a science which should have certain rules; these rules should be drawn from an evident principle; and this principle cannot really be known to us without the aid of mathematics."[19] And true to his Cartesian precepts, Rameau attempted to use mathematics to deduce from his first principle all the elements of musical practice. Even if the exact form and content of his theory varied over time, there was never any change in his deductivist strategy. From a single source Rameau was convinced it was possible to generate a complete theory of music. We can get a taste of Rameau's unvarnished Cartesianism in the following passage taken from the very same text approved by the Académie in which the composer attempts to mimic the philosopher's methodical doubt and search for "clear and evident" first principles:

Enlightened by the *Méthode* of Descartes which I had fortunately read and had been impressed by, I began by looking into myself. I tried singing much as a child might. I examined what took place in my mind and voice . . . I then placed myself as well as I could into the state of a man who had neither sung nor heard singing, promising myself even to resort to extraneous experiments whenever I suspected that habit . . . might influence me despite myself.[20]

Now in 1722, such explicit Cartesian rhetoric might scarcely have occasioned notice given the widespread acceptance Descartes's metaphysics enjoyed in the academies and colleges. But by 1749, things had changed considerably. In the *Essay Concerning Human Understanding* of 1690, John Locke attacked the concept of "innate ideas." He proposed instead a "sensationalist" epistemology wherein all human knowledge is traced to impressions received by the senses. Using the famous image of a "tabula rasa," Locke compared the human mind at birth to a blank slate that gradually accumulates information derived from the senses. The mind, upon reflection, analyzes and compares these sense impressions to form ever more complex ideas.

---

18 D'Alembert, *Preliminary Discourse*, 84.
19 *Traité*, Preface, n.p.; Gossett, xx.
20 *Démonstration*, 8–12.

The crucial point in Locke's epistemology is that since all knowledge derives from sensations of the outside world, there are no such things as innate ideas or *a priori* truths. Experience, therefore, takes ontological precedence over reason.

By mid-century, most of the French philosophes embraced Locke's psychological epistemology, seeing a triumphant application of its methodical empiricism in Newtonian science. Rather than rashly positing hypothetical principles as Descartes did, however "clear" or "evident" they may have been, Newton began (so argued the philosophes) by carefully observing nature. Only after this did Newton apply mathematical synthesis. But he never exceeded the boundaries sanctioned by observation and calculation. The difference, as the philosophes liked to put it, was between the "esprit de système" and the "esprit systématique."

Rameau's Cartesian posturing must have struck the Académie scientists, many of whom had by then converted to the Newtonian program, as amusingly quaint. It was not that anyone doubted that fundamental principles did exist, only that one could not presume the existence of these principles prior to their discovery and confirmation through observation, calculation, and experimentation. Rameau's almost obsessive concentration upon the generative structure of his theory thus *seems* to run counter to the restrained inductive empiricism expounded by most French philosophers and scientists at mid-century (although I will qualify this statement shortly).

But Rameau's anachronism goes far beyond that of an exuberant Cartesianism expressed within an apparently hostile Newtonian environment. His ideas proved to be far more eclectic than the single encompassing label "Cartesian" conveys. Over the course of his long theoretical career, Rameau continually developed and refined his theory, testing new formulations, and appropriating evidence and arguments from diversely related fields such as philosophy, natural science, ancient history, anthropology, architecture, and theology. At one time or another, Rameau cast his theory of the fundamental bass in the varied rhetorics of neoplatonism, Cartesian mechanism, Newtonian gravitation, Lockean sensationalism, and Malebranchian occasionalism. One might compare his approach to the Australian Bower bird which builds its nest out of any discarded bits of colored paper and shiny metallic objects that it can find.

Beyond this intellectual pilfering, Rameau could be surprisingly "un-enlightened" in his theorizing. For all his self-avowed ideal of scientific precision, his reasoning could be astoundingly convoluted, entangled as it was with glaring errors, painful sophistries, logical contradictions, and fallacious empirical evidence. His writings, far from epitomizing the elegance and clarity so highly prized in the eighteenth century, are often a vexing muddle of prolix and desultory prose challenging the patience and goodwill of his readers, French or not. Worse still, towards the end of his life, Rameau appeared to abandon whatever scientific pretenses he had made on behalf of his theory and retreated to a virtual hermeticist metaphysics – astonishing and angering his erstwhile supporters with quasi-Rosicrucian writings displaying the most conspicuous mystical and pantheistic sympathies.

Few of these puzzling contradictions were overlooked by his contemporaries. Even Rameau's most ardent admirers noted disconcerting quirks to his theory and bemoaned the composer's frequent lapses of clarity and logic. The scientist Jean-Jacques Dortous de Mairan, for instance, one of Rameau's staunchest supporters in the Académie, lamented to Gabriel Cramer in 1740:

> M. Rameau, to whom I conveyed part of my theory several years ago, summarized it in his book *Génération harmonique*. But to push the thing a bit further, one could wish that this author, whom one cannot refuse the distinction of being a great musician, had a bit more geometry and physics, or even a certain amount of metaphysics, along with the talent of expressing himself more clearly.[21]

In a not-too-subtly veiled reference to Rameau's penchant for extensive number manipulation, d'Alembert wrote in one of his many *Encyclopédie* articles:

> How much ought one disapprove of certain musicians who employ in their writings calculation on top of calculation, and believe that all this apparatus is necessary to their art? The urge to give their productions a false scientific air which could only fool the ignorant has led them into this error which renders their treatises much less useful and much more obscure. I believe that as a geometer, I will be forgiven for protesting here (if I may express myself in this way) against this ridiculous abuse of geometry in music.[22]

If there was one epistemological tenet that could be said to have enjoyed almost uniform consensus among the philosophes, it was that the scientist should always retain philosophical modesty by never speculating beyond the boundaries delimited by observation and calculation. With his audacious metaphysical claims, Rameau violated this rule, and eventually earned the censure of many erstwhile admirers such as d'Alembert and Rousseau. Despite their general confidence in Rameau's theory of music, the Encyclopedists found themselves engaged in a lengthy and bitter polemic with Rameau, from which we may read this rebuke offered by d'Alembert:

> One must not seek that striking evidence that is peculiar to geometry alone, and which can be so rarely obtained in those [sciences] mixed with physical properties. In the theory of musical phenomena, there will always be a kind of metaphysics that these phenomena implicitly take for granted, and that brings along with it a natural obscurity. What is called *demonstration* cannot be expected in such a matter.[23]

A consequence of this polemic was that Rameau's reputation was seemingly turned on its head. No longer the adulated *musicien-philosophe,* Rameau began to be satirized after mid-century as the deluded scientist *manqué* spinning webs of speculative musical nonsense. No other characterization has been more damning

---

21 Letter to Gabriel Cramer dated September 16, 1740; quoted in Abby R. Kleinbaum, "Jean-Jacques Dortous de Mairan (1697–1771): A Study of an Enlightenment Scientist" (Ph.D. dissertation, Columbia University, 1970), 188.

22 *Encyclopédie, ou Dictionnaire raisonné des sciences, des arts et des métiers, par une société de gens de lettres. Mis en ordre et publié Par M. Diderot . . . et quant à la partie mathématique, par M. d'Alembert . . .*, 17 vols. (Paris, 1751–65), vol. vii, s.v. "fondamental."

23 *Elémens de musique théorique et pratique suivant les principes de M. Rameau,* 2nd edition (Lyons, 1762), xiii.

and indelible than Diderot's merciless caricature of the elderly composer in *Le Neveu de Rameau* as the doddering old mystic listening in blissful delusion to the overtones of the church bells, and writing "so much visionary gibberish and apocalyptic truth about the theory of music – writings that neither he nor anyone else ever understood."[24]

Clearly this is a long way from the triumphant composer that Diderot had earlier praised as "singulier, brillant, composé, savant, trop savant quelquefois."[25] And one may well ask if he was talking about the same man. How do we reconcile Rameau the discoverer of the fundamental bass with the deluded mystic seer, or for that matter, Rameau the Newtonian with Rameau the Cartesian? What sense does it make to have, on the one hand, Rameau the paragon of Enlightenment clarity and rigor, yet on the other hand, Rameau the parody of that same Enlightenment – the blinded Cartesian and "would-be philosophe"?[26] Simply put, was Rameau truly as divided a music theorist as these paradoxes suggest, or is there a way we can piece the man together and still make sense of the whole?

I think there is indeed a way, but it requires us first to clear away many of the encrusted stereotypes of the French Enlightenment. Only by trying to reduce eighteenth-century French thought to a monochromatic Newtonian epistemology do we have trouble finding a comfortable place for Rameau. When, however, we see the French Enlightenment as a far richer and more complex intellectual and cultural *milieu*, the "problems" of Rameau's scientific eclecticism and "anachronism" appear far less severe than at first. And the best way to begin is by reassessing the character and function of science in the Enlightenment.

SCIENCE AND THE ENLIGHTENMENT

Few historical periods have been subject to more facile reduction and damning caricature than the high French Enlightenment. Despite a generation of sophisticated and detailed historiography on the eighteenth century that has time and again debunked the myth of a uniform "Enlightenment," most general history textbooks continue to convey a rather simplistic picture of the Enlightenment as consisting of an intrepid troop of secular materialists, fighting all the superstition, prejudice, and intolerance found in the *ancien régime* with the weapons of British empiricism, and marching into battle under the banner of the *Encyclopédie*.[27]

---

24 Denis Diderot, *Rameau's Nephew*, trans. Jacques Barzun and Ralph H. Bowen (Indianapolis, 1964), 10.
25 Denis Diderot, *Les Bijoux indiscrets* (Paris, 1747), in *Oeuvres complètes de Diderot* (Paris, 1975–), III, 70.
26 I borrow the last phrase from James Doolittle, "A Would-Be Philosophe, Jean-Philippe Rameau," *Publication of the Modern Language Association* 74 (1959), 233–48.
27 It would be futile to try to offer here any extensive bibliography on the Enlightenment. The secondary literature – already large enough in 1969 for Peter Gay to fill a 260-page bibliographic essay – has grown to unmanageable proportions (Peter Gay, *The Enlightenment: An Interpretation*, 2 vols. [New York, 1966–69]). Still, Roy Porter in his recent monograph has managed to compile a judiciously selected and intelligently annotated bibliography that can be a good starting point for the uninitiated: Roy Porter, *The Enlightenment* (Atlantic Highlands, N.J., 1990).

To be sure, this portrait is not without some foundation. Few other historical periods outwardly present to the historian so great a sense of coherence and identity as does the Enlightenment. There is an apparent unity of thought, one conveyed strongly by d'Alembert's *Discours Préliminaire*. We find a definable group of intellectuals – the philosophes – who largely shared the same religious skepticism, fought many of the same battles against the church and the censor, and united in prescribing an ambitious program of social reform. Much of their criticism was indeed aimed against the prevailing Cartesian orthodoxies and favored the new British empiricism embodied in the epistemology of Locke and the science of Newton. The culmination of their efforts is found in the monumental *Encyclopédie*, which, more than anything else, fostered the image of a united philosophical coalition, or as Diderot described it, a "société de gens de lettres."

Yet when we delve into the writings of the philosophes in any detail, this picture of solidarity rapidly dissolves. Rousseau, Diderot, d'Alembert, Condillac, Montesquieu, Voltaire, and La Mettrie (to say nothing of their British and German counterparts) each have such distinctive and original personalities and philosophies that one is hard pressed to find a single common intellectual denominator. Certainly "empiricism" fails the test. Even the *Encyclopédie,* when its articles are carefully read, testifies to deep philosophical disagreements among its many contributors.[28]

The philosophes, far from being a united coalition, were a diverse and divisive crew made up of both devout Catholics and deists (though rarely atheists), rationalists and sceptics, democrats and aristocrats, sentimentalists and cynics. Voltaire, probably the most celebrated and paradigmatic figure of the Enlightenment in most historians' eyes, has been shown to have held quite conservative political views, and a surprisingly pessimistic view of social progress.[29] On the other side of the political spectrum, Margaret Jacob has brilliantly brought to light a covert but tenuous "radical Enlightenment" consisting of pantheists, Freemasons, republicans, and outright atheists that ran as a sub-current underneath the more moderate high Enlightenment.[30] But the diversity of the Enlightenment is not manifest only in the opposition of factions. Individual philosophes such as Diderot and Rousseau espoused complex and mercurial views that cannot be facilely reduced to any stable constitution without Procrustean violence.

Let us consider the common characteristic of the Enlightenment as quintessentially "Newtonian." The philosophes, we are told, rejected Cartesian rationalism in favor of the empirical epistemology and philosophical modesty epitomized in Newton's experimental physics.[31] This popular view, while not entirely wrong, is misleading

---

[28] A thoughtful analysis of the problems facing the historian searching for a unifying theme within the Enlightenment can be found in Peter Gay's essay, "The Unity of the French Enlightenment," in the *Party of Humanity* (Princeton, 1959), 114–32. Also see Lester G. Crocker, "The Enlightenment: What and Who?," *Studies in Eighteenth-Century Culture* 17 (1987), 335–47.

[29] See, for instance, Henry Vyveberg's assessment in his important revisionist study, *Historical Pessimism in the French Enlightenment* (Cambridge, Mass., 1958), especially 170–88.

[30] Margaret C. Jacob, *The Radical Enlightenment: Pantheists, Freemasons and Republicans* (London, 1981).

[31] Representative works promoting this view are Frank E. Manuel, *The Age of Reason* (Ithaca, 1951), 23 ff.; Paul

for two reasons. First, this view falsifies the respective epistemologies of Descartes and Newton, neither of which can be placed as opposing ideologies on a rationalist–empiricist spectrum. There is no less an empirical element to Descartes's method than there are rationalist precepts to Newton's. To reduce these two scientists to a pair of Parliamentary peripatetics debating epistemological questions is to succumb to the simplest of historicist ideologies. In Chapter 2, we will have an opportunity to consider the respective scientific methodologies of Newton and Descartes in examining their relation to Rameau's music theory. There we will see how each was a rather more complicated figure than their respective detractors (and partisans!) often made them out to be.

Secondly, and to some extent as a consequence of the first point, the stereotyping of the Enlightenment as a "Newtonian" age simplifies the chronology and character of eighteenth-century thought. Many aspects of Cartesian metaphysics remained vibrant in the eighteenth century and proved compatible with "Newtonianism." Even that paragon of progressive thought, Denis Diderot, has been shown by one of his intellectual biographers to have been far more influenced by Descartes than he ever professed.[32] What conflict there was between the Cartesians and Newtonians in the eighteenth century tended to concern cosmological theories (vortices versus gravitation). In other ways, though, strongly Cartesian influences are apparent in the practices of many eighteenth-century scientists who claimed fidelity to Newton. Widely shared precepts including faith in the unity of knowledge, the mechanistic universe, and the power of mathematical deduction, can be traced back to Descartes (and beyond, for that matter). Ernst Cassirer has put the point nicely:

> It is evident that, if we compare the thought of the eighteenth century with that of the seventeenth, there is no real chasm anywhere separating the two periods. The new ideal of knowledge develops steadily and consistently from the presuppositions which the logic and theory of knowledge of the seventeenth century – especially in the works of Descartes and Leibniz – had established. The difference in the mode of thinking does not mean a radical transformation; it amounts merely to a shifting of emphasis. This emphasis is constantly moving from the general to the particular, from principles to phenomena. But the basic assumption remains; that is the assumption that between the two realms of thought there is no opposition, but rather complete correlation . . . the self-confidence of reason is nowhere shaken.[33]

D'Alembert is a perfect example of this eclectic rationalism. Despite being one of the most impassioned proponents of British thought in the *Discourse* to the

---

Hazard, *European Thought in the Eighteenth Century* (New Haven, 1954), 131; Isaiah Berlin, *The Age of Enlightenment* (New York, 1965), Introduction; Frederick B. Artz, *The Enlightenment in France* (Kent, Ohio, 1968), 13–15; and Norman Hampson, *The Enlightenment* (New York, 1968), 37 ff.

[32] Aram Vartanian, *Diderot and Descartes: A Study of Scientific Naturalism in the Enlightenment* (Princeton, 1953).

[33] Ernst Cassirer, *The Philosophy of the Enlightenment*, trans. Fritz C. A. Koelln and James P. Pettegrove (Boston, 1955), 22. There is actually a long and distinguished tradition in eighteenth-century historiography to see the Enlightenment as much more dependent upon the seventeenth century than its own spokesmen would have us believe. The classic monograph in this genre is Carl Becker's *The Heavenly City of the Eighteenth-Century Philosophers* (New Haven, 1932).

Encyclopédie, he was in practice one of the most thoroughly orthodox Cartesian scientists of the age.[34] And he was not an anomaly. Much of the greatest work in eighteenth-century science took place in those fields of rational mechanics most informed by Cartesian precepts.[35] (We will consider this scientific practice in more detail in Chapter 6.) The conclusion of most recent historians of eighteenth-century science is clear: the intellectual trajectory of the Enlightenment cannot be described simply as a process of Newtonian empiricism triumphing over Cartesian rationalism (despite the fact that many of the philosophes themselves asserted just that for their own political purposes!).

These are useful points for us to keep in mind, for they will help to explain how Rameau could project two such differing images that might seem to us to be irreconcilable. This is not to say that there were no epistemological tensions in Rameau's theory after all. But such tensions are less deleterious when understood in the context of analogous tensions in Enlightenment thought. This is why it was not a contradiction for Laborde to write that

> One can say that Rameau was both Descartes and Newton, since he did for music what these two great men together did for philosophy. Like Newton, he began with what existed in practice in order to find the principle. And like Descartes, he began with nature herself (that is to say, the phenomenon known as the *corps sonore*) in order to deduce along with all its consequences the principles and individual rules. By his efforts [music theory] has become elevated to a practical science whose mechanical operations are at once the most plausible and simple.[36]

The French Enlightenment is clearly too complex an affair to reduce to a single label. But the difficulties if not the impossibilities of finding a common intellectual denominator in the Enlightenment do not mean that the only avenue left is a kind of historiographic nominalism. Many scholars who recognize the diversity of Enlightenment thought have nonetheless identified unifying themes within it. The historians Peter Gay and Ira Wade, for example, have sought such unity not in any specific philosophical doctrine or program, but rather in a general attitude. Gay has defined this attitude as a "dialectic interplay of [the philosophes'] appeal to antiquity,

---

[34] As persuasively shown by Thomas Hankins in his study *Jean d'Alembert, Science and the Enlightenment* (Oxford, 1970).

[35] Clifford Truesdell, "A Program Toward Rediscovering the Rational Mechanics of the Age of Reason," *Archive for the History of Exact Sciences* 1 (1960), 1–36. For a good overview of Enlightenment science, with attention paid to its Cartesian roots, see Thomas Hankins, *Science and the Enlightenment* (Cambridge, 1985), 13–16; and J. V. Golinski's review-essay on the same: "Science in the Enlightenment," *History of Science* 24 (1986), 411–24. For an excellent bibliographic review of recent studies of scientific epistemology that convincingly debunks the myth of an omnipotent "Newtonian science" in the Enlightenment, see Rom Harré's contribution "Knowledge," in *The Ferment of Knowledge: Studies in the Historiography of Eighteenth-Century Science,* ed. G. S. Rousseau and Roy Porter (Cambridge, 1980), 11–54, but especially 35–47. Finally, a completely different aspect of Enlightenment science concerned with the life sciences is analyzed by Colm Kiernan in "The Enlightenment and Science in Eighteenth-Century France," *Studies on Voltaire and the Eighteenth Century* 59 (1973). Kiernan's study shows just how unhelpful labels like "Newtonian" and "Cartesian" ultimately are outside the physical sciences.

[36] Laborde, *Essai sur la musique ancienne et moderne,* III, 467.

their tension with Christianity, and their pursuit of modernity."[37] Wade, on the other hand, finds a more "organic" unity in the Enlightenment, rooted in a "new consciousness of self."[38] Other historians have tried to salvage a coherent intellectual description of the Enlightenment by distinguishing within it differing phases and levels. Henry May, for instance, identifies four different stages of Enlightenment thought that help account for the changing (and often overlapping) political attitudes of the time.[39]

Useful as such classifications may be, I do not think it is necessary to arrive at a single encompassing definition of the Enlightenment, however general or contingent, in order to situate Rameau effectively within its confines. This is not to say that no dominating trends can be identified when judiciously circumscribed by geographic, chronological, and social parameters. But it is by virtue of numerous competing and overlapping trends that I believe the Enlightenment attains its particular dynamic force. (Cassirer's characterization of Enlightenment thought as a dialectical struggle between rationalist and empiricist tendencies, while perhaps a bit narrow in its neo-Kantian bias, reflects quite well this dynamic quality.) Only by acknowledging and bringing out these many tensions and dissonances rather than repressing or resolving them can we begin to capture the full richness of eighteenth-century thought.[40] Obviously, one could object that such a dialectical characterization applies to any historical period. Yet rather than seeing this argument as counterfactual, I see it as validation. Before attempting any synthetic depiction of a historical period, it is first necessary to identify its many discordant components and competing forces.

For my purposes, I am not discomfited by a picture of the French Enlightenment as an intellectual *tourbillon*. However frustrating such a pluralistic portrait of the time may be to historians seeking to find coherence and unity, it allows us to understand the vicissitudes of Rameau's theory, without having, on the one hand, to accommodate them as aberrations from some fixed norm, or, on the other hand, to repress them as insignificant. For the totality of Rameau's theory – his many changes of scientific rhetoric, the shifting philosophical, historical, and aesthetic arguments; his struggles to balance empirical and systematic concerns; his speculative turn in his later years – can be traced to distinct and competing forces present in Rameau's culture to which he was responding.

---

37 Gay, *The Enlightenment*, I, 8.
38 Ira Wade, *The Structure and Form of the French Enlightenment*, 2 vols. (Princeton, 1977), I, xv.
39 Henry May, *The Enlightenment in America* (New York, 1976). Although May's study is obviously concerned with the American experience, his four stages of Enlightenment thought ("moderate," "skeptical," "revolutionary," and "didactic") are applicable – and indeed largely inspired by – the European Enlightenment.
40 Again, a remark by Cassirer seems appropriate here: "The true nature of Enlightenment thinking cannot be seen in its purest and clearest form where it is formulated into particular doctrines, axioms, and theorems; but rather where it is in process, where it is doubting and seeking, tearing down and building up. . . It cannot be presented in a summation of the views of these men, not in the temporal sequence of their views; for it consists less in certain individual doctrines than in the form and manner of intellectual activity in general" (*The Philosophy of the Enlightenment*, ix).

From this perspective, our story of Rameau's theory will be very much a kind of sociology of ideas.[41] This does not mean, however, that Rameau's theory lacked any internal coherence of its own, that we cannot, in other words, evaluate his musical arguments based upon criteria such as logical consistency, empirical adequacy, pedagogical efficacy, and the like. It does mean that we will better understand his arguments in light of the external (sociological and political) context within which they were formulated and received. In the following chapters, I will attempt to analyze the inception and development of Rameau's music theory by looking at both its "internal" motivations and its "external" constraints. The resulting picture, if not wholly a coherent and uniform one, will, I hope, do justice to the richness of Rameau's thought, and moreover be emblematic of the analogous intellectual complexity of the French Enlightenment, within whose cultural bounds, after all, it was situated.

[41] An insightful (and in many ways critical) analysis of the social history of ideas as practiced by some recent Enlightenment historians may be found in Robert Darnton, "In Search of the Enlightenment: Recent Attempts to Create a Social History of Ideas," *The Journal of Modern History* 43 (1971), 113–32. Darnton has put his advice into practice in a number of important studies, including *The Business of Enlightenment: A Publishing History of the Encyclopédie 1775–1800* (Cambridge, Mass., 1979); *The Literary Underground of the Old Regime* (Cambridge, Mass., 1982); and *The Great Cat Massacre and Other Episodes in French Cultural History* (New York, 1984).

2

RAMEAU AS MUSIC THEORIST

The *Traité de l'harmonie* would have been an extraordinary achievement for any music theorist, let alone the inaugural work of an obscure thirty-nine-year-old organist from the provinces. Until its appearance, Rameau's only other publication had been a small *recueil* of harpsichord pieces issued in 1706.[1] There was little to his background that betokened the colossal intellectual accomplishment that was the *Traité*. (But Rameau always seemed to be full of surprises; there was little to presage his triumphant debut as opera composer with the performance of *Hippolyte et Aricie* eleven years later in 1733.) How, then, did Rameau come to write the *Traité*?

Rameau's biographers have been continually vexed at the dearth of information we have concerning his early years.[2] Michel Chabanon, one of the first to try to compile information on the composer, bemoaned the fact that "The entire first half of his life is completely unknown. He reported no particulars to his friends, or even to Madame Rameau, his wife."[3] The little that we can piece together about his first forty years (that is, until the publication of the *Traité*) sheds almost no light on his theoretical background, and leaves many questions unanswered.[4]

We know from Rameau's own testimony that he was not particularly well educated. In the few years or so he spent at the Collège des Gordrans in Dijon (probably from 1695 to 1699), Rameau must have been exposed to the progressive humanist curriculum that was common to Jesuit education at the time. But except for whatever music instruction he may have received there, this education evidently made little impression upon the young musician.[5] Rameau never evinced any

---

1 *Premier livre de pièces de clavecin* (Paris, 1706).
2 Cuthbert Girdlestone's study, *Jean-Philippe Rameau: His Life and Work*, 2nd edition (New York, 1969), remains the standard work on Rameau's life and music. Unfortunately, Girdlestone makes short shrift of Rameau's theoretical writings.
3 Michel-Paul-Guy de Chabanon, *Eloge de M. Rameau* (Paris, 1764), 7. A translation of this work by Edward R. Reilly appears in *Studies in Music from the University of Western Ontario* 8 (1983), 1–24.
4 Besides the eulogy of Chabanon, there is only one other contemporaneous source of information of any substance concerning Rameau's life: an eulogy written for the Dijon Academy of Science by Hugues Maret: *Eloge historique de M. Rameau* (Dijon, 1766). A helpful inventory of all primary documents pertaining to Rameau's early years has been recently compiled by Neal Zaslaw: "Rameau's Operatic Apprenticeship: The First Fifty Years," *Jean-Philippe Rameau: Colloque International organisé par La Société Rameau*, ed. Jérôme de la Gorce (Paris, 1987), 37–50. (Henceforth cited as *Rameau Colloque International*.)
5 According to a story reported by Maret, Rameau so distracted himself in class by singing and writing music that the Jesuit Fathers eventually requested his departure (Maret, *Eloge*, 4).

sophisticated understanding of subjects outside of music. What knowledge of mathematics, physics, and philosophy he did glean seems to have been haphazard and relatively shallow, at least to judge from the desultory citations in his later publications. Perhaps the most conspicuous testament to Rameau's lack of schooling was the constant frustration he experienced in organizing his theoretical ideas clearly and putting them down on paper in good French. His writings were notorious for their prolixity and obscurity. Rousseau complained that he tried to read through the *Traité* once in convalescence, and after only a few pages had to stop for fear of a relapse. In a story reported by Maret, Rameau's earliest amorous pursuits were thwarted by the ridicule he received for his ungrammatical and infelicitous love letters. It should not be surprising, then, that we will so often find Rameau seeking the aid of others to help edit his theoretical writings.

Rameau's musical education was fortunately more thoroughly grounded. He came from a musical family, and learned to read music at an early age under the tutelage of his father, who was organist at Dijon cathedral. By the age of seven, according to Maret, Rameau could play at sight on the harpsichord. His first documented professional activity was in 1702 when he was appointed organist at the cathedral in Clermont-Ferrand – the provincial capital of the Auvergne in south-central France.[6] He stayed at this post until 1706 when he visited Paris for the first time in order to study under the celebrated organist Louis Marchand and have his first collection of harpsichord pieces published. Despite receiving a prestigious appointment while in Paris at the church of Sainte Madeleine after winning a heavily contested audition, Rameau declined the offer. For reasons we can only guess, he evidently felt unready to make a permanent move to the city. By 1709, we find our twenty-six-year-old organist back in his home town of Dijon in order to succeed his elderly father. Over the following years, Rameau moved several more times to take on a number of different jobs as organist, composer, and teacher. In 1715, he returned to Clermont-Ferrand.[7] His second Clermont residence lasted until 1722, the year in which he made his final move to Paris, there to remain for the rest of his life.

During all these years as an itinerant musician, there is no evidence that Rameau ever formally studied music theory.[8] But he always claimed to have had an interest in the subject, "drawn since my youth by a mathematical instinct to the study of an art for which I found myself destined, and which has singularly occupied me my entire life."[9] We do indeed have scattered anecdotes that testify to the young Rameau's interest in theoretical matters. For instance, in 1737 he related how "at the age of seven or eight I sensed that the tritone should be resolved by the sixth

---

[6] There were apparently musical activities that preceded Rameau's Clermont appointment, including a short stint as a violinist with a touring theatrical group, as well as a brief visit to Milan sometime in 1701. But the particulars of these travels are lost to us. See Zaslaw, "Rameau's Operatic Apprenticeship," 39.

[7] For the itinerary of Rameau during this period, see *ibid.*, 40–42.

[8] Although he does admit to having studied a little thorough bass as a youth in Montpellier with a organist named Delacroix. *CTW* VI, 42.

[9] *Démonstration du principe de l'harmonie* (Paris, 1750), 110.

and I made this into a rule."[10] But just how familiar Rameau was with the theoretical literature of his day is hard to gauge. He was certainly familiar with a few of the most important published writings of his immediate French predecessors such as Descartes, Masson, Saint-Lambert, and Brossard, all of whom he cites at various points in the *Traité*. He also seems to have read a little of Kircher's *Musurgia universalis* and Zarlino's *Istitutioni harmoniche*.[11] But he displayed such a consistent penchant for misreading and selectivity that one gets the impression he did not study these works with much discipline.

For better and for worse, the fundamental bass was worked out largely through Rameau's own imagination, insight, and effort. This is not to say that it was created *ex nihilo*. On the contrary, we will see over the following chapters just how much in Rameau's theory was indeed rooted in the seventeenth century. But his borrowings were always highly selective and syncretic. While many of the individual components that make up the fundamental bass enunciated in the *Traité* can be traced to the seventeenth century, their composite synthesis was hardly envisioned. By not subscribing to any one theoretical paradigm, Rameau felt himself at liberty to draw scattered ideas from disparate sources, and to meld them as he saw fit with his own. To be sure, this eclecticism would often result in confused and even contradictory arguments. But just as often it led Rameau to striking insights. A Cartesian suspicion of authority and a reliance upon his own reason and experience proved in the end to be a highly fruitful epistemology for our music theorist.

THE "CLERMONT NOTES"

We do not know what specific catalyst, if indeed there was one, caused Rameau to undertake the arduous task of writing the *Traité de l'harmonie*. The time and effort involved must have been extraordinary. At 479 dense pages of prose, the work is the longest treatise he would ever write, and incidentally, the longest to have been published in France since Mersenne's *Harmonie Universelle* of 1636. Obviously, Rameau must have spent many years working out his theory and drafting the text of the *Traité* before his arrival in Paris in 1722.[12]

---

10 *Génération harmonique* (Paris, 1737), 223. Rameau related another story that took place when he resided in Lyons (1713–15) that suggested he was by then well aware of the fundamental bass ("Réflexions de Monsieur Rameau sur la manière de former la voix et d'apprendre la musique," *Mercure de France* [October, 1752], 87–100; reprinted in Marie-Germaine Moreau, "Jean-Philippe Rameau et la pédagogie," *La Revue Musicale* 260 [1965], 50).

11 Given Rameau's linguistic ineptness, it would be surprising if he had been able to wade all the way through Zarlino's notoriously Baroque prose. Still, he may have picked up some knowledge of Italian during his brief sojourn in Milan in 1701, allowing him at least to peruse the treatise.

12 Apparently Rameau had sent the text to his publisher Ballard while he was still in Clermont. Rameau later reported that he was unhappy with the page proofs he received while in Clermont, and so hastened to Paris sometime in June 1722 in order to make a number of alterations and additions. These changes were eventually incorporated within a supplement and at least one new page revision that were printed and substituted before the book was bound (Zaslaw, "Rameau's Operatic Apprenticeship," 26). More specific information on the revisions can be found in Gossett's introduction to his translation: "Publication History," vii–xii. In the course of my analysis of the *Traité*, I will be considering a number of these revisions and Rameau's motivations for making them.

We can get an inkling of the intellectual struggle Rameau must have gone through in working out his ideas based upon a collection of manuscript notes, sketches, and student exercises originating from his second Clermont residence. The original manuscripts are unfortunately now lost, and are described only in a monograph by a former professor of music at the Ecole Nationale de Musique in Clermont-Ferrand, René Suaudeau.[13] From Suaudeau's study, we can follow Rameau's first adumbrations of his theory of the fundamental bass.

One note of caution, however: Suaudeau's scholarship is annoyingly imprecise. It is often impossible to tell from his jumbled and informal narrative whether something he reports is a faithful transcription of Rameau's text, or his own extrapolation. Further, Suaudeau seems to mix in ideas Rameau articulated in writings post-dating the *Traité*, without warning the reader of this fact. This makes the reconstruction of any autonomous "Clermont theory" difficult and perhaps even imprudent, lacking the original documents. Nonetheless, with appropriate circumspection, I think a few observations can be proffered.

The idea for the fundamental bass seems to have originated in Rameau's mind as a pedagogical tool. In the picture drawn for us by Suaudeau, we see Rameau the teacher searching for ways to simplify instruction in composition and thorough bass for his students. What guidelines and descriptions there were are generally ad hoc in nature and unsystematically worked out. According to Suaudeau, the fundamental bass comes across

> as a simple means of verifying harmony, a simple tool for instruction. He presented some rules on the subject, rules evidently quite arbitrary, often insufficient, in all ways empiric, and which were not of much more value than the precepts formulated by the ancient contrapuntists.[14]

Rameau begins with a well-established axiom of thorough-bass theory: the major and minor triads are the basic consonant structures of music. No theoretical justification or formal derivation is offered on their behalf; they are simply asserted as empirical givens. Rameau then goes on (according to Suaudeau's narrative) to consider the question of mode. If C major is assumed the tonic, F major and G major triads complement and define the tonic C. To distinguish their functions,

---

13 R. Suaudeau, *Introduction à l'harmonie de Rameau* (Clermont-Ferrand, 1960). An earlier draft of this essay exists in a mimeographed form: "Le Premier Système harmonique, dit clermontois, de Jean-Philippe Rameau."

The information Suaudeau provides in his published study concerning the manuscripts is frustratingly vague. It seems that at some point in the early eighteenth century, the native Clermontois composer, George Onslow (1784–1852), acquired theoretical papers stemming from Rameau's second Clermont residence. These papers were passed down to Onslow's descendants, in whose possession they were when Suaudeau studied them. Since that time, however, the Onslow estate has been dispersed among several descendants in England and South America. In the process, the Rameau manuscripts were apparently lost. (See Jacobi's report in *CTW* I, xviii ff.) Despite repeated attempts to trace them by such musicologists as Erwin Jacobi, Neal Zaslaw and myself, as well as officials of the Bibliothèque Nationale, their whereabouts remain unknown. The custodians of the former Onslow château at the *Centre Culturel de Valprivas Haute Loire* have disclaimed any knowledge of the manuscripts.

14 Suaudeau, *Introduction à l'harmonie de Rameau*, 12.

two characteristic dissonances are needed: an added sixth on F major, and a minor seventh on G major.[15] Together, these chords constitute the mode of C major, as well as representing three fundamental chord types: the consonant triad (*accord parfait*), the added-sixth chord (*accord de grande-sixte*), and the seventh chord (*accord de 7e de dominante*).[16] Several other kinds of dissonant chords such as the diminished-seventh chord are found by altering notes belonging to these three fundamental chord types.[17]

What is noteworthy about Rameau's "Clermont theory" up to this point is less the tripartite classification of chords he makes as much as the idea of a "fundamental" sound. The bottom note of each of these chords he calls the *basse fondamentale* – what musicians today refer to as a chord "root." Rameau does not yet speak of this bass as a "generator." He does make the important observation, though, that the fundamental bass grounds and defines these chords by remaining the same no matter in what inversion (*renversement*) the chord appears.[18] This is evidently possible since the octave position of any note in a chord does not alter that chord's identity.

There are apparently a number of additional ad hoc explanations Rameau offers in the Clermont notes concerning various dissonant chords of *supposition* (ninth and eleventh chords), the augmented-sixth chord, and the *double emploi*. (Although, again, it is not clear to me in all cases if Suaudeau's description refers exclusively to explanations drawn from the notes he was studying, or also to Rameau's later published writings.) The important point is that Rameau has radically reduced the plethora of figured-bass signatures to just a few fundamental types. However dubious or inconsistent his reductive procedure may have been, he was able to simplify the tedious process of learning the thorough bass. By further showing how the fundamental basses of his chord types succeed one another in a reduced number of models, Rameau makes the mastery of composition much easier. (These models are summarized by Rameau in ten basic rules of chord succession, and four cadence types.[19])

Such are the principal ideas conveyed in Rameau's "Clermont notes" (assuming Suaudeau's presentation is reliable). We see that the fundamental bass was conceived

---

15 *Ibid.*, 14.
16 *Ibid.*, 16. The inclusion in Suaudeau's narrative of an added-sixth chord as a fundamental harmony above the "sous-dominante" helping to define a mode is curious. Rameau did not formally discuss the subject of the subdominant in the *Traité*. Its presence here suggests either that Rameau had a sudden change of heart in 1722 and entirely abandoned the concept of the subdominant, only to reinstate it in the *Nouveau système* of 1726, or that Suaudeau was intermixing some of Rameau's later (published) ideas in his explication of the Clermont notes. It is not impossible, though, that Rameau may have thought of the notion of the subdominant well before the *Traité* was published, just as described by Suaudeau, but then decided for reasons of consistency and economy to omit it from this latter publication. As we will see in Chapter 7, in introducing the added-sixth chord as an independent fundamental harmony, Rameau contradicts his initial claim that there was only one source of dissonance: the seventh.
17 This aspect of Rameau's Clermont theory is further analyzed by Jacques Chailley in his article "Rameau et la théorie musicale," *La Revue Musicale* 260 (1964): 77.
18 Suaudeau, *Introduction à l'harmonie de Rameau*, 37.
19 *Ibid.*, 29–32.

by Rameau as a practical heuristic device to simplify music pedagogy. There is no indication that Rameau was trying to reduce music to scientific principles or deductive systems. As Jacques Chailley has pointed out, "The fundamental bass, the pivot of the entire Ramist system, appeared essentially as a *practical means* for coordinating and simplifying the rules of succession for the basso continuo, which had until then been taught exclusively by empirical formulas."[20] Suaudeau has summarized the practical motivation for Rameau's Clermont notes as follows:

> Well before the publication of his first treatise, the organist of Clermont cathedral, through the force of reflection, had already established his doctrine. It is general, and above all practical enough to dispense with the scientific, experimental, and deductive apparatus which encumbered his printed works. . . It was the vicissitudes of pedagogy which guided the musician to reflect, to learn, and finally to build a coherent body of theory.[21]

As subsequent publications would bear out, Rameau manifestly did want to build a theory incorporating some kind of "scientific, experimental, and deductive apparatus" in order to systematize the pedagogical rules and heuristics he had induced through practice. What he needed, though, was some means to generate and coordinate them in a coherent whole. In other words, what he needed to find was some *principle of harmony*. This was the task Rameau set out for himself in the *Traité de l'harmonie*.

THE *TRAITÉ DE L'HARMONIE*

The full title of Rameau's treatise is revealing: *Traité de l'harmonie reduite à ses principes naturels*. One word would have immediately struck educated French musicians in 1722: *harmonie*. For the first time in France, "harmony" was treated as a fully-fledged compositional discipline independent of counterpoint. To be sure, the subject of *harmonia* had been a topic of music theory since antiquity. But this was *harmonia* in the general sense of concordance, or as Zarlino defined it, "diversity of moving parts and consonances, brought together with variety."[22] So defined, *harmonia* entails any and all pitch relations, whether of intervals, melody, or chords.[23]

Rameau suggests a narrower interpretation of harmony in his *Traité* that is restricted to chords and their succession. Of course, the *Traité* was not quite a *Harmonielehre* as understood by nineteenth-century theorists; there is still a sense of the older *harmonia* in Rameau's conception of the *basse fondamentale*.[24] Understanding the mix of old and new that is to be found in the *Traité* demands a careful, historically informed exegesis that I shall attempt over the next several chapters. But first, it will be useful to offer a brief overview of the entire text so we may place it within a general theoretical-pedagogical context.

---

20 Chailley, "Rameau et la théorie musicale," 79.
21 Suaudeau, *Introduction à l'harmonie de Rameau*, 8.
22 Gioseffo Zarlino, *Le istitutioni harmoniche* (Venice, 1558); Book 3 translated as *The Art of Counterpoint* by Guy A. Marco and Claude V. Palisca (New Haven, 1968), 52.
23 Carl Dahlhaus, *Studies on the Origins of Harmonic Tonality*, trans. Robert O. Gjerdingen (Princeton, 1990), 18 ff.
24 A topic explored by Carl Dahlhaus, "Ist Rameaus 'Traité de l'harmonie' eine Harmonielehre?", *Musiktheorie* 1/2 (1986), 123–27.

TRAITÉ
DE
L'HARMONIE
Reduite à ses Principes naturels;
DIVISÉ EN QUATRE LIVRES.

LIVRE I. Du rapport des Raisons & Proportions Harmoniques.

LIVRE II. De la nature & de la proprieté des Accords; Et de tout ce qui peut servir à rendre une Musique parfaite.

LIVRE III. Principes de Composition.

LIVRE IV. Principes d'Accompagnement.

Par Monsieur RAMEAU, Organiste de la Cathedrale de Clermont en Auvergne.

DE L'IMPRIMERIE
De JEAN-BAPTISTE-CHRISTOPHE BALLARD, Seul Imprimeur du Roy pour la Musique. A Paris, ruë Saint Jean-de-Beauvais, au Mont-Parnasse.

M. DCC. XXII.
AVEC PRIVILEGE DU ROY.

Plate 2.1 Title page to the *Traité de l'harmonie*

The *Traité* is divided into two pairs of "Books" addressing theoretical and practical issues respectively. Book 1, "On the Relationship between Harmonic Ratios and Proportions," seeks to establish the fundamental structures that Rameau will need for the remaining portions of his text: chords. His essential goal is to validate chords as primary musical constructs. He does this by showing how all chords are generated from a single source. This "source" turns out to be that venerable tool of *musica speculativa*, the monochord. All the ratios Rameau needs to construct any and all chords can be generated directly from the monochord through string divisions that he describes in detail. He then posits two fundamental chord types: the consonant triad and the dissonant seventh chord. All other chords are derivative of these two harmonies through various theses such as inversional identity, supposition, borrowed roots and the like.[25] Rameau's essential point is that the monochord string itself is the "fundamental source" of these chords; it is the natural principle underlying and controlling all harmony, and hence all music.

Rameau's invocation of the monochord was somewhat unusual for the time. Few theorists of Rameau's generation employed this ancient instrument of the canonists.[26] Two reasons can be cited for its decline. First, in the course of the seventeenth century, the traditional function of the monochord – to plot and to demonstrate the numerical ratios of musical intervals and scales – was increasingly taken over by acoustics. That is, intervals traditionally defined and measured by string length ratios were now being described by the quantity of their individual frequencies.

Secondly, the variety of complex dissonant ratios, tuning systems, and temperaments explored by seventeenth-century theorists exceeded the monochord's practical capacity for easy presentation. To quantify their various systems of temperament, for example, many theorists found logarithmic computation to be the most effective means. As a tool for *musica theorica*, the monochord had become increasingly anachronistic.

In this sense, then, Rameau's employment of the monochord appears to be regressive; it hardly seems the mark of a revolutionary iconoclast. But Rameau never intended his use of the monochord to be revolutionary. For all the novel ideas he was to bring to the discipline of music theory, he always believed that these ideas were still grounded in theoretical tradition. It was natural that he would turn to the classical tool of *musica theorica* to demonstrate this. (Nonetheless, when we analyze Rameau's generation of chords in Chapter 4 in detail, we shall see that his employment of the monochord was unorthodox.)

In Book 2 ("On the Nature and Properties of Chords and on Everything Which May Be Used to Make Music Perfect"), Rameau grapples with the movement of these chords. Here the reader is introduced to the *basse fondamentale*. Rameau uses the fundamental bass to explain the behavior of the various chords he has constructed

---

25 The added-sixth chord claimed by Suaudeau to be in the Clermont notes is now absent as a fundamental harmony, but will be encountered again in his later publications. (See Chapter 7.)

26 It is in Germany, with its much more resilient scholastic tradition, that we find the monochord most often utilized in music-theoretical literature during the eighteenth century. (See Chapter 4, pp. 87–90 below.)

in Book 1. Of crucial significance in his search for the "natural principle" of harmony is his discovery that the interval ratios outlined by the fundamental bass are largely the same as those ratios by which the chords themselves were generated on the monochord. In this sense, Rameau's theory is indeed akin to the older tradition of *harmonia* described earlier. The same intervals that govern the construction of chords also turn out to control the succession of these chords.

Books 3 and 4, on composition and accompaniment, respectively, apply in a practical way the material presented in Book 2. Rameau's intention is to show that when one has mastered the theory of the fundamental bass, the writing and accompanying of music becomes much easier. These are obviously pedagogical sections, and can be read and understood without knowing or agreeing with the theoretical arguments of the first two Books.[27] (There is incidentally much material in these two Books that seems to overlap the "Clermont notes" as described by Suaudeau; it may well be that the bulk of the material therein was written at an earlier stage than the first two Books of the *Traité*.) The point is that the fundamental bass can be learned and profitably applied by a student who may not necessarily know the theoretical process by which it was established.

We see from this brief overview that the *Traité* is a syncretic work, encompassing both speculative and practical modes of theory. This juxtaposition of speculative and practical theory – what in Rameau's day was called *musica theorica* and *musica pratica* – constitutes a recurring and essential tension in Rameau's writings. They represent two distinct traditions in music theory that, until Rameau's *Traité*, had remained essentially separate from one another. As the dialectic between these two traditions would become a crucial one in Rameau's formulations, it will be useful to look briefly at their historical background in French musical thought.

THE LEGACY OF *MUSICA THEORICA*

We must not confuse "music theory" as we understand it today with *musica theorica* of the seventeenth century. The latter discipline was much more narrowly defined and, at least until Rameau's day, concerned itself with speculative matters. The disciplines of counterpoint, harmony, and thorough bass that we today consider a part of music theory were in most cases considered as components of *musica pratica*. To put matters simply, in the speculative tradition, the musician was concerned with the ontological nature of musical material, while in the practical tradition, with its application. Expressed in Aristotelian terms, speculative music theory concerned itself with formal causes, while practical music theory concerned itself with efficient causes. Obviously the precise agendas of the two traditions have changed over time so as to reflect the indigenous musical and intellectual climates in which

---

27 Both of these books were, in fact, independently published in English translation as autonomous composition and accompaniment texts during the eighteenth century. Indeed, they were the *only* theoretical works by Rameau that were ever translated before the twentieth century: *A treatise of music, containing the principles of composition. . . By Mr. Rameau* (London, 1737); *A treatise on harmony, in which the principles of accompaniment are fully explained and illustrated by a variety of examples* (London, 1795).

they have been articulated, thus precluding the drawing of any firm boundaries.[28] A few general characterizations can nonetheless be made that are relevant to the state of music theory in France during the generations immediately preceding Rameau.[29]

During the first half of the seventeenth century, French music theory was dominated by speculative concerns. Most theorists of the time were clerics with strong scholastic educations: Pierre Maillert, Salomon de Caus, Marin Mersenne, René Descartes, and Antoine de Cousu. As heirs of the tradition of *musica theorica*, these men were interested primarily in the origin and nature of all musical material: pitches, intervals, modes, prolations, and tunings. They found answers in a mixture of ancient authority (particularly Salinas and Zarlino), scholastic reasoning, and mathematical tools such as the monochord.[30] Among the problems they addressed were the classification of modes, the mathematical generation and hierarchy of intervals, and the evaluation of tuning systems. Occasionally these theorists would turn to more abstract topics such as the harmony of the spheres, modal affections, or the interpretation of ancient Greek music. But their primary focus was upon the *material* of musical practice.

It would be a mistake to believe that all authors of *musica theorica* were conservative. While it is true most speculative theorists employed traditional scholastic language in their analyses of music, it was in speculative theory that some of the most advanced revisions of consonance hierarchy, temperament, and modal theory took place. Further, a number of speculative theorists (notably Mersenne and Descartes) began to apply the fruits of the nascent scientific revolution and consider music in terms of a progressive mechanistic-acoustic model. Their work (to which we shall return in Chapter 4) marked a turning point in music theory in which many of the traditional problems of *musica theorica* began to be subsumed within the discipline of natural philosophy.

---

[28] One example: During the seventeenth century, counterpoint was typically classified as part of *musica pratica* by music theorists. It was concerned, as Brossard put it, "with the *execution* [of music], without concern for its reason, or the cause of the good effect of this execution" (*Dictionaire de musique* [Paris, 1703], s.v. "musica attiva"). By the eighteenth century, though, counterpoint became increasingly displaced by thorough bass as the primary discipline of *musica pratica*. The rules of counterpoint seemed to have played less a vital part of a musician's daily practice, and were confined to a very specific and conservative repertoire of liturgical music. Hence, counterpoint came to be seen more and more as a part of *musica theorica*. This was especially true in Italy, as shown by Renate Groth in "Italienische Musiktheorie im 17. Jahrhundert," *Geschichte der Musiktheorie*, vol. VII (Darmstadt, 1989), 324–25. But there was hardly any consensus on such matters; German-speaking theorists such as Fux, Marpurg, and Kirnberger continued to teach counterpoint as a purely practical skill.

[29] I shall continue to use the general term "music theory" in the twentieth-century sense (as encompassing both speculative and practical disciplines), and apply the designations "speculative" and "practical" when I wish to make more precise historical distinctions.

[30] For a comprehensive history of French music theory in the first half of the seventeenth century, see Herbert Schneider's excellent study, *Die französische Kompositionslehre in der ersten Hälfte des 17. Jahrhunderts* (Tutzing, 1972), a work, as will become clear in the footnotes over the following chapters, upon which I have profitably drawn. A more general survey of seventeenth-century French theory is found in Wilhelm Seidel's essay "Französische Musiktheorie im 16. und 17. Jahrhundert," *Geschichte der Musiktheorie*, vol. ix (Darmstadt, 1986), 1–140.

Independent of the speculative tradition (although not necessarily exclusive to it) stood *musica pratica* or *musica attiva*. Within this domain we find works written by musicians who may or may not have been interested in questions of *musica speculativa*. Their dominant concern was pedagogic; they sought to describe and codify empirical practice. Thus, the subjects of their treatises were counterpoint, chant, transposition, singing, and thorough bass. And while, as already noted, *musica pratica* and *musica theorica* need not be mutually exclusive – Mersenne and de Cousu, for instance, wrote encyclopedic works in which the two traditions intermingled – they were considered disciplines largely autonomous of one another.

By the second half of the seventeenth century, French music theory had become almost entirely practical in nature, epitomized in composition texts by Mignot de La Voye, Guillaume Nivers, Etienne Loulié, Marc-Antoine Charpentier, Michel L'Affilard, and Charles Masson – each one of these authors, incidentally, a practicing composer.[31] This is not to mention the dozens of other musical pedagogues who produced practical instrumental instructors, singing treatises, thorough-bass primers, methods for transposition, and dictionaries. Again it must be emphasized that "practical" theorists were by no means necessarily more progressive than speculative theorists. Many practical theorists of the seventeenth century proved to be the most intolerant curmudgeons when it came to accepting revisions of modal theory and temperament.

Rameau's most consequential intellectual accomplishment lay in the *rapprochement* he was able to effect between these two traditions. The *basse fondamentale* was at once a *theoretical* explanation of the origin of all musical material, as well as a *practical* description of that same material as used by musicians. To a degree not attained since Zarlino's *Istitutioni harmoniche* of 1573, Rameau was able to integrate practice and theory into a coherent whole. This is not to say, however, that Rameau's synthesis was accomplished without residual tensions.

THE CARTESIAN DILEMMA

We can detect such tensions quite clearly in Rameau's many discussions concerning *expérience* and *raison* that run throughout the *Traité*, and indeed, throughout just about all of his publications. Rameau is acutely ambivalent about the amount of emphasis to accord each of these *desiderata* in his theory. At times he insists upon the need to rely upon musical experience and the empirical judgment of one's ear in formulating any theory, while at other times he emphasizes the absolute necessity of reason and mathematical demonstration.

Reading the Preface to the *Traité de l'harmonie*, the innocent reader could hardly be faulted for assuming that Rameau's epistemology was purely rationalistic. We have already encountered in the last chapter his famous pronouncement that "music

---

31 Both Schneider and Seidel have noted the bifurcation of seventeenth-century French music theory into speculative and practical halves, respectively: Schneider, *Die französische Kompositionslehre*, 282–85; Seidel, "Französische Musiktheorie," 40–42, 88–94. Parallel developments in Italy are described by Groth, "Italienische Musiktheorie im 17. Jahrhundert," 311–18.

is a science which should have definite rules," and how "reason has lost its rights, while experience has acquired a certain authority." Rameau does not entirely depreciate experience, for he admits that it "can enlighten us concerning the different properties of music." But, he continues:

> it alone cannot lead us to discover the principle behind these properties with the precision appropriate to reason. Conclusions drawn from experience are often false, or at least leave us with doubts that only reason can dispel.[32]

And the means Rameau proposes for finding the true "principle behind these properties" is mathematics. Musicians who remain only at the level of practice without mathematical knowledge can never achieve a true understanding of music:

> Notwithstanding all the experience I may have acquired in music from being associated with it for so long, I must confess that only with the aid of mathematics did my ideas become clear and did light replace a certain obscurity of which I was unaware before.[33]

Rameau's rhetoric in this Preface, as we have observed earlier, is unabashedly Cartesian. This is most apparent in the general aim of the *Traité*: to demonstrate a single natural ("clear and evident") principle for music from which one can deduce the rules of musical practice with mathematical precision. Once he had discovered his principle, the way was clear:

> I then recognized that the consequences it revealed constituted so many rules following from this principle. The true sense of these rules, their proper application, their relationships, their sequence (the simplest always introducing the less simple, and so on by degrees), and finally the choice of terms: all this, I say, of which I was ignorant before, developed in my mind with clarity and precision.[34]

Now the Cartesian aspirations of Rameau have been no secret to music historians. He has been described with little variation as a "pure Cartesian" and "a true product of the Age of Reason."[35] For Charles Lalo, "Everything is there: the methodical, even hyperbolic, doubt; the revelation of a *cogito* which is here an *audio*."[36] One French music historian, Catherine Kintzler, has gone so far as to dedicate an entire book to the celebration of Rameau's "delectable" Cartesian rationalism in both his music and theory:

> [This Cartesianism] was not a simple manner of being, a figure of style, a fashionable dressing. It was not simply a partial borrowing of a few acoustical propositions and formulas of presentation. It was a complete Cartesianism, dedicated to orderly argumentation, a passion, an unmeasured love for intelligible forms which was applied everywhere.[37]

---

32   *Traité*, Preface; Gossett, xxxiii.
33   Ibid., xxxv.
34   Ibid.
35   The citations are from, respectively, Philippe Beaussant, ed., *Rameau de A à Z* (Paris, 1983), 23; and Albert Cohen, *New Grove Dictionary of Music and Musicians*, ed. Stanley Sadie (London, 1980), s.v. "Rameau."
36   Charles Lalo, *Eléments d'une esthétique musicale scientifique* (Paris, 1939), 80.
37   Catherine Kintzler, *Jean-Philippe Rameau: splendeur et naufrage de l'esthétique du plaisir à l'âge classique* (Paris, 1983), 45–46.

As we saw in the quotation cited in Chapter 1 (p. 12), Rameau himself did not disguise his intellectual indebtedness to Descartes. But if we leave our analysis of Rameau's epistemology at that, then we will miss the real richness and complexities to be found in his theory.

We might begin by reconsidering the role of reason in Rameau's theory. Despite the numerous incantations of this Cartesian codeword throughout the *Traité*, Rameau never denies the importance of empiricism in the formation of a credible music theory. Reliance upon a musician's experience and ear, he says frequently, is essential for the discovery and validation of any musical principle. Rameau even opens a chapter entitled "Observations on Establishing Rules" (Chapter 18, Book 2) with this empirical dictum: "We may judge music only through our hearing; and reason has no authority unless it is in agreement with the ear."[38] This is an appropriate caveat, since throughout this chapter (as well as the previous chapter "on license") he must continually resort to experience (often under the guise of *bon goût*) to sanction the numerous exceptions that run contrary to his already-established principles.

Much in Rameau's theory, as we know, was validated by musical experience and had little to do with any Cartesian reasoning. Examples are his explanations for the minor triad, octave identity, the function of the subdominant, and the need for temperament. There is nothing inherent in the string divisions of the monochord or resonance of the *corps sonore* that should lead to these formulations. Indeed, Rameau's main theoretical challenge, as we will see in subsequent chapters, was to relate these musical ideas in a non-forced way to his principle of harmony.

In Rameau's judicial system, experience seems to be the ultimate court of appeal, not reason. True, experience may offer us infinite diversity "in which we shall always lose our way," and it may "sow doubts everywhere." Yet, in the final account, reason has authority only "*as long as experience does not contradict [it]*."[39] In later years, Rameau would frequently cite with approval an aphorism of Cicero, "Superbissimum auris judicium" (The judgment of the ear is superior).[40]

We should hardly be surprised that Rameau paid such careful attention to experience in his theory. After all, he was first and foremost a practicing musician; in an active career spanning over sixty years, he was continually playing, composing, and listening to music, beginning with his humble church job as a youth and ending as the most renowned and prolific opera composer in France at the end of his life. For all his efforts spent on music theory, we must never forget that on an almost daily basis throughout his life he was constantly engaged in matters of practical music. His deep understanding of tonality was gained only through an almost unremitting immersion in practice. There was no aspect of his theory that was not a

---

38 *Traité*, 125; Gossett, 139.
39 *Ibid.*, 126; Gossett, 140. My emphasis.
40 Beginning with the *Nouvelles réflexions* (Paris, 1752), 51; *CTW* IV, xliv. Strictly speaking, Rameau used the aphorism not to elevate experience over reason, but rather to elevate hearing over all the other senses (a topic we will discuss in Chapter 8, pp. 215 ff.). Nonetheless, the increased priority he accorded to the ear is evidence of heightened empirical convictions.

product of – and tested against – this immense wealth of experience. More than once Rameau advised the student seeking to master the art of music to begin by learning to play and improvise at the keyboard.[41] Only in this way (that is, through practice), can one begin to develop one's ear, and thence, an understanding of music. One could never gain such an understanding through abstract theory.

There were other critical qualities essential to the composer that theory could not teach either. These were those quintessential qualities of French classical aesthetics: *bon goût, grâce,* and *sentiment.* As a composer of opera, Rameau knew his task was to underscore and express with music the rich gamut of passions suggested by his texts. In his famous letter to Houdar de la Motte of 1727 soliciting a libretto to set, the then-untested composer tried to distance himself from the "savant musicien" who, while skilful in combining notes with one another, is:

> so absorbed in these combinations that he sacrifices everything to them, common sense, wit, and feeling (*sentiment*). Such a one is but a school musician, of a school where it is a question of notes and nothing more.[42]

Rameau quickly added, however, that a more dispassionate understanding of music attained by the careful study of nature is still useful – indeed indispensable – for a composer. Repeating a doctrine made famous by Boileau, Rameau insisted that raw emotions that are the product of unmediated experience need to be filtered through reason in order to be effectively captured and expressed by the artist. Otherwise they will soon become enervated and tedious.

The fact remains, though, that before reason can have any meaningful application, the composer must first possess an abundance of experience, both of the passions he wishes to express and of the musical language by which he wishes to express them. For all of Rameau's emphasis upon reason, over and over again we find him ceding to experience, even when this forces him (as we will see it often will) to loosen the tight theoretical systems that he labored so intently to construct.[43]

One music historian who has recognized the true empirical character behind Rameau's epistemology is Marie-Elisabeth Duchez. In a number of perspicacious studies, Duchez has argued that the empirical side of Rameau's theory plays a far more critical role than does the deductive-rationalist side:

> The coherent system of hypotheses which forms the basis of Rameau's deductions results from an almost subconscious inductive synthesis comprising not only the results of the experience of harmonic resonance emitted by the *corps sonore*, but also the hypotheses with which his previous knowledge furnished him (definitions and properties of sound and its parameters, primary relations between sounds, etc.) . . . placed in connection with his empirical musical experience.[44]

---

41 *Nouveau système de musique théorique et pratique* (Paris, 1726), 91.
42 Quoted in Girdlestone, *Rameau*, 9.
43 Rameau continued to stress the necessity of experience and taste in the formation of one's musical skills in his later treatises. See, e.g., his remarks in the *Code de musique pratique*, 133.
44 Marie-Elisabeth Duchez, "D'Alembert diffuseur de la théorie harmonique de Rameau: déduction scientifique et simplification musicale," *Jean d'Alembert, savant et philosophe: Portrait à plusieurs voix*, ed. Monique Emery and Pierre Monzani (Paris, 1989), 486.

Duchez argues that the real basis of Rameau's theory was his daily experience as a musician, hence her preferred label: "épistémo-musicale."[45]

Was Rameau then being disingenuous by insisting upon the precedence of reason in the *Traité*? Was his Cartesian posturing mere rhetoric, or worse, was it that he was simply a bad Cartesian? For one American historian who has studied Rameau's writings, this is indeed the case. Charles Paul finds the label "Cartesian" to be more obfuscating than enlightening as applied to Rameau.[46]

Yet it is not impossible to reconcile Rameau's impassioned Cartesian professions with his equally impassioned exhortations to experience and practice. For the boundary between any "rationalist" and "empiricist" epistemology is never quite so clearly drawn. All rationalist theories, after all, must intersect at some point with empirical evidence, just as there can be no empirical observation completely devoid of theoretical precepts.[47] Descartes did not eschew observation or experimentation in his own scientific practice, despite the popular depictions of his commentators. For all his suspicion of the senses and reliance upon "clear and distinct" ideas innate in our minds, recent scholarship has shown beyond a doubt how "experience" actually constitutes a major part of the Cartesian method.[48] To be sure, in his more celebrated philosophical writings Descartes emphasized a rationalist, deductivist epistemology that appears to discount empiricism. But this can be seen as a rhetorical gambit.[49] Reason and experience are two essential components of any epistemology, and if either one is more accented than the other, it can hardly be at the complete exclusion of the other. It is thus naive to posit empiricism and rationalism as two opposing and irreconcilable methodologies, with all their related binary oppositions: inductive versus deductive, the "heart" versus the mind, or, ultimately, Newton versus Descartes.

CONDILLAC AND THE "NEWTONIAN METHOD"

One philosopher who was a contemporary of Rameau, the Abbé Condillac, recognized quite clearly the dialectical relation between reason and experience,

---

45 Marie-Elisabeth Duchez, "Valeur épistémologique de la théorie de la basse fondamentale de Jean-Philippe Rameau: connaissance scientifique et représentation de la musique," *Studies on Voltaire and the Eighteenth Century* 254 (1986), 130.

46 Charles Paul, "Jean-Philippe Rameau (1683–1764), The Musician as *Philosophe*," *Proceedings of the American Philosophical Society* 114/2 (April, 1970), 141.

47 Thomas Kuhn has exposed many of the fallacies inherent in a simplistic rationalist–empiricist bifurcation of scientific practice in his article "Mathematical versus Experimental Traditions in the Development of Physical Science," in *The Essential Tension: Selected Studies in Scientific Traditions and Change* (Chicago, 1977), 31–65.

48 For two studies emphasizing the empirical aspects of Cartesian science, see Desmond Clarke, *Descartes' Philosophy of Science* (Manchester, 1982), 24–30; and Géraud Tournadre, *L'Orientation de la science cartésienne* (Paris, 1982), 47–125.

49 A theme explored by William R. Shea, "Descartes and the Art of Persuasion," in *Persuading Science: The Art of Scientific Rhetoric*, ed. Marcello Pera and William R. Shea (Canton, Mass., 1991), 125–41; and Andrew E. Benjamin, "Descartes' Fable: the *Discours de la méthode*," in *The Figural and the Literal: Problems of Language in the History of Science and Philosophy*, ed. Andrew E. Benjamin, Geoffrey N. Cantor, and John R. Christie (Manchester, 1987), 10–30.

and offered a program for balancing the two that I believe is highly suggestive of Rameau's music theory. In his widely-read *Traité des systèmes* of 1749, Condillac prescribed a multi-stepped method by which any scientific, philosophical, or aesthetic system could be constructed and verified. His attempt can thus be considered the eighteenth-century equivalent to Descartes's *Discours de la méthode*.

Condillac defines a system as follows:

A system is nothing but the disposition of the different parts of an art or science in an order in which they all mutually sustain one another and where the last are explained by the first. Those parts which give reason to the others are called *principles*, and the system is so much the more perfect as the principles are few in number. It is even to be hoped that they may be reduced to a single one.[50]

A system in Condillac's view could be imaged as a chain in which all elements connect hierarchically, with a single governing principle at the top of the chain. In a well-ordered system, all the elements of a science should be disposed in as rigorous a manner as possible so that one could latch on to any part and descend or ascend the chain to any other point by induction or deduction. The task of all philosophy was to discover the principles that control a system. Condillac distinguished three ways in which this could be done: through (1) philosophical axioms, (2) undemonstrated hypotheses, and (3) facts verified by observation and experimentation.

The first kind of system results from the baleful *esprit de système*. Here the philosopher places his principle first and then tries to deduce its consequences. An example of such a "first principle" is the aphorism "it is impossible for the same thing to be and not to be." By rigorous analysis of the writings of four important seventeenth-century philosophers (Descartes, Spinoza, Malebranche, and Leibniz), Condillac attempted to show how this kind of system-building led to logical circularities and sophistries.[51]

The second of Condillac's systems was less invidious, although still prone to error. Here the scientist proposes hypotheses for various phenomena and then seeks to test his hypotheses against the "nature of things" through observation and experimentation. This method is commonly used by scientists, Condillac admits; in many cases it is the only method available. However, it can never lead to certainty. Scientific principles are never "demonstrated"; rather they are merely confirmed and thus given varying degrees of probability.

Condillac reserves only for his third system the title of a true philosophical system. This is the *esprit systématique*. One begins with the empirical data of observation and experimentation and proceeds through precise calculation until one has reached the principles of a science. This is the only certain means of "demonstration." Condillac describes the process as consisting of two steps:

---

50 *Traité des systèmes, où l'on en démêle les inconvéniens et les avantages* in *Oeuvres de Condillac*, 16 vols. (Paris, 1778), II, 1.
51 For a good discussion of Condillac's analysis of systems, see Ellen McNiven Hine, *A Critical Study of Condillac's "Traité des systèmes"* (The Hague, 1979).

The method I employ to make systems I call "analysis." One sees that it comprises two operations: "decomposition" and "composition." By the first, one separates all the ideas which pertain to a subject and examines them until one has discovered the idea which ought to be the germ of all the others. By the second, one disposes them following the order of their generation.[52]

Condillac's favorite illustration of this process was a watch. One can understand the inner workings of a watch only by carefully taking apart its pieces, examining and classifying them with meticulous care, and then reassembling them into a whole. In this way, one arrives at a precise understanding of its operations.

The first step, then, is to reduce a science to its simplest elements through empirical analysis. We will recognize that we have arrived at such a point when all the elements are at such an elementary and primitive state that they cannot be further reduced or defined without tautology. The second step after reduction is "composition." We must rebuild our simple elements back into more complex bodies. This is accomplished by assigning a precise "sign" to each component. Using a carefully formulated language appropriate to that science (ideally one that is quantitative), we can then piece together the elements one by one to form a system, and thereby understand the exact workings of that science. Indeed, this is the simplest part of the scientist's task. According to Condillac, with a properly "decomposed" science one need merely make a few simple calculations comparing and combining the various signs in order to discover its true principles.

It is not difficult to discover the source of Condillac's analytic-synthetic method – it is the very method propounded by Isaac Newton.[53] The philosophes were unanimous in crediting Newton with the most luminous method of investigating nature. Rather than having recourse to arbitrary hypotheses and *a priori* axioms, Newton used an empirical approach, which, according to d'Alembert, "consisted of deducing his reasonings and conclusions directly from phenomena without any antecedent hypotheses, by commencing with simple principles, deducing the first laws of nature from a small number of chosen phenomena, and using these laws to explain the other effects."[54] Newton's method was a bold synthesis of observation and mathematics. He introduced "geometry into physics," and "united experience and calculation." Moreover, he displayed judicious philosophical modesty by not seeking to explain phenomena beyond what could be known through empirical demonstration or mathematical calculation. It was enough that the inverse square law of gravitation could be shown to account for planetary orbits without having to explain the cause of attraction.

---

52 *Traité des systèmes*, 296–97.
53 The *locus classicus* of Newton's methodological credo is found in the Queries appended to the revised English edition of his *Opticks*: Isaac Newton, *Opticks,* 4th edition (London, 1730; reprint edition, New York, 1952), 404–05.
54 *Encyclopédie*, s.v. "Newtonianisme."

Of course Newton was not the first scientist to describe, let alone employ, the analytic-synthetic method. This procedure may be traced at least to Aristotle.[55] Throughout the Middle Ages, *resolutio* and *compositio* were standard modes of disputation among scholastic dialecticians. What is noteworthy, though, was that they were considered independent methods. Preference among logicians was given to the method of composition, wherein one begins, as in Euclidean geometry, with something known to deduce an unknown. It was not until the seventeenth century, especially in the writings of Francis Bacon, that a purely (if over-simplified) inductive methodology was articulated.

Newton's greatest accomplishment (so thought the philosophes) was his reconciliation of inductive and deductive strategies, which is to say, the empirical and rational methods.[56] Through careful empirical analysis of phenomena (the inductive approach), Newton was able to discover a number of regularities which led him to hypothesize several principles of optics and celestial mechanics. Having arrived at this point, Newton was able to generalize mathematically some of these principles into axioms by which other hitherto-unrelated phenomena could be discovered and explained (the deductive approach). Of course, in reality Newton's actual practice was neither as simple nor as consistent as this description implies.

There is no uniform "logic of discovery" or ideal "scientific method" that can be reconstructed in order to account for the complex and unpredictable processes by which scientists assembled theories, let alone one of Newton's stature. We must distinguish the "rhetoric of method" by which scientists and philosophers claim discoveries are made from the reality of the process, which is inevitably far messier, and influenced by a variety of psychological, social, and even political forces.[57] Nonetheless, the analytic-synthetic method described by Condillac and d'Alembert does at least capture part of the "Newtonian style" in that it offers a means of accommodating both the mathematical and experimental elements so conspicuous in his science.[58] And with suitable adjustments, it conveys a strong suggestion of Rameau's "style."

---

[55] Henry Guerlac, "Newton and the Method of Analysis," *Dictionary of the History of Ideas*, ed. Philip Wiener, 4 vols. (New York, 1973), III, 380.

[56] E. W. Strong, "Newton's Mathematical Way," in *Roots of Scientific Thought,* ed. Philip Wiener and Aaron Noland (New York, 1957), 412–32.

[57] The classic study espousing this view, of course, is Thomas Kuhn's *The Structure of Scientific Revolutions* (Chicago, 1962). While it is not possible here to explore any further this important and fascinating question, I will simply offer the titles of three different – and in some ways radically opposing – analyses of scientific practice that nonetheless share the same skepticism as concerns the positivists' claims of objectivity and uniformity in scientific method: Michael Polanyi, *Personal Knowledge* (Chicago, 1958); Paul Feyerabend, *Against Method* (London, 1975); and Bruno Latour, *Science in Action* (Cambridge, Mass., 1987). A number of interesting historical case studies of scientific rhetoric that also serve to disarm the positivists' position are to be found in the two volumes cited in footnote 49 above.

[58] For a good analysis of the Newtonian "style," see I. Bernard Cohen, *The Newtonian Revolution* (Cambridge, Mass., 1987), especially 52–154.

THE DIALECTICS OF THEORY AND PRACTICE

If we look from a distance at the content and evolution of Rameau's theory, it appears that the "method" he followed, such as one may call it, was analytic-synthetic. Rameau seemed to treat his own music and that of his contemporaries as a body of empirical evidence. Through astute analysis of this practice, he observed consistencies in its behavior, and posited a number of provisional hypotheses and heuristic arguments to explain it: the generative fundamental, octave identity, the seventh as source of all dissonance, the fundamental progression of the fifth, etc. (Much of this empirical basis is already evident in his Clermont notes as described by Suaudeau.) From this point, Rameau hypothesized a single master-principle to accommodate these observations. In the *Traité*, this principle was the division of a monochord string; in later works it was the resonance of the *corps sonore*.

Now this is obviously an idealized depiction of the development of Rameau's theory, which was in reality far more complicated and eclectic, not to say inconsistent. As we will see over the following chapters, Rameau's principles and theoretical formulations were not the result simply of his acute observational faculties or refined analytic mind. There were a number of *a priori* ideological biases he brought to his theory that delimited the kinds of observations he would make and the conclusions he would draw therefrom. Nonetheless, the analytic-synthetic model is useful in that it highlights the inherent tension between empirical and theoretical systematization that we will find runs constantly through Rameau's writings. And as I have already recorded in Chapter 1, many of the philosophes recognized his success at reconciling these two as a fully Newtonian accomplishment.

Condillac, significantly, singled out Rameau's theory as a model of the *esprit systématique* in his *Traité des systèmes*:

M. Rameau has built upon harmonic generation a system that can serve me as an example. He has reduced everything to the harmony of the *corps sonore*. In effect, it is evident that harmony consists of a single sound which makes heard its harmonics, previously [considered] only noise. Thus, when one observes analytically all the different combinations and movements which this harmony experiences, one will see it transformed into all phenomena, which seem to possess no other rule than the imagination of the musician. If this system suffers from difficulties, it is only that the parts have not all yet been thoroughly analyzed.[59]

Condillac's last point brings up a disturbing problem. Rameau's system, as complete and consistent as it appeared, still suffered from a number of empirical inadequacies. "Having cleared up the beginning of this difficult material in which a large number of questions did not appear susceptible to demonstration," d'Alembert noted, "[Rameau] was often faced, as he recognized himself, with multiplying the *analogies*, *transformations*, and *conventions*, in order to satisfy reason *as much as possible*

---

[59] *Traité des systèmes*, 296. Similar sentiments were expressed by Condillac in his *Essai sur l'origine des connoissances humaines* (Amsterdam, 1746), 73.

in the explanations of phenomena."[60] Does this mean that his principle of harmony is then to be rejected? Not at all, d'Alembert reassures us:

> In matters of physical science, where it is impossible to use any other arguments, except such as arise from analogy or convention, it is natural that the analogy should be sometimes more, sometimes less sensible, and we dare say that it is the mark of an unphilosophical mind not to be able to recognize and distinguish this gradation and its different nuances. . . But in the meantime it would not be less unjust to reject this principle, because certain phenomena appear to be deduced from it with less success than others. It is only necessary to conclude that, by future research, means may be found for reducing these phenomena to this principle, or that harmony has perhaps some other unknown principle more general than the resonance of the *corps sonore*, and of which this is only a branch, or, lastly, that we ought not perhaps to attempt the reduction of the whole science of music to one and the same principle.[61]

D'Alembert compared Rameau's theory of the fundamental bass to Newton's theory of gravity. Both theories accounted for a wide range of observable phenomena, although a small number of anomalies persisted. "[These anomalies] do not confute the fundamental bass as the *principle of harmony and melody*, just as the system of gravity is the principle of physical astronomy, although this system cannot explain all the phenomena observed in the movement of celestial bodies."[62] Rameau's theory had the preponderance of evidence supporting it, given the wide range of musical practice that it did explain. Rameau's fundamental bass may thus be accepted provisionally, if not demonstratively, as the principle of harmony, since from it one can deduce "by an easy operation of reason, the chief and most essential laws of harmony."

Finally, in designating Rameau's "method" as analytic-synthetic, I want to emphasize again that I do not mean to suggest that this process was in any way uniformly diachronic, as one might infer from Condillac's narrative. The process was really more of a dialectic in which Rameau was constantly attempting to mediate between the empirical appearances of musical practice and the synthetic demands of theoretical systematization. This fact explains better than any other, I think, why Rameau's writings display such variety and vacillation. If we take a step back and view the main theoretical oeuvre produced by Rameau over some forty years synoptically, it is possible to see this dialectic process quite clearly by dividing Rameau's most substantial publications and writings into practical and speculative halves, respectively (see Table 2.1).

---

60 Jean Le Rond d'Alembert, *Elémens de philosophie*, in *Oeuvres philosophiques, historiques, et littéraires de d'Alembert*, 5 vols. (Paris, 1821–22), I, 331.
61 *Elémens de philosophie*, xiv–xvii.
62 Ibid., 222.

Table 2.1 Rameau's theoretical writings

	"Practical" works	"Speculative" works
1716–21	"Clemont Notes"	
1722	Traité de l'harmonie (Books 3 and 4)	Traité de l'harmonie (Books 1 and 2)
1726		Nouveau système de musique théorique
1732	Dissertation sur les différentes méthodes d'accompagnement	
1737		Génération harmonique
1738–45	"L'Art de la basse fondamentale"	
1750		Démonstration du principe de l'harmonie
1760	Code de musique pratique	Nouvelles réflexions sur le principe sonore
1764		"Vérités également ignorées et interressantes"

Admittedly this bifurcation presents an over-simplified picture. No work was exclusively "practical" in content, just as none was exclusively "theoretical." (The *Génération harmonique*, for instance, includes a practical composition method, while, conversely, the *Code de musique pratique* has sections of quite a speculative nature.) But I think this division does capture the two fundamental epistemological forces that pulled upon Rameau.

In his "practical" works, we hear Rameau the organist, choir director, harpsichord teacher, and composer speaking. Beginning with the Clermont notes described by Suaudeau, and traversing the last two books of the *Traité*, the *Dissertation sur les différentes méthodes d'accompagnement* of 1732, the lengthy manuscript entitled "L'Art de la basse fondamentale" stemming from the early 1740s, and culminating in the *Code de musique pratique* of 1760, Rameau proves himself to be a keen and reliable observer of musical practice. In these practical writings, Rameau comprehensively lays out guidelines for the learning of thorough-bass accompaniment and the skills of composition (two disciplines that for most eighteenth-century musicians were related). All his analyses concerning harmonic "modulation," dissonance treatment, melody, counterpoint, ornamentation, operatic conventions, accompaniment, etc. are the product of a seasoned and perspicacious musical practitioner.

The "speculative" writings that seemed to alternate in regular rhythm with the practical works would always take as a starting point the empirical observations codified in these practical works, and attempt to synthesize and ground them within some coherent theoretical framework. Of course the nature of this framework changed for Rameau over time. The kinds of arguments and evidence he employed in the *Traité* of 1722 were not the same as in the *Démonstration* of 1750. As we will see over the following chapters, Rameau was always testing new scientific evidence, methods, rhetorics, and heuristics on behalf of his theory. As I have already suggested, there is no one uniform scientific model in the

Enlightenment to which Rameau aspired or by which we may judge his work. The various explanations he offered all shared some degree of endorsement in the eighteenth century. The important point is that his theoretical enterprise was an attempt to accommodate and account for the empirical practice of music using scientific models sanctioned in his day.

Rameau may never quite have attained his goal of complete reconciliation. But every work moved him a step closer; each publication built upon material developed in preceding works. From a strictly chronological perspective, the results may appear chaotic and desultory, making the analysis of any one work isolated from the others a precarious enterprise. This is why it is so difficult to derive a picture of Rameau's theory from any single publication, or even worse, to take all his writings and try to reduce them to a single and static form. (This is also surely why all redactors since d'Alembert and Rousseau have had such difficulties in distilling Rameau's ideas in their popularizations.) Rameau's theory is not so much a fixed doctrine as it is a dialectical process. In order to capture the full richness and dynamics of his theory, we must be able to follow the dialogue that he carried on with himself between theorist and composer.

To be sure, tensions between theory and practice are not the unique province of Rameau's writings. In any music theory there is necessarily a process of accommodation between the intractable facts of empirical practice and the synthetic demand of theoretical systematization. But never was this goal so ardently pursued as by Rameau, for never were the roles of composer and theorist more inextricably intertwined within one individual. Both the speculative and practical coexist in Rameau's theoretical universe in precarious balance. Each evolved *pari passu*, feeding off and in return nurturing the other in mutual symbiosis, each distinct from – yet bound to – the other.

3

PRECURSORS OF HARMONIC THEORY

For such a revolutionary work, the *Traité de l'harmonie* contains surprisingly few individual components that can be said to be original to Rameau. The fundamental bass, as I have suggested earlier, was not so much a discovery as a unification of received theoretical formulations and practical heuristics. Many of the most celebrated hypotheses comprising the fundamental bass – the triadic foundation of harmony, chordal inversion, the concatenation of dissonance, the parsing of music into cadential phrases, and the generative fundamental – are ones that can be found individually in seventeenth-century practical and speculative theory texts. Indeed, the obvious filiation of the fundamental bass to seventeenth-century theory led numerous critics in Rameau's own day to dispute its paternity.

One critic of Rameau's writings, for example, attributed the fundamental bass to Kircher, while another claimed that the fundamental bass was common knowledge in Paris thirty years before Rameau ever published a word about it.[1] The organist Gilbert Trouflaut reported that a "Mr. l'Abbé Dugré Maitre de Musique de l'Eglise Cathédrale de Paris" was told by Rameau himself that he (Rameau) was not the true discoverer of the fundamental bass, but learned of it as a child in Clermont from a "very old man who had long contemplated this art."[2]

While it is not quite true that the fundamental bass was a seventeenth-century invention, there were numerous adumbrations of it by theorists preceding Rameau in their treatises of composition and thorough-bass. If these theorists were not exactly giants upon whose shoulders Rameau stood (to borrow Newton's apt metaphor), they did offer a number of practical heuristics and informal guidelines that Rameau would use as a starting point. In the present chapter we will look at some of these precedents. In the following chapter we shall consider filiations of the fundamental bass to more speculative theoretical literature in the seventeenth century. We shall then be able to determine to what degree Rameau was dependent upon his predecessors, and what exactly was new in his theory.

---

1 *CTW* VI, 75, 38. The two critics were, respectively, Castel and Montéclair. We will shortly be looking in some detail at both these men's critique of Rameau's theory.
2 *CTW* VI, lii. The musician named was probably the Abbé Jean-Baptiste Guileminot Dugré who was *Maître de Musique* at Notre Dame from 1774 to 1790. While it is hardly likely that Rameau would ever have suggested such a thing to anyone, it does appear that Dugré was well acquainted with Rameau's theory – and possibly the composer himself – given the evidence of a short but faithful résumé of the fundamental bass in his own handwriting: "Principes de Composition de Mr. l'abbé DuGré" (F-Pn Rés F. 1433 fols. 38r-41v).

SEVENTEENTH-CENTURY TRIADIC THEORY

One of the most persistent shibboleths concerning Rameau's *Traité de l'harmonie* is that it was the first real "theory of harmony" ever to be written. Rameau, so the popular depiction goes, broke with the received models of contrapuntal pedagogy by positing harmony at the core of composition instruction.[3] Depending upon the historian's particular bias, the accomplishment may be either hailed or decried. For partisans such as Riemann and Fétis, Rameau's discovery of the fundamental bass opened a brilliant and fertile period of harmonic theory (to which they each naturally believed their respective music theory to be the culmination), while in the view of detractors such as Schenker and his followers, Rameau's theory inaugurated a period of darkness.[4] Neither position, however, can be countenanced by the facts. In both practical and speculative theory texts from the seventeenth century, there is ample evidence of clear "harmonic thinking."

Already in the first decade of the seventeenth century, the triad had assumed a central position in the theories of several pioneering Germans such as Joachim Burmeister, Otto Siegfried Harnisch, and above all, Johannes Lippius.[5] Music was understood and taught by these theorists not so much according to the intervallic relationship between independent voices but rather according to the articulation and disposition of individual chords. Taking their cue from Zarlino, who had canonized the *harmonia perfetta* in his hallowed *senario* (a result of the arithmetic division of the octave and fifth), they considered the major triad to be the most fundamental consonant construct of music (see p. 74). Lippius christened this chord the *trias harmonica*, and compared its perfection to the divine Trinity.

French music theorists at the beginning of the seventeenth century evinced little of the triadic awareness of their German counterparts. On the whole, we may say that until mid-century, French theorists tended to be rather traditional.[6] For example,

---

3   See, e.g., Hugo Riemann, *Geschichte der Musiktheorie*, 2nd edition (Leipzig, 1920), 474–75.

4   In an essay whose very title sets up one of the most specious polarities ever conceived by a music theorist, Schenker decried what he saw as the baleful effect of Rameau's fundamental bass upon the history of musical thought, by which the "seeds of death . . . penetrated into music theory and indirectly into composition": "Rameau oder Beethoven? Erstarrung oder geistiges Leben in der Musik?" *Das Meisterwerk in der Musik* 3 (1930), 492. But as Harald Krebs has shown, Schenker's antipathy towards Rameau is expressed only in his later writings. In his earlier essays, Schenker evinced a far more tempered – and in places, even charitable – assessment of the French theorist's accomplishments. See Harald Krebs, "Schenker's Changing Views of Rameau: A Comparison of Remarks in *Harmony, Counterpoint*, and 'Rameau oder Beethoven,'" *Theoria* 3 (1988), 59–72.

5   For a good overview of this history, see Joel Lester, *Between Modes and Keys: German Theory 1592–1802* (Stuyvesant [N.Y.], 1989), 28–52; and Benito V. Rivera, "The Seventeenth-Century Theory of Triadic Generation and Invertibility and its Application in Contemporaneous Rules of Composition," *Music Theory Spectrum* 6 (1984), 63–78. Even earlier precedents to these triadic theories have been identified by Professor Rivera in his article "Harmonic Theory in Musical Treatises of the Late Fifteenth and Early Sixteenth Centuries," *Music Theory Spectrum* 1 (1979), 80–95.

6   Which is not to say that German theory was uniformly progressive, either. Despite their widespread recognition and acceptance of the triad as an autonomous compositional construct, for example, most German theorists in the seventeenth century continued to teach the older modal system. Indeed, it was only in Germany that we find theorists in the eighteenth century passionately defending the modal system against the practice of major-minor tonality, long after the latter was accepted fully by theorists elsewhere on the continent (Lester, *Between Modes and Keys*, 47).

we find Zarlino's restrictive rules of counterpoint taught faithfully in France long after they were abandoned in most other countries.⁷ The reason for the conservative nature of French theory might be explained in part by a confluence of social and political factors in which the church, court, and music guilds sought to maintain tight control over musical practice by keeping at bay many of the innovations stemming from the Italian *seconda pratica*.⁸ And while these efforts proved only partially successful, they did have the effect of stifling most reforms of music theory and pedagogy. (Many of these conservative forces, we should also remember, were operative well into Rameau's day.)

Still, French music did not entirely escape the general evolution of musical style in the seventeenth century towards simpler, chordally-oriented textures obeying an incipient tonal syntax. A number of independent repertoires of early French Baroque music displaying these features can be identified: the *air de cour*, the Huguenot psalter, choruses from the *ballet de cour*, the *musique mesurée* of Jean Antoine de Baïf and his followers, and the improvised choral psalmody termed "fauxbourdon."⁹ In the numerous dance suites played by lutenists, guitarists, and clavecinists, we find clear evidence of an emerging "harmonic sensibility." Inspired by the chordal texture of Spanish guitar music that was imported via Italy, French instrumentalists in the seventeenth century adopted various Spanish homophonic dance genres within their instrumental suites: the *sarabande, passacaille, folie,* and *chaconne*. All this points to the emergence of a decided predilection for rich chordal sonorities that has continued to this day to be a hallmark of French musical taste.

In response to the ever-growing chordal textures of this music, a few theorists from the mid-century (such as Antoine Parran and Antoine de Cousu) began to incorporate triadic formulations in their pedagogy. They called the triad, translated from Zarlino, the *harmonie parfaite*.¹⁰ Ironically, this was just at the time some German theorists were abandoning the simple triadic pedagogy of Lippius and his generation. One reason suggests itself: the simple triadic theories of Lippius and his followers could not account for the increased complexity of dissonance treatment found in the more advanced Italian practice coming to be known in Germany at mid-century. Hence the primitive triadic theories found in the early part of the century became increasingly replaced by more contrapuntally oriented compositional

7 Albert Cohen, "Survivals of Renaissance Thought in French Theory 1610–1670: A Bibliographical Study," *Aspects of Medieval and Renaissance Music: A Festschrift for Gustav Reese* (New York, 1966), 82–95. The reader should note that in using the term "counterpoint," I do not necessarily restrict my meaning to genres and theories of polyphonic pieces like the fugue. I refer, rather, to a perspective from which musical structures can be understood as composite intervallic relations between individual voices and governed by definitive rules of voice-leading. It is thus possible to take a homophonic genre like the chorale and analyze it as a contrapuntal composition, just as it is equally possible to take a polyphonic genre like the fugue and analyze it as a harmonic composition.
8 For a lively discussion of the social forces shaping French music in the seventeenth century, see Robert Isherwood, *Music in the Service of the King: France in the Seventeenth Century* (Ithaca, 1973), especially 150–203.
9 Herbert Schneider, *Die französische Kompositionslehre in der ersten Hälfte des 17. Jahrhunderts* (Tutzing, 1972), 228–29.
10 *Ibid.*, 230. The term *trias harmonica* was never used by French theorists until the eighteenth century (e.g. by Brossard in his *Dictionaire*, s.v. "sysygia" and "trias harmonica").

theories. Paradoxically, the very triadic innovations of monodic recitative introduced by the Italians as a replacement for the polyphonic complexities of the sixteenth century had themselves soon evolved into a sophisticated harmonic language that could only be explained by a restoration of contrapuntal pedagogy, albeit with updated rules and licenses.

We thus find two parallel – and in many ways contradictory – developments in seventeenth-century musical style. On the one hand, there was a trend towards simplified triadic textures that displayed increasing tonal characteristics. On the other hand, there were, particularly in Italy, ever bolder explorations and employment of dissonance for expressiveness that appeared to complicate, if not undermine, this emerging tonality. In one fundamental sense, there was no contradiction here, as the development and effectiveness of the most extreme "theatrical" dissonance was to some degree predicated upon a clearly-implied triadic tonality. In any event, since French music tended to remain more insulated from the *seconda pratica* during the seventeenth century, these French theorists could deal with their indigenous triadic practice with far fewer of the difficulties encountered by musicians elsewhere. And nowhere does this triadic awareness emerge more strongly than in their pedagogy for the thorough bass.

FRENCH THOROUGH-BASS PRACTICE

Thorough bass was a practice conducive to a harmonic conceptualization of music, since its primary charge was to "fill in" or double various musical textures by the sounding of chords above the bass. These chords either were indicated by the composer with the use of figured-bass notation, or, as was more common in the seventeenth century, were inferred "sopra la parte" by the performer reading the *partitura* or the simple unfigured-bass line. A consequence of this practice was that the composer and performer learned to parse the music into discrete vertical units that could be encoded by a shorthand notation of signatures. Even highly complex polyphonic textures could be expressed harmonically through the thorough bass.

For the political reasons described above, the French were relatively late in adopting the Italian thorough bass. The first work by a French composer calling for it was not published until 1652.[11] When the thorough bass finally did arrive after mid-century, though, it spread quickly. One suspects that the reason for this had to do with the way in which this new compositional device proved congenial to the French predilection for full harmonic sonorities. Not coincidentally, perhaps, the instruments favored by the French for the realization of the thorough bass during the seventeenth century were just those instruments most suited for producing strongly chordal textures: the family of strummed instruments such as the lute, theorbo, and above all, the guitar.[12]

---

[11] The *Cantica Sacra* of Henry Du Mont.
[12] A point well-emphasized by Albert Cohen in his article "A Study of Instrumental Ensemble Practice in Seventeenth-Century France," *Galpin Society Journal* 15 (1962), 3–17.

The solo dance pieces indigenous to the Spanish five-course guitar were primarily homophonic in texture, and were played using a technique of rapid strumming called *rasgueado*. (As mentioned earlier, a number of the most popular dance genres cultivated by the French in the seventeenth century had their origins in Spanish guitar music.) Even if more contrapuntal textures would be played by more proficient guitarists using the technique of *punteado* (plucking), the general textures of these pieces remained mostly chordal.[13] The theorbo, a particularly favored strummed instrument for the "petit chœur" of the Opéra continuo section, could produce more elaborate contrapuntal textures than the guitar on account of its greater size and number of strings. Still, few theorbo composers and performers could resist adding to their solo music sections of chordal strumming to exploit the distinctively rich and deep resonance of the instrument.

The importance of all these various strummed instruments to French thorough-bass practice in the seventeenth century is underscored by comparing the number of thorough-bass manuals published before 1700 written for guitarists and theorbists to those written for keyboardists. Whereas there are eight such thorough-bass manuals aimed at guitarists and theorbists, there are only three works for harpsichordists and organists. And of the latter, the only substantial one was subtitled "for the Theorbo and Harpsichord."[14]

Seventeenth-century French thorough-bass treatises

A. For guitar, lute, and theorbo

Fleury, Nicolas. *Méthode pour apprendre facilement à toucher le theorbe sur la basse-continue*. Paris, 1660.

Bartolimi (Bolognese), Angelo Michele. *Table pour apprendre facilement à toucher le theorbe sur la basse-continue*. Paris, 1669.

Carré, Antoine, sieur de La Grange. *Livre de guitarre . . . avec la manière de toucher sur la partie ou basse continue*. Paris, 1671.

Corbetta, Francesco. *La guitarre royalle*. Paris, 1671.

Grénerin, Henry. *Livre de guitare . . . avec une instruction pour jouer la basse continüe*. Paris, 1680.

Perrine. *Livre de musique pour le lut. Contenant une métode nouvelle et facile pour aprendre à toucher le lut sur les notes de la musique . . . et une table pour aprendre à toucher le lut sur la basse continüe*. Paris, 1680.

Grénerin, Henry. *Livre de théorbe . . . avec une nouvelle méthode très facile pour apprendre à jouer sur la partie les basses continues*. Paris, 1682.

Derosier, Nicolas. *Les principes de la guitare*. Paris, 1690.

---

13 I have explored the theoretical implications of this practice in an article, "The Spanish Baroque Guitar and Seventeenth-Century Triadic Theory," *Journal of Music Theory* 36/1 (1992), 1–42.

14 If we expand our survey to include French-language publications produced outside of France, we could also cite the short résumé of rules compiled by the Belgian organist Lambert Chaumont, "Petit Traité de l'accompagnement," appended to the *Pièces d'orgue sur les 8 tons* (Liège, 1695).

B. For harpsichord and organ

Denis Delair, *Traité d'accompagnement pour le théorbe et le clavessin*. Paris, 1690.

Guillaume Gabriel Nivers, "L'Art d'accompagner sur la basse continue pour l'orgue et le Clavecin," *Motets a voix seule accompagnée de la basse continue*. Paris, 1689, 149–70.

Jean Henry d'Anglebert, "Les Principes de l'accompagnement," appended to the *Pièces de Clavecin*. Paris, 1689.

There were crucial theoretical ramifications to the practice of thorough-bass realizations using strummed instruments: performers on guitars and theorbos tended to play and think of music in strongly vertical (harmonic) terms, and formulated their notation and pedagogy accordingly. Most of the realizations prescribed in the tutors listed above were strongly chordal, sometimes to the point of entirely discounting voice-leading considerations. One example of this extreme verticalism can be seen in the informal rule of thumb found in most thorough-bass treatises for harmonizing a diatonic bass line. The basic rule states that a "perfect" (5/3) chord was assumed above any bass note unless it was *supra mi*, in which case a 6/3 chord was to be played, so as to avoid the forbidden mi–fa tritone.[15] Plate 3.1 shows a typical illustration of this rule that employs "alfabeto" notation, in which the respective letters indicate a particular chord to be strummed. (These chords are intabulated in tables usually found at the beginning of most guitar instructors. The particular intabulation specified in this example – from a collection of solo pieces by the guitar virtuoso Francesco Corbetta – is transcribed at the bottom of Plate 3.1.)[16] By means of such "scale triads," a continuo player could learn to provide a simple harmonization to almost any diatonic bass line.

Plate 3.1 Table and transposition of "scale triads"

---

15 Carl Dahlhaus, *Studies on the Origin of Harmonic Tonality*, trans. Robert O. Gjerdingen (Princeton, 1990), 120.
16 Appended to Francesco Corbetta, *Varii Capricii per la ghitarra spagnuolo* (Milan, 1643).

Elementary as these scale triads may be, they are noteworthy for suggesting an informal kind of harmonic awareness. Each scale degree of a mode is understood to support some appropriate chord. Scale triads thus reflect the beginnings of a subtle but ultimately decisive shift in music theory, in which a melodic conception of mode based upon the ordering and articulation of particular pitches (*ambitus* and *species*) gave way to a tonal conception of key based upon the context and function of its indigenous harmonies. As we follow the evolution of these scale triads as prescribed in thorough-bass primers during the course of the seventeenth century, we are in essence observing the emergence of a scale-degree based conceptualization of tonality – a kind of primitive *Stufentheorie*, if you will.[17]

The popularity of strummed instruments within the French continuo ensemble was largely confined to the seventeenth century. At least one treatise from the early eighteenth century, however, still reflects this tradition: François Campion's *Traité d'accompagnement et de composition selon la règle des octaves de musique* (Paris, 1716). Campion was himself a theorbist and guitarist, and his rules for accompaniment were very much a reflection of this background. Campion's treatise constitutes the final chapter of French guitar-theorbo continuo practice before its eventual usurpation by the keyboard.

The most important feature of Campion's treatise, the *règle de l'octave* – the "rule of the octave" – turns out to be an updated version of the scale triads found in seventeenth-century thorough-bass treatises for strummed instruments. Example 3.1 gives one version of Campion's *règle* in C major and A minor. The idea behind

Example 3.1 Campion's *règle de l'octave*

---

17 Many keyboard thorough-bass treatises from the seventeenth century also contained versions of these scale triads. (Examples by Banciardi, Banchieri, and Sabbatini are given by Franck T. Arnold in *The Art of Accompaniment From a Thorough-Bass* [Oxford, 1931], 75, 83–85, and 112–21, respectively.) But in line with the more contrapuntal orientation characteristic of keyboard practice, these are prescribed less as bona fide triads to be played above each scale degree than as intervallic progressions.

the *règle* is identical to that behind scale triads; it represents a utilitarian means by which a performer could realize a diatonic unfigured bass line *sur la partie*. Instead of the very awkward parallel triads found in earlier treatises, though, we now have a more elegant and a smoother progression largely consisting of sixth chords that help to define each scale degree. Only the tonic and dominant take triads, while all the other scale degrees support some variety of sixth chord. By knowing which particular sixth chord belongs to which scale degree, one has a means of harmonizing every diatonic scale progression. At the same time, by means of differing characteristic dissonances, one can orient a given chord within any key. So, for example, the 6/4/2 chord (the *accord du triton*) uniquely defines the fourth scale degree descending to a 6/3 on $\hat{3}$ (carrying the *accord de la petite sixte* in major). If however we play the *accord de la grande sixte* (6/5/3), we are defining the fourth scale degree ascending to the dominant. Should we raise this chord's lowest note a half-step, thus creating a diminished fifth (figured 6/5/3 – the *accord de fausse-quinte*), we are defining a new leading tone (*notte sensible*). With only a few exceptions, we can continue in this manner with each scale degree – whether in a major or minor key, whether in an ascending or descending format – and find a chord that distinguishes it from other scale degrees. We will see in Chapter 7 of what theoretical consequence the *règle de l'octave* was to be in Rameau's theory.

By the beginning of the eighteenth century, as I have noted, the harpsichord had largely supplanted strummed instruments in the French continuo. Nonetheless, I think we can detect the legacy of these strummed instruments in the chordal realizations that were prescribed for keyboardists in their own thorough-bass primers. This quality emerges most clearly in the heuristics by which French keyboardists realized the more complex dissonant figures increasingly found in eighteenth-century music.

In order to learn to play these many dissonant chords, thorough-bass instructors often posited the triad as a fixed structure from which more complicated signatures could be derived, either by inversion, by adding dissonant notes below or above the chord, or by altering the notes of the triad itself. Thorough-bass pedagogues began to adopt this strategy with increasing frequency in the course of the eighteenth century. A good example can be found in one text Rameau knew well and quoted in his writings (although not always with citation!): Michel de Saint-Lambert's short treatise, *Traité de l'accompagnement du clavecin, de l'orgue et de quelques autres instruments* (Paris, 1707).[18] In one section entitled "Réduction des Accords chiffrez aux Accords parfaits" ("Reduction of figured chords to perfect chords"), Saint-Lambert advises the student to learn to realize these dissonant figures by playing some consonant triad in the right hand above the bass note played by the left hand:

[18] Gossett has identified a number of short passages from the fourth Book of the *Traité* ("On Accompaniment") that are cribs of Saint-Lambert's treatise (Gossett, xiii–xiv). Strangely, though, none of the cribs concern any sophisticated theoretical ideas, but are quite pedestrian passages. I should add that in my reading of all of Rameau's writings, I have come across no other passages that I have been able to identify as cribbed. In any case, the passages under consideration deal with rather ordinary technicalities of accompaniment. It may seem odd that Rameau would choose to plagiarize them. Yet it was undoubtedly because of their rather pedestrian nature that he obviously felt no qualms in doing so.

Those who are learning Accompaniment usually have more difficulty understanding & remembering by heart figured chords than [they do] perfect chords. But it is easy to make this less difficult, by pointing out that when a [bass] note has several figures that assign to it an unusual chord – this chord (though unusual for that particular bass note) is often the perfect chord of another [bass] note. When an Ut, for example, is figured with a 6, the chord denoted by 6 on Ut is the perfect chord on La; if it is figured with Four & Six 6/4, this is the perfect chord on Fa; if it is figured with 7, or with 7/5, or with 7/5/3, this is the perfect chord on Mi, etc. In order, therefore to give the Reader all possible assistance on the above matter, I am going to teach him how to imagine the majority of dissonant chords indicated by these figures as perfect chords.[19]

Saint-Lambert goes on to take more dissonant figures (such as 6/♯4/2 and 9/7/4) and show how this strategy simplifies their realization.[20] In these last cases, the chord can be found by playing a triad one step higher and lower, respectively, than the notated bass.

The implications for Rameau's theory are striking: as a simple heuristic, students were taught to think of triads as the fundamental building blocks of harmony. All other chords, even the most dissonant, were implicitly derivative. We should not exaggerate the point, though. Saint-Lambert was not saying, as Rameau would, that in any *formal* sense all harmony could be derived from a fundamental harmonic source. His was an entirely practical rule of thumb.

RAMEAU'S PEDAGOGY OF THE THOROUGH BASS

Thorough-bass practice was the catalyst by which Rameau discovered the fundamental bass. Through his experience playing and composing the thorough bass, Rameau learned to conceive of music as discrete harmonic units that were controlled by a temporal bass line. It was a practice he recommended strongly for every music student. "The shortest and surest means for becoming properly sensitive to harmony," he wrote in 1726, "is by accompanying on the harpsichord or organ, since one will always hear a most regular succession of full harmonies."[21] This is why accompaniment was always such an important topic to Rameau, and why he returned to it again and again in his writings.[22] One reviewer of Rameau's own day recognized the importance of this discipline to the development of his theory:

The art of accompaniment is in a sense the primer of the author and that by which he began to be renowned. It is the key that has opened to him the most secret sanctuaries of music.

---

19 *A New Treatise on Accompaniment*, translated and edited by John S. Powell (Bloomington, 1991), 42–43.
20 Other thorough-bass theorists who follow a similar method are Denis Delair, *Traité d'accompagnement* (Paris, 1690); and Gottfried Keller, *A Compleat Method for Attaining to Play a Thorough Bass* (London, 1707). For a description of Keller's method, see Matthew Shirlaw, *The Theory of Harmony* (London, 1917), 448–53. Arnold is generally dismissive of this heuristic, calling it "worse than useless" (*The Art of Accompaniment*, 183).
21 *Nouveau système*, 91.
22 Besides the fourth Book of the *Traité*, advice to the student accompanist can be found in the *Dissertation* of 1732, "L'Art de la basse fondamentale" of the 1740s, and the *Code de musique pratique* of 1760.

It is in this that we should expect to receive from him ideas that are the most precise, the most naive (if I may use this term), the most developed and the most methodical.[23]

Thorough-bass accompaniment was not unlike composition, since the performer must be able to play harmonies without hesitation following the very rules that guide the composer. Hence Rameau could write in 1760 that "the principles of composition and accompaniment are the same but in an entirely opposite order."[24] Learning the former skill, he explained, is like studying a tree by starting at its roots, while in the latter, one begins with the branches.

We have seen through Suaudeau's study of Rameau's Clermont notes how the fundamental bass was initially conceived as a practical aid for learning to realize chords above a continuo bass. If many of the signatures of the figured bass were shown to be related, and indeed could be played using identical fingerings in the right hand, then the mastery of accompaniment is much simplified. As we have just seen, this was the approach that Saint-Lambert took. Rameau would adopt Saint-Lambert's idea in the fourth Book ("On Accompaniment") in his *Traité*, but pursue it far more systematically. Rameau suggests that by knowing only two basic chordal structures – the consonant triad and the dissonant seventh chord – an accompanist can realize any signature, provided he knows which triad or seventh chord to place above the given note in the bass.

We can see this process clearly illustrates in Example 3.2, taken from a "Carte générale de la basse fondamentale" written by Rameau to serve as a summary of his theory.[25] While Rameau wrote this example several years after the *Traité* was published, it accurately reflects ideas he articulated in Book 4 of that work. We can see that by utilizing only the consonant triad and three different seventh chords (and making a few adjustments for the minor mode), Rameau is able to generate thirty-two separate chords. The "fundamental bass" indicated below the basso continuo part reveals the true foundation of each chord, determined by the bottom note of the respective triad or seventh chord that forms its core. The first three chords are all considered to be consonant since they are products of the tonic triad. The second group of chords is derived from the dissonant minor seventh chord built on the second scale degree ("la septiéme de la seconde note du ton"). Here Rameau is able to generate twelve separate chords by placing different notes in the basso continuo. Two chromatic alterations are also included so as to produce a secondary dominant in the major mode, and a "French" augmented sixth chord in the minor mode. (The notes designated with black noteheads are to be omitted when the chord is sounded in order to avoid unacceptable octave doublings and dissonant clashes.) The chord figured 4 is another exception noted by Rameau. He still considers the chord to be a kind of seventh built on D even though a non-chord tone (G) is sounded in the basso continuo. This latter note of "supposition" is analyzed by Rameau as standing outside of the chord (an "hors d'œuvre"). Similar instances are

---

23 *CTW* I, xlviii. The reviewer was Castel, an eccentric Jesuit whom we will encounter again in Chapter 5.
24 *Code de musique pratique*, 24.
25 "Carte générale de la basse fondamentale," *Mercure de France* (September, 1731); *CTW* VI, 64.

1. tonic triad   **2. seventh chord on the second scale degree**
                     major mode   minor mode

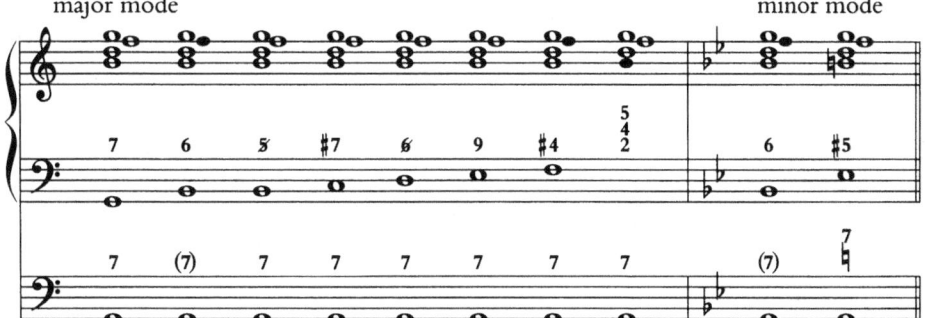

3. dominant-seventh chord
major mode   minor mode

4. diminished-seventh chord
minor mode

Example 3.2 Rameau's "General Table of the Fundamental Bass"

found in those chords figured as ♯7, 9, and ♯5.[26] The remaining two groups involve the dominant-seventh chord and the diminished-seventh chord on the leading tone (minor mode only). We can see that with but a few licenses related to chromatic alterations, omitted notes, and "supposed" basses, there are just four basic chord types involved and hence just four fundamental basses.

Rameau's fundamental bass is thus a great simplification of accompaniment since one must only know how to finger four chords in the right hand. Moreover, voice leading is made much easier since one need only know how to prepare and resolve these four chord types. Two basic rules are laid out by Rameau: (1) the seventh of each dissonant chord (the "minor" dissonance as he calls it) is usually – but not in all cases – prepared as a consonance in the previous chord and resolves downwards by step, and (2) the leading tone of a dominant-seventh chord and diminished-seventh chord at a cadence (the "major" dissonance) resolves upwards by step to the tonic note. Rameau offers an exercise to practice these rules in the *Traité* (see Example 3.3).[27]

In this example, Rameau writes out a chain of dissonant seventh chords in order to show how the seventh is prepared as a consonance and resolved downwards by step to another consonance in the following chord. (The only exceptions to this "rule of the seventh" are in the first measure, and in m. 6 where two sevenths are displaced by chromatic motion.) The added-sixth chord figured in m. 7 is interesting since it is assigned its own fundamental bass. (We will see in Chapter 5 how Rameau was acutely ambivalent in the *Traité* about the true nature of this chord.) Because the added sixth is here considered by Rameau to be a "major" dissonance, it resolves upwards by step to the third of the following triad, just as does the leading tone.

The striking feature Rameau wishes to illustrate by this example is the unification of voice-leading rules possible through the fundamental bass. By showing a variety of possible basso continuo lines that could conceivably support this harmonic progression, Rameau is demonstrating that there are really only a very limited number of fundamental chord progressions, despite the diversity of dissonant figures one may find above the basso continuo. In a real sense, all the myriad rules of dissonance treatment found in typical thorough-bass treatises are redundancies. One simply needed to know *how* a given dissonance progression was related to the fundamental seventh chord. We should note that Rameau did not propose these various continuo lines as viable bass parts that a composer might choose; he admitted that many of them were quite awkward. Rather, they were illustrations of the variety of signatures that could be related to each of these seventh chords depending upon the particular bass voice used in the continuo. The example was thus a kind of thesaurus of harmonic vocabulary not unlike the chords itemized in

---

[26] We will consider the theoretical arguments related to these chords in Chapter 5 along with Rameau's theory of "supposition."
[27] *Traité*, 419; Gossett, 432.

Example 3.3 *Traité*, 419

Example 3.2, except that now these chords were connected together in a variety of sequential patterns.

Despite this extraordinary revision of thorough-bass pedagogy, Rameau does not entirely reject more traditional approaches for learning accompaniment. Indeed, for most of the lessons contained in the fourth Book of the *Traité*, Rameau has recourse to received empirical rules of voice leading and counterpoint measured above the continuo bass (as opposed to the fundamental bass), as well as mnemonic formulas such as the *règle de l'octave*. He cites the *règle* in Chapters 6 and 7 (which he calls "une progression diatonique de la basse, tant en montant qu'en descendent d'une octave").[28] The *règle* proved useful for Rameau, since it helped him clarify the tonal context of his seventh chords and inversions, that is, it showed which chords were typically to be found above which scale degree. So as one example, we find Rameau recommending that the "chord of the small sixth" (6/4/3) usually occur over the second scale degree of any mode and resolve upwards by step to the simple "chord of the sixth" (6/3) on the mediant.[29] Yet later he discusses the same progression in terms of his fundamental bass, which is to say as a dominant-seventh chord with its fifth in the bass resolving to a tonic triad with its third in the bass.[30] The result is an eclectic system of accompaniment, relying upon traditional methods of pedagogy and his new fundamental bass.

Over the following years, Rameau evidently continued to refine his system of accompaniment, for by 1729 we find him engaged in a lively dispute over this very topic. This will be only the first of many quarrels we will see the temperamental Rameau involving himself in concerning his theory. The dispute (known as the "Conference") involved "two well-known musicians who met at the home of someone whose daughter is a skilled harpsichordist in order to discuss together several points of harmony upon which they disagree."[31] Although the two disputants are referred to throughout the controversy as the "first" and "second" musicians, respectively, it becomes quite clear that Rameau is the "first" musician in question. As to the identity of the second musician, the most likely candidate is the composer and pedagogue Michel-Pignolet de Montéclair (1666–1737).[32]

---

28   *Traité*, 382.
29   *Traité*, 393; Gossett, 406.
30   *Traité*, 413; Gossett, 426.
31   The "Conference" was reported in the pages of the *Mercure* (June, 1729), 1,281–89. This was followed by a series of increasingly-vituperative open letters penned by the two participants that was also published in the *Mercure* over the following two years. The complete exchange is reprinted in *CTW* VI, 29–65.
32   Rameau and Montéclair were well-known rivals in their days, not only as music pedagogues, but as opera composers. And a contemporaneous annotation in a copy of the *Mercure* now at the Bibliothèque Nationale indicates that the "second" musician was indeed Montéclair (Cuthbert Girdlestone, *Jean-Philippe Rameau: His Life and Work*, 2nd edition [New York, 1969], 486). But the case for Montéclair is not conclusive. For one thing, he never published any pedagogical works on harmony or accompaniment. (His pedagogical writings are all elementary primers on singing and the violin.) Moreover, it is known that Rameau had enough regard for Montéclair's music to have borrowed a number of passages from the opera *Jephté* (1732) in his own *Hippolyte et Aricie*, produced only one year later. See Robert Fajon, "Le Préramisme dans le répertoire de l'opéra," *Rameau Colloque International*, 307–29.

While there were a number of issues involved in the dispute between Rameau and Montéclair, one subject quickly assumed capital importance: what means was the most efficacious for teaching accompaniment – the fundamental bass or the *règle de l'octave*? Rameau was by now growing ever more confident in regards to his theory, and he believed he could now construct a method of accompaniment that was exclusively built upon the fundamental bass. It is "the first and only principle to which everything else leads in music and from which proceed rules as definite as they are simple."[33] With the fundamental bass, it is possible for the student to play any signature without hesitation, and moreover, know how to connect that harmony to the next without any faults. With the *règle de l'octave*, on the other hand, the student is faced with learning by memory hundreds of individual chords and patterns – 1,584 to be precise (given that there are twenty-two different chords in the *règle* to be memorized in 3 different hand positions in 24 keys – resulting in a grand total of 1,584 chords!).[34] And even then, there are so many exceptions and progressions contrary to common practice in the *règle*, that it is rendered all but useless:

> The number of these exceptions is prodigious. The knowledge and practice of them are filled with almost insurmountable difficulties on account of the quantity of chords, the infinite variety of their accompaniment, and the constant surprise caused by the different types of progressions to which each chord is individually susceptible contrary to habits often already formed. There is a confusion between fundamental rules with those of taste and an emptiness too often suffered by the harmony because of the impoverished resources available to the ear in learning the real progress of sounds. There is finally the servile subjection to frequently incorrect figures and false applications to which none of the many rules and innumerable exceptions can be subjected.[35]

Compare this, Rameau challenges, to his own theory of the fundamental bass, which reduces all harmonies to but two basic building blocks: the consonant triad and the dissonant seventh chord.

Montéclair answered Rameau's charges by defending the utility of the *règle* and in turn accusing Rameau's system of suffering itself from pedagogical difficulties and exceptions to practice.[36] Among the criticisms raised by Montéclair were that

---

33   *CTW* VI, 49.
34   Of course Rameau's calculations are misleading, as many of the harmonies in all the various *règles* are identical; hence, there are far fewer than the 1,584 separate chords Rameau claimed. In any event, Rameau misrepresents the pedagogy of the *règle*, as Campion emphasizes not the memorization of individual chords in separate keys but rather the memorization of common harmonic progressions and finger patterns that can be called upon spontaneously by the player.
35   "Observations sur la méthode d'accompagnement pour le clavecin qui est en usage, & qu'on appelle Echelle ou Règle de l'Octave," *Mercure de France* (February, 1730), 253–54; *CTW* VI, 45. Rameau develops his critique of the *règle* further in his *Dissertation*, 53–58.
36   The vigor with which the second musician defends the *règle* from Rameau's attacks raises the intriguing possibility that the disputant in question is not Montéclair at all, but the most prominent advocate and "discoverer" of the *règle*: Campion! It may be of significance that it was just at this time that Campion published two works that served as clarifications and propaganda on behalf of the *règle*: *Lettre du sieur Campion à un philosophe disciple de la règle de l'octave* (Paris, 1729); and *Addition au traité d'accompagnement et de composition par la règle de l'octave* (Paris, 1730). It is true that in the first of these publications Campion offered somewhat elliptical praise for Rameau's fundamental bass. But this need not have precluded his still engaging in a debate with Rameau over the merits of the *règle*.

Rameau's system resulted in clumsy realizations and mechanical voicings that were often faulty. Moreover, his system was difficult for the student to learn, and even more difficult to put into practice. Not willing to concede any point, Rameau pressed on to develop his method. Indeed, within one year after the conclusion of this dispute, Rameau published his important treatise of accompaniment, the *Dissertation sur les différentes métodes d'accompagnement pour le clavecin* of 1732. Building upon ideas first enunciated in the "Conference," Rameau outlines a complete system of accompaniment by which one could learn to play the basso continuo without even knowing how to read music!

Rameau's "nouvelle méthode" consists of two parts. The first is a new notation for the basso continuo. Figures used by composers today, Rameau bemoans, are both too numerous and too imprecise. A single figure 6 or 7 in the basso continuo, for instance, might refer to any one of a dozen possible chords. Rameau insists that the accompanist needed to know how to play only seven different kinds of chords with the right hand (thus expanding by three the list given in Example 3.2). He did not need to worry about doubling the bass line with the left hand, since another continuo instrument would play that part. Here are the seven chords and their new symbols according to Rameau's system:

Chord Name	Symbol
Tonic Triad (C–E–G)	C
Dominant Seventh (B–D–F–G)	X
Minor Seventh (C–D–F–A)	2
Added Sixth (C–E–G–A)	aj
Four Three (C–E–F–A)	4/3
Four (C–D–G)	4
Seven (C–E–G–B)	7

By knowing these seven chord types, Rameau argues, it is possible to realize almost any diatonic progression. The triad was the only one of these chords that could be transposed (indicated by its letter name). But the other chords were fixed within the given mode. Naturally music changes keys, thus one needed to know all these chords in all possible keys. (Key changes were to be indicated by designating the letter name of the key in the basso continuo.) Finally, if a chord needed to be played that could not be found on this list, it would be easy to play and notate it through the diatonic or chromatic displacement of notes belonging to one of these chords.

The second part of Rameau's new method consists of a series of rules for connecting chords. Essentially it involves keeping the right hand in as closed a position as possible while fingering a chord, keeping all common tones between chords, moving by stepwise and contrary motion between outer voices whenever possible, and having all dissonances resolve downwards by step (except when the dissonance is an added-sixth, in which case the sixth resolves upwards). To indicate any irregular resolutions, Rameau employs a notation of dots to direct the keyboardist's finger movements. Depending upon the placement and number of dots, the performer

Plate 3.2 Rameau's figured-bass notation for Corelli's sonata Op. 5 no. 3

was to move one or two fingers downwards at the prescribed moment. We can see an illustration of this notation in the one example Rameau provided from a sonata by Corelli (see Plate 3.2).[37] The rhythmic placement of each chord can be

---

[37] *Dissertation*, 64.

determined by the beats of the measure marked underneath the respective chord symbols.[38]

With Rameau's new method, continuo playing was purely a mechanical process of chord placement and finger movement, or, as he proudly noted, just a "méchanique des doigts." By vastly reducing the plethora of chord signatures, and further by prescribing a few simple rules of chordal connection, Rameau had ostensibly made one of the most daunting and time-consuming tasks of musical practice accessible to everyone. What had previously taken years of practice to perfect could now be accomplished in only a few months' time.[39]

It probably need not be pointed out that Rameau's method is logically inconsistent. As only the most obvious example, one may demand why Rameau chooses the seven chord types he did, given that a number of other functional types (e.g. any chord of the mediant or leading tone) are omitted. We must agree with Montéclair that his method really was both too mechanical and too cumbersome to be of practical value.[40] His symbols were ultimately insufficient in accommodating the more complex harmonic vocabulary required of accompanists in the eighteenth century, and his limited rules of voice leading resulted necessarily in clumsy and often faulty progressions. But Rameau was not blind to this fact either.[41] He never did, after all, employ his new notation in any of his own compositions (nor, as far as I can tell, did any other composer).

And when he returned to the question of accompaniment in his *Code de musique pratique* thirty years later, he admitted that this method was inadequate.[42] He retained most (but not all) of the traditional figures for notating the basso continuo line as well as reinstating many of the older contrapuntal rules of voice leading. Reflecting

---

38 For a more detailed discussion of Rameau's method of accompaniment, as well as a transcription of the Corelli example, see Deborah Hayes, "Rameau's 'Nouvelle méthode,'" *Journal of the American Musicological Society* 27/1 (Spring, 1974), 61–74.

   Rameau's notational reform, we should note, was only one of many proposed in the eighteenth century. Numerous other "methods," "machines," "secrets," "tables," and the like were offered by authors seeking to satisfy the public's demand for means to facilitate learning to read and play music. Two in particular may be mentioned: Demoz de la Salle, *Méthode de musique selon un nouveau système très-courte, très facile et très-sûr* (Paris, 1728); and Jean-Jacques Rousseau, "Projet concernant de nouveaux signes pour la musique lu par l'auteur à l'Académie des sciences, le 22 août 1742" (Genève, 1781). Even Montéclair caught the reformist virus and proposed a new system of notation in 1736 that he believed greatly simplified the reading of music, as well as helping the student intone pitches more accurately: "Abrégé d'un nouveau système de musique," in *Principes de musique* (Paris, 1736). For a comprehensive description of these many notational reforms in the eighteenth century, the reader is encouraged to consult Johannes Wolf's still-authoritative *Handbuch der Notationskunde*, 2 vols. (Leipzig, 1913–19) II, 335–86.

39 *Dissertation*, 62.

40 Rousseau later remarked that Rameau "corrected a fault" with his system of figured-bass notation "only by substituting for it another" (s.v. "chiffres," *Dictionnaire de musique*).

41 In the Bibliothèque Nationale there is a copy of the *Dissertation* (call number Vm8 X4 [3]) with substantial annotations and corrections penned in the margins. These seem to be by Rameau and suggest that he was at some point thinking of revising the work.

42 *Code de musique pratique*, 74. It is ironic, then, that the *Dissertation* was the only work of Rameau's to enjoy a second edition in the eighteenth century with a reprinting around 1772 by Bailleux. A reviewer of this edition rightly expressed his puzzlement about the need for reissuing a work that was clearly so obsolete (*CTW* V, 91).

his new-found fascination with sensationalist ideas, Rameau replaced his mechanical method with a new approach to accompaniment that emphasized the performer's *feeling* his way to a proper realization ("feeling" in the sense of both touch and innate *sensibilité*). Yet his goal stated in the *Dissertation* of reducing all chords and voice leadings to a small number of paradigmatic constructs was never abandoned as an ideal. It simply required refinement. And despite Montéclair's scathing criticisms of Rameau's system, it is telling evidence of both the practical appeal of the fundamental bass and its rapid dissemination that Montéclair nonetheless accepted its basic heuristic. Never once did he deny that chords might have a common fundamental bass; he only thought that the particular basses Rameau assigned to some chords (such as the suspended fourth and ninth) were wrong.

The thorough bass was the chrysalis in which Rameau's theory of the fundamental bass was born; it furnished him with the major pedagogical problems he sought to solve, the notation and nomenclature to do this, and finally, the practice to which he would continually return in order to test his solutions. It is not too much of an exaggeration to say, I think, that Rameau's system of the fundamental bass is a theory of the thorough bass. But as we will see over the following chapters, it was one whose ramifications were far from restricted to the thorough bass.

HARMONIC COUNTERPOINT

It was not only in French thorough-bass pedagogy that we can observe a growing sensitivity among music theorists to harmony. The same awareness is manifest in practical composition treatises of the later seventeenth century. As has already been noted, for the first half of the seventeenth century, French compositional theory was relatively conservative. Writers such as Salomon de Caus (1610), Mersenne (1636), Antoine Parran (1639), and Antoine de Cousu (1658) essentially restated the rules of counterpoint found in Zarlino's third book of the *Istitutioni harmoniche* with little change.[43] Music was conceived as a composite counterpoint between individual voices, the specific intervallic relationships following a conservative grammar codified by the norms of the *prima pratica*.

After mid-century, though, a notable shift can be detected in French music theory that parallels the harmonic maturation of French musical style that we have already noted above. Pedagogues beginning with La Voye Mignot (1656), and then René Ouvrard (1658), Guillaume-Gabriel Nivers (1667), Marc-Antoine Charpentier (c. 1692), Etienne Loulié (1696), and Charles Masson (1697), formulated a distinctive pedagogy of counterpoint that was harmonically influenced, even while they retained the outward shell of the received contrapuntal paradigm. Two-part counterpoint was now held to be the scaffolding of a three- or four- part progression of chords, even if those chords were only implied. Counterpoint, in other words, was seen as a kind of "figured harmony." As La Voye Mignot expressed it, "Counterpoint, whether simple or figured, is nothing but the art of presenting

[43] Schneider, *Die französische Kompositionslehre*, 220–23.

well-regulated chords."[44] While Masson observed, "by the term counterpoint, one should understand harmony."[45]

An example of such a two-part harmonic counterpoint by Etienne Loulié is given in Example 3.4.[46] This progression is really a kind of fourth-species diminution on the *règle de l'octave*. Even though no chords are sounded vertically, a clear harmonic succession is implied. Since full harmonies could now be inferred in two-part progressions, theorists began to allow the imperfect consonance of the third as an opening and closing interval. Nonetheless, any such two-part progression was understood to be "imperfect" since, as Masson noted, it lacked the full harmonic sonority of a "perfect" three- or four-voiced progression.[47]

A further indication of the new harmonic perspective was the importance assigned the bass voice. No longer was the tenor the part against which all other voices were measured and composed; the bass now assumed this important task. This can be seen as one consequence of the thorough bass. Moreover, as Masson notes, it is the bass voice that constitutes the harmony:

Example 3.4 Example of "harmonic" counterpoint by Loulié

The part that sings below the other parts in music is the base and foundation of the other parts, since one builds them upon it. In effect, the harmonies are what they are only because of the relation they have with it.[48]

44 *Traité de musique*, 2nd edition (Paris, 166), Part 4, 2.
45 Charles Masson, *Nouveau Traité des règles de la composition de la musique* (Paris, 1699), 31. The French were by no means the only ones to reinterpret counterpoint harmonically, though. Joel Lester has looked at the writings of a number of German Baroque theorists, including Niedt and Fux, and showed how their contrapuntal rules were strongly influenced by the new harmonic thinking (*Compositional Theory in the Eighteenth Century* [Cambridge, Mass., 1992], especially Chapter 2, "Species Counterpoint and Fux's *Gradus*").
46 Quoted in Richard Semmens, "Etienne Loulié and the New Harmonic Counterpoint," *Journal of Music Theory* 27/2 (1984), 76.
47 *Nouveau Traité*, 29.
48 Ibid., 31.

One of the most important catalysts for French theorists in their development of a pedagogy of harmonic counterpoint was the repertoire of homophonic dance forms such as the *passacaille, chaconne,* and *folia.* As we saw, many of these dances were introduced early in the seventeenth century by performers playing the Spanish five-course guitar, and became wildly popular in France by mid-century. Each one of these dances is characterized by a relatively simple harmonic formula that the composer would elaborate upon with numerous diminutions and variations. Binary dance forms like the *sarabande* or *menuet,* on the other hand, were sometimes embellished by the composer in written-out repeats (called "doubles"), or as was more frequently the case, by the performer improvising his own ornamentations. This practice helped to cultivate further the idea of "harmonic counterpoint."

The French did not entirely neglect traditional counterpoint in their practice and pedagogy. But the cultivation of strict counterpoint – *contrepoint pressé* – was never as strong in seventeenth-century France as it was in either Germany or Italy. Even outwardly polyphonic genres like the fugue were treated by French composers in a unique way. The fugue never became the forum for the display of contrapuntal virtuosity as it did in Germany (at least not before the French Conservatory started holding fugal competitions and exams). Rameau's prescriptions for the fugue in his *Traité,* for instance, have to do less with the contrapuntal manipulations to which a theme may be subjected than with the harmonies by which imitative voices should enter.[49] This is one reason French discussions of the fugue in the eighteenth century are often so difficult to reconcile with their German and Italian counterparts.[50] A fugue by Lully or Rameau (in one of their "French overtures," for example) could revert to purely homophonic textures in lively dance rhythms after the initial entries of the individual voices were finished.[51]

Perhaps the most noteworthy theoretical consequence of this harmonic sensibility is to be found in the interpretation of dissonance. Consider the two-part progression shown in Example 3.5. The dissonant fourth resolving to an even more dissonant diminished fifth was widely employed by seventeenth-century musicians. But this progression could not be easily explained by traditional rules of strict counterpoint.[52] The *Figurenlehre* by which German theorists such as Christian Bernhard explained such "theatrical" styles of dissonance treatment was foreign to French theorists of the seventeenth century. Instead, the French tended to explain such dissonances as the product of harmonic figuration – the outlining of an underlying harmonic progression.

---

49 See Chapter 44 of Book 3.
50 Alfred Mann, *The Study of Fugue* (New Brunswick, 1958), 50–52. An enlightening analysis of Rameau's fugue "technique" is found in Jean Duron, "Le Grand Motet: Rameau face à ses contemporains," *Rameau Colloque International,* 331–70.
51 Not coincidentally, the one piece in the entire *Traité* for which Rameau offers a fundamental-bass analysis (i.e. a "harmonic reading") is one of his own fugal motets: "Laboravi Clamans" (*Traité,* 341–55; Gossett, 358–66).
52 Schneider, *Die französische Kompositionslehre,* 251.

Example 3.5 Example of two-part dissonant resolution

The interpretation of dissonance as a harmonic event marks a watershed in musical thought. Whereas for Renaissance musicians dissonance was an interruption of a consonant progression, many seventeenth-century musicians began to interpret dissonance as an essential component of musical structure.[53] It was necessary, in Masson's view, not only for the smooth and proper connection of harmony, but also the expressiveness of melody.[54] We recall how Campion's *règle de l'octave* employed characteristic dissonances on most of the sixth chords (on scale-degrees 2, 4, and 7 ascending; 6, 4, and 2 descending) in order to define each respective scale degree and reciprocally orient a chord within a mode. Dissonance was also useful for smoothing out voice leading by preparing common tones between successive harmonies. Dissonance, in other words, was neither a disruption nor a darkening of some consonant chord progression; rather, it was an artful and even necessary means of defining that progression. Because two-part structures were understood to imply fuller harmonies, localized transgressions of strict counterpoint rules (cross-relations, accented dissonances, hidden parallels, unprepared and unresolved dissonances, etc.) could be tolerated provided that the underlying harmonic progressions made sense.

Of course French theorists did not dispense entirely with contrapuntal analysis in favor of chordal analysis; they did not yet have the conceptual framework or vocabulary to do this. Masson's important treatise of composition, for instance, still relied mostly upon traditional – if heavily modified – rules of counterpoint.[55] What is striking, though, is how theorists like Masson taught these contrapuntal rules in harmonic contexts – as vertical counterpoint, if you will. The following examples illustrate some of the various ways theorists accounted for unusual dissonance treatments or voice leadings by invoking implied harmonic structures.

In the excerpts from Masson's composition treatise given in Example 3.6, the various unprepared and unresolved diminished fifths are tolerated since they can be heard as implying a full – and presumably less harsh – harmony.[56] Charpentier allows the Example cross relations between E and B♭ in Example 3.7 on account of the agreeable harmonic progression it outlines.[57]

The increased acceptance of harmony as the essential determinant of musical structure led French theorists to formulate a species of dissonance that would be

---

[53] Ibid., 246–47. [54] Charles Masson, *Nouveau Traité*, 59.
[55] For further information on Masson and his treatise, see Herbert Schneider's fine study, "Charles Masson und sein *Nouveau Traité*," *Archiv für Musikwissenschaft* 30/4 (1973), 245–74.
[56] Rameau quoted the second of these progressions (among others) from Masson's treatise in his own *Traité* as an example of two – voiced counterpoint expressing a single harmony. We will look at Rameau's analysis of Masson's counterpoint in Chapter 5 (p. 119 below).
[57] Quoted in Wilhelm Seidel, "Französische Musiktheorie im 16. und 17. Jahrhundert," *Geschichte der Musiktheorie*, vol. ix (Darmstadt, 1986), 108.

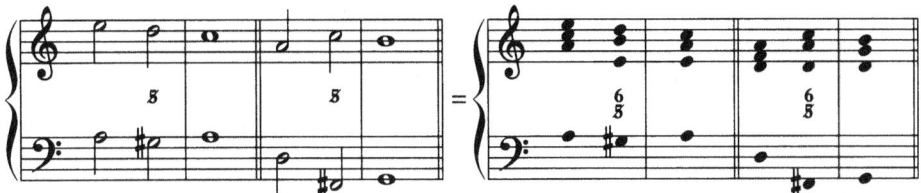

Example 3.6 Two-part counterpoint implying fuller harmonies. Charles Masson, *Nouveau Traité*, 74–75

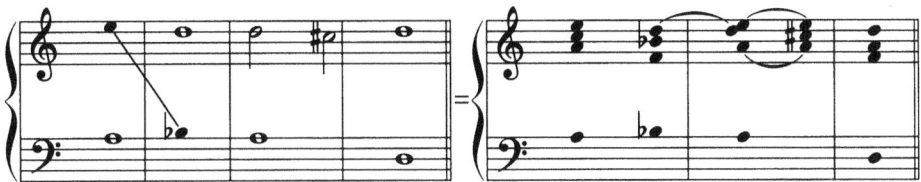

Example 3.7 Cross relation allowed by Charpentier

crucial to Rameau's theory: *supposition*. Supposition was initially defined in the seventeenth century as a melodic dissonance caused by passing tones and ornamentation.[58] Brossard tells us:

> Supposition occurs when one part holds a note while the other part has two or more notes of lesser value that move by conjunct degrees against the first note. It is one of the ways of ornamenting the counterpoint that is called *Contrapunto sciolto* by the Italians, *Celer progressus* by others, and *Ornement du Chant* by still others. One of the most important uses made of supposition occurs when we treat the most dissonant sounds like [consonances].[59]

While this meaning was retained right through the eighteenth century (Rameau, for instance, referred to the supposition at one point in the *Traité* as a "dissonance pour le goût du chant" [p. 320]), a harmonic flavor to the term came to be inferred towards the end of the seventeenth century. Here is Nivers's definition:

> The [supposition] is an activity that occurs in, and consists of, two notes of equal value sounded one after the other in conjunct motion, of which a dissonant one substitutes for its neighbour which is consonant. And in this manner dissonances are acceptable on the second, third or fourth parts of a measure, and even on the first. But one of the parts must hold firm against the dissonance, which should always be preceded and followed by a consonance.[60]

Supposition, in other words, could be understood as a kind of *non-harmonic* tone. Loulié considered it a category of "dissonances par harmonie."[61] For René Ouvrard,

---

58   Albert Cohen, "*La Supposition* and Changing Concepts of Dissonance in Baroque Theory," *Journal of the American Musicological Society* 24 (1971), 63–84. Mersenne's use of the term was somewhat idiosyncratic and will be discussed in relation to Rameau's theory of supposition in Chapter 4.
59   Brossard, *Dictionaire*, s.v. "supposition."
60   Guillaume Gabriel Nivers, *Traité de la composition de musique* (Paris, 1667); trans. Albert Cohen (Brooklyn, 1961), 30.
61   Cohen, "*La Supposition*," 76.

the author of a composition primer entitled *Secret pour composer en musique* (Paris, 1689), *supposition* was a dissonance in two-part composition that was to be understood as a displacement of some consonance within a four-part, bass-oriented harmonic scaffolding.[62] In the second edition of his important thorough-bass treatise, Denis Delair called the consonant triad the "accord fondamental." All other dissonant harmonies, he tells us, are "suppositions." Every non-triadic dissonant interval "supposes" a consonant one: 4 supposes 3, 6 supposes 5 (!), and 7 and 9 suppose the octave.[63] Supposition can also occur in the bass voice. In Example 3.8, the accented passing tones in the bass are to be heard against a "natural melody" revealed by Delair in the bottom line.[64] This natural melody implies a simple harmonization against which the "supposed" dissonance is to be heard. The crucial point is that supposition came to be a means of accounting for melodic dissonance through harmony. Dissonances were measured according to some present or implied consonant chord of resolution.

Exemple des Supositions

Chant suposé

Chant naturel

Example 3.8 Example of melodic supposition in the bass

If we need any further evidence of this fact, we need only consider what was probably the most ubiquitous example of supposition to be found in French Baroque music: the various species of long appoggiaturas described in eighteenth-century singing treatises (*port de voix, coulé, cadence appuyée,* etc.). These ornaments constituted a compendium of appoggiatura types utilized by French singers to enhance important notes of phrases at almost all cadential points (see Example 3.9).[65]

---

62 Seidel, "Französische Musiktheorie," 102.
63 Denis Delair, *Traité d'accompagnement pour le théorbe et le clavessin*, 2nd edition (Paris, 1723), Preface.
64 Ibid., 61.
65 For a helpful inventory of vocal embellishments common to the music of Rameau's day, see Nicholas McGegan and Gina Spagnoli, "Singing Style at the Opéra in the Rameau Period," *Rameau Colloque International*, 209–26.

Example 3.9 Common French vocal embellishments

Their expressiveness was achieved precisely because of the explicit consonant harmonies against which they sounded and ultimately resolved. The excerpts from the operas of Lully and Rameau cited in Chapters 5 and 8 require constant embellishment of the vocal line, even if these embellishments are not always indicated in the notation. The reader must not misconstrue the above examples as exhaustive of the kinds of dissonance analysis to be found in French composition texts in the seventeenth century. The studies of both Schneider and Seidel have shown us just how dependent French theorists from the later seventeenth century remained upon the contrapuntal rules bequeathed by Zarlino. But the examples do convey some of the new harmonic attitudes that were brought to that older theory. Schneider writes:

In summary, it is evident that in practice an empirical attitude reigned as far as dissonance treatment was concerned that had distanced itself from classical polyphony (without however achieving the freedom of Italian music) and that [this practice] can be viewed as a transitory stage on the way to functional-harmonic composition using self-sufficient chords.[66]

By the beginning of the eighteenth century, a harmonic sensibility had permeated French musical practice and theory. It was in this well-tilled harmonic soil that Rameau's theory of the fundamental bass was to germinate.

THE INVERSIONAL DERIVATION OF TRIADS

It is quite natural that an informal notion of triadic inversion should have arisen in seventeenth-century thorough-bass pedagogy, particularly for performers on strummed instruments such as the guitar and theorbo. (Nowhere, however was the term "inversion" ever used by theorists to describe this practice.) Because of the peculiar tuning of these instruments, a given chord notated in the tablature might actually end up being played in a variety of positions, spacings, and doublings. This was

---

[66] Schneider, *Die französische Kompositionslehre*, 254.

because these instruments either used double courses that were sometimes tuned in octaves, or tuned the top strings an octave lower (so-called "re-entrant" tuning). Thereby a note written higher than another might actually be sounded an octave lower, or vice versa. Consequently, when a guitarist or theorbist realized a given figure, the sounding chord could overlap the basso continuo line and create awkward voice-leadings.[67] Pedagogues for these instruments generally discounted these overlappings and voice-leading violations as unimportant.[68] Keyboardists, too, would have found the notion of octave transposition familiar given that on most harpsichords and organs one could change the octave registration of a chord by the simple drawing of a stop or coupler. In general, we can say that performers of the thorough bass in the seventeenth century were concerned more with the *functional sonority* of a chord than with its particular voicing. If the bottom note of some realization failed to coincide with the basso continuo line, this was rarely a problem so long as the resulting harmony still contained the required pitches.[69]

Octave complementation was also a familiar technique in *musica theorica* to derive intervals on the monochord. For Zarlino, any interval and its octave complement possessed the same nature ("una istessa natura"), since the one was merely the inverse of the other.[70] The German theorists mentioned earlier in this chapter applied the technique of octave transposition to the triads they had reified.[71] Johannes Lippius offered perhaps the most explicit enunciation of this doctrine:

The *diffusa* [triad] is that whose parts or root voices, less mutually neighbors to one another, are dispersed to different octaves than that which their proper root requires. Indeed, either only one part may be transferred from the fundamental [position], the other two remaining the same; or two [parts can be transferred], one constant; or all three [can be transferred]. Yet all of these conjunctions sound together perfectly because of the direct root whence they arise according to elegant proportions . . . And, moreover, that triad is always sweeter, fuller, and more perfect, whose prime is firmly in place lowest and deepest, the remaining notes above . . .[72]

The term Lippius uses to describe the "root" of the triad (*radix*) would find favor among subsequent German theorists. (Werckmeister, for instance, would refer to the *Wurtzel* of a 6/3 triad lying a third below its lowest note.[73]) But there was nothing of the generative implications to this concept comparable to Rameau's *son fondamental*, as we will see in the next chapter.

---

67   I have illustrated and analyzed such tablature "overlappings" in my article "The Spanish Baroque Guitar."
68   Nigel North, *Continuo Playing on the Lute, Archlute and Theorbo* (London, 1987), 163.
69   One reason why the "inversions" played by guitarists and theorbists were not necessarily apparent in performance was that the bass line was usually doubled (by a bassoon, for example). This helped to cover up any of their overlappings.
70   *Dimostrationi harmoniche* (Venice, 1571), 89–90. They did not, however, necessarily possess the same degree of consonance. All major imperfect consonances, for example, were considered more closely related to one another than to their respective inversions. The same was true for all minor imperfect consonances.
71   Lester, *Between Modes and Keys*, 31–45.
72   Quoted in *ibid.*, 40.
73   *Harmonologia Musica* (Frankfurt, 1702), 76.

English theorists of the seventeenth century also invoked practical heuristics by which to teach chordal inversions. In his *A New Way of Making Fowre Parts in Counterpoint* (London, c. 1613), Thomas Campion points out that when sixths are notated above bass notes, "such Bases are not true Bases, for where a sixt is to be taken ... the true Base is a third lower."[74] He illustrates this by notating two sixth chords above E and F♯ respectively, and then indicating in the following measure the "true Bases" of C and D. Other seventeenth-century English writers who illustrated similar kinds of chordal inversions, complete with suggestions of chord roots, were Roger North and Christopher Simpson.[75]

If somewhat belatedly, French composition teachers in the seventeenth and early eighteenth centuries also pointed out inversional derivations of certain triads. For instance, Masson noted that the sixth chord commonly sounded on *mi* was derived from the same (triadic) harmony found above *ut*. Likewise, the sixth chord on *fa* was related to *re*.[76] In a treatise by the famous organist Louis Marchand (1669–1732) that exists in manuscript, we find a description of three "consonant chords" whose relations were due to inversion: the "natural" 5/3, the "bonne quarte" (6/4), and the "sixte" (6/3), of which Marchand pointed out "Il faut remarquer que tous ces accords se trouvent de trois maniere[s] differentes sous la main par raport à la basse."[77] Notably fewer theorists, however, mentioned the seventh chord in regard to its inversions. This was not because they failed to follow the logic of triadic inversion; rather, they simply did not believe the seventh to be a fundamental chord like the triad.[78]

Another of the catalysts leading to the acceptance of chordal inversion was the recognition by theorists that certain scale degrees played critical tonal roles. Depending upon the context, these scale degrees retained their function no matter in which voice they appeared. The clearest example of this was the leading tone (*notte sensible*). All theorists agreed that the leading tone was critical at cadential points for the definition of the *finales* or *tonique*. Thus Jacques Hotteterre, in his 1707 flute treatise (which, despite its title, contains much on harmony and "modulation"), gave the excerpts shown in Example 3.10 employing the leading tone.[79] In the first excerpt, he tells us, the third of the first chord is the leading tone, while in the second excerpt it is in the bass. (Note, incidentally, how Hotteterre fails to resolve the bass in the last example on account of the parallel octaves it would create with the soprano.) The two chords were nonetheless seen by Hotteterre to be functionally related.

74 Percival Vivian, *Campion's Works* (Oxford, 1909), 204.
75 Barry Cooper, "Englische Musiktheorie im 17. und 18. Jahrhundert," *Geschichte der Musiktheorie*, vol. ix (Darmstadt, 1986), 216–17.
76 *Nouveau Traité*, 35.
77 "Regle pour la Composition des accords à 3. Parties par Mr. Marchand," F-Pn Ms. Rés Vm8 21, fol. 39r. A direct influence by Marchand upon Rameau is highly plausible, given that Rameau, as we noted in Chapter 2, p. 22 above, was a great admirer of Marchand, and studied under the elder organist during his first stay in Paris in 1706. See Girdlestone, *Rameau*, 4 and 18–19.
78 However, see the revealing suggestions by de Cousu quoted in Schneider, *Die französische Kompositionslehre*, 155.
79 Jacques Hotteterre, *Principes de la flute traversière* (Paris, 1707), 46.

Example 3.10 Jacques Hotteterre, *Principes de la flûte traversière*, 46

Now, it is important to make a distinction in these descriptions between inversional *derivation* and inversional *equivalence*. For virtually every seventeenth-century music pedagogue, whether a practical thorough-bass instructor, composition teacher, or speculative theorist, 6/3 and 6/4 chords were not considered "equivalent" to the perfect 5/3 triad, since the very quality that determined the perfection of the 5/3 triad – the harmonic division of the octave and fifth – would disappear as soon as the *bassus* was transposed into an inner voice. The triad would lose its *luogo naturale* as Zarlino called the disposition of the *harmonia perfetta*. This is why inversions were designated by theorists with names that emphasized their subordinate nature: *diffusa* (Lippius), *imparfait* (Boyvin), *Versetzung* (Werckmeister), or *Verkehrung* (Heinichen).

Zarlino had drawn the analogy between the four voice parts and Aristotle's four elements. The bass was equated with the earth, while the tenor, alto, and soprano corresponded to water, air, and fire, respectively:

> As the earth is the foundation of the other elements, the bass has the function of sustaining and stabilizing, fortifying and giving growth to the other parts. It is the *foundation of harmony* and for this reason is called bass, as if to say the base and sustenance of the other parts. If we could imagine the element of earth to be lacking, what ruin and waste would result in universal and human harmony! Similarly a composition without a bass would be full of confusion and dissonance and would fall into ruin.[80]

What sense would it make to exchange the places of earth and water in this peripatetic world? When a bass voice is "transposed" to an inner voice, it thereby forfeits its role as "sustainer" and "stabilizer" of the other parts. In order for the concept of octave transfer to become inversional "equivalence," a brand new idea born of tonality needed to be introduced: the generative fundamental. For only with the notion of a chord fundamental could one begin to speak of inversions as somehow consanguineous by virtue of having been generated by an identical source. But this would require a change in theoretical perspective for which practicing musicians of the seventeenth century were not yet prepared. The way was being forged, though, in several speculative theoretical tracts, some of which would eventually influence Rameau in his formulation of the *basse fondamentale*. It is to these developments that we now turn.

---

[80] Gioseffo Zarlino, *The Art of Counterpoint*, trans. Guy A. Marco and Claude V. Palisca (New Haven, 1968), 179.

4

THE GENERATIVE FUNDAMENTAL

The transformation of a *bassus* into the *basse fondamentale* entailed a profound reconceptualization in which the lowest note of the *accord parfait* was to be heard not only as the *foundation* of the harmony, but also as the generative *source* – what we today call a chord root. Only in this way could all spacings or inversions of the triad be related back to its original position. Yet the concept of chord root was not an intuitive one for musicians before Rameau. If the *bassus* was to be compared to the earth, as Zarlino's Aristotelian analogy suggests, how was it also to be understood as generator? In Aristotelian physics, after all, the earth is inert and immovable. How could the earth (the *bassus*) generate the elements of air or fire (upper voices), let alone exchange places with one of them? Obviously, Aristotelian physics did not offer a conducive intellectual model for conceiving the fundamental bass.

But there were alternative intellectual models available in the seventeenth century that did suggest the idea of a generative source for harmony. When these were integrated with emerging acoustical knowledge concerning the production of pitch, scientists and music theorists had at hand a wide assortment of analogies by which the notion of a "generative fundamental" could be conceived. As these forerunners to Rameau's doctrine of the *basse fondamentale* have gone virtually unstudied by music historians, unlike the practical precedents discussed in the previous chapter, I will examine them in some detail here.

NEOPLATONISM AND THE CANONIST TRADITION

Plato had taught that nature was a hierarchical continuum arranged in incremental levels of perfection. Christian neoplatonists fused to this idea the theme of divine creation: God was at the top of this ladder (or if a circular metaphor was used, in the center), from which all else emanated.[1] Not surprisingly, music theorists who were most influenced by Platonic doctrines were convinced that music participates in this cosmic plan, and they attempted to order musical materials on a graded scale of perfection. The primary musical constituents that interested most of these music theorists were naturally those which they understood to be the essential elements of musical composition: intervals and modes. And the means by which these

---

[1] C. A. Patrides, "Hierarchy and Order," *Dictionary of the History of Ideas*, ed. Philip Wiener, 4 vols. (New York, 1973), II, 439.

intervals and modes could be compared was that venerable tool of *musica theorica*, the monochord.

For neoplatonists of the seventeenth century like Johann Kepler, Athanasius Kircher, Robert Fludd, and Marin Mersenne, the monochord was more than a didactic tool of *musica theorica;* it was a microcosm of universal harmony. In Plato's *Timaeus*, the demiurge creates the world-soul and corporeal universe modeled upon simple numerical proportions and geometric forms. We can see a seventeenth-century allegorical rendition of this tale in the striking illustration reproduced in Plate 4.1 from Robert Fludd's mammoth text of Rosicrucian theology, *Utriusque cosmi*. God is here shown to be the "pulsator monochordii," tuning the monochord string, which, when set into motion, sounds the harmonic ratios of the universe – the *musica mundana*.[2]

Of course, there were more practical ways music theorists were able to use the monochord in order to generate intervals, scales, and tuning systems. (Music theorists who utilized the monochord for such purposes were historically referred to as "canonists.") This was usually accomplished by two different procedures.[3] The first (and evidently oldest) way was to divide the single monochord string manually into successive aliquot (equal) divisions of decreasing size, and compare the results. One would begin by bisecting the string and compare the half (½) back to the whole (1). The resulting ratio (½ : 1) is dupla (2 : 1) and sounds the octave. (It was also possible, of course, to begin with two strings of identical length, thus allowing one to sound the interval simultaneously.) The next division is one third of the string (⅓). This would be compared back to the half, resulting in a sesquialtera ratio (⅓ : ½ or 3 : 2) of the perfect fifth. One continues in this manner and produces an ascending series of superparticular ratios: 2 : 1, 3 : 2, 4 : 3, 9 : 8, 16 : 15, etc. By comparing these intervals, more complex ratios could be found that would otherwise be cumbersome to plot out independently. For example, the Pythagorean semitone (256 : 243) is easily found as the difference between the perfect fourth (4 : 3) and two major whole tones (9 : 8): $\frac{1}{3} \div \frac{9}{8} \times \frac{9}{8} = {}^{256}/_{243}$.

A second technique for plotting intervals on the monochord that was widely used by Medieval and Renaissance canonists (although it too can be traced to ancient Greek authority) reversed this process by beginning with the lower pitch (larger string length) and comparing it to higher (smaller) aliquot string divisions. This produces a series of subsuperparticular ratios: 1 : 2, 2 : 3, 3 : 4, 8 : 9, etc. It will be noted that these two approaches result in harmonic and arithmetic divisions, respectively.[4] (For explanations of the arithmetic and harmonic proportions, see Appendix 1.)

[2] Peter J. Ammann, "The Musical Theory and Philosophy of Robert Fludd," *Journal of the Warburg and Courtauld Institutes* 30 (1967), 224. It should be mentioned that both Kepler and Mersenne were outspoken critics of Fludd's ideas. Nonetheless, both shared Fludd's basic belief – however differently it was articulated – in a kind of *musica mundana* that could be modeled on a monochord or, in the case of Kepler, inscribed as polygons within circles.

[3] For a more detailed description of historical monochord procedures, see Cecil Adkins, "The Technique of the Monochord," *Acta Musicologica* 39 (1967), 34–41.

[4] In Article 6 of Chapter 3 (Book l) of Rameau's *Traité*, these respective techniques are all illustrated.

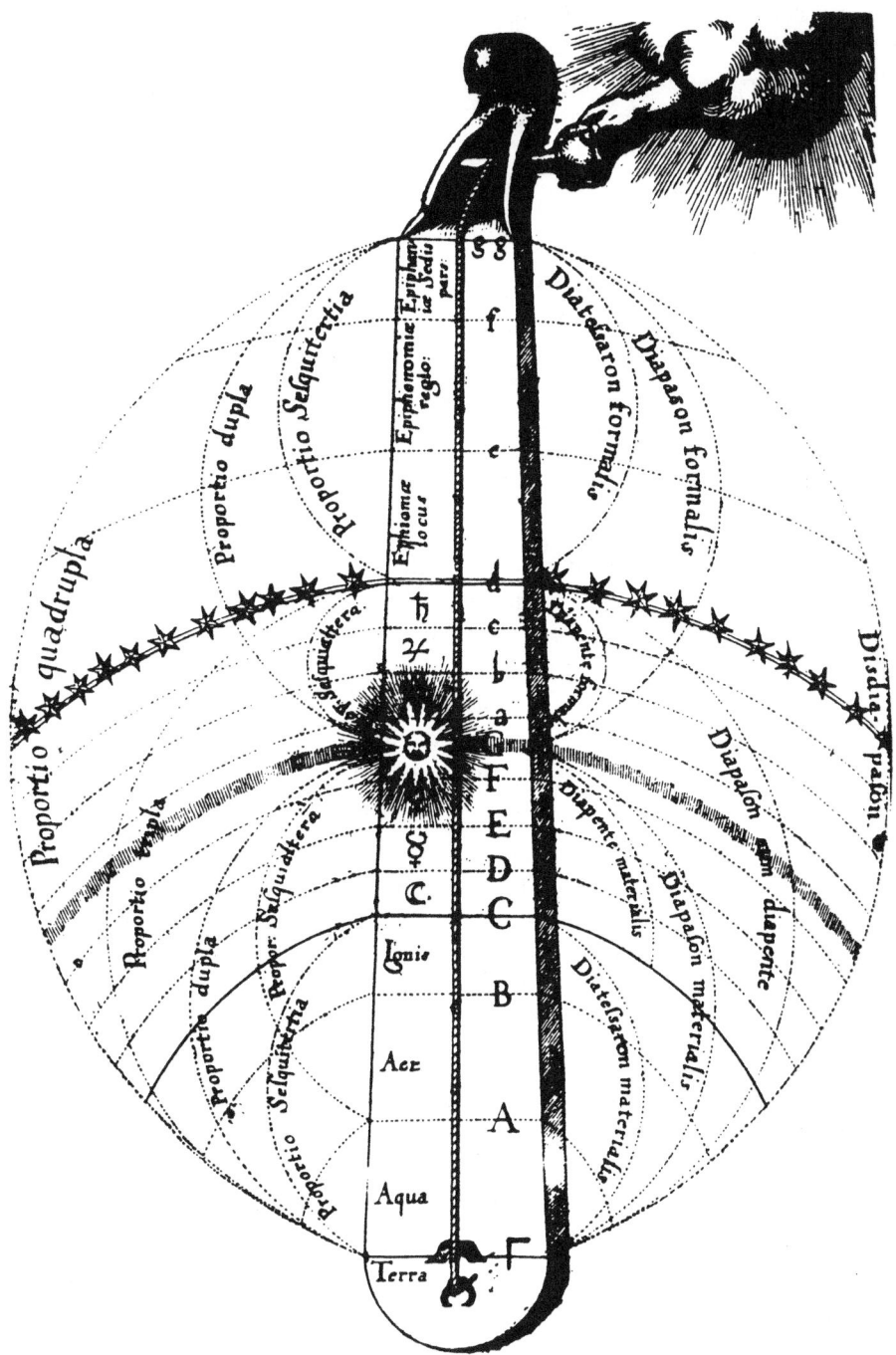

Plate 4.1 Fludd's monochord

There was a third technique for dividing the monochord that differs substantially from both the ascending and descending techniques just described. It entailed dividing a string and comparing the parts *to one another*. But the actual pitches produced by such a procedure proved less suitable for purposes of tuning or scale construction. It is really only useful when the theorist wishes to describe and illustrate individual interval ratios in isolation. Hence, we rarely find this technique utilized in canonic theory.

The succession of aliquot divisions produced on the monochord provided a convenient classification and ranking of intervals. Those intervals generated by the simplest superparticular ratios were considered the most perfect: the octave (2 : 1), perfect fifth (3 : 2), perfect fourth (4 : 3), major third (5 : 4), and minor third (6 : 5). The major and minor sixths, both of which were accepted by sixteenth-century musicians as consonant, were ranked lower on the hierarchic order owing to their superpartient ratios (5 : 3 and 8 : 5, respectively). Because they were composites of simple (superparticular) intervals, they were not heard as fundamental intervals themselves.

Zarlino limited the ratios of consonance to the first six integers since he believed the number six to possess metaphysical significance.[5] (There are six sides of a cube, six planets in the sky, and six days of creation. Moreover, six is the first integer that is the sum of all numbers of which it is a multiple: $1 \times 2 \times 3 = 6$; $1 + 2 + 3 = 6$.) He canonized this series as the *numero senario*. Not only does the *senario* contain all the primary superparticular consonances, it determines their order of perfection on the basis of their closeness to their origin in the number one. "The thing that is nearest to its origin or cause," Zarlino wrote in strongly Aristotelian language,

retains the greatest part of the nature of that cause and is more perfect in that class than the things that are distant from it. This may be seen in the case of light. The part nearest to its origin and cause, which is the sun, has more clarity, shines more brightly, and is more perfect than more remote parts. So the interval nearest to the cause and origin of consonance – the unison – which is contained in the proportion of equality and is among the unisone combinations is more perfect than any other consonance.[6]

But one difficulty with this hierarchy became painfully apparent by the seventeenth century: the canonist ranking of interval ratios did not reflect accurately the empirical judgment of musicians. First of all, most musicians by 1600 did not accept the perfect fourth (4 : 3) as more consonant than the major third (5 : 4) or minor third (6 : 5). Secondly, the ratio of the minor sixth required the number eight (8 : 5). But this went beyond the number six that Zarlino had laid down as the limit of his *senario*.

Zarlino offered a number of ad hoc explanations to account for these embarrassing discrepancies. The perfect fourth, for example, while being more perfect than the major third, is "less pleasing." The ratio 8 : 5 could be included within the *senario in potenza* since eight is the double of four. Later on he explained

---

[5] Gioseffo Zarlino, *Le istitutioni harmoniche* (Venice, 1558), Part 1, Chapter 14.
[6] Gioseffo Zarlino, *The Art of Counterpoint*, trans. Guy A. Marco and Claude V. Palisca (New Haven, 1968), 17.

The generative fundamental

it was really a composite of the perfect fourth and minor third – both consonances contained within the *senario*. But the essential conflict between empirical judgment and rational ordering was not thereby resolved. We will see these very same problems resurfacing in Rameau's theory over a century and a half later.

For now, though, it is important to observe that Zarlino saw the *octave* as the generator and source of all consonance, since its ratio was the beginning of the harmonic series that in successive divisions produced the just ratios necessary to construct the syntonic diatonic tuning (see Plate 4.2). By dividing the octave harmonically, one produces a perfect fifth with the perfect fourth as a remainder. The perfect fifth can then be itself harmonically divided to produce the major and minor thirds respectively. Dissonances could be found by adding and subtracting the consonant ratios that lay within the *senario*. Thus by subtracting the perfect fourth from the perfect fifth, one produces the large whole tone ($^3/_2 \div ^4/_3 = ^9/_8$) while the small whole tone could be derived as the difference between a minor third and the perfect fourth ($^4/_3 \div ^6/_5 = ^{10}/_9$). (Although both these whole tones could also be derived by harmonically dividing the major third: $^5/_4$ or $^{10}/_8$.) Sevenths could be found by squaring perfect fourths, or as Zarlino preferred, adding thirds to perfect fifths. However one derived dissonance, all intervals could still be said to originate with the first interval that could be divided: the octave. Zarlino compared the octave to a line in geometry that can be divided. "We may conclude

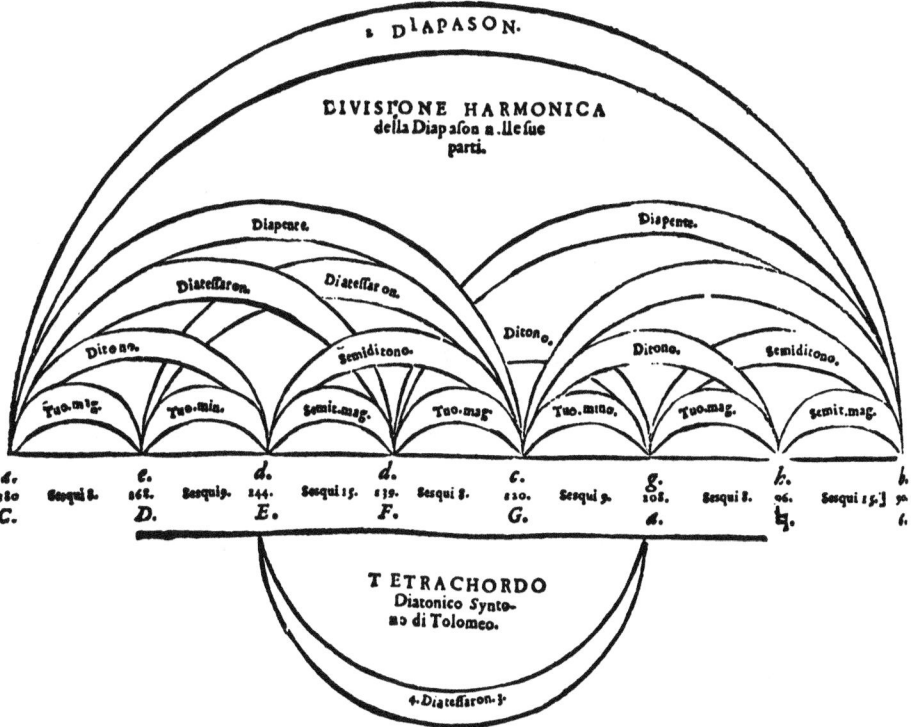

Plate 4.2 Zarlino's syntonic-diatonic divisions of the octave

that it is simple and non-composite. It is the *mother and generator*, fount and beginning, from which every other consonance and interval is derived."⁷

The unison was rejected by Zarlino as the generator of these intervals, even though it could be their "cause." He justified this very scholastic distinction on the fact that one could not plot any kind of division between a ratio of equality (1 : 1). Indeed, it was questionable whether the unison was even an interval at all, since it lacked the crucial defining characteristic of a true musical interval: an appreciable contrast of pitches. Zarlino compared it to the point in geometry:

> Equality is never found in consonances or intervals, and the unison is to the musician what the point is to the geometer. A point is the beginning of a line, although it is not itself a line. But a line is not composed of points, since a point has no length, width, or depth that can be extended, or joined to another point. So a unison is only the beginning of consonance or interval; it is neither consonance nor interval, for like the point it is incapable of extension.⁸

Earlier, we saw that Zarlino did refer to the unison as the "cause and origin" of consonance. But he meant this in the Aristotelian sense of *formal* cause, since formally all intervals are made up of single *unisones*. But the unison itself is not the *efficient* cause of consonance, since by the famous conundrum first proposed by Parmenides and the Eleatics, "one" (unity) cannot simultaneously be the source of "many" (diversity) without contradicting its nature. The true *efficient* cause of intervals must remain the octave, since only it can be divided so as to generate all the consonances.

> Therefore I say that in a cause-effect relation the cause will possess more of the quality described than the effect. For example, the hand is warmed by the fire; hence the fire is warmer than the hand. Similarly, the octave is simple by virtue of the unison; hence the unison is simpler than the octave. But musicians do not consider the unison a consonance, rather a basis for consonances. So we can say that the octave is the simplest, first, and most perfect of the consonances. It is so, in fact, and every other interval owes its being to it.⁹

One might think of the role of the unison like the prime in arithmetic. The ancient Greeks did not accept "one" as a true number, since, according to Aristotle, "one" is the measure (*monas*) by which all numbers are known. "One" cannot possess the quality of "number" since this presupposes a quantity of homogeneous units for comparison and counting.¹⁰ Nicomachus expressed the paradox this way:

> Unity, then, occupying the place and character of a point, will be the beginning of intervals and numbers, but not itself an interval or a number, just as the point is the beginning of a line, or an interval, but is not itself line or interval. Indeed, when a point is

---

7   *Ibid.*, 7, emphasis mine.
8   *Ibid.*, 24. Rameau would agree with Zarlino in rejecting the unison as a real interval, "as it does not fulfil the necessary condition for one, i.e. a difference in the sounds with regard to low and high" (*Traité*, 6; Gossett, 8).
9   Zarlino, *The Art of Counterpoint*, 24.
10 Stephan Gaukroger, *Explanatory Structures: Concepts of Explanation in Early Physics and Philosophy* (Atlantic Highlands, N. J., 1978), 101. Rameau's otherwise curious remark makes more sense when read from this perspective: "The unit is the source of numbers, and 2 is the first number" (*Traité*, 6; Gossett, 8).

added to a point, it makes no increase, for when a non-dimensional thing is added to another non-dimensional thing, it will not thereby have dimension.[11]

Neoplatonic doctrines thus were the origin of Zarlino's – and Rameau's – convictions that the single monochord string was both unity and source in music.

DESCARTES'S *COMPENDIUM MUSICAE*

A procedure for deriving intervals on the monochord that differed in interesting ways from previous canonist methods was described by René Descartes in his small treatise, the *Compendium Musicae*. Descartes's monochord techniques would have profound implications for the hierarchy of octave-generated intervals we have looked at, although they were implications of which he could scarcely have been aware.

Written in 1618 when Descartes was only twenty-two (but not published until after his death in 1650), the *Compendium* represents the young philosopher's first tentative attempts at articulating and testing his nascent mechanistic epistemology.[12] While heavily indebted to Zarlino's *Istitutioni harmoniche*, which he had recently read at the Jesuit college of La Flèche,[13] Descartes treated the monochord in a critically different way: the string divisions he plotted were for Descartes *real physical entities*. Zarlino, faithful Platonist that he was, had considered these string divisions only *images* of the numerical ratios he believed to be the cause of musical consonance. Descartes turned this ontology around: string segments were now the true foundation of sounds, and numbers were only a description. Essentially, then, Descartes was substituting a mechanical (acoustical) model of music for the older Pythagorean (numerical) model. In crucial ways, this anticipates the analogous mechanistic explanations he would propose for the entire cosmos some years later.

Hence, after asserting in the very first sentence that "the basis of music is sound" (not number!), Descartes proceeds to show how the divisions of a monochord string represent real, appreciable sounds. In a famous passage that Rameau would quote approvingly one hundred years later, Descartes wrote:

Pitch is related to pitch like string to string. Each string includes all strings that are shorter than itself, but not longer ones. Each pitch contains, therefore, all higher pitches; but lower pitches are not contained in a high pitch. It is therefore clear that the higher pitch of a consonance must be found by division of the lower one.[14]

Because each string division corresponded to a specific pitch, Descartes could argue that these sounds are truly "contained" in the single monochord string. It was just a matter of calculation to divide the string in order to find these sounds. He proceeds to do so using the traditional canonist procedure of dividing the string into aliquot

---

11 Nicomachus of Gerasa, *Introduction to Arithmetic*, trans. Martin D'Ooge, 2 vols. (New York, 1926) II, Chapter 6, 237.
12 Bertrand Augst, "Descartes's Compendium on Music," *Journal of the History of Ideas* 26/1 (1965), 124.
13 André Pirro, *Descartes et la musique* (Paris, 1907), 14.
14 René Descartes, *Compendium of Music*, trans. by Walter Robert (American Institute of Musicology, 1961), 16.

78   Rameau and Musical thought in the Enlightenment

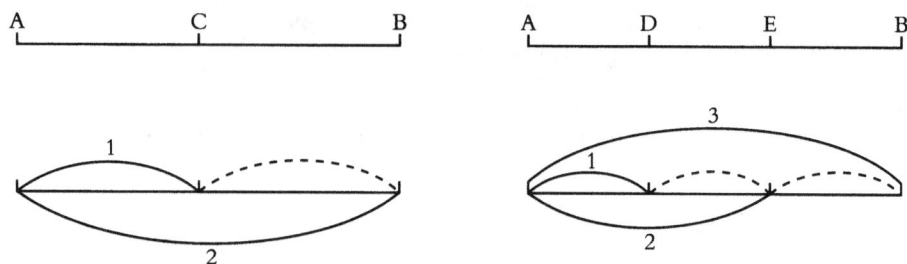

Figure 4.1 Descartes's first monochord division

parts. But instead of comparing these divisions to one another, he takes the novel – but on the basis of his physical postulate, perfectly logical – step and compares these divisions *back to the whole string*. (Zarlino and most other canonists, as we have seen, previously had compared string divisions only to one another.[15]) So taking the whole string AB as illustrated in Figure 4.1, Descartes first divides the string in half (AC), and compares this to AB, resulting in the octave 1 : 2. AB divided into thirds (D and E) produces a perfect twelfth (AD : AB = 1 : 3), and a perfect fifth (AE : AB = 2 : 3). Descartes continues in this manner producing an interval series that runs from the octave through the perfect twelfth, double octave, major seventeenth, and ending with the perfect nineteenth (doubly compounded perfect fifth). He stops at this point, since "the ear would not be keen enough to distinguish greater differences of pitch without effort."[16] While it is noteworthy that Descartes resorts to sense perception in justifying the limit of the *senario* (rather than any neoplatonic justification concerning the perfection of the number six), his argument is weakened by the fact that he will indeed need to go beyond the *senario* in order to generate the major sixth and dissonant intervals.

In any case, Descartes notes how the six intervals he has produced are octave compounds of "simple consonances." Since the octave is the "first" and "largest" of all consonances, and further, since its duple ratio is the only one "which can be multiplied by itself" such that it "does not increase the number of proportions when it enters into the composition of other consonances, as all other consonances do," these "other consonances" should be reduced to simple ratios that are "contained" within the octave.[17] To show how this is so, Descartes goes back to his monochord and tries a second method of interval derivation, one related to the older "descending series" described above.

Descartes begins by plotting an octave on the monochord string AC : AB (1 : 2), as shown in Figure 4.2. This octave is itself divided in half (AD). The resulting ratio (AC : AD = 2 : 3) sounds the perfect fifth. The "remainder" of this division

---

15 This monochord technique did not entirely originate with Descartes, however. As far back as the Pythagoreans, similar string comparisons were made (a Medieval example being the author of the *Scholia Enchiriadis*. But the compound (multiplex) intervals produced by comparing string segments with the undivided string would have had less practical value to musicians wishing to build and test scales or tuning systems.
16 Descartes, *Compendium*, 17.
17 Ibid., 19.

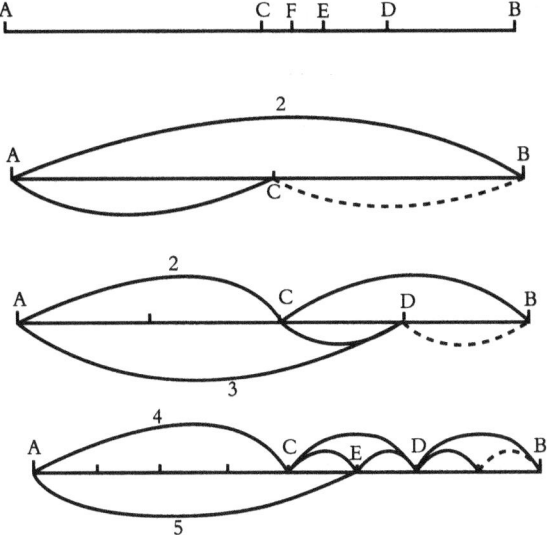

Figure 4.2 Descartes's second monochord division

(AD : AB = 3 : 4) produces the perfect fourth, which consequently holds a lower status than the perfect fifth. In Descartes's memorable metaphor, it is the "shadow of the fifth" and the "unhappiest of consonances."[18] He also briefly alludes to the phenomenon of upper partials in suggesting that "no pitch is heard without its higher octave somehow sounding audibly" – hence the fourth is naturally perceived as a kind of acoustical resultant when the fifth is sounded.[19] But he never pursues this line of thought further.

He continues: "After dividing the distance CB at D, I can in the same way divide CD at E. The immediate result is the major third" (AC : AE = 4 : 5). The resultant of the major third is of course the minor sixth (AE : AB = 5 : 8). From these divisions, Descartes concludes, "There are only three interval-numbers, to wit: 2, 3, and 5. 4 and 6 are multiples of these, and are therefore only secondary interval-numbers."[20] The three primary interval-numbers correspond to the octave, perfect fifth, and major third, respectively, which he then labels as primary consonances. From the comparison of these primary consonances to the upper octave, two secondary consonances (consonances *per accidens*) are found: the perfect fourth and the minor sixth. The minor third – also a secondary consonance – arises from a different comparison: as the difference between the major third and the perfect fifth.

The major sixth presents a problem, though. Since the minor third is a difference within a perfect fifth, Descartes cannot then turn around and take *its difference* from an octave. Therefore, instead of relating the major sixth to the minor third as he earlier related the minor sixth to the major third, he derives it (as Zarlino did) by adding the perfect fourth to the major third – a somewhat embarrassing but unavoidable consequence of his determination to stay within the *senario*.[21]

[18] Ibid., 24.   [19] Ibid., 18.   [20] Ibid., 22.   [21] Ibid., 27.

So for young Descartes, the octave remained the generator of all intervals. In this sense, his theory remains firmly within the traditional canonist paradigm. But there were aspects to Descartes's procedure that were novel, and threatened to upset this generative hierarchy. By equating his string divisions to sounding pitches, and further comparing these back to the whole string, Descartes made a powerful suggestion that the monochord string itself (unity) was the physical source of these intervals. But he was not able to complete this connection, since he was not able to reconcile his physical intuition of pitch with the canonist-mathematical definition of interval. Such connections were being made, though, by scientists outside France. Descartes would soon learn about these developments from his friend Mersenne.

ACOUSTICAL REVISIONS

A new chapter concerning the subject of interval ranking was opened in the late sixteenth century. Around 1563, the Italian scientist Giovanni Battista Benedetti reported in a letter to the composer Cipriano de Rore that sound was propagated to the ear through the air by a series of rapid pulses initiated by any periodic vibrational disturbance. Benedetti argued that pitch was a direct result of the frequency of these vibrations: the faster the frequency, the higher the pitch. He deduced from this that the length of a vibrating string is inversionally proportional to its frequency.[22] This has the effect of reversing the received harmonic and arithmetic divisions: an octave measured by string lengths in the ratio of 2 : 1 when measured by vibrational frequency becomes the ratio 1 : 2. What is an arithmetic division in one becomes the harmonic division in the other, and vice versa.

Independently of Benedetti, both Galileo Galilei and the Dutch scientist Isaac Beeckman began to study the vibrational nature of pitch. Galileo made some preliminary attempts to explain the isochronic behavior of the vibrating string by analogy with a pendulum. Beeckman recorded related observations in his private journal, and soon communicated them to his friend Descartes. (Descartes had incidentally penned the *Compendium* as a gift to Beeckman, who was one of his earliest scientific acquaintances.) Mersenne, who engaged in a voluminous correspondence with just about every major scientific figure in Europe, quickly learned of these investigations and incorporated them within his *magnum opus*, the *Harmonie Universelle* of 1636.[23]

Not all these scientists were in agreement as to how these different frequencies were propagated to the ear. Galileo, for example, believed that sound was propagated as waves through the air in direct proportion to the displacement of the vibrating object. On the other hand, Beeckman thought that sound was propagated

---

[22] Claude V. Palisca, "Scientific Empiricism in Musical Thought," *Seventeenth Century Science and the Arts*, ed. H. H. Rhys (Princeton, 1961), 105.

[23] For an excellent history of these scientists' work on music theory and acoustics, the reader is encouraged to consult H. F. Cohen's enlightening study, *Quantifying Music: The Science of Music at the First Stage of the Scientific Revolution 1580–1650* (Dordrecht, 1984), especially Chapter 5, "Contacts and Criticisms," 180–204.

as atomistic corpuscles.[24] In other words, Beeckman believed that air consisted of countless Democritan atoms that individually respond to a discrete frequency, and would be physically propelled to the ear when the respective frequency was initiated. (We will encounter an analogous atomistic sound theory resurrected in the eighteenth century when considering the acoustical theories of Dortous de Mairan in Chapter 6.) But however they explained sound propagation, most scientists agreed by the second quarter of the seventeenth century that pitch was a product of the regular and periodic vibrations of some displacement force.

The significance of this acoustical revision to music theory was twofold. First of all, it seemed to undermine the traditional canonist linking of pitch and string length. The "efficient" cause of musical pitch sounded on a monochord turned out to be not its string length but rather the frequency of its vibrations. Hence, Descartes was not quite accurate when he concluded that lower sounds contain higher sounds because longer string lengths contain shorter ones. (The physics of harmonic overtones by which Descartes's original analogy might in fact be validated was not yet understood by scientists.) Interestingly, though, the new acoustics did nothing to weaken the Pythagorean doctrines associated with canonist theory. The simple numerical ratios discovered by the canonists on the monochord had been threatened with imminent demise through the demonstration of Vincenzo Galilei (father of Galileo) that the ratios of musical intervals could be expressed in terms other than string lengths. When, for instance, one measured an octave on the monochord by comparing tensions in the string (as opposed to length), the ratio was quadruple (1 : 4) not duple (1 : 2). Even more irrational ratios resulted from measurements of pipe conics or string densities. The new understanding of pitch proved to be a kind of vindication of the received Pythagorean ratios, even if these ratios were now in inverted form and shorn of much of their mystical symbolism.

The second and most important consequence of an acoustical reconceptualization of pitch was that it led to a new theory of consonance based upon the relative simplicity of frequency ratios; the more the respective frequencies of two pitches coincide, the more consonant the interval will sound.[25] The explanation for this theory presumably lay in some physiological reaction within the ear, wherein the greater coincidence of individual pulses impinging upon it (whether explained by Galileo's wave theory or Beeckman's atomistic theory) creates a lesser sense of irritation. This could be measured precisely through mathematical calculation. One only needed to multiply the terms of any interval ratio; those with the smallest products were the most consonant. Hence, a precise ranking of intervals could be produced (as shown in Table 4.1).

---

[24] *Ibid.*, 87 and 120.
[25] Cohen's study contains a detailed history and analysis of the "coincidence theory" of consonance in the seventeenth century: *Quantifying Music*, 73 ff.

Table 4.1 Interval rankings

Interval	Ratio	Product
Unison	1:1	1
Octave	1:2	2
Perfect 12th	1:3	3
Double Octave	1:4	4
Major 17th	1:5	5
Perfect 5th	2:3	6
Perfect 4th	3:4	12
Major 6th	3:5	15
Major 3rd	4:5	20
Minor 3rd	5:6	30
Diminished 5th	5:7	35
Minor 6th	5:8	40

There were several interesting consequences to this rigorous mathematical ranking. For one, the unison could now be accepted as a consonance since its ratio was as mathematically valid as any other. Secondly, by defining consonance with acoustical criteria, the confines of Zarlino's *senario* were breached.[26] The distinction between consonance and dissonance turned out to be only one of gradation; there was no acoustical reason for sanctioning the limit of consonance at the number six. Finally, an acoustical ranking of consonance based upon frequency ratios overturned the received hierarchy of consonance. It can be seen, for example, that the superparticular ratios of Zarlino's *senario* were less perfect than their octave compounds. The perfect twelfth ($1 \times 3 = 3$) was more consonant than the perfect fifth ($2 \times 3 = 6$), as was the major seventeenth ($1 \times 5 = 5$) versus the major third ($4 \times 5 = 20$). (We will see this mathematical ranking of consonance resurrected virtually unchanged by Euler some 150 years later, with interesting implications for Rameau's thesis of octave identity.) More critically, it suggested that the perfect fourth ($3 \times 4 = 12$) was more consonant than the major third ($4 \times 5 = 20$), and that the diminished fifth ($5 \times 7 = 35$) was more consonant than the minor sixth ($5 \times 8 = 40$).

In order to account for the discrepancies between musical judgment and acoustical ranking, some scientists posited two different kinds of evaluation.[27] In a letter to Mersenne, Descartes explained this as a difference between the simplicity of ratios (*douceur* or *excellence*) and pleasingness to the ear (*agrément*).[28] By this

---

[26] Palisca, "Scientific Empiricism," 109.

[27] In his annotations to the Mersenne correspondence, Cornelis de Waard provides a good summary of the differing rankings assigned to intervals by several seventeenth-century scientists. See *Correspondance du P. Marin Mersenne*, ed. Cornelis de Waard, 16 vols. (Paris, 1932–86) III, 219–21.

[28] Letter dated January, 13, 1631, *Correspondance*, II, 25. Descartes was hardly the first to recognize conflicts between objective and subjective judgment in music, however. The heated arguments that raged in the Renaissance over tuning systems were demarcated by whether one accepted the Pythagorean ratios as

distinction, the fourth is more "perfect" though less "agreeable" than the major third, as is likewise the diminished fifth in relation to the minor sixth. Unfortunately, such subjective criteria opened the doors to a position of empirical relativity that Descartes found disconcerting. Since pleasingness appeared to be a capricious judgment of the senses, he saw that it would vary from person to person, place to place, and time to time. Asking someone to explain his preference for an interval was like asking someone "why fruit is not more agreeable to the palate than fish."[29] In certain musical contexts, quite dissonant intervals could be pleasing. Then, too, the most perfect consonances such as the octave and perfect fifth would become wearisome if over used. In two other letters to Mersenne, Descartes invoked a different gustatory analogy to explain this: Honey is certainly sweeter to the palate than are olives, but it is also less agreeable to eat honey in quantity than it is to eat olives.[30] Quite simply, Descartes distrusted judgments based upon our senses – faculties that he believed to be unreliable and even deceiving. Only analysis through reason offered a truly secure way. So skeptical was Descartes about the possibility of ever subjecting music to this kind of reasoned analysis that he eventually gave up any hope of erecting a truly objective system of music theory. Music was relegated to the domain of taste; Descartes wanted to concentrate upon those sciences that could be treated with mathematical certainty.[31] It is thus not surprising that he never formally addressed the subject of music theory in any of his writings after the *Compendium* of 1618.

By defining pitch acoustically, seventeenth-century scientists had radically and irreversibly altered the metaphysical grounding of music theory. The received models by which pitch had been understood and analyzed (Pythagorean ratios Aristotelian essences, etc.) were replaced by a rigorously mechanistic model. In one important sense, of course, there was no change; intervals could still be expressed in terms of numerical ratios. Indeed, the acoustical revision offered a firmer foundation for traditional consonance theory than scholastic philosophy could. But one critical ingredient of canonist theory was also lost: a generative hierarchy. Whereas it was easy for canonists to show on the monochord how the octave when divided could generate subsequent intervals, no such demonstration was available when intervals were understood only as ratios of frequencies.

To be sure, one could rank intervals as to their degree of coincidence, thus granting the unison the primacy of first place. But one could not thereby say that the unison *generated* other intervals. To retain the notion of interval generation

---

sacrosanct in determining consonance (i.e. allowing as consonances only those intervals whose ratios were comprised of integers up to four) or whether one should accept the judgment of the ear as did Bartolome Ramos in 1482 when he allowed just major thirds (ratio 4 : 5) into his tuning system. Zarlino also recognized something along the lines of these two kinds of evaluation in speaking of "fuller" intervals such as the perfect fifth, and "more pleasing" intervals such as the major third (*The Art of Counterpoint*, 18).

29   Letter dated March 4, 1630. *Correspondance*, II, 408.
30   Letters dated January 13, 1631, and October 1631. Mersenne, *Correspondance*, III, 25 and 212.
31   Pirro, *Descartes et la musique*, 99.

(and lacking for now the understanding of harmonic overtones), music theorists needed to reintegrate elements of Platonic philosophy within this new mechanistic model of pitch. This is what Mersenne would try to do.

MERSENNE AND THE GENERATIVE UNISON

In contrast to Descartes, Mersenne was reluctant to accept any division between "agreement" and "excellence." Having faith in the uniformity of God's universe, the truth of mathematical calculation, and confidence in the perfectibility of human judgment, he felt that one's perception of interval purity could and should follow the ranking mathematics assigns. If we did not hear intervals that way, it was because of our corrupted state. Mersenne believed – or at least hoped – that through education of the mind and piety of the soul, one could learn to recognize the intervals in their natural order.[32] Ideally, agreement and excellence should coincide.

Mersenne had an ulterior motive here. Hoping to create a perfect language through which men could communicate perfectly and be morally elevated, he believed music to be the key. The ranking of consonances was more than just a scholastic dispute. Only if musical intervals could be assigned to fixed gradations would such an ideal language be possible. It was for this reason that Mersenne spent so much effort exploring whether a "perfect song" could be composed (and likewise, a "perfect musical instrument" constructed and a "perfect performance" executed). While he optimistically believed that the answer was affirmative in all cases, he admitted these accomplishments were perhaps beyond his own ability.[33]

Faith in the rational order of music was a direct reflection of Mersenne's deep-seated neoplatonic philosophy (or more precisely, Plato as filtered through Augustine). Mersenne was convinced that the universe was a perfect creation based upon God's perfect design, hence it was rational, orderly, and harmonious – a *Harmonie Universelle*. But Mersenne was also a mechanist; like his friend Descartes, he believed the visible universe consisted of extended matter governed by precise mechanical laws of motion and impact, not any elusive Aristotelian tendencies or occult forces. And the means to discover and describe this mechanistic order was with mathematics.

While Mersenne agreed that God's mind and plans are inscrutable to man, we could still understand His creation through careful analysis and observation, contrary to the pernicious arguments of the Pyrrhonists and skeptics against whom he would tirelessly polemicize.[34] Music became one of the most important models

---

[32] More detailed discussions of Mersenne's views on interval ranking may be found in Albion Gruber, "Mersenne and Evolving Tonal Theory," *Journal of Music Theory* 14/1 (1970), 42–50; and Hellmut Ludwig, *Marin Mersenne und seine Musiklehre* (Halle, 1935), 58–64.

[33] For Mersenne's program of a universal language, see Robert Lenoble, *Mersenne ou la naissance du mécanisme* (Paris, 1943), 514–31. Dean Mace has analyzed the musical aspects of Mersenne's language theory in "Marin Mersenne on Language and Music," *Journal of Music Theory* 14/1 (1970), 2–34.

[34] An excellent study of Mersenne's syncretic theology may be found in Peter Dear, *Mersenne and the Learning of the Schools* (Ithaca, 1988).

for Mersenne's cosmology, as it manifested more clearly than anything else this mechanistic-harmonic order. And just as the universe could be arranged in a hierarchy descending from God the source and prime mover, so too could music. What was the analogous source for music? For Mersenne, it was none other than the humble unison.

In his *Harmonie Universelle*, Mersenne spends some thirty dense pages discussing the unison – the longest section devoted to any one topic in all of the text.[35] Unlike Zarlino and Descartes, Mersenne believed that the unison was not only a true consonance, but the most perfect of all consonances. Clearly, it must be so, he argued, for it represents the first and most perfect of all ratios: equality. It "surpasses all the contentments which come from other intervals, since it is the image of divine harmony and the source of the said pleasures."[36] He explores in peripatetic fashion the ontological priority of the unison, and draws a host of analogies comparing the unison to everything from equilibrium in mechanics and light reflecting from a mirror to the incorruptible virtue of God and divine love.[37] If it does not please the ear as much as other intervals, that is only because we mortals cannot appreciate its perfection directly, much as we cannot look directly into the sun although it is undoubtedly the most perfect source of light.

Given the perfection and equality of the unison, all other intervals must necessarily be corrupt in varying degrees due to their inequality and distance from unity, including the octave. But this leads to a paradox. In the Platonic universe, as we have seen, there was an orderly and continuous descent from perfection to corruption that encompassed all creatures and matter. The belief in a graded ordering of the universe that could be imaged as a single continuous ladder that began with God at the top – transmuted as the "Great Chain of Being" in the eighteenth century – was to be one of the central metaphysical axioms of Enlightenment thought.[38] But the question arises for Mersenne, as it did for any neoplatonist, how God who is incorruptible, immutable, and perfect can beget something that does not have these qualities.[39] Mersenne seems to have arrived at the same quandary in which Zarlino and Descartes had found themselves when they considered the unison as a source for musical intervals.

In Proposition 7 of his "Traitez des Consonances," Mersenne sought "to determine if the idea of inequality comes from the idea of equality, and consequently if all the consonances have the unison as their source and origin."[40] It seems paradoxical,

---

35 *Harmonie Universelle contenant la théorie et la pratique de la musique* (Paris, 1636), "Traitez des consonances," 5–34.
36 *Ibid.*, 17. A partial translation of the section on the unison is found in Edward Lippman, *Musical Aesthetics: A Historical Reader*, 3 vols. (New York, 1986), I, 105–17.
37 "Traitez des consonances," 12, 22, 29, 30. Mersenne's obsession concerning the unison must be understood in the context of an ancient – but in his day still vital – Patristic doctrine that equated the perfection of God with the simplicity of unity in number. The long discussion of the unison found in the *Harmonie Universelle* is really only a continuation of a subject begun in several of his earlier theological publications. See Dear, *Mersenne and the Learning of the Schools*, 104–09.
38 Recall Condillac's description of the "correct" philosophical system from Chapter 2.
39 Peter A. Bertocci, "Creation in Religion," *Dictionary of the History of Ideas*, I, 571–73.
40 *Harmonie Universelle*, "Traitez des consonances," 30.

he admits, for a ratio of equality to produce unequal ratios, since it appears that "unity is indifferent to production, and generates (*engendre*) nothing but itself." Unity either divided or multiplied will only make another unity.

It is here that Mersenne reverts to scholastic argumentation. Aquinas had taught that God was a single indivisible Being who nonetheless comprehended the diversity of His creation, since God "knows all possible ways in which its own divine essence can be imitated."[41] Mersenne took this as an analogy for the simplicity of unity generating numbers. Peter Dear paraphrases Mersenne's reasoning:

> Creatures draw their perfections from God just as numbers draw theirs from unity, "to which they add nothing new"; as the being of creatures represents participation in the divine being, so the numerality of numbers represents the participation of unity, "on which they depend, such that it is impossible that they exist without it."[42]

Mersenne also proffered an adaptation of Anselm's ontological proof of God: from our finite and movable nature we are able to imagine an infinite and immovable Being who must therefore exist and be the cause of our creation. The unison must therefore presuppose all other intervals, just as equality must presuppose inequality:

> It follows that the idea of equality and the unison are not the principles of inequality and consonance properly speaking, but only that the unison which comes from the equality of vibrations or the movements of air which strike the ear is simpler and easier to conceive than the other consonances and that it is not possible to consider the proportions of inequality without supposing that of equality . . .[43]

Unity, in other words, must be the *material* cause of numbers since, as Aristotle had argued, all numbers are collections of unities. But Mersenne goes a step beyond Zarlino and grants the unison a privileged place in the hierarchy of consonances. As the most perfect of intervals, the unison must logically be the generator of all other intervals – "la première consonance, ou la racine des accords."[44]

Despite Mersenne's skill in scholastic argumentation, the fact remained that, acoustically, the unison was more like a single pitch than a real interval, and mathematically, it could not be divided by traditional canonist techniques. Thus, by the following chapters, when Mersenne finally moves on to consider the derivation of other consonant intervals, we find him retreating from his earlier position and calling the octave the "source and origin" of intervals, since it is the first interval of inequality from which are derived other intervals.[45] Mersenne ultimately seems to have been unable to overcome the basic problem faced by previous canonists. The ratio of equality – the unison – could not in any mathematical sense

---

[41] Quoted in Dear, *Mersenne and the Learning of the Schools*, 70.
[42] Ibid.
[43] *Harmonie Universelle*, "Traitez des consonances," 33. Salinas earlier made an analogous scholastic distinction between the unison and octave, the former being "principium a quo omnes numeri derivantur," while the latter was "principium per quod." *De Musica Libri Septem* (Salamanca, 1577), 63.
[44] *Harmonie Universelle*, "Traitez des consonances," 139.
[45] Ibid., 60.

generate terms of inequality.⁴⁶ Only the octave could. Yet for aesthetic and theological reasons that Mersenne found difficult to resist, he also believed that the unison could still be considered the true origin of these intervals. As with so much else in Mersenne's writings, he never satisfactorily resolved these contrasting positions, and left them as paradoxes. We will nonetheless see the seductiveness of the neoplatonic ideal of generative unity penetrating into the eighteenth century in the theory of Rameau, even if the exact genealogy of the concept had become obscured along the way.⁴⁷

A GERMAN EXCURSUS

In the generations separating Mersenne and Rameau, little interest was shown by French music theorists concerning the problems of interval generation, owing, as we have already noted in Chapter 2, to the decline of *musica speculativa* in the second half of the seventeenth century. Lest we think that such questions lay completely dormant during this period, however, we may observe that outside of France where *musica speculativa* remained more vibrant, the topic of interval generation and ranking was granted more attention. This was especially true in Germany with its rich scholastic heritage. Few German writers added anything substantially new to the discussion. Indeed, most of them simply troped the writings of classical authorities. Still, it is noteworthy that such questions were considered vital ones.

Andreas Werckmeister (1645–1706) may serve as a good example. He was perhaps the most prominent and certainly the most prolific exponent of German *musica speculativa* in the late seventeenth century. Certainly no one better epitomizes the paradoxical mix of conservative and pragmatic thinking that was characteristic of German music theory at the time. His obsession with *Ordnung* and *Ratio* reflects less enlightened rationalism than the conservative scholastic tradition characteristic of the provincial German Latin schools in which he spent his life, overlaid with an almost cabalistic mysticism derived from Lutheran eschatalogy. The *trias harmonica*, as for Lippius, represented an acoustical icon of the holy trinity. Musical harmony, consisting of varied dispositions of the triad, was nothing less than a divinely inspired art created to instil piety in man and recognition of the number and order by which God created the world.⁴⁸ It is not surprising in this regard that the

---

46 If he had put more credence in the harmonic series of pitches produced by a natural trumpet and the harmonic overtone series, it might have been possible for Mersenne to suggest a physical model of sound generation, as Rameau would eventually do. But Mersenne never saw these as consistent or uniform phenomena from which he could generalize. (We will return to this topic in more detail in Chapter 6.)

47 One other writer who seemed to have been persuaded by Mersenne's arguments was Brossard, who calls the unison the source (*principe*) of all intervals in the same way *unité* is the *principe* of all numbers (*Dictionaire*, s.v. "unissone").

48 The partial title of Werckmeister's last publication is illustrative of this attitude: *Musicalische Paradoxal–Discourse oder ungemeine Vorstellungen wie die Musica einen hohen und göttlichen Uhrsprung habe, und wie hingegen dieselbe so sehr gemissbrauchet wird. . . So wohl denen so ihre Music zur Ehre Gottes gedencken anzuwenden auch andern Gott-, und Kirchen-Music Liebenden zum weitern nachdencken mathematicè historicè und allegoricè durch die musicalischen Proportional-Zahlen* (Quedlinburg, 1707).

question of temperament played such a central role in his writings. If music was a reflection of divinely-ordered numerical proportions, then a musician cannot wantonly alter these proportions without profound consequences.[49]

Like Mersenne, Werckmeister held that unity was the source of number and music, and an image of the divine creator. "If we compare the days of creation with music," he wrote, "we see that in the beginning God created heaven and earth in the first days. This beginning is the unity or *unisonus* out from which all consonances and dissonances flow. Indeed, God Himself is unity – a beginning without beginning or end."[50] Elsewhere he wrote: "Just as unity is compared to the one God, so is a harmony originating in this unity and that contains in itself at once all the consonances in harmony perfectly complete."[51] Werckmeister liked to repeat the Augustinian axiom that the "closer a thing is to unity or equality, the more perfect and appreciable it is."[52] In traditional canonist fashion, he demonstrated how the monochord string represents this equality by generating all musical intervals through successive string divisions. The monochord, he exclaimed, is "an inexhaustible font of musical elements."[53] However, it is significant that Werckmeister saw in the natural tones of the trumpet a better manifestation of the harmonic series than that provided on the monochord. The trumpet was a more "natural" source than the artificial divisions of a string; it showed us "how nature has implanted in even inanimate objects the characteristics of musical proportions." The fundamental tone of the trumpet is thus the true physical *unisones* that manifests God's single, eternal Being.[54]

Yet how far we still are from Rameau's fundamental bass becomes apparent when we consider Werckmeister's heuristic for chordal inversion. Since any chord was measured according to its distance from the fundamental unity, a chord "inversion" could hardly be considered equivalent to a "root-position" chord that included the fundamental as its *bassus*. It is true that in places Werckmeister did

Example 4.1 Werckmeister's *Haupt-Formal Clausulen*

49   Yet it was a sign of Werckmeister's pragmatic nature that he realized that some sort of temperament was necessary. While he could not bring himself to adopt equal temperament (although he was well aware of it), he calculated several tuning systems that could accommodate a chromatic gamut of twelve keys.
50   *Musicae mathematicae hodegus curiosus* (Frankfurt, 1687), 142.
51   *Musicalische Paradoxal-Discourse*, 99.
52   *Musicae mathematicae hodegus curiosus*, 30.
53   Ibid., 23.
54   Ibid., 57 and 146.

recognize a derivative relationship between progressions that resulted from the transposition of voices. In his thorough-bass treatise of 1698, he illustrated various voicings of the authentic perfect cadence with a 4–3 suspension (called by him *Haupt-Formal Clausulen*).[55] His paradigmatic models of the cadence are shown in Example 4.1. He then shows how the bass voice can also be interchanged with the upper voices, resulting in cadences like those given in Example 4.2.[56] He notes from this that the resolutions of the dissonant second and seventh "are nothing else but the *clausulae formales*."

Example 4.2 "Inversions" of Example 4.1

Still, this is not Rameau's idea of inversional equivalence. The operation Werckmeister describes (called *Versetzung*) really derives from the traditional art of invertible counterpoint. Chordal "inversions" could not be considered equivalent by Werckmeister, since their respective distances from unity varied, and thus so did their respective degrees of perfection. (This is why Heinichen, incidentally, used the term *Verkehrung* rather than *Umkehrung* to translate Rameau's term, *renversement*; chord inversions were literally perversions of the harmonic triad.) The 6/3 chord (5 : 6 : 8) is closer to perfection than the 6/4 chord (6 : 8 : 10), since its proportion "more closely approaches the number one." But neither attains the perfection of the harmonic triad (4 : 5 : 6). (Of course if we follow this reasoning literally, the 6/4 chord 3 : 4 : 5 should be more perfect than the harmonic triad 4 : 5 : 6.)

The kind of scholastic theorizing epitomized in Werckmeister's writings continued to flourish in Germany during the eighteenth century. Under the influence of Leibnizian rationalism (as transmitted especially by his disciple Christian Wolff), music theorists like Johann Heinrich Buttstett, Lorenz Mizler, and Meinrad Spiess continued to promote a canonist program that addressed many of the problems – and used much the same language – of seventeenth-century German *musica speculativa*, including the priority of the generative unity. Ironically, the persistence of a conservative theoretical tradition in Germany may help to explain the comparatively more favorable reception Rameau's writings initially enjoyed there during the first half of the century than in his own homeland.

---

55 *Die nothwendigsten Anmerckungen und Regeln wie der Bassus Continuus oder General-Bass wol könne tractiret werden* (Aschersleben, 1698), 38. Carl Dahlhaus discusses this same example in *Studies of the Origins of Harmonic Tonality*, trans. Robert O. Gjerdingen (Princeton, 1990), 116–18.
56 Werckmeister warns us that all voices are not equally exchangeable. The bass line $\hat{1}$–$\hat{5}$–$\hat{1}$, for instance, does not make an effective descant line.

For now, we can see that in the generations preceding Rameau, many of the components of the *basse fondamentale* were already in place. There was a practical tradition in composition and thorough-bass theory that encouraged musicians to think of music in largely chordal terms. Moreover, there were informal heuristics by which these chords could be related by inversion and supposition to the consonant triad. On the other side of the theoretical spectrum, there was a speculative tradition rooted in neoplatonism by which the harmonic triad and its "inversions" were seen to be generated from a single monochord string, and against which they were graded in perfection based upon their respective distances from this source. What was needed was the unification of these overlapping musical and philosophical concepts in a single theoretical system. This was achieved by Rameau, whose writings we now consider in more detail.

RAMEAU'S *SON FONDAMENTAL*

Rameau's use of the monochord in the first book of the *Traité* betrays close kinship to Zarlino's *Istitutioni harmoniche* and Descartes's *Compendium,* both of which he quotes from at the beginning of Chapter 3. From Zarlino, Rameau learned of the *senario* as the limit of consonance. The first six divisions of the monochord string generate all the consonant intervals available (with the problematic exception, of course, of the minor sixth). From Descartes, Rameau got the pregnant idea that higher sounds are "contained" in lower sounds, just as shorter strings are contained in longer ones.[57] Still, Rameau's actual use of the monochord differed in crucial ways from both Zarlino's and Descartes's. For Rameau, the monochord was a musical – not a mathematical – instrument. In other words, the actual string divisions plotted on the monochord represented not so much numerical ratios (as they did for Zarlino) or the physical string segments (as for Descartes) as actual pitches. This is an important point to keep in mind, for it explains why Rameau felt at liberty to manipulate the ratios of his string divisions as freely as he did. Numbers did not have the same ontological significance for him as they would have for a neoplatonist like Zarlino, to say nothing of a scientist like Descartes. Hence they could not be subject to exclusively mathematical confirmation or refutation.

By choosing to found his theory upon monochord string divisions, Rameau finds himself in a quandary. Specifically, we know his primary goal was to validate chords as fundamental entities. But the monochord, as we have also seen, was traditionally used to measure intervals. In order to produce the various chords he wanted, Rameau had to find a means to combine these intervals in some logical way. By validating chords through intervallic structures instead of the other way around, Rameau was essentially reversing the derivational equation he wanted. After the *Traité,* it was a procedure he would never again try. But it was a necessary consequence of wishing to stay for now within the canonist paradigm.

[57] Rameau read the 1688 translation of Descartes's *Compendium* by Nicolas Poisson (published as *Traité de la mechanique composé par Monsieur Descartes. De plus l'abrégé de musique du mesme autheur mis en françois* ([Paris, 1688]).

The generative fundamental

Rameau finds a partial solution to his dilemma with the notion of a *son fondamental* – the "fundamental sound." Every interval, he will try to show, is generated by some single sound that may or may not coincide with its lowest term. Those intervals that share common fundamental sounds may be combined into chords, while conversely, chords can be analyzed as composites of intervals sharing the same fundamental sound. The real value of the monochord to Rameau can now be understood: the single monochord string will be the fundamental sound of his intervals and chords; it will serve as the natural source and principle of harmony whose discovery he had earlier announced as his professed goal in the Preface to his *Traité*. Much as Descartes had already shown, the monochord string becomes the physical source of the pitches produced by its divisions:

> These divisions clearly prove that each part of the divided strings arises from the first string, since these parts are contained in that first, unique string. Thus the sounds which these divided strings produce are generated (*engendrez*) by the first sound, which is consequently their source and their fundamental.[58]

Because the fundamental sound generates all the intervals that together comprise harmony, it is the *principle* of harmony.[59] To emphasize his point visually, Rameau redrew the diagram in the *Supplément* he had originally printed in the text showing Descartes's first monochord division (given in Figure 4.1) with the illustration reproduced in Figure 4.3. This new illustration shows more graphically how the whole string AB literally encompasses and hence generates these divisions.

Figure 4.3 Rameau's revised illustration of his monochord division

As did Mersenne, Rameau makes "one" the measure of the monochord string. He waxes rapturous over the generative power of the fundamental sound. At times, his prose is redolent of Mersenne's hyper-Platonism. "All properties of this octave, of sounds in general, of intervals, and of chords rest finally on the single, fundamental source, which is represented by the undivided string or by the unit[y] (*unité*)."[60] In adopting Mersenne's position, Rameau appears to be undaunted by his predecessor's difficulties in having established "unity" as a generative source for intervals. Rameau obviously did not want the octave to be his generator, since he will

---

58 *Traité*, 5; Gossett, 7–8. The verb *engendrer* has a different nuance from the acoustical *générateur* that is the resonating *corps sonore* of Rameau's later writings. Strictly speaking, a monochord generates only single intervals in succession, while a vibrating string generates the entire spectrum of upper partials that comprise its overtone series. The former is an artificial kind of generation, whereas the latter occurs naturally – an aesthetic distinction that will soon become critical in Rameau's theory.

59 The French term Rameau uses – *principe* – can be translated as either "principle" or "source" – an ambiguity deliberately conveyed by Rameau's usage.

60 *Traité*, 9; Gossett, 12–13. *Unité* is much more expansive a concept than conveyed by Gossett's translation as "unit." Recalling how for Mersenne the number one had a paradoxically dual nature of prime as well as unity, I think a better translation for *unité* is precisely its literal English cognate: unity.

need to maintain the strict identity of octaves to support his thesis of inversional derivation. But what new arguments could Rameau offer on behalf of a generative unity?

The answer lay in Descartes's initial monochord technique: take the received series of aliquot string divisions and compare them *back to the original string*. All such intervals will thus have the numerator one fixed as their base: the octave (1 : 2), perfect twelfth (1 : 3), double octave (1 : 4), major seventeenth (1 : 5), etc. Rameau claims this is the "natural" order of interval generation (see Plate 4.3). Like his predecessors, Rameau must also skip over the seventh division, explaining "it cannot give a pleasant interval as is evident to connoisseurs."[61]

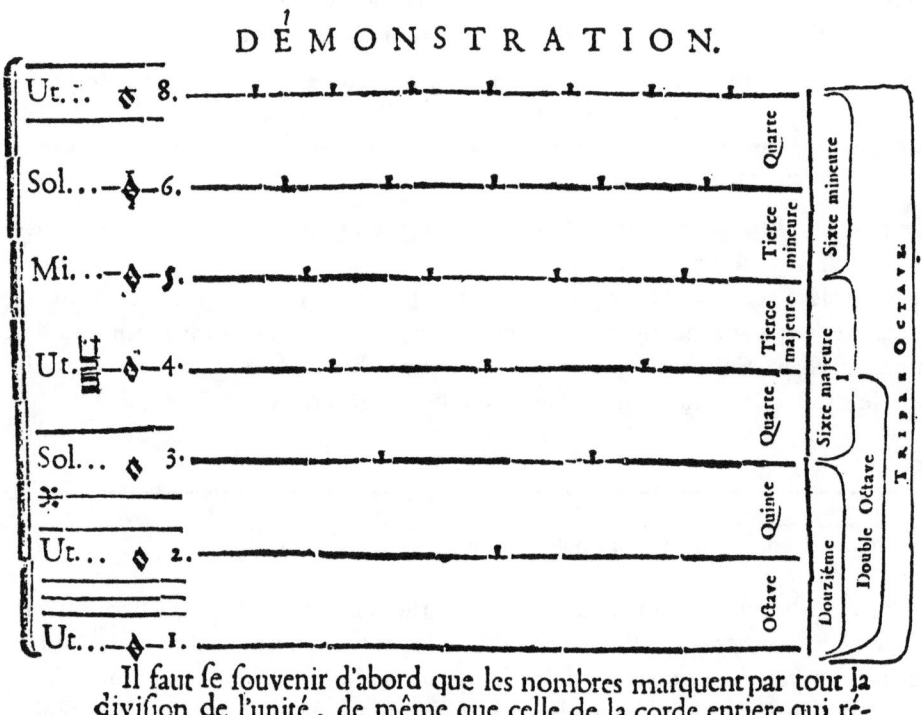

Plate 4.3 *Traité*, 4. Rameau's string divisions

By relating all string divisions to unity, Rameau necessarily had to notate them as fractions. But this created mathematical complications, since it would have been awkward to subject fractions to the extensive multiplications and divisions he is shortly to undertake. Rameau might have avoided the problem by doing what most canonists before him had done and treating the monochord string as a *composite* of divisions. One computes the smallest common denominator of the string divisions utilized, and designates it as one. The resulting string composites may then number 864 (Zarlino), 3,600 (Mersenne), and, in the case of Salomon de Caus, 17,280![62]

---

61 *Traité*, 4; Gossett, 6.
62 Salomon de Caus, *Institution harmonique* (Frankfurt, 1615), 13.

But Rameau wanted the string to be equated with the number one for the same reason Mersenne posited unity as the source of all numbers. In order to salvage the concept of generative unity while avoiding the fractional harmonic series, Rameau inverted these fractions by treating all string segments as *multiplications* of the original string. In other words, what were previously parts of the string (½, ⅓, ¼, etc.) were now multiples of that string (2, 3, 4, etc.). This has the effect of inverting the harmonic series into an arithmetic series.

Unfortunately, this also creates a logical inconsistency. Rameau wished to adopt Descartes's thesis that higher notes are contained in lower notes as string divisions are contained by the whole. Yet he also wished to adopt Mersenne's thesis that unity was the source of all numbers. Essentially, then, Rameau was trying to combine two differing and ultimately irreconcilable models for the monochord: a physical model where string divisions represent parts of the whole string, and a numerical model where string divisions represent integers generated from a fundamental unity. Rameau tries to make amends in later writings by resubstituting fractions for these multiples. But this only has the deleterious effect of confusing his terms and muddling up his subsequent calculations.

The precariousness of this position was not lost upon Rameau, who admitted that "the numbers measuring the lengths of string, however, follow a progression which is the inversion of the first progression, thus destroying some of the rules of arithmetic, or at least obliging us to invert them, as we shall see later."[63] But for both practical and aesthetic reasons, he chooses to use the "natural" (arithmetic) series of whole numbers, noting that "since the choice between these operations does not affect the harmony, we shall use only those in which the numbers follow their natural progression, for everything then becomes much clearer."[64]

Rameau thus arrives back at Mersenne's numerical model of interval generation (as opposed to Descartes's physical model) where unity is the generator and source of all subsequent whole integers. It follows from this position that the only directly generated intervals are those with the prime as base: the octave (1 : 2), perfect twelfth (1 : 3), double octave (1 : 4), major seventeenth (1 : 5), and perfect nineteenth (1 : 6). How can Rameau take other smaller intervals that do not have one as their base (e.g. the perfect fifth 2 : 3) and claim that they too are generated by the same fundamental sound? Rameau's answer was to invoke the notion of octave replication.

In a lengthy discussion contained in Article 3 of Chapter 3 ("On the Octave"), Rameau offers a number of seemingly ad hoc mathematical, empirical, and acoustical justifications why two pitches separated by an octave represent essentially the same sound: the duple ratio is "the first to be understood"; "male and female voices naturally intone the octave, believing themselves to be singing a unison or the same sound"; and strings naturally resonate in octaves. The conclusion is that any number doubled (i.e. any pitch compounded by an octave) "always represents

---

[63] *Traité*, 3; Gossett, 5.
[64] *Ibid*.

the same sound, so to speak, or rather gives the replicate of that sound which is the root" (*racine*).[65]

These are not particularly persuasive arguments, at least by the criteria Rameau had established. For a mathematician, the notion that a number doubled is equivalent to itself is ludicrous. This is why, incidentally, Euler will take such strong exception to Rameau's ideas concerning the octave. But for now these are the only arguments Rameau can offer.[66] With the axiom of octave replication, it follows that any two intervals that are compounds can be posited as equivalent. Consequently, we can accept the octave 1 : 2 as a product of the fundamental sound, as well as its "replicates": 2 : 4 and 4 : 8. Likewise, the next division of the string following the octave – the perfect twelfth (1 : 3) – can be replicated by the perfect fifth (2 : 3), since 2 is the octave duplication (duple multiplication) of 1. In this manner the perfect fifth can be said to be directly generated from the undivided string, even though "1" is not represented in either of its terms. By the same reasoning, the major seventeenth (1 : 5) can be equated with the major third (4 : 5).

Rameau now has three intervals directly generated from the fundamental sound – the octave, perfect fifth, and major third. They correspond to Descartes's three primary numbers 2, 3, and 5. When combined, they produce the *accord parfait* (4 : 5 : 6) – Zarlino's *harmonia perfetta*. It is critical to recognize, though, that Rameau does not believe the triad to be perfect because it reflects harmonic divisions of the octave and fifth (as did Zarlino), but because it originates in the arithmetic series generated directly from the fundamental unity.

From here, Rameau is able to generate a series of secondary intervals that result from the differences of these primary intervals when taken against the octave. Descartes, as we saw, called these "remainders" and "residues." They comprise the perfect fourth (3 : 4) and minor sixth (5 : 8). Rameau repeats Descartes's evocative metaphor referring to the perfect fourth as "the shadow of the fifth."[67] Likewise, Rameau derives the minor sixth (5 : 8) as a remainder of the major third. But significantly, Rameau considers the fourth and sixth to be essentially the same as the fifth and third. How could Rameau hold such a belief? By virtue of the generative fundamental. Since all pitches are generated from some fundamental sound, and secondly, since this fundamental sound may be compounded by virtue of octave replication, it follows that comparing that pitch to any octave compound of the fundamental sound cannot alter its intervallic quality.

[It] has only those properties communicated to it by the fundamental sound which generated it. In other words it remains the same sound, transposed to its octave or to its

---

[65] *Traité*, 7; Gossett, 9. One should not misconstrue Rameau's use of the term "root" with its present-day connotation. A *racine* in Rameau's sense here was a mathematical term meaning the uncompounded version of some note, interval, or chord. Our chord "root" was always called by Rameau the *son fondamental*.

[66] The difficulty is that the phenomenon of octave identity is in part a psycho-acoustical phenomenon and in part a cultural convention of Western tonality that in either case cannot be explained by recourse to simplistic mathematical or mechanistic arguments. We will return to this problem in Chapter 8 in our discussion of Rameau's debate with Euler.

[67] *Traité*, 11; Gossett, 14.

replicate, or multiplied [geometrically], in order to determine from all sides the intervals characteristic of each sound generated by the fundamental sound. This does not, however, alter the original properties of those sounds generated by the initial comparison made with the fundamental sound.[68]

In this garbled explanation, Rameau is making an extraordinary claim: octave duplications of any musical sonority are fundamentally identical. Descartes, as we saw, allowed only that "compounded" intervals could be reduced to "simple" intervals using the octave. But one could not thereby go beyond this and have the octave trespass the space of the simple interval in order to produce an "inversion" since the octave was inviolable. The "inversion" of an interval could only be a "remainder" for Descartes. By claiming that inversions were in fact kinds of replicates, Rameau offers a justification for the informal principle of chordal inversion we have observed invoked by composition and thorough-bass pedagogues in the seventeenth century. Inversions of triads are not only related to one another as derivatives, but they are identical by virtue of sharing the same generative fundamental. It did not matter – as it did to someone like Werckmeister – that an inversion was "further away" from unity. All were equally products of the same generative source.

A serious problem arises with the minor third and major sixth, though. Just as the perfect fourth is the difference between the perfect fifth and octave, the minor third E–G is the difference between the major third C–E and perfect fifth C–G. By Rameau's reasoning, then, its fundamental source should be the same as the major third C–E. However, Rameau is not willing to allow the minor third to be a resultant since he needs it to serve another purpose: as the lower third in the minor triad E–G–B. Since the minor mode was accepted by Rameau and his contemporaries as equal to the major mode, the generative fundamental of the minor triad presumably deserved as much validation as the fundamental of the major triad. Quite simply, he wants the fundamental of E–G to be E, not C. But the arithmetic division of the perfect fifth (measuring string multiples) produces the major third first, not the minor third. No harmonic or arithmetic division of the octave will generate a minor third until the nineteenth division, and even then the interval is closer to a flat augmented second than a true minor third.

To salvage his theory of numerical generation for the minor triad, Rameau concocts the following argument: the minor third 5 : 6 (E–G) generated from the fundamental sound (C) can be the minor third of a triad if we take the octave 5 : 10 as the new base against which to measure it.[69] Presumably, then, we are to be persuaded that the minor third is still a directly generated interval on par with the major third. But this is contradictory, at least according to his original criteria of numerical generation. One cannot arbitrarily transfer the privilege of the fundamental sound to a note that is one of its own products.

---

[68] *Traité*, 8; Gossett, 11.
[69] *Traité*, 15; Gossett, 18.

Rameau is hardly oblivious to his predicament. For in the very same article, he makes an astonishing *volte-face* and tells us that the order of thirds in a chord is really arbitrary; it is the fifth that is the most important determinant of harmony.

The fundamental sound uses the fifth to form all the chords, the construction of which is immediately determined by the union of the fifth with the third. As the fifth is made up of a major third and a minor third, these thirds cannot simultaneously be related to their source. Only one of them need appear to be generated directly, however, for us to attribute the same privileges to the other, since this difference of major and minor does not alter the interval; it remains a third.[70]

In other words, the minor third, by virtue of sharing the space of the perfect fifth with the major third, may enjoy the "privilege" of occupying the lower half. In the *Nouveau système*, Rameau expressed this idea even more succinctly:

Since the fifth is the most perfect of all consonances, along with the octave, and since it may be composed of a major third and a minor third, the order of those thirds must be immaterial. At least this is what the ear decides, and no further proof is necessary.[71]

This constitutes an entirely new method of analyzing triads. Whereas Rameau had just laboriously established a strict "numerical" derivation of intervals using the arithmetic series, he now offers a less formal notion of generation that David Lewin has labeled "triadic parallelism."[72] This new idea, however, is not congruent with the principle of numerical generation. By following the logic of "triadic parallelism," one could just as well say that the perfect fourth could occupy the lower position within the octave instead of the perfect fifth.

Rameau might have attempted to explain the minor triad by invoking the harmonic proportion, much as Zarlino invoked the arithmetic proportion for the same purpose. (Remember that Rameau was measuring string multiples, while Zarlino was counting divisions.) But he rejects this solution after lengthy consideration in Chapter 4, since the use of two differing proportions representing both string multiples and divisions would contradict the numerical priority he was assigning the generative unity. Only in later writings when he dropped the canonist apparatus in favor of an acoustical model of generation would he again reconsider such a dualist argument.

All these difficulties in finding a consistent and meaningful way to generate the minor triad leads Rameau to confess unhappily that "the source of the minor third appears to be different from that of the major third, the fifth, or the octave."[73] But I think Rameau's arguments are not as nonsensical as some later commentators have made them out to be.[74] From a tonal viewpoint, Rameau was arguably justified in seeing the ordering of thirds as being less strictly determined within the perfect

---

70 *Traité*, 12–13; Gossett, 15.
71 *Nouveau système*, 21.
72 David Lewin, "Two Interesting Passages in Rameau's *Traité de l'harmonie*," *In Theory Only* 4/3 (1978), 4.
73 *Traité*, 13; Gossett, 16.
74 Shirlaw is particularly critical of Rameau's reasoning here.

fifth than was that of the perfect fifth within the octave. (Canonists had always recognized that a fifth could be divided by either harmonic or arithmetic means and remain consonant; the same was not true for the octave.)

Not yet willing to adopt the harmonic division in order to generate the minor triad, Rameau found the notion of "third building" within the tonal framework of the perfect fifth to be musically intuitive. As we will soon see when considering the motion of the fundamental bass, Rameau grants the perfect fifth a special status in tonal music different from either the octave or third. Thus its position as a fundamental tonal structure *within which* thirds may be juggled is a reasonable deduction. And it was one he would be able to apply fruitfully, if at times recklessly, in the following chapters where he proceeds to use the same principle to build various dissonant chords.

The obvious goal of Rameau's convoluted reasoning here is to end up with three directly generated intervals (the perfect fifth, the major third, and the minor third), and three inversional resultants (perfect fourth, major and minor sixths). With these intervals established, he can then go on in Chapter 7 to posit the major and minor triads as *directly* generated from the fundamental sound. In Chapter 8, Rameau argues that by virtue of the common generative source and the principle of octave identity, all inversions (*renversements*) of each triad are accepted as equivalent to the original: the *accord parfait* (4 : 5 : 6), the *accord de sixte* (5 : 6 : 8), and the

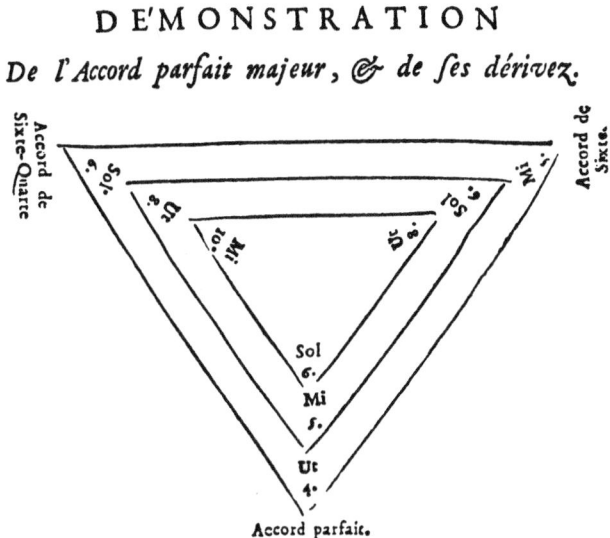

Plate 4.4 *Traité*, 36. Rameau's demonstration of the inversional equivalence of triads.

accord de sixte-quarte (6 : 8 : 10). This is shown in the famous illustration reproduced in Plate 4.4. For the minor triad, Rameau uses the proportions dubiously built upon the octave from which he had obtained his minor third: 10 : 20. Together these constitute the two fundamental consonant constructs in music.

THE GENERATION OF DISSONANCE

Rameau generates dissonance following a tried and true canonist method by subjecting consonant interval ratios to a variety of simple mathematical manipulations. Subtracting the perfect fourth from the perfect fifth produces the major (whole) tone, for example, while adding the minor third to the perfect fifth produces the seventh. By squaring the ratio of the major third, we get an augmented fifth, while by cubing the minor third, we get a diminished seventh. In this ad hoc manner, Rameau is able to produce all the dissonant intervals he needs.

The generation of dissonant chords proved more problematic, as here there was less precedent to follow. It was eminently reasonable for Rameau to have reduced all consonant chords to two fundamental triads given the widespread acceptance of the major-minor tonal system by 1722. But there was no precedent in contrapuntal theory or thorough-bass practice for reducing dissonances to any single fundamental structure. After all, if dissonance was indeed a product of consonance, how can any dissonant structure be considered fundamental? Nonetheless, Rameau boldly asserts that there is indeed a fundamental dissonant structure: it is the [dominant] seventh chord – a major triad with an added minor third.

Rameau is not particularly clear in explaining how or why the seventh chord enjoys this privileged status in the first Book of the *Traité* except to say that it is the "most perfect of all dissonant chords" since it is the source of both "major" and "minor" dissonances. (The reason for the special status granted to the seventh chord will become apparent only in the following Book when he deals with the progression of the fundamental bass, a subject that we will consider in detail in the next chapter.) For now, Rameau's readers must accept his statement on faith.

As with major and minor triads, the seventh chord is generated from a fundamental sound. Since the interval of the seventh cannot be derived by either procedures of "numerical generation" or "triadic parallelism" given the confines of the *senario* that he had earlier accepted, Rameau offers yet another kind of root attribution that David Lewin has aptly called "Suitable Combinations of Thirds." Major and minor thirds may be added to triads in "suitable combinations" so as to produce chords musicians commonly use. Such an arbitrary operation, evidently, does not weaken the identity of the triad's original fundamental.

To make matters simpler, we could consider thirds for the time being as the sole elements of all chords. To form all dissonant chords, we must add three or four thirds to one another. The differences among these dissonant chords arise only from the different positions of these thirds.[75]

---

[75] *Traité*, 33; Gossett, 39. A number of critics – particularly Riemann – have seized upon this idea, and exaggerated its importance in Rameau's theory. Third stacking, as can be seen, was only one heuristic offered

Thus, over several articles in Chapter 8, Rameau proceeds to construct the most common seventh chords found in Baroque music practice by adding major or minor thirds above or below major and minor triads. Just as with triads, all seventh chords may be inverted, resulting in the dissonant figures 6/4/2, 6/4/3, and 6/5/3. The chord of the added sixth that apparently had been granted equal status in the Clermont notes is now explained as an inversion of the fundamental seventh (although it will make a spectacular comeback in Rameau's subsequent writings). Through various ingenious, if at times precarious, explanations, Rameau will try to show how all dissonant chords can be explained by the fundamental seventh chord.

Ninth and eleventh chords, for instance, are derived through the theory of *supposition*. We noted in Chapter 3 how supposition was a term used by French theorists in the seventeenth century to describe melodic appoggiaturas and non-harmonic tones sounding against a consonant (triadic) harmony. Rameau now uses it to account for "non-harmonic" tones sounding against the fundamental *seventh chord*. Since, by the axiom of octave replication, any chord exceeding the boundary of the octave represents a compound, Rameau argued that these ninth and eleventh chords cannot be fundamental; they are actually seventh chords with thirds added *beneath* the fundamental bass that "suppose" the true fundamental.[76] By this reasoning, then, the ninth chord in Example 4.3 is really a seventh chord on G, with E the supposed bass a third below.[77] Because the added note is "supernumerary," it cannot participate in inversion, and must remain at all times in the lowest voice.[78]

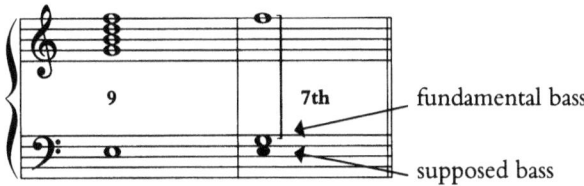

Example 4.3 A ninth chord with a "supposed" bass

---

to justify his fundamental bass for dissonant chords – and it was an explanation he rarely cited after the *Nouveau système*. It was Rameau's unfaithful German exegetes (beginning with Marpurg) who carried the notion of third stacking to such unreasonable extremes.

76   *Traité*, 33; Gossett, 38.
77   Some English-speaking musicologists have proposed the term "sub-position" as a better translation for "supposition" in order to emphasize that the bass is placed *below* the fundamental bass (e.g. Joan Ferris, "The Evolution of Rameau's Harmonic Theories," *Journal of Music Theory*, 3/1 (1959), 236; Joel Lester, *Compositional Theory in the Eighteenth Century* [Cambridge, Mass., 1992], 108–09). I prefer to retain the literal English cognate *supposition*, first because of its etymological relation to the older sense of *supposition* meaning a dissonant non-harmonic tone (something lost by using the term "sub-position"), and secondly, because it conveys more evocatively the idea that this added note *feigns* ("supposes") the real fundamental bass lying above it. In the "Table des termes" prefacing the *Traité*, Rameau reminds us that the terms "sous-entendre" (imply or feign) and "supposer" are necessarily synonymous (*Traité*, xxi; Gossett, xlv) .
78   *Traité*, 76; Gossett, 89.

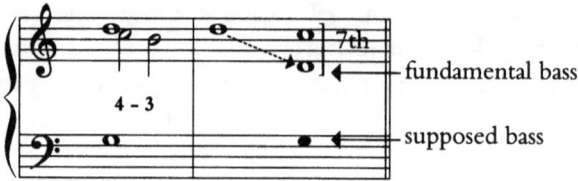

Example 4.4 A chord of suspension with a "supposed" bass

Rameau also finds supposition a useful concept to account for dissonant suspensions. The 4–3 suspension in Example 4.4, for instance, represents a seventh chord on D with the G supposed as a bass a fifth below. The perfect fourth in this example cannot truly be a fourth since it would then necessarily be heard as the consonant inversion of the perfect fifth. Instead, argues Rameau, the fourth is really an eleventh above the supposed bass transposed down an octave. It is what he calls "heteroclite" as the chord "is not divided as are the other chords," meaning it is not divided into thirds.[79]

There are obviously a number of difficulties with Rameau's theory of supposition, both empirical and logical. But his reasoning here is not quite as precarious as later critics have made it out to be; there were compelling reasons that led Rameau to develop the notion of supposition, many of which we will consider in more detail in Chapter 5.[80] The important point Rameau wishes to stress in Book 1 of the *Traité* was that all dissonant figures could be ultimately reduced *somehow* to a seventh chord above the fundamental bass. Thus, the seventh must be the origin of all dissonance.

Example 4.5 A diminished-seventh chord with a "borrowed" fundamental bass

Rameau gives the diminished-seventh chord a special derivation. Because it cannot be built using either a major or minor triad, Rameau finds it by taking a regular chord of the dominant seventh and raising the fundamental a half step. The root of the chord is thus "borrowed" (*empruntez*).[81] While the B♭ in Example 4.5 feigns the role of fundamental, the true fundamental bass of the chord is A.[82] In

---

[79] Ibid.

[80] Rameau's ideas on supposition, we may note, are more closely related to Mersenne's use of the term than those of Nivers and Delair cited in Chapter 3. Mersenne describes supposition as an adjunct consonance intuited above or below a consonant interval related by the natural arithmetic series. For example, the lowest note of a perfect fourth (3 : 4) "supposes" the fifth below (2 : 3) and the major sixth above (3 : 5), or contrariwise, the upper note "supposes" the octave below (2 : 4) or the major third above (4 : 5) (*Harmonie Universelle*, "Traitez des consonances," 102–03). For Mersenne, then, the "supposition" is a note that is understood by virtue of its presence *inside* the perfect arithmetic ordering from which each interval is derived, while for Rameau supposition is understood precisely because a note stands *outside* the closed system of triads and seventh chords. For both theorists, though, the supposed note is seen as a kind of appendage to the harmony.

[81] *Traité*, 43; Gossett, 50.

[82] To confuse matters, though, in subsequent publications Rameau will usually take the leading tone of the diminished-seventh chord as the fundamental bass. See, for illustrations, Examples 5.9 and 9.12.

Table 4.2 Summary of Rameau's chord derivations

Chord-type		Ratio	Chord fundamental	Derivative chords of "supposition"	Senses of root	Chapter
1. Parfait majeur (MAJ)	C–E–G	4–5–6	C	—	NG	8/1
2. Parfait mineur (MIN)	A–C–E	10–12–15	A	—	TP	8/2
1. Dominante-tonique (MAJ + MIN3)	A–C#–E–G	20–25–30–36	A	F (3/#5/7/9) D (5/#7/9/11)	NG SC3	8/3
2. Dominante (MIN + MIN3)	A–C–E–G	10–12–15–18	A	F (5/7/9) D (7/9/11)	TP SC3	8/4
3. Septiéme superflue (MAJ + MAJ3)	C–E–G–B	8–10–12–15	C (E)	A (5/7/9) F# (♮7/7/9/11)	NG SC3	8/5
4. "Half-diminished"[a] (MIN3 + MIN)	E–G–B♭–D	25–30–36–45	G?	C (3/5/♭7/9) A (5/7/♭9/11)	TP SC3	8/6
5. Septiéme diminuée (DIM + MIN3)	B♭–C#–E–G	108–125–150–180	(B♭) (A)	F (♭4/#5/7/9) D (♭6/#7/9/11)	BOR SC3	8/7

[a] Rameau does not give the "half-diminished" chord a label since it is a product of "modulation."

addition, and unlike chords of *supposition,* the diminished-seventh chord can be freely inverted.

Rameau thus offers a profusion of ingenious, if not always consistent, ways to construct all the chords he needs. He summarizes his procedures for chordal generation in Chapter 8 by reviewing the seven basic harmonies dealt with in the first Book: the two consonant triads, and five types of dissonant seventh chords. Table 4.2 shows these procedures borrowing the designations proposed by Lewin: NG (numerical generation), TP (triadic parallelism), SC3 (suitable combinations of thirds), SUP (supposition), and BOR (borrowed fundamentals). Every dissonant chord is shown to be formed by a consonant triad to which dissonances are added, borrowed, or supposed.

It need hardly be emphasized that Rameau's generation of chords is eclectic. His loose use of numbers seems to justify the reprimand he received from d'Alembert that his theory was such an "abuse of geometry." But at least three points can be made in his defense. First of all, the derivation of dissonant intervals and chords through the manipulation of consonant intervals is not an altogether unreasonable idea, and indeed, it is a very musical one. There is ample historical evidence to suggest that dissonance began to be employed precisely in this way. At the very least, the juggling of interval ratios was an acceptable and long-established procedure in the canonist tradition.

Secondly, we must recall the observation made at the beginning of this chapter, to wit, that Rameau considered these numbers to represent not so much mathematical entities in themselves as real pitches. In order to produce the *musical* result he wanted, Rameau sometimes needed to subject his numbers to strained manipulations. There was an inevitable tension between the canonist procedures of interval plotting and the tonal notion of chordal generation, the latter being an acoustical not a mathematical ontology. Rameau was using a tool and technique of *musica theorica* that was ultimately ill suited to his needs. We should not be surprised that as soon as he discovered a way to generate his chords and dissonances acoustically, he did not hesitate to drop the canonist apparatus. He obviously knew his arguments in the first book of the *Traité* were vulnerable (and admitted in the Preface they were dispensable to the musician). Rameau was trying to justify something of which he had a secure musical intuition but a weak mathematical understanding.

Finally, from a purely pedagogical viewpoint, Rameau offered a real (if imperfect) simplification of harmonic theory. There were two fundamental chord-types – the consonant triad and the dissonant seventh, both of which were generated from a single source. All compounds, inversions, added notes, suspensions, and chromatic alterations of these chords could be reduced to these two chords, and hence back to a common fundamental source. It was this idea, at once so elementary yet so revolutionary, and conceived as a didactic aid for composers and accompanists, that Rameau struggled to articulate and formalize in the first Book of the *Traité*. But the real fruits of his struggles will be seen when we consider how the various chords he has generated behave in musical context.

5

THE FUNDAMENTAL BASS

THE MECHANIZATION OF NATURE

Arguably the distinguishing characteristic of the scientific revolution at the beginning of the seventeenth century was the rapid and widespread acceptance of the mechanistic universe. As described by Descartes, the most important spokesman of the mechanical philosophy, nature consists of infinite space occupied by matter existing in one of two basic states: inertia or motion. In Descartes's view, all appreciable phenomena can be reduced to a mechanistic equation of matter impacting upon matter. Qualities like color, odor, sound, and taste are "secondary" since they are not essential to matter itself, but perceptions of the mind. To be sure, a mechanistic interpretation of nature was not the discovery of the seventeenth century; many of its tenets can be traced back to the atomistic materialism propounded by ancient philosophers such as Democritus and Lucretius. But seventeenth-century philosophers provided a radically new metaphysical framework in which this materialism was situated. Mathematics became for them the key to decoding nature.[1] Any material body could be quantified as to extension, shape, and weight, while its position, movement, and collision with respect to another material body could be measured as a kind of physical geometry. All of nature, it was believed, could be reduced to mathematics. In Galileo's memorable image, mathematics was the language in which the book of nature was written.

To appreciate how truly revolutionary this new perspective was, we need only recall some of the received doctrines by which natural phenomena had been hitherto explained. Aristotle, as the most important authority to Renaissance thinkers, had claimed that all matter possessed innate "substances," "qualities," and "affinities" by which its essence and behavior could be known. Platonists, on the other hand, saw in nature a reflection of a perfect order governed by number and ideal forms such as the circle. Renaissance naturalists, animists, and hermeticists, drawing upon a mix of these doctrines, believed nature to be a mysterious and bubbling cauldron of unknown spirits and occult forces.

The mechanistic philosophy did away with most such innate qualities, ideal forms, and occult forces. (Although as Mersenne's case demonstrates, some aspects of Platonic idealism could be harmonized quite easily with the mechanistic

---

[1] E. A. Burtt, *The Metaphysical Foundations of Modern Science*, revised edition (Garden City, N.Y., 1954), 115–21.

outlook.) The universe was now understood as an infinite Euclidean space occupied by countless tiny impenetrable corpuscles in various states of composition and motion.[2] The only acceptable "causes" for motion were efficient ones – matter acting upon matter. In a delightful little dialogue published in 1686 for the purpose of explaining and popularizing the Cartesian cosmology, the poet and future secretary to the Parisian Académie Royale des Sciences, Bernard le Bovier de Fontenelle, compares the workings of the universe to the machinery that operates backstage at the opera:

> Imagine all the Sages at an opera – the Pythagorases, Platos, Aristotles, and all those whose names nowadays are dinned into our ears. Suppose that they watched Phaeton lifted by the winds, but they couldn't discover the wires and didn't know how the backstage area was arranged. One of them would say: "Phaeton has a certain hidden property that makes him rise." Another: "Phaeton is composed of certain numbers that make him rise." Another: "Phaeton has a peculiar attraction to the top of the theater, and he is uneasy if he's not up there." Still another: "Phaeton wasn't made for flying, but he would rather fly than leave a vacuum in the upper part of the stage." And there are a hundred other notions which I'm astonished haven't destroyed the reputation of the whole of Antiquity. Finally, Descartes and some other moderns would come along, and they would say: "Phaeton rises because he's pulled by wires, and because a weight heavier than he is descends." Nowadays we no longer believe that a body will move if it's not affected by another body and in some fashion pulled by wires; we don't believe that it will rise or fall except when it has a spring or a counter-weight. Whoever sees nature as it truly is simply sees the backstage area of the theater.[3]

Mechanics thus became the paradigmatic science to which all the other sciences were to be reduced. Natural phenomena ranging from planetary orbits and magnetism to human illnesses and the passions were explained by mechanistic means.[4] Not all scientists in the seventeenth century were in agreement concerning the precise mechanical design of the universe. Nor was mechanistic causation successful in explaining problems like gravitation and certain biological processes (although Descartes was particularly creative in hypothesizing elaborate mechanisms that did). Nonetheless, as a general metaphysics, most scientists of the time accepted that nature was essentially mechanistic, and that their task was to uncover and describe mathematically these mechanisms. Where mechanistic explanations were lacking, the scientist could still quantify effects (as Newton did with gravity) without seeking to hypothesize an explanation, on the assumption that some mechanism would eventually be discovered.

We have already noted in Chapter 4 one way in which this mechanistic philosophy affected music. Sound was one of the earliest natural phenomena to be

---

[2] An intellectual transformation chronicled in Alexander Koyré, *From the Closed World to the Infinite Universe* (Baltimore, 1957).

[3] Bernard le Bovier de Fontenelle, *Conversations on the Plurality of Worlds*, trans. H. A. Hargreaves (Cambridge, 1990), 11–12.

[4] Richard S. Westfall, *The Construction of Modern Science: Mechanisms and Mechanics* (Cambridge, 1977), 25–42.

analyzed in mechanistic terms, since its production was relatively easy to explain and quantify as matter in motion. Indeed, sound became something of a paradigm of mechanization. Both Francis Bacon and Galileo used musical acoustics as subjects to test their respective (although quite differing) scientific methods.[5] Pitch was understood by most physicists to be a purely material consequence of periodic vibrational disturbances that were propagated to the ear by waves through the medium of air. Consonance, as we saw, was analyzed as a physiological perception dependent upon the greater coincidence of frequencies striking the ear.

Despite these acoustical revisions, though, there was still something lacking that was necessary for a fully mechanistic explanation of music: a motive agent. The mechanistic universe, after all, consisted not of simple extended matter in stasis, but of matter that was in constant flux due to motion and impact. All physical change could only be attributed to material bodies acting upon other bodies following immutable mechanical laws (such as those codified in Newton's famous three laws of motion).

Scientists in the seventeenth century had taken the first steps towards a mechanistic explanation of music by discovering the material basis of pitch. But they failed to explain why these material pitches combined and succeeded one another as they did except by recourse to the older Aristotelian notion of interval progression. In Medieval and Renaissance music theory, contrapuntal motion was ascribed to a natural tendency for intervals to progress towards ever-increasing degrees of perfection: from dissonance to imperfect consonance to perfect consonance.[6]

Rameau complained that such contrapuntal rules did not constitute a true explanation of harmonic succession:

All the rules that are taught, whether on the progression of the bass, whether on that of the octave of the given key, whether on the manner of preparing and resolving dissonances, whether on composition in general, do not agree in explaining the movement from one single chord to another.[7]

It was one of Rameau's great insights to see how a mechanistic explanation could be found for the motion of the fundamental bass. Had he been content to stop at the end of Book 1 of the *Traité*, his theory, however significant it was for the classification of tonal harmony, would not have signified any qualitative change from the acoustical theory of consonance formulated in the seventeenth century. Both were physical explanations of musical material. What Rameau did – and herein is the real parallel between his music theory and seventeenth-century science – was find a mechanistic cause to explain the motion of this musical material analogous to the causes that explained the motion and impact of material bodies in mechanics. It seems odd, perhaps, that a mechanistic explanation came as late as it did in music theory, given the attention paid to music in the early part of the scientific

---

5 Frederick V. Hunt, *Origins in Acoustics* (New Haven, 1978), 78ff. Further discussion of this topic will be found in Chapter 6.
6 Carl Dahlhaus, *Studies in the Origin of Harmonic Tonality*, trans. Robert O. Gjerdingen (Princeton, 1990), 86ff.
7 *Dissertation*, 10; *CTW* V, 16.

revolution by mechanistic scientists like Galileo, Descartes, Mersenne, Hooke, and Huygens. But the reason for the delayed application is easily explained: the tonal harmonic language upon which the fundamental bass was predicated had not coalesced in musical practice until the end of the seventeenth century. Music theory had to wait until someone came along who was both fluent with this tonal practice as well as sympathetic to the mechanistic philosophy. This someone was to be Rameau.

THE MECHANIZATION OF HARMONIC MOTION

Rameau concluded Book 1 of the *Traité* having established chords as the primary elements of music. The next task, to which he devotes the whole of Book 2, is determining how and why these chords connect with one another, or more accurately, by what causative agent they are impelled. As Rameau sees it, music is comprised of physical entities we call chords following one another in temporal succession. As nothing moves in the mechanical universe without physical causation, there must be some such causation present in music – the tonal equivalent of Galileo's *vis motrix*. To discover what this cause might be, Rameau begins naturally enough by analyzing how the fundamentals he has found for each chord connect with one another.

He initially observes that chord fundamentals progress primarily "by those consonant intervals obtained from the first divisions of the string."[8] These would be the consonances of the perfect fifth, major third, and minor third (plus their respective inversions):

> Without abandoning the principle that has just been enunciated, then, we shall strengthen it even more by adding to it the principle of the undivided string. The latter contains in its first divisions those consonances which together form a perfect harmony. Thus, when we give a progression to the part representing this undivided string, we can only make it proceed by those consonant intervals obtained from the first divisions of this string. Each sound will consequently harmonize with the sound preceding it.[9]

From this perspective, it seems that the same intervals generated by the fundamental string also guide chord progressions. According to Carl Dahlhaus: "Chord structure and chord progression – the coherence of tones in the triad and the coherence of triads in harmonic movement – are of the same stuff."[10] David Lewin expresses much the same thought: "the *principe* thus generates its part in time just as it has already done in harmonic space."[11] The observations of Dahlhaus and Lewin underscore how Rameau's principle affords tonal music the same kind of coherence as Zarlino's *senario* does for modal practice – each provides the quality of *harmonia* wherein the intervals of chords are related to those of melody. But any such notion

---

8 *Traité*, 50; Gossett, 60.
9 *Traité*, 49–50; Gossett, 59–60.
10 Carl Dahlhaus, "Ist Rameaus *Traité de l'harmonie* eine Harmonielehre?," *Musiktheorie* 1/2 (1986), 124.
11 David Lewin, "Two Interesting Passages in Rameau's *Traité de l'harmonie*," *In Theory Only* 4/3 (1978), 10.

of *harmonia* would have been found by Rameau insufficient in explaining the succession of chord fundamentals, since it could not offer any mechanistic agent to impel these fundamentals to move. Rameau would find such a mechanistic agent, though, in musical dissonance.

We saw in Chapter 4 how music theorists in the seventeenth century hierarchically ranked intervals based upon the respective coincidences of their constituent frequencies. Differences between consonance and dissonance tended thus to lie on a continuum. Rameau made a radical break from this hierarchy by sharply distinguishing consonance and dissonance. (More properly, we might say that he *reinstated* the sharp distinction between consonance and dissonance that had been weakened in the seventeenth century.) Each was a single and inviolable category. Just as there were but two states in which an object could exist in classical mechanics – stasis and motion – so too did tonal music possess two and only two absolute states: consonance and dissonance. In Rameau's mechanistic image, consonance is like equilibrium in mechanics; it constitutes a state of perfect repose and stability. Dissonance is a displacing force, and hence a disruption of this repose.

This change in conception is remarkable, and mirrors precisely the metaphysical shift in seventeenth-century conceptions of matter. No longer are consonances and dissonances simply gradations in interval quality along some Aristotelian continuum; rather, they represent categorically contrasting ontological states. Rameau explicates his mechanistic model by first considering the etymological derivation of the term *syncope* (syncopation or suspension). Brossard, Rameau reports, derives the term in his Dictionary from the Greek word *synkopto* meaning "to hit" (*frapper*) or "collide" (*heurter*).[12] Rameau agrees that this derivation is suggestive. But he feels Brossard does not pursue its consequences fully. "[Brossard] speaks only of a secondary cause arising without doubt from the supposed collision (*choc*) of the sounds."[13] The root of Rameau's complaint is that Brossard's analysis deals with the syncopation only in metric terms – as a "collision with the natural beats of a measure." In fact, Rameau notes, "the effect resulting from this so-called collision of sounds has much in common with the collision of solids."

To show how this is so, Rameau quotes two "propositions" from a physics text of Ignace-Gaston Pardies, a widely-read Cartesian physicist from the seventeenth century. Pardies's two propositions state that "A moving body meeting another body which is at rest gives the body at rest all its motion and remains immobile itself"; and "A hard body which strikes an immovable body will be reflected together with all its motion."[14] Both of these propositions were widely accepted axioms of seventeenth-century mechanics. What is new here is the analogy Rameau draws between the physical behavior of colliding bodies and the behavior of prepared and unprepared dissonances in music. Here is Rameau's analysis:

12 M. de Brossard, *Dictionaire de musique* (Paris, 1703), s.v. "syncope."
13 *Traité*, "Supplément," 6; Gossett, 79.
14 *Oeuvres du R. P. Ignace-Gaston Pardies*, 2 vols. (Lyons, 1709), Book 2: *Un discours du mouvement local*, Proposition 18, p. 155; Proposition 23, p. 161.

In order to judge the effect in question, we need only notice that in [Example 5.1], dissonance B is at rest when consonance A strikes it. Immediately after the collision, the consonance becomes immobile and obliges the dissonance to pass to C. This is effectively the place to which the consonance itself could have passed but can no longer do so, since the dissonance has taken its place. The consonance seems to have given all its motion to the dissonance. Consonance D, however, which seems to be immobile, after having collided with dissonance F obliges it to return to G, from where it started. The dissonance here seems to be reflected with all its motion, after having struck an immovable consonance.[15]

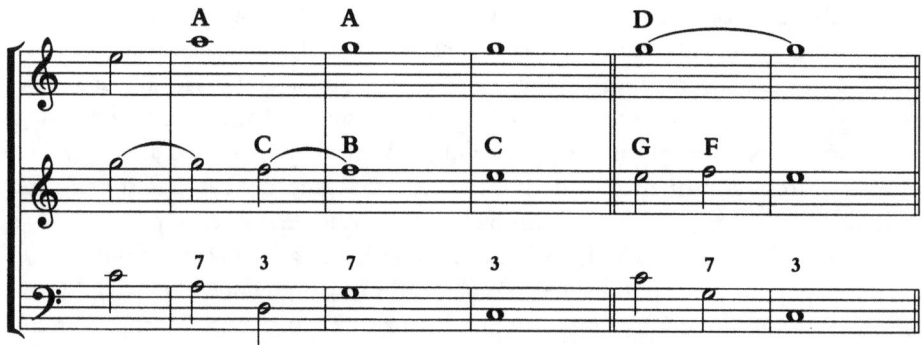

Example 5.1 Rameau's illustration of "colliding" dissonances

The analogy Rameau draws is obviously imperfect, and raises a host of philosophical problems that are left unresolved or unaddressed. In an ideally perfect mechanistic model, all objects in motion must continue onwards or transfer their motion to another object upon impact. Theoretically, though, this would suggest that music could never come to a state of equilibrium or rest, i.e. resolve to a consonance. One could also demand to know from whence comes the initial dissonant impetus to begin any musical motion. Still, the image of notes as moving and colliding objects was appealing to a mechanistically inclined mind like Rameau's, and one that would suggest to him a number of fruitful insights into the behavior of tonal music.[16]

It is curious that the lengthy mechanistic analogy was apparently added by Rameau only after the completion and printing of the main text. In Chapter 2, I have already briefly described the publication history of the *Traité*. We recall how Rameau had sent the text to Paris for publication while still residing in Clermont. Before the entire book was printed and bound, though, Rameau saw fit to make a number of last-minute changes that required his coming to Paris. Most of these

---

15   *Traité*, "Supplément," 7; Gossett, 79.
16   The East German musicologist Hans Pischner was one of the few historians to recognize the "mechanistic materialism" underlying Rameau's theory in the *Traité (Die Harmonielehre Jean-Philippe Rameaus* [Leipzig, 1963]; and "Jean-Philippe Rameau und die französische Aufklärung" in Hans Pischner, *Musik, Theater, Wirklichkeit: Ausgewählte Schriften und Reden* [Berlin, 1979], 7–29). Unfortunately, Pischner never analyzed the manifestations of this "mechanischer Materialismus" beyond the rather crude Marxist reductionism that was lamentably so typical of the scholarship common to his political culture.

changes were eventually incorporated within a seventeen-page supplement that was appended to the text before final binding. And of all the changes, the most significant relate to Chapter 7 in Book 2. Rameau completely revised and expanded this chapter, fully tripling its size. Among the additions were the citations of Pardies and the mechanistic analysis of the suspension that we have just examined. Why did Rameau make these particular changes at the last minute? While we cannot say with certainty, it is possible to suggest one plausible scenario that involves the entrance of a new character into our story: the Jesuit scientist, journalist, and amateur musician Louis-Bertrand Castel (1688-1757).

FATHER CASTEL

Castel is the first of many scientists to whom Rameau would turn for support and advice over the course of his theoretical career. Rameau may have first heard of Castel while in Clermont, where the Jesuit father had taught physics and rhetoric between 1711 and 1713.[17] It was not until Rameau arrived in Paris in 1722, though, that he first personally made Castel's acquaintance "through a mutual friend."[18] That Castel would be interested in Rameau's music theory was quite understandable. Castel was an avid Cartesian and mechanist. Even in the face of growing Newtonianism in France in the second quarter of the eighteenth century, he remained faithful to Cartesian precepts. Indeed, Castel became one of the most outspoken critics of Newtonian physics in France, using his position of associate editor in the *Journal de Trévoux* to launch progressively more scathing attacks on the Newtonians.[19]

Castel was also deeply interested in music and wrote frequently on the topic. One of Castel's most novel accomplishments related to music was the design and construction of an "ocular harpsichord"; Castel subscribed to a rigidly mechanist theory of synaesthesia, and believed it was possible to replicate the effects of music visually by assigning specific colors to each individual pitch. His "clavecin oculaire" was designed precisely to demonstrate this correspondence. Although not commercially successful and ridiculed by many other scientists, his invention did attain a certain notoriety in his day. (We will be crossing paths with Castel and his synaesthetic ideas again in Chapter 6.)

Castel's interest in Rameau should thus be clear. Not only did Rameau's theory concern a subject that the Jesuit loved and about which he would frequently write, it was overtly Cartesian in its content and form. Castel thus became the first important convert to Rameau's theory, and more importantly, its first propagandist. In the October and November 1722 issues of the *Journal de Trévoux,* he provided a detailed résumé of the *Traité*. There, he expresses unabashed enthusiasm for the work, declaring that its four Books reveal four sides of Rameau's genius:

17 Donald S. Schier, *Louis Bertrand Castel: Anti-Newtonian Scientist* (Cedar Rapids, Iowa, 1941), 3.
18 "Lettre de M. Rameau au R. P. Castel," *Journal de Trévoux* (July, 1736), 1,691; *CTW* VI, 86.
19 See Schier, *Castel,* 4–58 for a narration of the many anti-Newtonian polemics and quarrels in which Castel engaged.

In the first, he studies the primitive and intelligible nature of sounds, intervals and chords as a mathematician. In the second he reasons [about music] using examination and experimentation as a philosopher. In the third he derives the whole art of composition as a master. Finally, in the fourth he offers advice concerning the finest points of the art in accompaniment as a consummate practitioner.[20]

The element of Rameau's theory that Castel emphasizes the most strongly in his review, though, is its methodical concision. Like a good Cartesian, Rameau worked out his theory in geometric order:

The intelligent reader will recognize the good analytic order leading [Rameau] from practice to the rule, from the rule to reasoning, from reasoning to the principle and reason itself. . . All these steps show what genius guided the author who had for his synthesis no other teacher than analysis.[21]

In his review of the *Nouveau système* published six years later, Castel appears to recognize the mechanistic significance of Rameau's theory: "It seems that before Rameau the progression of sounds was not ordinarily mentioned, and only the progression of certain sounds and dissonances was considered in detail."[22] By explaining not only the origin (generation) of musical chords with the fundamental bass, but also the progression of these chords, Rameau is able to offer a systematization of music theory that is in all respects scientific:

With this author, music has become a regular and coherent entity that can be treated as one does a speech or discourse, analyzing it, tracing its design, following it through.[23]

I think it is quite possible that Castel could have been responsible for Rameau's hastily adopted mechanistic analogy between the suspended dissonance and colliding rigid bodies. In later years, Castel claimed that he conveyed a number of useful ideas to the composer in the course of their initial conversations in 1722.[24] Pardies's laws of impact were just the kind of scientific knowledge Castel would have possessed, and the mechanistic analogy could well have occurred to him as he discussed with Rameau the theory of the fundamental bass.[25] Additionally, Pardies was a fellow Jesuit, and Castel was always an unflagging booster of any member of his order.

Whether or not Castel suggested this particular mechanistic analogy to Rameau, though, it is clear that the fundamental bass offered a mechanistic model of musical motion that must have been highly appealing to Castel. In one sense, Rameau had succeeded in constructing a perfect model of mechanization. It was a model Castel would try to emulate two years later in his own portrayal of the mechanical cosmos,

---

20 *Journal de Trévoux* (October, 1722), 1,720; *CTW* I, xxx.
21 *Ibid.*
22 *Ibid.* (March, 1728), 480; *CTW* II, xx.
23 *Ibid.*
24 "Remarques du P. Castel sur la Lettre de M. Rameau," *Journal de Trévoux* (September, 1736), 2,015; *CTW* VI, 98.
25 Although this may have actually happened even earlier. Given the speed with which Castel's comprehensive review followed the publication of the completed *Traité*, one might guess that he had access to an advance copy of the text. Could Castel have read part of the manuscript on behalf of the publisher Ballard, and made suggestions and changes that required Rameau's trip to Paris? While we have no evidence to support this scenario, Castel's abilities as both journalist and musician would have made him a plausible candidate for such a task.

the *Traité de physique sur la pesanteur universelle des corps*.[26] (It is not surprising in this light, incidentally, that Castel would become increasingly critical of Rameau's theory as it took on a more Newtonian hue with recourse to experimentation and notions of gravitational attraction. But that is a development we will defer discussing until Chapter 7.)

Rameau, for his part, was of course delighted with his new found champion. There can be little doubt that the encouragement and promotion of his theory by so influential a journalist and scientist as Castel must have been a real boon. Castel was only the first of many scientific figures whose patronage Rameau would cultivate. But by any account, he was probably the most important, for he came to the composer's assistance at a particularly precarious and vulnerable moment: when Rameau was yet to be tested as either a composer or theorist. Were it not for Castel, one wonders whether Rameau would have found the confidence to continue his theoretical research with such energy. Finally, and most importantly, Castel provided Rameau with some scientific information that would profoundly impact the development of his theory – the *corps sonore* and the geometric progression. Each of these ideas would be incorporated and developed by Rameau in his next publication, the *Nouveau système* of 1726. But these topics will be treated in due course (Chapters 6 and 7, respectively). We need first to return to the *Traité* and finish considering Rameau's mechanistic analysis of the fundamental bass.

THE SEVENTH AS FUNDAMENTAL DISSONANCE

Having satisfied himself in Chapter 7 of Book 2 concerning the motivating capacity of dissonance, Rameau naturally wanted to know whether all dissonances could be reduced to one fundamental harmony, just as all consonances could be reduced to the triad. As we saw in Chapter 4, Rameau found such a fundamental harmony in the seventh chord. But as we also saw, this reduction required some creative explanations on his part.

Prior to Rameau, the seventh chord had not enjoyed any particularly important status as a dissonance. Unlike the major and minor triads, both of which had been accepted since Zarlino as privileged chords, the seventh was not ranked above any other dissonant chord. If we recall how the canonists traditionally derived dissonances by comparing and combining consonant string divisions, the "first" dissonances to be produced were the major and minor whole tones (9 : 8 and 10 : 9), followed by the major semitone (16 : 15). Sevenths were produced only secondarily, usually as additions of the perfect fifth and minor third. This is why Zarlino treated the seventh as the last interval in his discussion of dissonance, calling it merely the "diapente plus diatone."[27]

In thorough-bass treatises before Rameau, we find a similar if less formal hierarchy. Dissonant signatures were typically ordered and taught according to

---

[26] Jean Ehrard, *L'Idée de nature en France dans la première moitié du XVIIIe siècle* (Paris, 1963), 116–19.
[27] Gioseffo Zarlino, *The Art of Counterpoint*, trans. Guy A. Marco and Claude V. Palisca (New Haven, 1968), Chapters 22 and 23. Descartes proposes a similar derivation for the seventh.

ascending interval size. Thus, the first dissonances to be introduced were chords of the second (4/2; 5/4/2; 7/4/2, etc.) followed by the augmented fourth and diminished fifth, and only then by various kinds of seventh chords.[28]

If the canonists had allowed themselves to include the seventh division in their calculations, one might think that the natural seventh should occupy the first rank of dissonances. Indeed, Mersenne seriously considered this possibility; the question of the natural seventh was a continual subject of concern in his correspondence with Descartes.[29] But Mersenne was eventually forced to concede (as did Rameau) that such a seventh was far too flat to have any practical value. Few canonists saw a way to relate the natural seventh (4 : 7) to the seventh found in practice (which was usually tuned closer to the ratio 5 : 9 or 9 : 16).[30] Only later in the eighteenth century did a few theorists attempt to integrate the natural seventh into their tuning systems.[31]

Rameau's positing of the seventh as a fundamental dissonance thus needed some justification, and he struggled mightily in the *Traité* to offer one, although his reasoning was neither very clear nor consistent. Our first encounter with this interval in his text is inauspicious; the seventh is shown to be the product of the minor third and perfect fifth ($5/6 \times 2/3 = 10/18$) and alternatively as the square of the perfect fourth ($3/4 \times 3/4 = 9/16$).[32] The seventh chord, as we saw, is generated by the addition of a third to the major triad. All other types of seventh chords are formed through analogous additions of thirds to triads, as was shown in Table 4.2.

By virtue of these derivations, one might conclude that the *third* is the true source of dissonance. And when Rameau refers to the two dissonant components of the seventh chord, he speaks of them in terms of "the quality of the thirds by which they are generated."[33] The lower major third of the seventh chord constitutes the "major dissonance" while the upper minor third added above the triad constitutes the "minor dissonance." Elsewhere, though, Rameau seems to derive the seventh as an inversion of the second. The second can be considered the first dissonance since it is the first to arise from the comparison of perfect consonances.

---

28 A French thorough-bass treatise following this ordering is Denis Delair, *Traité d'accompagnement* (Paris 1690).

29 Hellmut Ludwig, *Marin Mersenne und seine Musiklehre* (Halle, 1935), 63.

30 For a more detailed history of the natural seventh in French music theory, see Martin Vogel, *Die Naturseptime* (Bonn, 1991), 109–42.

31 The first theorist in France to advocate a justly-tuned seventh for the dominant-seventh chord was Charles Levens, *Abrégé des règles de l'harmonie pour apprendre la composition* (Bordeaux, 1743). Subsequent advocates of the natural seventh were Charles-Louis-Denis Ballière de Laisement, *Théorie de la musique* (Paris, 1764); T. Jamard, *Recherches sur la théorie de la musique* (Paris, 1769). Among the non-French theorists and scientists to concern themselves with the natural seventh may be mentioned Sorge, Euler, Kirnberger, and Tartini.

32 *Traité*, 24; Gossett, 29. Rameau was unique in recognizing only one basic kind of seventh, corresponding to our "minor seventh." Just as there is only one form for each perfect consonance, he argued, there is also just one kind of seventh that could be modified by augmentation (*superflüe*) or diminution (*diminuée*). Hence what others call the "septiéme majeure" (8 : 15) is for Rameau the "septiéme superflüe." (The second, as the inversion of the seventh, is likewise recognized by Rameau as existing in only one basic form.) See the discussion in Chapter 29 of Book 2 of the *Traité*, 163–68; Gossett, 180–85.

33 *Traité*, 81; Gossett, 95.

Further, the second is the first interval to be generated in the natural arithmetic series (8 : 9) aside from the unusable natural seventh.[34]

Rameau thus finds a plethora of contradictory sources for the seventh.[35] One can almost sympathize with Mattheson, who complained:

> Mr. Rameau makes such a fuss in his *Traité de l'harmonie* concerning the seventh, that I believe he must drink to its health everyday. I cannot refrain from taking the opportunity to mention that in various passages he holds his beloved seventh to be the source of all dissonances. But then he says that it is a composite of two fourths, which he then immediately contradicts by asserting that the second [is fundamental], and from the inversion of this second arises the seventh. How can it be the origin of all dissonances when it is itself derived from fourths and inverted seconds?[36]

Rameau's real reason for considering the seventh as a fundamental dissonance cannot be understood by following his tortuous logic in generating the interval as a single autonomous unit. Rather, it must be seen as a functional dissonance in the empirical context of a moving harmonic progression, and specifically in the context of the *cadence parfaite*. It is in this latter construct that Rameau finds the single most important paradigmatic chordal progression in all of tonal music.

THE CADENTIAL MODEL AND THE FUNDAMENTAL BASS

"Cadence" is one of the most malleable concepts in music theory. Generally speaking, most musicians use the word to designate some sort of closing, although the criteria by which such a closing is defined and categorized have varied over the centuries (e.g. whether considered in relation to a particular voice, the kinds of intervals used at the closing, or the scale degree upon which the closing interval occurred).[37]

French theorists in the seventeenth century found the concept of cadence to be of particular importance, and they devoted lengthy discussions to it in their composition treatises. Strictly speaking, they used the term in two ways. First of all, a cadence could designate the specific ornamentation found at some melodic closing.[38] Since the penultimate note of such a closing was typically ornamented by a trill, the trill came to be called a "cadence."[39] Secondly, a cadence could indicate a structural closing, one defined by the scale degree upon which the bass voice ended or the interval by which the bass moved. Three basic categories were recognized in the seventeenth century to accommodate such endings.

---

34 *Traité*, 113; Gossett, 127.
35 And this is only in the *Traité*. In his subsequent writings he will expand further his list of derivations for the seventh.
36 Johann Mattheson, *Kleine General-Bass-Schule* (Hamburg, 1735), 199.
37 See the comprehensive inventory of cadence-types in the article "Kadenz" by Siegfried Schmalzriedt in the *Handwörterbuch der Musikalischen Terminologie*, ed. Hans Heinrich Eggebrecht (Wiesbaden, 1974).
38 Ibid., 11–12.
39 Rameau uses the term "cadence" in this sense when describing embellishments in the prefaces to his various collections of harpsichord pieces (1706, 1724, 1728).

1. *Cadence parfaite* (Perfect cadence). This cadence type was uniformly defined as the bass voice moving to the final of a mode. Some theorists, like Nivers and Hotteterre, prescribed a falling-fifth (or ascending-fourth) bass progression (dominant to tonic) as the optimal motion of this cadence, while others, like Masson, simply specified that the resolution should be to an octave in the outer voices.[40]

2. *Cadence rompue* (Broken cadence). This term was generally used to designate the avoidance of an expected *cadence parfaite*. La Voye Mignot described two types of avoidance: from the dominant of the mode the bass ascends a second, or it descends a third to the mediant.[41]

3. *Cadence imparfaite* (Imperfect cadence). Nivers defined the imperfect cadence as one in which the bass ascends a fifth in contradistinction to the *cadence parfaite* in which the bass descends a fifth.[42] Nivers does not restrict this cadence to a tonic closing, though (corresponding to the Italian *cadenza plagale*). He allows that a tonic can move to a dominant note and still be considered "imperfect." La Voye Mignot, however, calls this a "half" cadence (*cadence attendante*).[43] Masson is more conservative in his definition, and calls imperfect any cadence in which an interval other than the octave is sounded at the closing. To designate the cadence of an ascending fifth in the bass, Masson uses the term *cadence irréguliere*.[44]

What is critical for us to note is that for these French theorists, a cadence was an event that was not restricted to the ending of a piece or phrase. Since a cadence was defined by the specific motion of a bass or intervallic progression, it could occur at any point in the music. The high priority French theorists gave to the cadence was a direct reflection of a compositional practice that favored the clear declamation of vocal lines as well as the frequent employment of dance rhythms. Both these features entailed precise articulations of phrase structure delineated by frequent cadential caesuras. French Baroque music thus tended to be more homophonic and periodic, with cadential points defined by clear vocal closings of line, metrical articulations of harmony (the *plié* and *élevé* inherent to dance music), and leaps in the bass voice. Indeed, the mannered – one might almost say galant – articulation of cadential units set off by leaps in the bass was a hallmark of French music noted by many observers in the eighteenth century, especially when this style was placed in comparison to the more continuous motor rhythms and thick textures characteristic of Italian music, with the latter's emphasis upon scalar motion in the bass.[45]

---

[40] Guillaume Gabriel Nivers, *Traité de la composition de musique* (Paris, 1667); Charles Masson, *Nouveau Traité des règles de la composition de la musique* (Paris, 1699), 50.

[41] La Voye Mignot, *Traité de musique pour bien et facilement apprendre à chanter et composer* (Paris, 1656), Chapter 17.

[42] Nivers, *Traité de la composition*, 23–24.

[43] La Voye Mignot, *Traité de musique*, Chapter 17.

[44] Masson, *Nouveau Traité*, 24.

[45] One of Rameau's recommendations to the beginning composer is to begin with a bass that contains as many leaps as possible, "for the natural progression of a bass is to proceed by consonant intervals rather than by diatonic ones" (*Traité*, 291; Gossett, 309).

This background in French cadential theory and practice will be useful to us in understanding Rameau's emphasis upon the cadence in his own writings. When Rameau proclaims that all music is but an imitation of cadences in the *Traité*, he is merely pursuing to its logical conclusion ideas widely shared by French theorists in the preceding generations. Indeed, we will see that Rameau appropriated without substantial change the three fundamental categories of cadence described above. What Rameau did offer that was new was a reinterpretation of these three cadential categories that follows logically upon the harmonic principles he laid down in Book 1 of the *Traité*.

For Rameau, a cadence becomes a *harmonic* event entailing the instigation and release of tension by means of dissonance. The *cadence parfaite* is Rameau's paradigmatic model of this dynamic. He defines it as a seventh chord resolving to an *accord parfait* by a descending-fifth fundamental bass. This is an interesting change, since prior to Rameau, few theorists considered the seventh to be a fundamental element of any cadential progression. The normative intervallic progression of some *clausulae* consisted of an imperfect consonance moving to a perfect consonance (e.g. 6–8 or 3–1).[46] At most, the seventh might come into play as a suspension of the imperfect sixth (7–6–8), or it might be introduced as a passing tone on a weak beat. But the direct succession of a seventh to the third was sanctioned only as a license.[47] Why did Rameau posit a progression with such little theoretical and empirical validation, then?

The answer is simple. The perfect cadence, Rameau informs us, entails the most fundamental harmonic motion in tonal music, as well as containing the two most fundamental dissonances. It thus constitutes the model from which all other cadential progressions are derived and "suffices to justify all the rules of music."[48] In a later publication, he summarizes this idea succinctly:

The single perfect cadence . . . is the origin of the diversity that may be introduced in harmony. This cadence may be inverted, broken, interrupted, imitated, and avoided, from which all variety in harmony is drawn.[49]

Rameau analyzes the *cadence parfaite* in Chapter 5 (Book 2) of the *Traité*. As illustrated in Example 5.2, the progression consists of three essential components: (1) a fundamental bass descending a perfect fifth from the dominant to the tonic; (2) a dissonant seventh ("minor" dissonance) above the dominant that must resolve *downwards* to the third of the tonic triad; and (3) the leading tone ("major" dissonance) above the dominant that resolves *upwards* to the tonic note.[50] Because of the unique position and behavior of this dissonant seventh chord, Rameau reserves

46 As illustrated in Masson, *Nouveau Traité*, Chapter 5.
47 Clérambault was one of the few theorists prior to Rameau to recommend the seventh on the dominant triad at a *cadence parfaite*, but only in conjunction with a 4–3 suspension ("Règles d'accompagnement," fol. 6). Denis Delair, however, advised that a seventh could be added to any triad that descends a perfect fifth to another triad (*Traité d'accompagnement*, fol. H).
48 *Traité*, "Table des termes," x; Gossett, xl.
49 *Code de musique pratique*, 93.
50 *Traité*, 56; Gossett, 66.

for it the name *dominante-tonique,* that is, the dominant chord that defines the tonic. By inverting the perfect cadence, one finds all the most common two-part dissonant progressions taught in counterpoint treatises. The "minor" dissonance becomes the source of all dissonances that descend at resolution such as 2–3, 4–3, ♭5–3, ♯4–6, and 7–6. The "major" dissonance (or leading tone) becomes the source of all dissonances that resolve upwards such as the augmented fifth and ascending suspensions.[51]

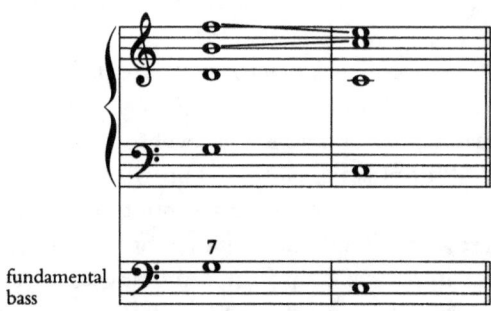

Example 5.2 The "perfect cadence"

This perfect cadence is not limited to the scale degrees of dominant and tonic, however. It is possible to place a seventh chord (with the appropriate diatonic adjustments) on any scale degree and have it descend by a fifth. These, too, are *dominante* chords, Rameau claims. Of course not all seventh chords behave like the *dominante-tonique,* that is, they do not all resolve downwards by a perfect fifth. For that matter, the *dominante-tonique* itself does not always resolve by the descending fifth progression Rameau prescribes as normative. How does he account for these discrepancies? By invoking the secondary cadence types utilized by his seventeenth-century predecessors.

Rameau brings in La Voye Mignot's category of *cadence rompue* to describe a *dominante-tonique* seventh chord that ascends a second to the sixth scale degree (see Example 5.3). While this progression does indeed follow the essential voice leading of the perfect cadence, in that both major and minor dissonances above the dominant resolve properly, the ascending second in the fundamental bass appears to violate the fundamental fifth motion he had just prescribed for all cadences. Rameau tries to save appearances by analyzing the chord of resolution as an inverted tonic chord. The sixth, he argues, is really just a "substitution" for the dominant note of the tonic triad (see Example 5.4).[52] Since all other aspects of the voice leading remain unaltered, and the substitution is only of a consonant interval, Rameau can claim that the *cadence rompue* is still a variety of the *cadence parfaite* granted by license.

---

51 Properly speaking, Rameau's analysis should lead to the conclusion that the tritone (diminished fifth) in the dominant seventh chord is the true motivating dissonance of tonal music, just as Fétis would assert some one hundred years later. But we must remember that as Rameau measured all intervals from the fundamental bass, the tritone was not a directly generated interval, and thus could never be considered fundamental.

52 "cette sixte que nous supposons à la quinte," *Traité,* 62; Gossett, 71.

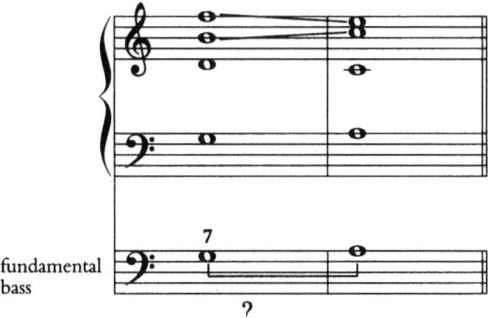

Example 5.3 The "broken cadence"

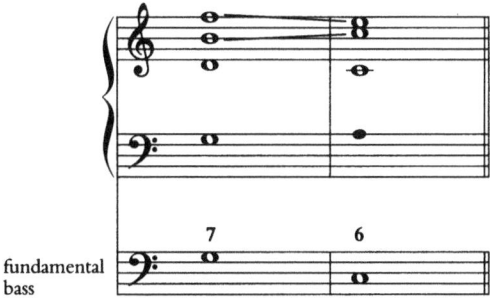

Example 5.4 Rameau's analysis of the "broken cadence"

There are obvious inconsistencies with Rameau's analysis of this cadence. Not only must he invert the tonic triad and substitute its dominant note, he must deny the obvious perception of this chord as representing the sixth scale degree ("submediant"). In fact, Rameau goes on in the same chapter to acknowledge that this chord can indeed be understood as a triad on the sixth scale degree.[53] And in later writings, this is exactly how he would continue to analyze the deceptive cadence.[54] But at this point in the *Traité,* Rameau seems intent upon preserving a fundamental fifth motion in all cadential patterns.

The next variety of cadence Rameau discusses – the *cadence irréguliere* – causes him even more headaches. Rameau defines the irregular cadence as one where a bass leaps by an ascending fifth at the close. This definition conforms to Masson's for this cadence (and what most other theorists called the *cadence imparfaite*). Like both the *cadence parfaite* and the *cadence rompue,* the *cadence irréguliere* ostensibly represents a dissonant chord resolving by a fundamental fifth progression to a consonant triad, with the exception that the fifth progression is inverted. A critical distinction, though, is the dissonance Rameau posits for the "dominant" chord of the irregular cadence. A seventh cannot resolve properly by step when the bass ascends by a perfect fifth. If, however, one adds a sixth to create a 6/5 chord, the new dissonance can resolve *upwards* when the bass moves by an ascending fifth. In

[53] *Traité,* 62; Gossett, 71. [54] See Chapter 15 of the *Génération harmonique,* and the *Code de musique pratique,* 61.

essence, the added sixth becomes a "major" dissonance.⁵⁵ And like the seventh of the perfect cadence, the added sixth of the irregular cadence resolves to the *mediant* of the following triad (see Example 5.5).

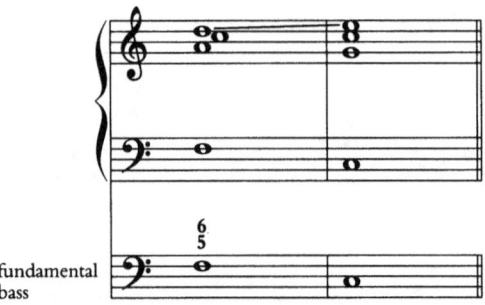

Example 5.5 The "irregular cadence"

Rameau was profoundly ambivalent about this cadence. For one thing, he could not decide whether the cadence was restricted to the fourth scale degree resolving to a tonic (corresponding to our "plagal" cadence), thus making it a kind of inversion of the perfect cadence, or whether it was also possible to include a tonic moving to its dominant (our "half" cadence), thus making it a retrograde of the perfect cadence. By considering the motion from tonic to dominant as an irregular cadence, Rameau obscures the functional qualities he had just posited in which the tonic was equated with absolute consonance and repose, and the dominant with dissonance and motion.⁵⁶ More critically, it introduces a new kind of fundamental dissonant structure hitherto unencountered: the chord of the added sixth (the *accord de la grande sixte*). By his theory of chordal inversion enunciated in Book 1 of the *Traité*, the chord of the added sixth should be a first inversion of a simple *dominante* chord. It is one thing to speak of the sixth as substituting for the fifth as he does in regards to the broken cadence. It is quite another thing to claim that the added sixth is itself a fundamental dissonance analogous to – but independent of – the fundamental seventh. Rameau wavers on this question in all his writings; sometimes he analyzes the 6/5 chord as a fundamental and independent dissonant structure, and other times he calls it only an inversion of the seventh.⁵⁷ It is telling of his uncertainties on this question that the chapter in which he introduces the irregular cadence (Chapter 7 of Book 2) is the same heavily revised chapter that included the mechanistic descriptions of dissonance using Pardies's laws of impact. In the original and shorter form of Chapter 7, Rameau justifies the chord of the added sixth as an inversion of the fundamental seventh chord, but one that resolves

---

55   *Traité*, "Supplément," 7; Gossett, 81.
56   While Rameau was unclear about this in the *Traité*, in later writings he resolved the problem by declaring any added-sixth chord to be subdominant. If the tonic moved to the dominant as an irregular cadence, then the progression really constituted a modulation. See the discussion in Chapter 7, pp. 183–84.
57   In his Clermont notes, it will be recalled, Rameau apparently allowed the 6/5 to be a fundamental dissonant chord on a par with the seventh.

"irregularly."[58] Of course, if this were literally true, then the fundamental bass of Example 5.5 should be D *descending* a major second to C. Such a progression, though, violates his previously established rules governing the proper motion of the fundamental bass and the resolution of dissonance. This is why Rameau feels the need to revise his arguments in the supplement.

Essentially, Rameau argues that the chord contains a "new dissonance which has not yet been discussed, although the majority of skillful musicians use it successfully."[59] This chord, he admits, can be derived as an inversion of the seventh. But it is better to understand it as "original," whereby the fundamental bass (in Example 5.5) remains an F. The "dissonant" sixth "resolves" upwards to the mediant of the following triad, just as the dissonant seventh of the *dominante-tonique* resolves downwards to the same mediant.[60] He illustrates this behavior by taking a four-part cadential progression of Masson and analyzing the fundamental bass of its first three chords (see Example 5.6).[61] Rameau criticizes Masson for failing to recognize that this progression actually represents an inverted irregular cadence. For Masson, the A in the tenor needs to resolve upwards because it forms an augmented fourth against the bass. For Rameau, on the other hand, the A resolves upwards because it constitutes the major dissonance of the added-sixth chord on C.

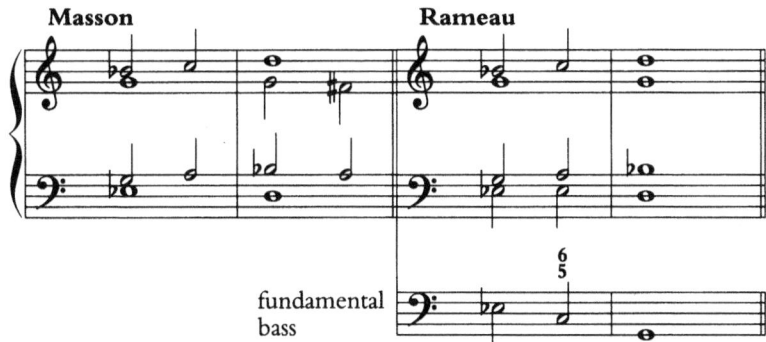

Example 5.6 Rameau's analysis of a cadence by Masson

Of course in designating the added-sixth chord as an autonomous dissonant structure parallel to – but independent of – the dominant-seventh chord, Rameau now is contradicting his previously enunciated stipulation that the seventh is the single source for all dissonance. His wish to reduce all dissonant structures to the

---

58 *Traité*, 64.
59 *Traité*, "Supplément," 3; Gossett, 73. Actually, musicians had discussed this chord earlier, as Rameau surely knew. In his thorough-bass treatise of 1690, for instance, Denis Delair recommended the addition of a sixth to any triad that ascends by a perfect fifth in the bass to another triad (*Traité d'accompagnement*, fol. H).
60 In his later writings (most specifically, the *Génération harmonique*), Rameau would discover a number of other appealing symmetries in both the generation and behavior of these two dissonant structures. As I will argue in Chapter 7, much of the impetus for Rameau's new views on this question can be credited to his coming into contact with various Newtonian ideas related to the theory of gravity.
61 Masson, *Nouveau Traité*, 99; Rameau, *Traité*, "Supplément," 4; Gossett, 76.

fundamental seventh directly conflicts with his wish to reduce all cadential fundamental-bass motion to the perfect fifth. Moreover, by allowing the irregular cadence to move from tonic to dominant, Rameau undermines the tonal stability he had just claimed as the exclusive prerogative of the tonic. He thus finds himself in a bind from which he never successfully extricates himself in the *Traité*. It was only in the *Génération harmonique* that Rameau was able to resolve these paradoxes with any success by refining his ideas on mode and modulation. But these are developments we will consider in due course.

Having established these three cadences in the *Traité* as constituting the primary motion of the fundamental bass, Rameau can now proceed to show the mechanistic process by which the fundamental bass motivates all harmonic motion. The answer turns out to lie in the paradigmatic dynamic of the perfect cadence. Rameau wants to show how any harmonic progression can be analyzed using the model of a dissonant seventh chord resolving to a consonant triad by the fundamental bass motion of a perfect fifth (presumably ignoring for now the contradictions inherent in the irregular cadence!). The force that drives all tonal music onwards, in other words, is the tension created by the dissonant seventh needing to resolve. All music, it follows, is but a concatenation of these three cadences:

> The three cadences discussed in the last three chapters contain all the most essential matters of harmony. Not only may all the chords and their progressions be derived from them but, in addition, true modulation originates there. All consonant chords are contained in the perfect chord and all dissonant chords arise from a new sound added to this perfect chord, forming a seventh chord which contains all the dissonant chords.[62]

To illustrate Rameau's idea, let us look at what is perhaps the most celebrated musical analysis in the entire corpus of Rameau's theory: the famous monologue from Lully's *Armide*. Rameau discussed and analyzed this monologue no less than three times in his treatises: in the *Nouveau système* of 1726, the *Observations sur notre instinct pour la musique* of 1754, and the *Code de musique pratique* of 1760. In the last two publications, Rameau cites the monologue to respond to criticisms raised by Rousseau concerning French operatic practice and the relative expressive powers of harmony and melody. (We will consider some of these questions in Chapter 8.) Rameau's initial concern with Lully's *récitatif ordinaire* in the *Nouveau système*, though, was to show how it constitutes a perfect usage of "modulation."[63] By modulation, Rameau means the articulation of related scale degrees by means of his primary cadential models. Through the fundamental bass, one can easily see this cadential structuring. In the opening four bars of the music, reproduced in Plate 5.1, Lully writes a harmonic progression modulating quickly from E minor to G major by use of a *cadence irréguliere*. (The 6/4 figured above the C in m. 2 is a misprint; Lully's original figuring was a simple 6 here, from which Rameau inferred a complete 6/5 so as to clarify the cadential function of this chord.[64]) In m. 3, Rameau's analysis

---

[62] *Traité*, "Supplément," 7; Gossett, 81.
[63] *Nouveau système*, 41.
[64] See Cynthia Verba, "The Development of Rameau's Thoughts on Modulation and Chromaticism," *Journal of the American Musicological Society* 26/1 (1973), 73.

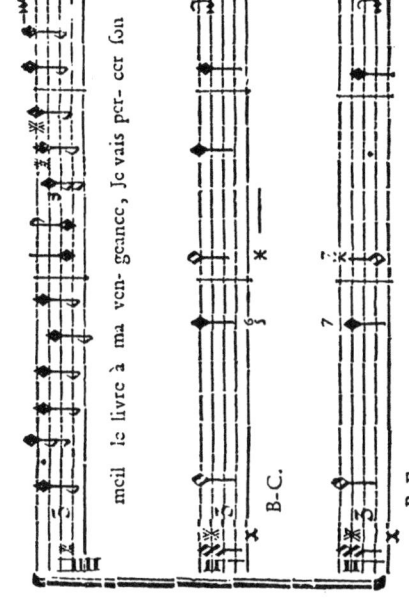

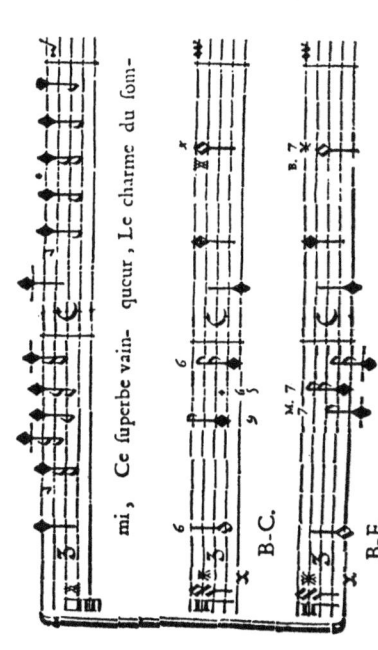

Plate 5.1 *Nouveau système*, 80–81. Opening of Rameau's analysis of the monologue from Lully's *Armide*

shows that G major is reconfirmed as tonic by means of a *cadence parfaite*. From here, the music moves on to A minor by means of another *cadence parfaite*. Rameau's analysis continues along these lines by revealing modulations to all the primary key relations of E minor: G major, A minor, B minor, C major, and D major. While there is much more that can be said concerning Rameau's notion of "modulation" – and we will return to consider this topic in more detail in Chapter 7 – the crucial point to keep in mind here is how Lully's recitative can be parsed into discrete cadential units. These cadences are delimited by chains of dissonant dominants "imitating" the motion of the perfect cadence leading ultimately to a *dominante-tonique* (or on occasion, an added-sixth chord) that resolves to a consonant *tonique* by means of a perfect fifth in the fundamental bass. Of course not all *dominante-tonique* chords resolve immediately to a consonant triad. For this reason, Rameau introduces the concept of "evaded" cadence.

In Chapter 54 (Part 3) of his *Istitutioni harmoniche*, Zarlino describes how a composer can avoid having some two-part counterpoint cadence on the expected octave or unison by substituting a third, fifth, or sixth at the resolution. (This was what Masson meant by his *cadence imparfaite*.) Zarlino calls such a process "evading cadences" (*fuggir la cadenza*). Rameau borrows this idea in Chapter 9 of Book 2 (entitled "How to avoid cadences while imitating them"), and applies it to his three harmonic cadence types. There he shows how any one of these cadences can be evaded by adding either a dissonant seventh or sixth to the chord of resolution, thus creating another dissonant chord that itself needs to resolve. Theoretically, one could construct entire chains of such "dominants."

To show what such a chain of evaded cadences would look like, Rameau writes out the chord progression shown in Example 5.7.[65] Throughout this rather awkward chord progression (which he admits is "not very regular"), Rameau distributes a number of cadences that are evaded by virtue of a dissonance added to the expected consonant chord of resolution, thus compelling the progression to move forward. In Example 5.7 we find two evaded perfect cadences (AB, GH), an evaded irregular cadence (FG), and four evaded "broken cadences" (BC, CD, OP, RS).[66] In between we find three properly resolved perfect cadences (HJ, LM, TV), a "passing" tonic (N), as well as sequential chains of simple (diatonic) dominants (AAA, DEF, QR, ST). However stilted this example is, its meaning is unmistakable. We see from the fundamental bass analysis how virtually the entire harmonic progression is moti-

---

[65] *Traité*, "Supplément," 8; Gossett, 86. It should be noted that like Chapter 7, Chapter 9 was also heavily revised in the supplement, including the example given here. Matthew Shirlaw and Carl Dahlhaus both cite the original version of this example unaware that it differs in important respects from the revised version printed in the supplement: *The Theory of Harmony*, (London, 1917), 122; *Studies*, 26–27.

[66] It is of course somewhat contradictory for Rameau to speak of a "broken" cadence being evaded, since he has just finished describing the *cadence rompue* as itself a kind of evaded perfect cadence. The ambiguity is apparent in the fundamental bass assigned to chords C and D. Whereas chord C is figured as an added-sixth chord above F in the basso continuo – suggesting an evaded perfect cadence between chords B and C – Rameau indicates a fundamental bass of D, since a fundamental-bass progression of F to E (connecting the chords labeled C and D) would be unacceptable. The progression C–D is also considered an evaded broken cadence by Rameau, although of a different kind in that it lacks a *dominante-tonique* at C and a regular *dominante* at D.

Example 5.7 Chain of "evaded cadences"

vated by dissonant chords and their need to resolve to a consonance. To return to the mechanistic analogy Rameau drew in Chapter 7, the percussive effect of the dissonant seventh is the causative agent impelling the music onwards to a final consonant resolution.

SUPPOSITION AND THE SUSPENSION

We can now begin to see why Rameau believed all other dissonant chords such as ninths, elevenths, and chords of suspension (to say nothing of his added-sixth chord) should ultimately be derived from the seventh chord. It was not that he did not see how most of these dissonances could be explained as displaced consonances. He knew well enough that suspensions were melodic retardations of consonances. In all counterpoint and thorough-bass treatises, after all, suspensions were always taught in the contexts of their resolutions (e.g. 4–3, 9–8, or 6/4–5/3). This is why in Chapter 31 ("On the Eleventh Chord, called the Fourth") Rameau reminds us that "chords by supposition serve only to suspend sounds which should be heard naturally."[67] But this was not a satisfactory explanation for Rameau. He wanted to

[67] *Traité*, 280; Gossett, 299.

understand *theoretically* why specific notes in a chord lent themselves more easily to suspension than others. Moreover, why did suspended notes in most cases resolve downwards by diatonic step? Rameau found an answer by applying in a new way the traditional means French theorists had accounted for displaced consonance in the seventeenth century: *supposition*.[68]

In essence, Rameau observed that all suspensions behave suspiciously like the minor seventh, that is, they each normally prepare and resolve in identical ways. He suspected that the seventh might indeed be the source of the suspension if one allows that the continuo bass "supposes" the true fundamental of the chord that actually lies above it. The argument is not – as it is often made out to be by historians – simply that the octave is the "boundary" of all intervals.[69] While Rameau indeed made this point, the real issue for him was that dissonance should be reduced to a single source if at all possible, and the seventh seemed to serve as that source.

In Example 5.8, adapted from the *Traité*, the various ninths, elevenths, and fourths figured in the continuo line can be analyzed as seventh chords with the true fundamental bass supposed a third and fifth above the continuo bass, respectively.[70] Each measure thereby "imitates" the fundamental cadential progression of a falling fifth: the *cadence parfaite*. I think it must be admitted, if nothing else, that there is a logical consistency behind Rameau's analysis. But it is also a musically sensitive insight. It is not hard to hear, for instance, the "chord of the augmented seventh" in measure 4 – a typical eighteenth-century harmonic appoggiatura – as an A dominant seventh built over a pedal tonic which then resolves to the tonic triad. The D can be heard as anticipating (or "supposing") the resolution. Even if one wants to argue that the fundamental bass is tonic in the first beat rather than dominant, there is a clearly-implied clash between the two functions. This is implicit in Rameau's analysis. In just this way, the "chord of the augmented fifth" heard in

Example 5.8 Rameau's illustration of "supposition"

---

68 See the discussion in Chapter 3, pp. 64–67.
69 Shirlaw makes this argument, and thereby entirely misrepresents Rameau's ideas concerning supposition: *Theory of Harmony*, 87–90.
70 *Traité*, 75; Gossett, 90.

m. 3 – one of the most characteristic and expressive harmonies of French Baroque practice – can be analyzed as a composite of dominant and tonic functions. The F in the bass can be heard as representing the mediant of the tonic. It is not an unreasonable inference then – and it is indeed a theoretically consistent and insightful one – for Rameau to recognize in m. 5 a derivative situation with the 4–3 suspension. The D *theoretically* represents the seventh of an E minor "dominant" chord above the root of the A major resolution. Of course the E minor triad is not sounded in full, thus weakening its functional identity.[71] But Rameau's important insight is that this dissonance still can be understood as a species of the essential seventh, and that such suspensions are commonplace and satisfying to the ear precisely because they replicate the essential dynamic of tonal motion – a dissonant seventh resolving to a consonance over a falling fifth in the fundamental bass.

What must be remembered in all this is that Rameau never denies that the suspension could also be analyzed as a simple melodic displacement. In all of his published writings, he includes analyses which show suspensions such as the fourth in the fundamental bass. The question arises, then, how Rameau could reconcile two seemingly contradictory perspectives. While it is possible to infer an answer from reading between the lines in Rameau's earlier writings, it is in the practical composition treatise from the early 1740s entitled "L'Art de la basse fondamentale" that he tries to disentangle the concept of supposition from the suspension. There he explains himself as follows:

The suspension is nothing but the retardation of what would naturally be heard according to the most perfect fundamental succession by fifth. This suspension is frequently drawn from the same principle as supposition, but in practice it is better to consider the note which forms it as a note of taste . . . This note of taste in principle is only a dissonant fourth or ninth. The fourth suspends the third, and the ninth suspends the octave.[72]

The important point is that the suspended dissonance, from a practical point of view, is a "note de goût" (or as we would say today, a "non-harmonic" tone) that resolves over a single fundamental bass, whereas from a theoretical point of view, it represents the essential dissonance of a seventh and implies a change of fundamental bass at resolution. In his practical works, Rameau does not see it necessary to use the supposition as an explanation of the suspension; a simple linear description is more efficient. Thus he could write that since

71 This fact, among others, led Montéclair to loudly condemn Rameau's notion of the supposition. *CTW* VI, 39.
72 "L'Art de la basse fondamentale," fol. 85v. "La suspension n'est autre chose que le retardement de ce que devoit s'entendre naturellement, selon l'ordre de la plus parfaite succession fond[amentale] par quinte. Cette suspension se tire souvent du même principe que la supposition mais dans le pratique il vaut mieux y considerer la note qui la forme comme une simple note de goût . . . Cette note de goût dans son principe n'est jamais que quarte dissonante ou la neuvième. La quarte suspend la tierce et la neuvième suspend l'octave."
   Pietro Gianotti edits Rameau's prose as follows: "L'origine de la suspension est souvent la même que celle de la supposition; mais dans la pratique, il vaut mieux s'attacher à la consonnance qui la sauve (& qui est justement celle qu'on auroit dû entendre d'abord,) qu'à la suspension même, qu'il ne saut considérer pour lors, que comme note de goût. Cette note de goût, n'est jamais que quarte dissonante, ou neuvième. La quarte suspend la tierce, & la neuvième suspend l'octave." *Le Guide du compositeur* (Paris, 1759), 268–69. (For information on Rameau's composition treatise and its relation to Gianotti's text, see Appendix 2.)

a suspended note is only a [product] of taste; it has no fundamental bass, and if one assigns one to it, it is only in order to satisfy oneself in seeing that its origin is most often to be drawn from the supposition. But as this is of no use in practice, it is better to recognize the note of suspension as counting for nothing [by itself] and assigning it the fundamental bass of the consonance that it suspends and that immediately follows it.[73]

In the "Art de la basse fondamentale," Rameau itemizes precisely which chords are best analyzed as chords of supposition and which as suspensions (see Table 5.1).[74]

Table 5.1 Chords of supposition and suspension

Scale degree	Chords of supposition	Chords of suspension
Tonique	♯7	4 9 9 – 4– 3
Tonique d'un ton mineur	♯7 6	
Sus-tonique	9 4	4– 5 – 9 – 8 7 – –
Médiante d'un ton mineur	♯5 ♯5 4	
Médiante d'un ton majeur	9	9– 8 7 –
Sous-dominante	9	9– 8 7 –
Dominante-tonique		6 6– 5 4 4 –

The difference between supposition and the suspension, Rameau remarks, is that the chord of supposition is normally complete, while in the suspension it is incomplete (i.e. the seventh chord of the fundamental bass is not fully stated).[75] More importantly, in a suspension the dissonance is normally in an inner voice and the basso continuo will normally sustain the fundamental note of the chord for its duration, whereas in the supposition the basso continuo is always the dissonant

---

[73] "L'Art de la basse fondamentale," fol. 86r. "La note de suspension n'est que de goût, elle n'a point de basse fond[amentale] et si on luy en donne une ce n'est seulement que pour la prouver la satisfaction de voir qu'elle tire le plus souvent son origine de la supposition. Mais comme cela n'est d'aucune utilité dans la pratique il vaut mieux en reconnoissant la note de suspension la compter pour rien et luy donner pour basse fond[amentale] celle de consonance qu'elle suspend et qui la suit immédiatement."

    Gianotti's version is as follows: "Car à dire vrai, la suspension n'a point de basse fondamentale; & si on lui en donne une, ce n'est que pour voir le plus souvent, qu'elle tire son origine de la supposition. Or comme cette connoissance ne sert de rien dans la pratique, il vaut mieux en reconnoissant la note de suspension, la compter pour rien, & lui donner pour basse fondamentale celle que doit avoir la consonnance suspendue," 271.

[74] "Art," fols. 149v–150r; Gianotti, Guide, 236–39. I have slightly reordered Rameau's lists for greater clarity.

[75] In the Code, Rameau distinguished the supposition from the suspension by claiming that the dissonant seventh of the supposition was always prepared by a consonance, while the dissonant interval of the suspension was prepared by a dissonance except in the case of the cadential 6/4 (p. 129).

Example 5.9. Gianotti's illustration of "double suspensions"

(non-harmonic) tone. So in Example 5.8, the dissonant chords in m. 2, 3, and 4 would be considered chords of supposition, that in m. 5 a suspension.[76]

We can see a clearer illustration of Rameau's distinction in Example 5.9, taken from Gianotti's *Guide*, that also can serve as a good example of his mature fundamental bass.[77] The specific article to which the example applies concerns double suspensions and the staggering of their resolution (e.g. the delayed cadential 6/4: 6/4–5/4–5/3). Such a double suspension is found right away in the second measure of Example 5.9. The fundamental bass analysis of this cadence shows Rameau considers the suspension to be an elaboration of the *dominante-tonique* on E. But the cursors indicated below the fundamental bass indicate alternative harmonizations available (a tonic and a supertonic harmonization, respectively). In m. 4, however, Rameau analyzes the suspended voices of beats 1 and 2 as chords of supposition, since unlike the second measure, the complete dissonant chords suggested by each of the fundamental basses are present above the "supposed" bass. This creates a unique series of descending thirds in the fundamental bass that constitutes neither a change of key nor a series of interrupted cadences, but rather "intentional suspensions dictated by taste."[78] The "resolution" of this progression at m. 5 to the chord of an augmented fifth is another example of supposition since the complete *dominante-tonique* on E is implied above the basso continuo in conjunction with the melody (creating a ninth). (A progression similar to m. 4–5 is found in m. 12–13 but in the key of the relative major.) At m. 6 and 10, the notes of suspension figured in the basso continuo resolve without change of fundamental bass above a *dominante-tonique* in both cases. The reason Rameau chooses to analyze the 6/4 chord in m. 18 as an inverted tonic rather than a suspended dissonance has to do with the *double-emploi* introduced in the previous measure – a subject we will defer discussion of until Chapter 7. Finally, the tonic pedal at m. 22–24 reveals a combination of supposed chords and suspensions, depending, again, whether the complete dissonant chord is realized above the basso continuo or not. As the 6/♯7 chord in m. 22 shows, it is also possible to suppose a diminished-seventh chord built on the leading tone above a tonic pedal.

Obviously, there is a residual tension here between Rameau's two explanations of the suspension. In the *Code de musique pratique* of 1760, the only published work

---

[76] Although it is not clear that Rameau would have actually chosen to call the progression in measure 5 a suspension in 1722. In his polemic with Montéclair, Rameau was still arguing that the simple figures 4 and 9 ought to be considered chords of supposition, even though he presumably also recognized that they represent a different category of supposition, one he was soon to designate as a suspension (*CTW* VI, 30). Perhaps it was Montéclair's criticism that provoked Rameau to revise his thoughts on supposition.

[77] Gianotti, Example 18, Plate 38. Gianotti's example and text summarize the discussion found in fols. 92r–94v of the "Art."

[78] Gianotti, *Guide*, 296. "On voit donc ici la nécessité de la marche fondamentale par tierce en descendant, sans qu'il s'y agisse ni de changement de ton, ni de cadence interrompue, mais simplement de suspension volontaires dictées par le goût."

Rameau's original text from the "Art" (fol. 93v) reads as follows: "On voit par la necessité de faire descendre de tierce la basse fond[amentale] dans un cas où il n'y a ni de changement de ton, ni de cadence interrompue que sans doute cela regarde des suspensions volontaires dicteés par le seul goût."

in which Rameau discusses the supposition and suspension in any detail, he seems to backtrack by offering a number of contradictory statements and analyses concerning the suspension – at times analyzing it as only a "play of fingers" ("jeu de doigts"), and other times as a chord of supposition.[79] And one might argue that the notion of supposition is a cumbersome and ultimately expendable analytic artifice. But we can see how from a purely generative point of view, it was both musically plausible and systematically reasonable for him to attribute the source of these dissonances to the seventh. The dissonant seventh could now be held as the *causa prima* of harmonic motion, the displacing agent (*vis motrix*) of the tonal universe.

THE DYNAMICS OF TONALITY

Rameau's application of his mechanistic analogy does not stop here, though. He suggests at one point that harmonies within a mode can be analyzed using an analogous mechanical model. Just as the dissonant seventh is compelled to resolve to a consonant perfect triad, so too are all non-tonic harmonies compelled to return eventually to the equilibrium of the tonic. This is why Rameau insists that every non-tonic scale degree carries a seventh chord: he sees musical motion as a chain of falling seventh chords moving inexorably onwards to the one consonant chord of repose: the tonic.

The ideal tonal motion in Rameau's *Traité*, then, would be a sequence of "dominants" descending by a circle of fifths to the final tonic.[80] This is the "prescribed order of nature" and "the essence of the most natural harmony . . . to which we often become habituated before understanding it."[81] Of course, not all tonal motion is quite so direct and simple; intermediate "modulations" might temporarily disrupt the move to the tonic. Likewise, subsidiary cadential motions and fundamental chords (such as the added-sixth chord on the subdominant) will be introduced by Rameau that will defy the normative falling fifth motion of the fundamental bass. Most of these exceptions can be seen in Example 5.10. But within a given mode, every non-tonic scale degree is ultimately analyzed by Rameau as a seventh chord, even if the seventh must be imputed by the performer or listener.[82]

Now, the notion of imputed dissonance above chords has long been a controversial component of Rameau's theory, particularly when it leads Rameau to

---

79 See e.g. the discussion on pp. 56–61, and the musical examples in Plate 3. One of these analyses from the *Code* is examined in Chapter 9, p. 289.
80 *Traité*, 204: Gossett, 224. Rameau writes out two circles of fifths using diatonic seventh chords as keyboard exercises in Book 4 (*Traité*, 394–96; Gossett, 408–09). (One of these was quoted in Chapter 3 as Example 3.3.) Similar progressions are to be found in the *Code de musique* of 1760 (Lesson 7, Example B, Plate 1). A few of his followers also took the sequential circle of fifths as the essential paradigm of harmonic motion upon which they premised their teachings. See, e.g., Giorgio Antoniotto, *L'arte armonica; or a Treatise on the Composition of Musick* (London, 1760), who calls such a progression the "skip of the cadence."
81 *Traité*, 204, 297; Gossett, 224, 410. I have slightly altered Gossett's translations here.
82 The one exception is apparently the dominant of the mode, which when not preceding the tonic (and hence not functioning as the *dominante-tonique* of a perfect cadence) may be a consonant triad without the defining seventh (*Traité*, 388; Gossett, 399).

Example 5.10 Rameau's analysis and refiguring of Corelli's basso continuo

refigure the basso continuo parts of works by Corelli and Lully. In the Lully excerpt given in Example 5.7, we find a number of such refigurings. Both the 6/5 in m. 2 and the 9 and 6/5 in m. 3 are not found in Lully's original score.[83] An even more striking example can be seen in Example 5.10 from the *Nouveau système,* where Rameau "corrects" a continuo line of Corelli the better to reveal its true harmonic meaning derived from the fundamental bass.[84] The simple ascending 5–6 sequence Corelli figures is condemned by Rameau as "an evasion which almost all musicians make use of quite willingly, and by which one can accuse them of not knowing what they have practiced in such cases." Rameau shows the true fundamental bass to be a diatonic circle of fifths, and hence demands the figuring in the basso continuo shown at the bottom of the example.

One cannot deny that Rameau's is a most inelegant figuring, producing a clumsy and thick realization utterly inappropriate for Corelli's delicate music. But before we too hastily condemn Rameau's arguments here, we should keep in mind some of the aesthetic and philosophical motivations. His insistence in his polemic with Montéclair (and later with Rousseau) that an accompaniment should be a complete replication of harmony is partly a consequence of the strict neo-classical doctrine that art should imitate nature. And as his theory has presumably shown, there is nothing more natural than the consonant triad and dissonant seventh. Further, and perhaps more importantly, his mechanistic model requires dissonance as a causative force. An accompanist is required to play as complete a realization as possible so as to convey a full imitation of nature as well as the essential impetus of musical motion. By omitting notes from the chords demanded, or playing vaguely-defined harmonic progressions, presumably the accompanist weakens these features.

[83] For a detailed comparison between Lully's original score and Rameau's refigurings, see Cynthia Verba, "The Development of Rameau's Thoughts on Modulation," 80–81. Verba shows, incidentally, that in a later analysis of this music (contained in the *Observations*), Rameau made yet *more* changes to Lully's figured bass in order to bring the music into even closer alignment with his evolving theory.

[84] *Nouveau système*, 99–100. This example is just one of several passages of Corelli that Rameau analyzes and criticizes in Chapter 23. A complete translation with extensive commentary on this chapter is given by Joel Lester in the Appendix to his book *Compositional Theory in the Eighteenth Century* (Cambridge, Mass., 1992), 305–19.

But despite his impassioned arguments on behalf of a full figuring of harmony, Rameau never actually figured his own basso continuo this way. In any basso continuo part from one of Rameau's own compositions (as seen, for instance, in Example 8.1) we find quite lightly figured bass lines that do not suggest the complete fundamental bass presumably underpinning these progressions. Even in works composed around the time of the *Nouveau système*, for instance the solo cantata *Le Berger fidèle* (1728), Rameau writes extensive passages of Corelliesque sequences that are sparsely figured.

I believe that Rameau no more expected the basso continuo to be realized in practice following his "corrections" any more than he would expect to be sounded the many "interpolated" fundamental basses he reads between the basso continuo in order to reveal an idealized motion of fifth progressions (such as can be observed in measure 2 of Example 7.1). The point he was making, if put a bit too unsubtly, was that since sevenths are necessary mechanistic agents for impelling and directing chordal motion towards a tonic, every non-tonic harmony must therefore be a seventh, even if the seventh be suppressed in notation or performance.[85]

The importance of the dissonant seventh as a mechanistic motivating agent in Rameau's conception of tonality as presented in the *Traité* can scarcely be overstated. Alone among historians, Carl Dahlhaus has recognized this fact, and also how Rameau's ideas relate back to the older notion of "interval progression" found in Renaissance theory:

A traditional component of Rameau's theory, the factor of linking chords by dissonances, is based on the principle of the variation of intervallic quality. And one of the basic ideas of contrapuntal theory from the 14th through the 17th century is that the variation of intervallic quality – the tendency of dissonance toward consonance, or of imperfect consonance toward perfect consonance – forms the driving force behind music's forward motion. A chain of sixths striving toward the perfection of an octave differs of course in degree, but not in principle, from Rameau's progression of seventh chords whose goal is a triad – an *accord parfait*.[86]

In the *Génération harmonique* of 1737, Rameau modified this rigorously mechanistic and directional model of harmonic motion (a change Dahlhaus and most other historians who concentrate upon the *Traité* overlook). The cascading series of sevenths so evident in all the fundamental-bass analyses in the *Traité* gives way to a more entropic – and, as we will see in Chapter 7, Newtonian – tonal model wherein the tonic is symmetrically defined by two opposing harmonic poles, the subdominant and dominant. Each of these opposing polarities is *drawn* toward a

---

85 This leads to the problematic issue of defining the fundamental bass. Is it an empirical paraphrase of a harmonic progression, or is it an interpretive model of ideal motion? Rameau, I think, meant it to represent both. For an interesting discussion of the linguistic issues lurking behind this problem, see Allan R. Keiler, "Music as Metalanguage: Rameau's Fundamental Bass," *Music Theory Special Topics*, ed. Richmond Browne (New York, 1981), 83–100.
86 Dahlhaus, *Studies*, 29.

central tonic by a kind of gravitational pull, as opposed to being *impelled* in a single downwards direction by the percussive force of the dissonant seventh. But this is a development Rameau only hints at in the *Traité* (as in his discussion of the irregular cadence).

The heart of Rameau's theoretical revolution lay with the fundamental bass, not in his principles of string divisions or the *corps sonore*. Ontologically, these principles differ little from Zarlino's *senario* in that they are all static sources of musical *harmonia*. What the fundamental bass offered was a profoundly new *dynamic* model of musical coherence. Those notes notated underneath the harmonies of some musical passage, in other words, were there not only to show the abstract origin of the various harmonies, but to show how these harmonies together constitute a directed progression obeying a unified and coherent set of structural laws. It was a mechanistic model of musical motion, to be sure. But it was also one that revealed more precisely than any theory hitherto conceived how music was a fully dynamic process that unfolded over real time. (This is why, incidentally, Rameau always notates his fundamental bass using rhythmic values corresponding to the meter of the music under consideration.) Nothing could be more wrong, then, to condemn Rameau's theory as "static" and "rigorously vertical."[87] It is unfortunate that so many exegetes of Rameau (such as Shirlaw) lose themselves in his labyrinthine arguments concerning the generation of harmony, when in fact the more important and revolutionary feature of his theory involves the activation and succession of these chords over time. As Elisabeth Duchez correctly notes, the fundamental bass fulfills both structural and operational functions; it not only reveals the rational organization of music, but serves as a kind of cognitive model of the musical experience.[88] No theorist was ever more obsessed by the "horizontal" dimension of music than was Rameau, and no analytic apparatus was ever devised that more vividly projects this dimension than the fundamental bass.

The real revolution that was the *Traité de l'harmonie* and the fundamental bass lies, I believe, in this unification of the structural and the temporal. While Rameau would refine the mechanisms of the fundamental bass over his various publications, offer new ideas as to its origins, and adjust or test new theoretical deductions, the central claim of the *Traité* remained unaltered and unchallenged: music is a coherent and intelligible succession of directed harmonies over real time that can be both defined by and modeled with the fundamental bass.

---

[87] As do many Schenkerian theorists such as Hellmut Federhofer in his *Akkord und Stimmführung in den Musiktheoretischen Systemen von Hugo Riemann, Ernst Kurth und Heinrich Schenker* (Vienna, 1981), 150.

[88] Marie-Elisabeth Duchez, "Valeur épistémologique de la théorie de la basse fondamentale de Jean-Philippe Rameau: Connaissance scientifique et représentation de la musique," *Studies on Voltaire and the Eighteenth Century* 254 (1986), 122.

6

THE *CORPS SONORE*

In his lengthy review of the *Traité,* Castel made a passing remark that must have immediately caught Rameau's attention. He noted that the aliquot string divisions Rameau used as his principle of harmony occur naturally in any vibrating string:

> Not only may a string produce at the same time two sounds an octave apart, but additionally three and four [sounds], and without doubt the six [sounds], UT, UT, SOL, UT, MI, SOL. It is a fact attested to by M. Sauveur that when one plucks a long string in the still of the night, one hears the 12th UT, UT, SOL, and often even the 17th UT, UT, SOL, UT, MI, and in trumpets, one may even hear further, so that in physics, nature gives us the same system which M. Rameau has discovered in numbers...[1]

The phenomenon Castel makes reference to is of course that of the harmonic overtone (or upper partial) series produced by many uniformly vibrating bodies.

Rameau must have been astounded by this revelation. Had he known of this fact when writing the *Traité*, there is every reason to suspect he would have cited it to support his principle of harmony, as he indeed did after Castel's disclosure. Not only did this phenomenon seem to offer a more "natural" origin for the harmonic series Rameau had generated through aliquot string divisions, it also provided a more convincing definition of the fundamental bass. The *son fondamental* of the monochord was nothing less than an acoustical generator.

We may wonder indeed why Rameau had not noticed the partial series earlier, either by his own observations of violin strings and experiments with organ stops, or at least through his readings of Mersenne, who frequently mentions the phenomenon. Yet overtones were not well-understood by scientists in 1722. It is quite comprehensible why Rameau would have been ignorant of their existence while working on the *Traité*, or, at the very least, unclear as to how these strange and apparently inconsistent acoustical by-products related to his music theory. The fact is that although the harmonic series of upper partials seems to offer a more empirically convincing and aesthetically satisfying notion of harmonic generation, it by no means solves all of the theoretical paradoxes and inconsistencies we observed in the *Traité*. If anything, it poses a number of new, even more intractable problems that Rameau would wrestle with in almost all his subsequent publications.

[1] *CTW* I, xxxv.

But before we consider what these consequences were, it is first necessary to provide a little scientific background. For the forty-year period in which Rameau struggled to explicate and integrate the phenomenon of harmonic upper partials within his theory coincided almost exactly with the research of numerous continental scientists on the subject. These scientists – Jean-Jacques Dortous de Mairan, Daniel Bernoulli, Leonhard Euler, Jean Le Rond d'Alembert, and Joseph Lagrange – engaged in intensive and often contentious competition with one another to solve the problem of overtones. Their findings proved to be some of the most fruitful and consequential in the whole eighteenth century, opening up diversely related fields of vibrational mechanics, differential calculus, and psycho-acoustics. Whereas overtones were a bizarre and ill-understood acoustical phenomenon at the beginning of the eighteenth century, by mid century these scientists were able to offer the basic mathematical and physical principles by which they could be explained. To a surprising degree, this research impinged upon Rameau's own theoretical efforts (of which all the above-mentioned scientists were quite aware). The story of Rameau's music theory after 1722 is inextricably tied with the progress and polemics of these scientists. Many of the composer's most sophisticated theoretical formulations after the *Traité* (including his derivations of the minor triad, dissonance, and mode) were predicated upon – and thus can only be understood when analyzed alongside – the research of these scientists. As this research changed during his lifetime at an unprecedented rate, Rameau was likewise forced to change those relevant portions of his theory. To be sure, some scientists objected strenuously to Rameau's appropriation of their research; but there were just as many who were more than willing to lend a hand to the composer in his quest for an acoustical explanation of tonal harmony.

To begin this fascinating story, though, we must return several generations before Rameau, and consider the received understanding of two scientific problems that were initially considered as independent, but were eventually recognized as being closely related: (1) finding a formula for the fundamental frequency of a vibrating string; and (2) arriving at an intuitive understanding of overtones. As the history of this research has been treated elsewhere in detail, it will be necessary here to review only briefly the main historical developments leading up to the time of Rameau.[2]

---

[2] There are a number of comprehensive studies of early vibrational mechanics and acoustics in the seventeenth and eighteenth centuries. Two of the most detailed are Clifford Truesdell, "The Rational Mechanics of Flexible or Elastic Bodies, 1638–1788," in *Euleri Opera Omnia* (Leipzig, etc., 1912–), Series 2, vol. XI/2; and Sigalia Dostrovsky, "Early Vibrational Theory: Physics and Music in the Seventeenth Century," *Archive for History of Exact Sciences* 14 (1975), 169–218. Some of the musical implications of this research have been discussed in two works cited earlier: Claude Palisca, "Scientific Empiricism in Musical Thought," *Seventeenth Century Science and the Arts*, ed. H. H. Rhys (Princeton, 1961); and H. F. Cohen, *Quantifying Music: The Science of Music at the First Stage of the Scientific Revolution, 1580–1650* (Dordrecht, 1984).

THE FORMULA FOR THE VIBRATING STRING

In 1563, Giovanni Battista Benedetti made the intriguing suggestion that a vibrating string's pitch was determined by its vibrational frequency. As we already saw in Chapter 4, Benedetti's hypothesis led the way to the development of the "coincidence theory" of consonance. But it also challenged scientists to find a definitive formula for any vibrating string, whereby given its known physical parameters – length, density, and tension – one could accurately predict its frequency. A number of scientists accepted the challenge, among them Galilei father and son, Beeckman, Francis Bacon, Descartes, and Mersenne. Finding such a formula proved difficult, however. Through patient empirical measurements, Mersenne was able to derive a number of approximate proportions between a string's frequency and its length, tension, and linear density.[3] Subsequent research by Christian Huygens and Robert Hooke modified Mersenne's findings in various ways. But the establishment of an exact formula for determining the frequency of any vibrating string was not possible until more powerful mathematical tools were made available.

With the development of the calculus at the end of the seventeenth century, such a means was now at hand. Based upon the long-accepted assumption that the oscillations of any string were pendular (isochronic), the English scientist Brook Taylor concluded in 1713 that the ratio of the curvature of the string at any point is proportional to its distance from the axis, and hence, the acceleration (restoring force) of any point on the string will be directly proportional to its curvature.[4] By integrating this proportion, Taylor was able to produce an accurate formula for the frequency of any vibrating string of uniform construction. Figure 6.1 gives Taylor's

$$F = \frac{1}{2l}\sqrt{\frac{T}{\alpha}}$$

Figure 6.1 Taylor's formula for the fundamental frequency of a vibrating string

formula in modern notation. Here l is string length, T the string tension, and α the mass per unit length of the string. He concluded that the overall shape of the vibrating string must be sinusoidal, or as he termed it, a "companion of the cycloid." While this is untrue, as we will see, Taylor's formula is nonetheless correct for the fundamental mode, and seemed to have definitively solved the problem of the vibrating string.

HARMONIC OVERTONES

While studying the vibrating string, Mersenne had noticed an unusual phenomenon: a plucked string sounded a number of faint pitches above the fundamental tone. These were, of course, the string's overtones. Although overtones had been known to

---

[3] Marin Mersenne, *Harmonie Universelle contenant la théorie et la pratique de la musique* (Paris, 1636), "Traitez des instrumens," 120–26.
[4] Brook Taylor, "De Motu Nervi Tensi," *Philosophical Transactions* 28 (1713), 26–32.

musicians since Aristotle, it was only with Mersenne that they were first investigated systematically.[5] Mersenne was fascinated by these strange sounds, and made frequent reference to them in his published writings and correspondence. At times he claimed to hear distinctly the upper twelfth (octave plus perfect fifth) and major seventeenth (double octave plus major third), while at other times he perceived partials that were inharmonic or dissonant (such as the seventh partial, sounding a sharp twentieth above the fundamental).[6] Unfortunately, he was unable to find a satisfactory explanation for these sounds. He queried his many correspondents for possible explanations. Numerous suggestions were offered, including a Democritan theory of atomistic sound propagation (Beeckman), the sympathetic resonance of nearby strings (Christopher de Villiers), and inequalities in the mass of the taut string (Descartes).[7]

Eventually the correct theory occurred to Mersenne, to wit: "it seems it is entirely necessary that [the string] beat the air five, four, three, and two times in the same time." But Mersenne rejected this idea as "impossible to imagine" and "against experience."[8] His confusion over the issue was exacerbated by the inconsistent series of overtones he heard in bells and organ pipes. Mersenne had no empirical evidence to suggest that every vibrating system yielded a stable and homogeneous family of partials.[9]

Little progress was made in the understanding of overtones by the generation following Mersenne. Toward the end of the century, though, a phenomenological explanation was found. The English mathematician John Wallis reported in 1677 that two Oxford scientists, William Noble and Thomas Pigot, had discovered that a string may vibrate in aliquot divisions.[10] By placing tiny paper riders upon a single monochord string, and then plucking a second nearby string tuned to some aliquot division of the first string, one may demonstrate the existence of nodes (points upon the vibrating string that remain relatively stationary); every paper rider not on a nodal point would be shaken off because of sympathetic resonance. By this simple experiment, it was shown that the vibrations of a string are not necessarily uniform; rather a string may vibrate in successive aliquot parts. Strangely, though, Wallis did not associate this discovery with overtones. Nor did Brook

---

5 For an exhaustive history of the discovery of overtones, see Burdette Green, "The Harmonic Series from Mersenne to Rameau: An Historical Study of Circumstances Leading to its Recognition and Application to Music" (Ph.D. dissertation, The Ohio State University, 1969). Also Palisca, "Scientific Empiricism," 96–100; and Dostrovsky, "Early Vibrational Theory," 193–96.

6 Dostrovsky, "Early Vibrational Theory," 194.

7 *Correspondance du P. Marin Mersenne*, ed. Cornelis de Waard, 16 vols. (Paris, 1932–86), III, letters 251, 263, 277, and 291.

8 *Harmonie Universelle*, "Traitez des instrumens," 210. Descartes made a similar suggestion in a letter dated July 23, 1633 (in Mersenne, *Correspondance*, III, letter 263), as did Deschamps in another letter dated March 26, 1642 (letter 1,075).

9 For an analysis of Mersenne's writings on overtones, see Green, "The Harmonic Series," 327–74; and Frederick Hyde, "The Position of Marin Mersenne in the History of Music" (Ph.D dissertation, Yale University, 1954), 184–245.

10 "A Letter to the Publisher concerning a New Musical Discovery," *Philosophical Transactions* 12 (April, 1677), 839–42.

Taylor appear to have been familiar with Wallis's report. The connection between overtones and the motion of a vibrating string would not be drawn until Sauveur did so at the beginning of the eighteenth century.

Joseph Sauveur (1653–1716) is one of the most important figures in the history of acoustics. Despite an apparent hearing defect, Sauveur made the study of acoustics his specialty.[11] His contributions were many. But perhaps his most consequential work for music theory was his study of overtones. As early as 1697, Sauveur had observed that "in string instruments and bells . . . besides the principal sound, one hears the octave, the fifth, the third, etc."[12] In his unpublished manuscript, Sauveur offers no further explanation of this observation. He evidently spent the next four years working out an answer, for in an extensive acoustical study presented to the Académie Royale des Sciences in 1701, Sauveur provided an explanation of these "petit sons."[13] First of all, he pointed out (unaware of Wallis's report) that any vibrating string possesses nodal points. From this he made the crucial connection that Wallis failed to make: the nodes corresponded to a string's overtones (which he called "sons harmoniques"). Thus, the very thing Mersenne found "impossible to imagine" was shown indeed to be true: a string can vibrate in several ways *at once*. Sauveur concluded that overtones must always be harmonic, otherwise they would suffer immediate decomposition. He further made the incredible claim that if one listened attentively, one could hear up to the 128th partial.[14] Sauveur did not attempt to explain mathematically how these different nodes and oscillations could coexist on the same vibrating string; his was entirely a phenomenological description. In later papers he elaborated upon his observations, attempting to show why the series of harmonic overtones corresponds to the natural tones of a trumpet. He was also the first to state that tone color was determined by the composition of partials.[15]

As was customary, Fontenelle summarized Sauveur's work in the annual *Histoire* of the *Académie*. Fontenelle recognized the significance of harmonic partials for the theory of harmony. After noting that Sauveur had determined that a sounding body emits harmonic overtones, he marveled:

It seems then that each time nature makes by herself, so to speak, a system of music, she employs only these kinds of sounds. . . . It is not that nature has not sometimes forced

---

11 For information on Sauveur, see Robert E. Maxham, "The Contributions of Joseph Sauveur (1653–1716) to Acoustics" (Ph.D. dissertation, University of Rochester, 1976); and Albert Cohen, *Music in the French Royal Academy of Sciences*, 24–29. A useful compendium of Sauveur's writings on acoustics has been compiled and edited by Rudolf Rasch: *Collected Writings on Musical Acoustics (Paris 1700–1713)* (Utrecht, 1984).

12 Joseph Sauveur, "Traité de la théorie de la musique," F-Pn MS n.a. fr. 4674, fol. 188; transcribed in Richard Semmens, "Joseph Sauveur's 'Treatise on the Theory of Music': A Study, Diplomatic Transcription and Annotated Translation," *Studies on Music from the University of Western Ontario* 11 (1986), 1–202.

13 "Système général des intervalles des sons & son application à tous les systèmes & à tous les instrumens de musique," *Mémoires de l'Académie royale des sciences*, 1701 (Amsterdam, 1707), 390–482.

14 Ibid., 466. Sauveur nonetheless emphasized – as would Rameau – that the third and fifth partials were the most conspicuous: "sur tout la nuit, on entendoit dans les longues cordes, outre le son principal, d'autres petits sons qui étoient à la douziéme & la dixseptiéme de ce son." Ibid., 393.

15 "Application des sons harmoniques à la composition des jeux d'orgues," *Mémoires de l'Académie royale des sciences*, 1702 (Paris, 1704), 308–28.

musicians to fall into the system of harmonic sounds, but they have fallen into it themselves guided only by their ear and their experience.[16]

Such was the scientific understanding concerning overtones, then, when Castel informed Rameau of their existence. Our composer was not slow in recognizing their relevance to his theory. Before the ink barely had time to dry in the *Traité*, he was at work on a second treatise to announce his new principle of harmony. This was to be the *Nouveau système de musique theorique* of 1726. Not coincidentally, the title he chose was taken from Fontenelle's report on Sauveur's work: "Sur un nouveau système de musique."[17] Rameau began his *Nouveau système* with these portentous words:

There is actually in us a germ of harmony which apparently has not been noticed until now. It is nonetheless easily perceived in a string or a pipe, etc. whose resonance produces three different sounds at once. Supposing this same effect in all sonorous bodies, one ought logically to suppose it in the sound of our voice, even if it is not evident.[18]

The three sounds contained in the fundamental frequency of every *corps sonore*, Rameau insisted, are always the octave, the perfect twelfth, and the major seventeenth.[19] The perfect octave and double octave that are also generated by the fundamental sound are barely distinguishable on account of their "equisonance." According to Rameau, they are therefore not included among the fundamental sounds of the *corps sonore*. With great self-confidence, he concluded, "We believe we are thus able to propose this experiment as a fact which will serve us as a principle for establishing all our consequences."[20]

Despite all the fanfare, Rameau did not really develop his new principle of harmony in the *Nouveau système*. The remainder of the treatise served as a supplement and elaboration of the *Traité*.[21] Important new theoretical ideas were introduced in the *Nouveau système*, among them the geometric progression and the subdominant function (both of which we will examine in Chapter 7). However, there was no real theoretical investigation of the *corps sonore*. Rameau evidently needed time to

---

16 "Sur l'application des sons harmoniques aux jeux d'orgues," *Histoire de l'Académie royale des sciences*, 1702 (Paris, 1704), 92. About a century earlier, Mersenne had also noticed the correspondence between overtones and triadic harmony: "Strings and all other kinds of bodies make three or four different sounds at the same time which blend together... This is worthy of great consideration, for it seems that the harmony of chords is imprinted in the nature of each thing that is employed for the praise of its author." Quoted in Lloyd Farrar, "The Harmonic Series in Seventeenth-Century Scientific and Musical Thought (Descartes to Rameau)" (Master's Thesis, University of Illinois, 1956), 28.
17 *Histoire de l'Académie royale des sciences*, 1701 (Amsterdam, 1707), 155–75. It should be noted that a "system" for Sauveur and Fontenelle meant dividing the octave for tuning purposes. Sauveur does not consider a system of music in any way related to a theory of harmony as Rameau does.
18 *Nouveau système* (Paris, 1726), iii.
19 Ibid., 17. The term *corps sonore* was widely used by seventeenth-century scientists to refer to any periodically vibrating system. Rameau used the term in his *Traité* in such a sense (Book 1, Chapter 4), but obviously without being aware of the overtone series. After the *Nouveau système*, Rameau defined the *corps sonore* as any vibrating system that emitted exclusively the harmonic overtones of the perfect twelfth and major seventeenth.
20 Ibid.
21 The *Nouveau système* was in fact subtitled "pour servir d'introduction au Traité de l'harmonie" and bound with a reissue of the *Traité*.

work out the musical implications of his new acoustical principle. It was not until 1737 that he published a treatise on harmony fully exploiting the *corps sonore* as a theoretical basis.

DORTOUS DE MAIRAN

Shortly after arriving in Paris in 1722, Rameau had made the acquaintance of the scientist Jean-Jacques Dortous de Mairan (1678–1771). Mairan had been censor for the *permis d'imprimer* at the time Rameau published his second book of *Pièces de clavecin* in 1724.[22] Rameau's friendship with Mairan would prove to be of great consequence in future years. Mairan had long interested himself in acoustics, writing on the subject as early as 1715. Although one of the last major defenders of Cartesian physics in the Académie, he was acquainted with much of Newton's work and in fact early in the century helped promote his optical theories.[23] It was in reading Newton's *Opticks* that Mairan conceived a new theory of sound propagation that was inspired by Newton's theory of light transmission.

Newton had argued that light was the product of minute corpuscules that were transmitted directly to the eye. This theory was in contradistinction to the then widely accepted wave theory (as advocated, for instance, by Newton's arch-rival Robert Hooke) that explained light as the infinitesimal and instantaneous undulations of an ether, much as sound was the product of vibrations propagated through the air. Newton rejected the wave theory since light always was found to move rectilinearly (in straight lines), and never bent around obstacles as did waves in water.[24] Light must be a material substance, Newton argued, otherwise it too could bend around objects.

Mairan thought that Newton's corpuscular emission theory might also hold true for sound, with suitable adjustments. And in a lengthy paper read before the Académie in 1737, Mairan described how this might be so.[25] The main problem Mairan wished to solve was the paradox of simultaneous pitch propagation:

It always seemed to me impossible to conceive how many differing pitches could be perceived at the same time; how different voices singing in parts in a concert, for example, let alone differently tuned strings imparting their tones to the immediately surrounding air . . . could each be transmitted faithfully and without confusion to the ear . . . For example, let one strike a major triad C, E, G. If the air is to convey the impression of the fundamental sound, C, it ought to make 100 vibrations per second, 125 for the third, and 150 for the fifth . . . But how can the same mass of air make 125 and 150 vibrations at the same time it is making just 100?[26]

---

22 Cuthbert Girdlestone, *Jean-Philippe Rameau: His Life and Work*, 2nd edition (New York, 1969), 522, fn. 5.
23 Henry Guerlac, "The Newtonianism of Dortous de Mairan," *Essays and Papers in the History of Science* (Ithaca, 1981), 479–90.
24 A. I. Sabra, *Theories of Light from Descartes to Newton* (Cambridge, 1981), 231ff.
25 "Discours sur la propagation du son dans les différens tons qui le modifient," *Mémoires de l'Académie royale des sciences*, 1737 (Amsterdam, 1740), 1–87.
26 *Ibid.*, 4–5.

140   Rameau and Musical Thought in the Enlightenment

To solve this riddle, Mairan proposed a theory of sound transmission that was modeled upon Newton's corpuscular theory of light emission (although his theory also drew upon the atomistic theories held by such seventeenth-century scientists as Beeckman, Gassendi and de La Hire). Mairan hypothesized that the air is a composite of different-sized atomic particles, each particle capable of vibrating at a single distinct frequency depending upon its size.

I say that the air, as a vehicle of sound, is an assemblage of an infinite number of particles of different elasticity, whose vibrations are analogous in their duration to the different pitches of the *corps sonore*. Among all these particles, only those of the same type, the same duration of vibration, and in unison with the *corps sonore* are capable of producing the same vibrations and of transmitting these to the ear. The smallest mass of perceptible air contains many of these various particles.[27]

The propagation of sound, then, was essentially a chain reaction of sympathetically vibrating particles. Only in this way, Mairan argued, can sounds of differing pitch (as well as differing timbre and dynamic) reach the ear without interference.

Mairan was convinced that his hypothesis solved a host of acoustical paradoxes insoluble by competing theories. It showed not only how differing pitches can be propagated through the air, but also suggested how the ear can recognize these pitches. Mairan described the basilar membrane that carpeted the inner ear as a "veritable musical instrument." Each fiber of the basilar membrane is tuned – just like an air particle – to respond to a unique frequency.[28]

In a claim that must have attracted Rameau's intense interest, Mairan asserted that his hypothesis explained the mystery of harmonic overtones. He reported that, "in the presence of a very competent musician," he plucked a string and was able to hear an octave, twelfth, double octave, and seventeenth above the fundamental.[29] "What is the cause of this extraordinary effect?" he asked. "It is clear that this cause cannot reside in the *corps sonore* or in the sound itself, in the string, or in the air." Objecting that something cannot vibrate simultaneously at different frequencies, Mairan concluded that this phenomenon must originate in the sympathetic resonance of commensurate air particles. In other words, the vibrations of the string will also agitate those particles whose frequencies are integrally related in harmonic proportion to that of the original sounding frequency, just as we observe in the sympathetic resonance of harmonically tuned strings. "This is why a string which itself can excite in the air only a unison or its octaves, may on occasion make heard the fifth and the third of their octaves." Mairan concludes:

This is one of the experiences that in my opinion is inexplicable by any other system. One finds here at the same time the principal laws of harmony dictated by nature itself; the major triad founded on the correspondence that the harmonic particles of the air possess

---

[27] *Ibid.*, 3.
[28] This is essentially a description of the modern physiological "resonance" theory. Rameau repeats this idea as "Proposition 7" of his *Génération harmonique*.
[29] "Discours sur la propagation du son," 15.

between themselves and a fecund source of rules, which art and calculation can extend, and which all philosophy will admit.[30]

Mairan's explanation of our instinct for harmony is surprisingly Lockean coming from such a strong Cartesian. Perhaps the triad is not implanted in our minds as an innate idea, he admits. But hearing tones with their concomitant harmonics of the third and fifth, and "repeated millions of times since our birth, forms in us a habit that can justly be called a natural sentiment for harmony." This is clearly cause for contemplation, and perhaps even a basis for developing a theory of music.

But I shall refrain from entering into this in detail, as a celebrated musician of our day, to whom my ideas and my hypothesis are not unknown, will imminently give the public a treatise on music which aims at this goal, and is based upon these same principles.[31]

THE *GENERATION HARMONIQUE*

The treatise Mairan refers to is Rameau's *Génération harmonique*, published in 1737. In this work, Rameau adopted Mairan's hypothesis as the explanation for harmonic overtones heard in the *corps sonore*:

Ten or twelve years ago, Mr. de Mairan, whose name alone is occasion for praise, while discussing my system with me, informed me of [his] reflections concerning the particles of air. He explained his idea to me in great detail . . . But not then concerned with that area, I did not know how to profit from this idea, and even forgot about it until Mr. de Gamaches [another Academy scientist] reminded me of what Mr. de Mairan had told me. And through kindness for which I cannot sufficiently acknowledge him, I was made to see the relation of this principle to those upon which I had already founded my system such that I finally appropriated it.[32]

Rameau's adoption of Mairan's theory would have a number of profound consequences for his own music theory (not all of them favorable) that we will shortly examine. At the outset, however, Mairan's theory did seem to offer a secure scientific foundation for his principle of the *corps sonore*.

"Harmony," Rameau began his treatise, "which consists of an agreeable mixture of several different sounds, is a natural effect, the cause of which resides in the air agitated by the percussion of each individual *corps sonore*."[33] Rameau proceeded to detail Mairan's theory in twelve "propositions." He then augmented the theory with seven of his own "experiments," ostensibly to serve as confirmation or consequences of the atomistic hypothesis. For the most part, these experiments consisted of the sounding of various instruments: violoncello and monochord strings, trumpets, organ pipes, and even a pair of tongs. Here is part of Rameau's second *expérience*:

Take a viol or violoncello and tune two of its strings a twelfth apart. Bow the lower string; you will see the higher string vibrate and perhaps even hear it. You will certainly hear it if you touch it with your fingernail while it is vibrating.[34]

30 *Ibid.*, 18–19.   31 *Ibid.*, 19.   32 *Génération harmonique*, 3–4.
33 *Ibid.*, 1.   34 *Ibid.*, 8.

And from the fourth *expérience*:

> Take the organ stops called *Bourdon*, *Prestant*, or *Flute*, *Nazard*, and *Tierce*, which form among themselves the octave, twelfth and major seventeenth above the *Bourdon*, in the ratios of 1, ½, ⅓, ⅕. Press one of the keys using only the *Bourdon* stop sounding, and pull out in succession each of the other stops. You will hear their sounds blend successively with one another. You may even be able to distinguish one stop from another while they are sounding together. But if you improvise on the keys so as to distract yourself for a moment while all these stops are sounding and then return to the original single note [you played earlier], you will hear only a single sound . . .[35]

Rameau's point was to show how every musical tone contains two upper partials corresponding to the perfect twelfth and major seventeenth, respectively. Musical pitch, in other words, is compound: "An appreciable sound is not singular by nature, rather, it is harmonious, and its harmony represents this proportion: 1, ⅓, ⅕."[36] And again: "Until now the sound taken as the physical object of music was always considered to be singular and solitary, whereas it is actually triple in nature."[37]

NEWTONIAN OPTICS AND EXPERIMENTAL SCIENCE

Rameau repeatedly emphasized the discovery that pitch is compound in nature, expecting that his readers would make a connection with another well-known scientific discovery: Newton's demonstration that light is also compound. The Cartesians, it will be recalled, had argued that white light is naturally pure, and colors just modifications and corruptions of it. Newton turned this relation around by showing in the most famous single experiment contained in the *Opticks* (the so-called "experimentum crucis") how sunlight, when refracted through a prism, breaks up into a spectrum of seven colors. If one of these colored rays is in turn refracted, however, no change is observed. Newton concluded from this that the primary constituents of light were colors, and white light was only a compound of these colors.

Rameau was not the first to call attention to the surprising correlation between sound and light. Scientists and musicians throughout the seventeenth century had suggested many parallels. Hooke had claimed, for instance, that individual colors were the product of differing infinitesimal undulations transmitted to the eye through an ether, much as pitch was the product of frequencies propagated to the ear through the air. Newton, who rejected Hooke's wave theory of light propagation, obviously could not accept this explanation. Instead, he proposed that color was the result of the velocity and mass of individual light corpuscles. Most intriguingly, though, Newton saw a startling correspondence between the seven colors of his spectrum and the seven notes of a diatonic scale. He found that when

---

[35] *Ibid.*, 13.
[36] *Ibid.*, 28–29. Rameau did not associate the upper partials of a tone with its timbre since he was convinced that overtone content was uniform for every musical pitch.
[37] *Ibid.*, 30.

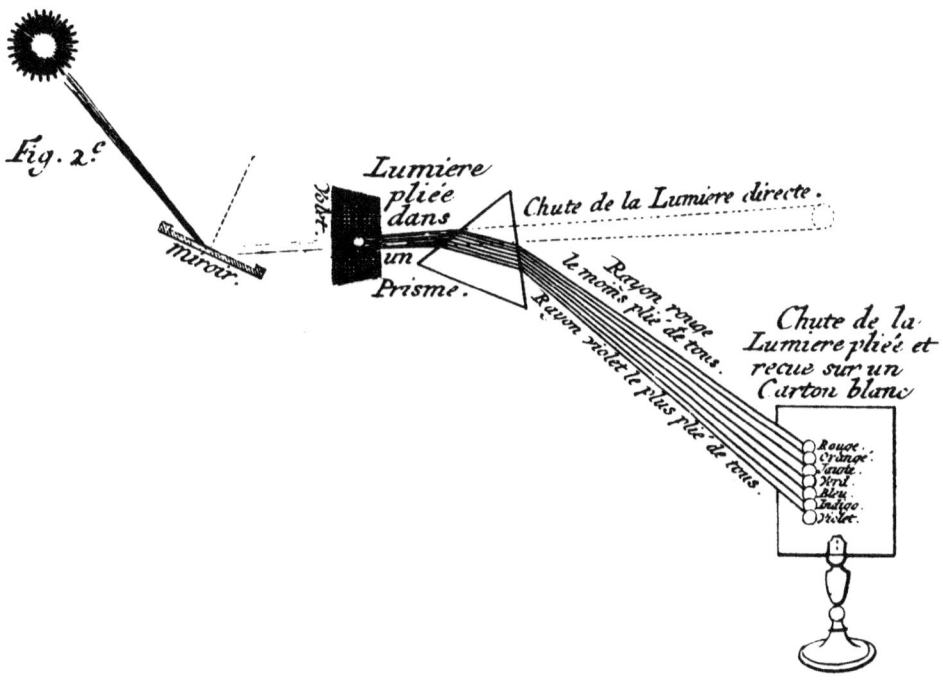

Plate 6.1 An illustration of Newton's "experimentum crucis" demonstrating the refraction of light into a spectrum of seven colors. From Abbé Pluche, *Le Spectacle de la nature* (Paris, 1732), IV, 164

light was refracted through a prism, the sines of the seven individual colors of the spectrum paralled the ratios of those found between the seven notes of the diatonic scale.[38] Newton never pursued his analogy further than this, and for good reason. The correspondence proved ultimately to be illusory. As Penelope Gouk has shown, Newton had to fudge some of his arguments with *ad hoc* mathematical calculations and contradictory physical hypotheses in order to make the analogy work out.[39] She even suggests that Newton's conclusion that there were seven primary colors in the spectrum (as opposed to the five he initially saw) may have come about from his wish to demonstrate an underlying unity and symmetry between sound and color. (So much for Newton the dispassionate empiricist![40])

But if Newton never pursued the analogy, his followers were not so reluctant. The correspondence between sound and color seemed too fortuitous to be ignored

---

38 Isaac Newton, *Opticks*, 4th edition (London, 1730; reprint edition, New York, 1952), 211–12, fn. 45.
39 Penelope Gouk, "The Harmonic Roots of Newtonian Science," *Let Newton Be! A New Perspective on His Life and Works,* ed. John Fauvel (Oxford, 1988), 101–25.
40 A suggestion disputed by David Topper, however: "Newton on the Number of Colors in the Spectrum," *Studies on the History and Philosophy of Science* 21/2 (1990), 269–79.

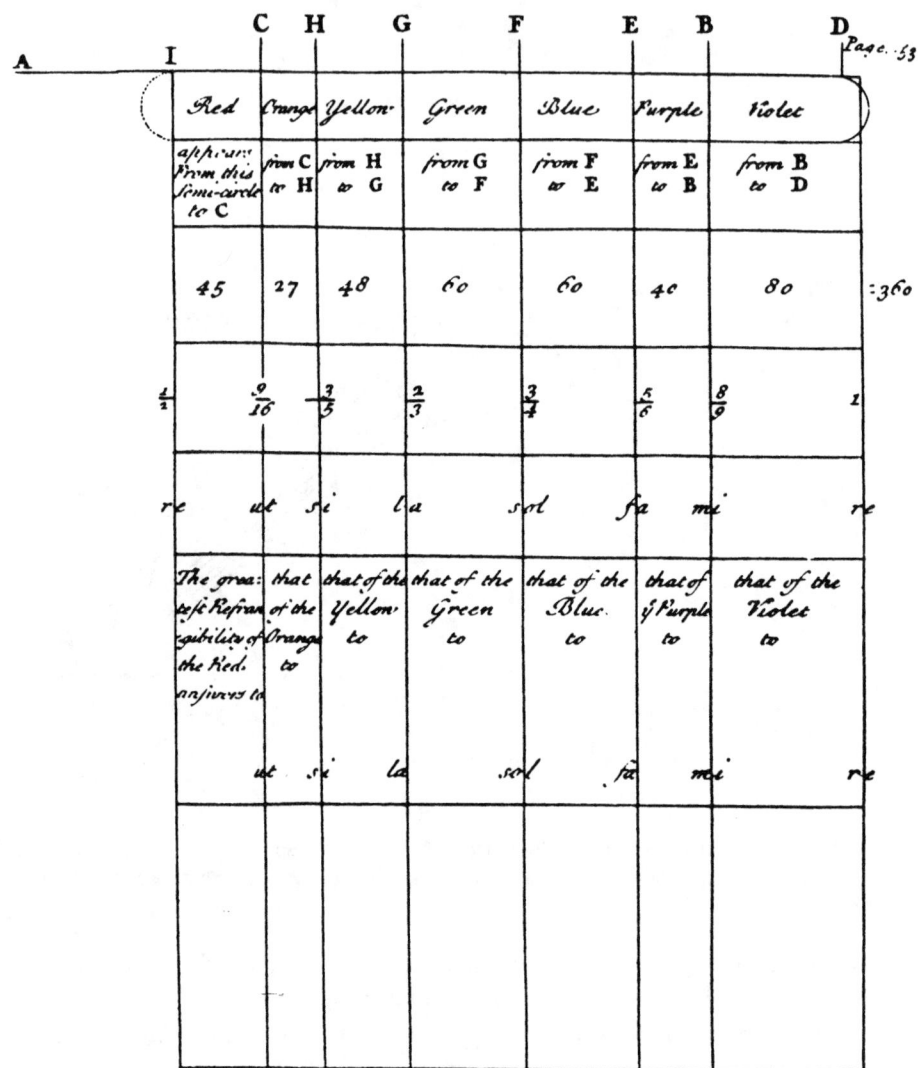

Plate 6.2 Voltaire's correlation between Newton's color spectrum and the seven notes of the diatonic scale. From the English edition of Voltaire's *Eléments de la philosophie de Neuton* (*Elements of the Philosophy of Newton*, London, 1754), 53.

by Platonically inclined thinkers who were convinced of the harmonic unity of nature. On account of the great prestige of Newton's endorsement of the idea, French scientists, including Mairan and Buffon, and philosophes like Malebranche, Condillac, Voltaire, Diderot and Rousseau (to say nothing of Germans like Goethe!) enthusiastically debated the color–sound analogy, although not all were equally convinced of its validity.[41]

[41] Synaesthetic correspondences between color and sound were not the only ones considered in the eighteenth century, however. One writer, a certain Polycarpe Poncelet, tried to establish a spectrum of odors corresponding to the diatonic scale (!) in his *Chimie du goût et de l'odorat* (Paris, 1755).

Castel, as we have earlier noted, developed and built an ocular harpsichord based upon synaesthetic theories. But being the arch anti-Newtonian he was, he rejected most of the elements of Newton's optical theories concerning the nature and transmission of light. Instead of the seven primary colors proposed by Newton, Castel believed there were only three: blue, yellow, and red, of which the other colors were compounds.[42] Interestingly, one of Castel's most frequently cited arguments in favor of his theory was that musical pitch, too, was triune in nature. He equated the fundamental, twelfth, and seventeenth of Rameau's *corps sonore* with the colors blue, red, and yellow, respectively, and even wrote of the "génération harmonique des couleurs."[43] Differing as the optical theories of Castel and Newton were, though, it is noteworthy that both men used musical analogies to buttress their respective ideas.[44]

However striking the parallel between sound and light seemed, the correspondence breaks down at a number of critical points where Rameau's theory is concerned. First, not all musical pitches possess the uniform overtone content Rameau claimed. As we will soon learn, many musical instruments produce *inharmonic* partials. Secondly, Rameau made a number of faulty observations, particularly concerning the sympathetic resonance of lower-tuned strings. (I will return to this topic in a moment.) In what sense, then, can the observations and experiments in the *Génération harmonique* be considered truly scientific? Why the outward show of objective empiricism if so much of it turns out to have been contrived?

The answer, I think, is this: Rameau's gambit to open his *Génération harmonique* with thirty pages of propositions and experiments was a calculated emulation of the then-in-vogue "experimental" science. His strategy would have been unmistakably recognized by all Académie members and educated lay persons as Newtonian in character, and, more specifically, as modeled upon the very source from which Mairan derived his atomistic theory of sound propagation: Newton's *Opticks*.

Throughout the eighteenth century, the *Opticks* was considered a model of experimental science. Unlike the forbidding *Principia* with its difficult and intimidating mathematical abstractions, the *Opticks* was a relatively accessible work; it took a common-sense, empirical approach to natural science that even those with

---

[42] For more on Castel's color theories, see Donald S. Schier, *Louis-Bertrand Castel: Anti-Newtonian Scientist* (Cedar Rapids, Iowa, 1941), 135–96. A good description of Castel's "clavecin oculaire" is given by Anne-Marie Chouillet-Roche, "Le Clavecin oculaire du Père Castel," *Dix-Huitième Siècle* 8 (1976), 141–66.

[43] Louis-Bertrand Castel, *L'Optique des couleurs* (Paris, 1740), 69.

[44] Rameau never seemed to have been particularly interested in Newton's color–sound theory, even though he must have learnt of it through Mairan. The only mention he ever makes of it was in a relatively late publication in which he criticizes Newton for equating colors with the diatonic scale rather than looking for a truly generative origin of colors analogous to the generative system he had himself found with his *corps sonore* (*Nouvelles Réflexions*, 63–64; *CTW* V, 130–31). Presumably Castel's theory was more to his liking as it emphasized the relationship between color and the *corps sonore*. Rameau makes a complimentary reference to Castel's ocular harpsichord in the *Nouveau système*, p. v. Of course, one cannot push the analogy too far. Rousseau was only the first to note that colors cannot be transposed as can scale degrees (or, for that matter, the *corps sonore*). This and a number of other criticisms of Castel's ideas are detailed in Beatrice Didier, *La Musique des lumières: Diderot – L'Encyclopédie – Rousseau* (Paris, 1985), 163–64.

no scientific background could follow.[45] Beginning with a few easily explained definitions and axioms, Newton moves progressively through a series of "experiments" using mirrors, lenses, and prisms in which the reader is invited to join. They serve to demonstrate one by one the refrangibility of light, the particle theory of emission, the nature of colors, and so on.

The *Opticks* was by no means the first text of experimental science. British scientists throughout the seventeenth century had cultivated "experimental physick" inspired by Francis Bacon's vision of science as an empirical, experimental, and, above all, communal enterprise. Dutch scientists, too, seemed particularly drawn to the experimental sciences. By the end of the seventeenth century, even a few French scientists began to try their hands at "physique expérimentale."[46]

But it was with the publication of Newton's *Opticks* in 1704, and more specifically with its French translation in 1720, that the vogue for experimental science took off in France.[47] The *Opticks* was the first work of Newton to be widely read there.[48] With its many dramatic and incredible demonstrations of refrangibility, diffraction, and colors, the *Opticks* was ideally tailored to attract a large and curious audience. (It would also inspire the poetic imagination as no other scientific work ever had[49]). Its overwhelming authority and empirical puissance convinced French scientists quickly of both its arguments and the advantages of its measured, inductive approach to scientific investigation. Within a generation, many imitations of the "méthode Newtonienne" appeared in publication.[50] While French scientists (to say nothing of Newton himself) by no means abandoned their rationalist theories or deductive methodologies, the experimental approach was seen – whether rightly or not – as an alternative to Cartesianism.

Sound was a discipline ideally suited to the new experimental approach. Along with optics and electricity, it made for some of the most spectacular empirical demonstrations. Using pneumatic devices such as the air pump, one could measure degrees of sound propagation through air of various densities and composition. (This could be done by, among other means, suspending a small bell inside a glass container and pumping air out until there was a vacuum.) Demonstrations of the speed of sound, echoes, amplification using a speaking trumpet, sympathetic resonance (e.g. the shattering of a wine glass by a high-pitched voice), and of course the overtone series, made entertaining public spectacles, and were described in most texts of experimental physics and science popularizers in the eighteenth century.[51]

45 A point emphasized by I. Bernard Cohen in his Preface to Newton, *Opticks*, p. xviii.
46 Most notably Pierre Poliniére, *Expériences de physique* (Paris, 1709).
47 Ira Wade, *The Structure and Form of the French Enlightenment*, 2 vols. (Princeton, 1977), I, 516–82; Thomas Hankins, *Science and the Enlightenment* (Cambridge, 1985), 46–80.
48 Henry Guerlac, *Newton on the Continent* (Ithaca, 1981), 78–163.
49 Marjorie Hope Nicolson, *Newton Demands the Muse* (Princeton, 1946).
50 The most important are Abbé Pluche, *Le Spectacle de la nature*, 8 vols. (Paris, 1732); André-François Boureau-Deslandes, *Discours sur la meilleure manière de faire des expériences* (Paris, 1736); and the Abbé Nollet, *Leçons de physique expérimentale*, 6 vols. (Amsterdam, 1745).
51 Pierre Poliniére, *Expériences de physique*, 2nd edition (Paris, 1718), 230–44; and Nollet, *Leçons de physique expérimentale*, III, 395–486.

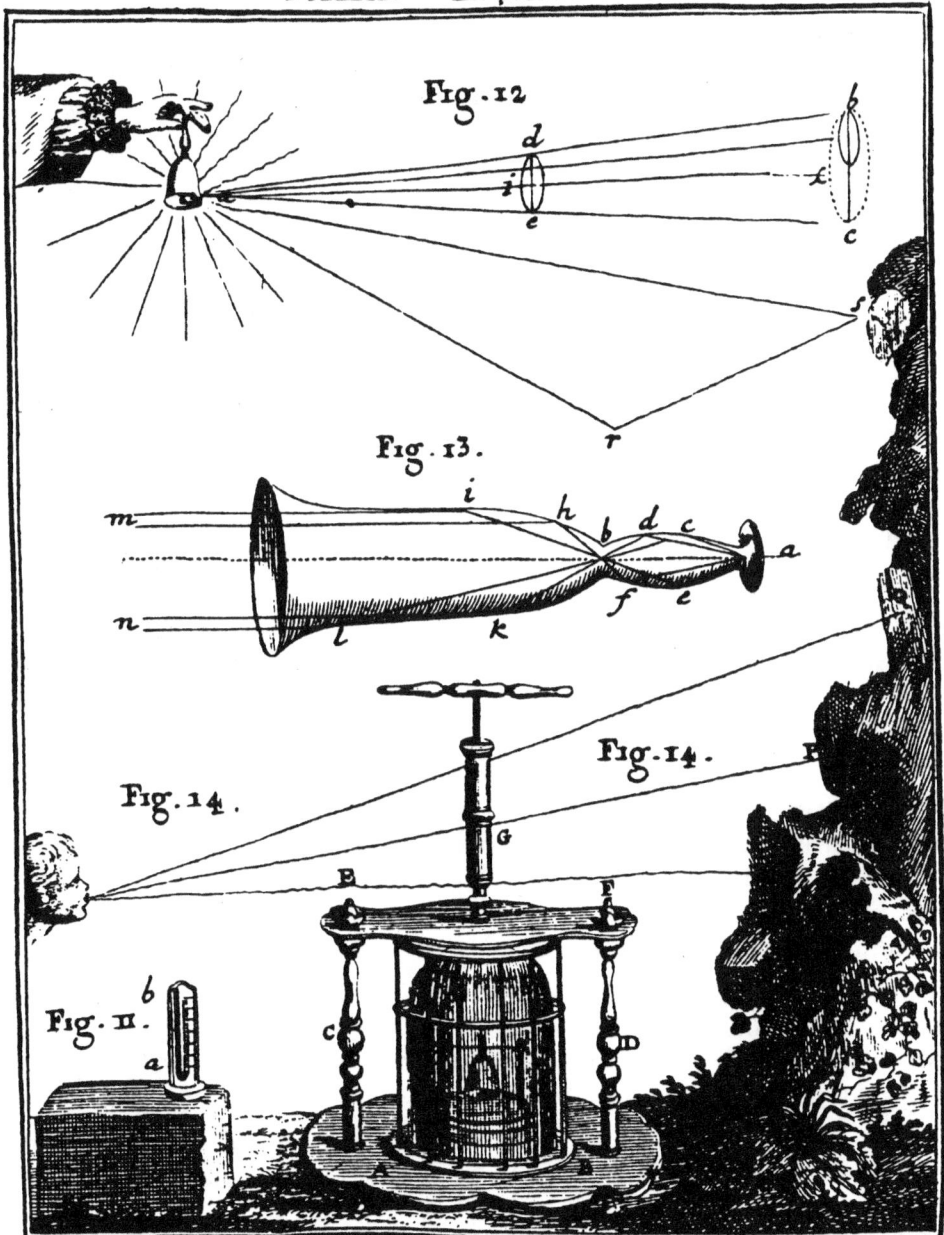

Plate 6.3 Illustration of some acoustical experiments from Abbé Nollet, *Leçons de physique expérimentale* (Amsterdam, 1745), III, 438

The *Génération harmonique,* then, was clearly to be understood as an example of Newtonian experimental physics. By his many experiments, Rameau hoped to endow the *corps sonore* with the same empirical legitimacy Newton had for his optical theories. Even more, perhaps, Rameau hoped to persuade his reading public of the validity of his theory *independent* of the actual epistemological relation of his experiments to its construction. The correspondence between the two, as we are about to see, was tenuous at best.[52] In parts of the *Génération harmonique*, Rameau quite blatantly misinterpreted Mairan's thesis in order to make it support all the musical consequences he wished. One anonymous critic complained that Rameau adopted a physical hypothesis of which he had neither understanding nor need,[53] only, the critic cynically suggests, to secure a favorable review of his treatise by the Académie – a not entirely improbable suggestion![54]

Perhaps the most glaring example of Rameau's suspect experimentation was his derivation of the minor triad. In proposition 5, Rameau suggests that a sounding string will not only activate higher partials through the agitation of air particles whose natural frequencies are integral multiples of the fundamental (sounding the major triad), but also activate those air particles whose frequencies are divisions of the fundamental:

> A sonorous body set in motion communicates its vibrations, not only to the particles of air capable of the same vibrations, but also to all the other particles which are commensurable to the first particles. In turn, these different particles react on the same sonorous body, as well as on surrounding bodies. The particles of air not only draw from the first body the different sounds of its different aliquot parts, thus causing it to produce sounds which are higher than the sound of its totality, but also agitate all surrounding bodies which are capable of the same vibrations, and, sometimes, even cause them to resound.[55]

By Rameau's reasoning, this would produce the reciprocal (arithmetic) series of a lower octave, perfect twelfth, and major seventeenth, sounding (if C were the fundamental) a lower F and A♭, respectively. Rameau's point with all this is that the minor triad (in this case F minor) is as much a product of "harmonic generation" as is the major triad. Of course there was really little empirical evidence to confirm the theory. Rameau admitted that

> the slowest vibrations have more power over the fastest than the latter have over the former, and in consequence, because the fastest vibrations can only agitate the slowest vibrations weakly, they cannot give those bodies sufficiently strong agitation for the sound to be transmitted to the ear.[56]

In order to verify the existence of the slower vibrations and make them perceptible, Rameau tells us in his second experiment to tune two strings a twelfth apart. If

---

52 Although this is not necessarily unusual in the annals of experimental science. Experimental reports in scientific papers have often served more as heuristic strategies to *persuade* the reader of some theory than as means by which that theory was arrived at. See Geoffrey Cantor, "The Rhetoric of Experiment" in *The Uses of Experiment*, ed. David Gooding, Trevor Pinch, and Simon Schaffer (Cambridge, 1989), 159–80.
53 *Observations sur les écrits modernes* 10 (1737), 68–86; *CTW* VI, 127–33.
54 But Mairan was quick to come to the composer's defense: "M. Rameau should neither be accused of imprudence nor of harboring any illusions in having employed my idea." "Eclaircissement de M. de Mairan," *Ibid.*, 355; *CTW* VI, 136.
55 *Génération harmonique*, 4–5.
56 *Ibid.*, 5.

you bow the higher-sounding string, "you will not only see the lower sound vibrate as a whole, you will also see it divide itself into three equal parts, forming three anti-nodes of vibrations between two nodes or fixed points."[57] We can verify that the string is vibrating as a whole, says Rameau, by touching it at one of these nodal points. We will be able to feel that these nodes are not perfectly stationary, thus "proving" that the string is indeed vibrating as a whole. (I will term this Rameau's "sympathetic resonance" theory of the minor triad.[58])

Rameau concluded from all these propositions and experiments that a single vibrating *corps sonore* is indeed the acoustic generator of both the major triad and the minor triad. He admits, though, that the minor triad possesses an origin "less perfect and less natural than the original harmony,"[59] requiring as it does "the artificial means of facilitating the perception of a sound imperceptible by itself."[60] But wishing to establish a theory of "harmonic generation" for both the harmonic and arithmetic proportions, Rameau must insist that the origin of the minor triad is as natural as that of the major triad.

Rameau's sympathetic resonance theory, of course, is false, as he was soon to realize. Strings tuned a twelfth and seventeenth below a sounding string will not vibrate in their totality, but only in aliquot divisions corresponding to a unison with the sounding string.[61] Rameau's concern, though, was with harmony, not physics. Thus whether willfully or out of sheer ignorance, he misread his evidence in order to provide the minor triad with as firm an acoustical base as the major triad.[62]

Notwithstanding the difficulties with the minor triad, though, Rameau was perfectly justified in defining the *corps sonore* using Mairan's atomistic hypothesis. Overtones were a well-confirmed property of most vibrating systems. As no scientist in 1737 was yet able to explain conceptually how a *corps sonore* such as the vibrating string could vibrate in such a manner as to emit several frequencies at once, Mairan's hypothesis was a reasonable one, if a bit naively mechanical. Around this time, though, a number of scientists working outside of France were taking the first steps toward an understanding of vibrational superposition, steps which would eventually lead to the correct explanation of overtones.

---

57 *Ibid.*, 9.
58 I choose the label "sympathetic resonance theory" instead of "undertone theory." The latter term erroneously suggests the Riemannian proposition that the vibrating string itself emits lower frequencies analogous to its "overtones," whereas Rameau explicitly attributes these frequencies to motions occurring outside the string itself, namely, the collision of commensurable air particles.
59 *Ibid.*, 32.
60 *Ibid.*, 23.
61 As proven, for example, in 'sGravesande's important physics treatise of 1720. See W. James 'sGravesande, *Mathematical Elements of Natural Philosophy Confirm'd by Experiments,* trans. J. T. Desaguliers, 2 vols. (London, 1747), II, 57.
62 It is interesting how the notion of "lower harmonics" proved attractive to many scientists. For instance, Euler, despite the differences he had with Rameau that are examined in Chapter 8, found the notion useful to his optical theories. In one of his works he posited a reciprocal series of "under-colors" (*colores derivati*) complementing the "over-colors" generated in the spectrum: Casper Hakfoort, *Optica in de eeuw van Euler* (Amsterdam, 1986), 108ff.

TOWARD A THEORY OF VIBRATIONAL SUPERPOSITION

As we have noted, Taylor's formula assumed that the fundamental shape of any vibrating string would be sinusoidal. This would account for the string's fundamental frequency, but not its overtones.[63] It was precisely upon the basis of this assumption that Mairan sought the cause of overtones in a source *outside* the vibrating string. Taylor was wrong, though; the shape of a vibrating string is much more complex than a single sine curve. As Sauveur discovered, any string possesses many possible forms (or "modes") of vibration. What Sauveur could not conceive (nor could anyone else at the time) was how these modes could be superimposed to form a single complex motion without disturbing the individual component vibrations (frequencies). The answer to this puzzle was soon found through the study of simple vibrating systems.

While analyzing what scientists call the "dangling chain," the Swiss physicist Daniel Bernoulli (1700–82) came to an important realization in 1733: a vibrating system possesses as many modes of vibration as the system has degrees of freedom.[64] This can be demonstrated by setting up a freely dangling string loaded with a small number of equally-spaced weights (the weights being analogous to the links of a "dangling chain"). With only one weight at the end of the string, there is but one mode of motion possible. A pendulum is a good example of this. With the addition of another weight, though, one additional degree of freedom is possible, and consequently one more mode of vibration. The process continues, theoretically, *ad infinitum*. Figure 6.2 reproduces Bernoulli's representation of the respective modes of a string loaded first by two and then by three weights.[65]

Bernoulli concluded from his observations that all upper modes of vibration contained nodes; for an object with k degrees of freedom, there would be $k-1$ nodes. He further realized that these findings could be generalized to any flexible body. The vibrating string behaved like a dangling chain loaded with infinitely many small weights adjacent to one another. Thus, the vibrating string had potentially an infinite number of degrees of freedom, giving a correspondingly infinite number of nodes. Finally, Bernoulli realized that the frequency of each mode was directly proportional to the number of its nodes. At this point, though, Bernoulli was not ready to say that such modes could coexist. The concept of vibrational superposition must have appeared improbable to Bernoulli, much as it

---

[63] Taylor, it is worth pointing out, never made any mention of overtones in his study of the vibrating string. Ironically, in later years he read and reported on Rameau's *Nouveau système* for the British Royal Society. But even in his report – incidentally a quite favorable one – Taylor makes no mention of Rameau's new acoustical principle (Leta E. Miller, "Rameau and the Royal Society of London: New Letters and Documents," *Music and Letters* 66/1 [1985], 25–26).

[64] "Theoremata de oscillationibus corporum filo flexili connexorum et catenae verticaliter suspensae," *Commentarii Academiae Scientiarum Imperialis Petropolitanae* 6 (1732–33), 108–22. This article is reprinted with an accompanying English translation in the appendix to John T. Cannon and Sigalia Dostrovsky, *The Evolution of Dynamics: Vibration Theory From 1687 to 1742* (New York, 1981).

[65] *Ibid.*, 141.

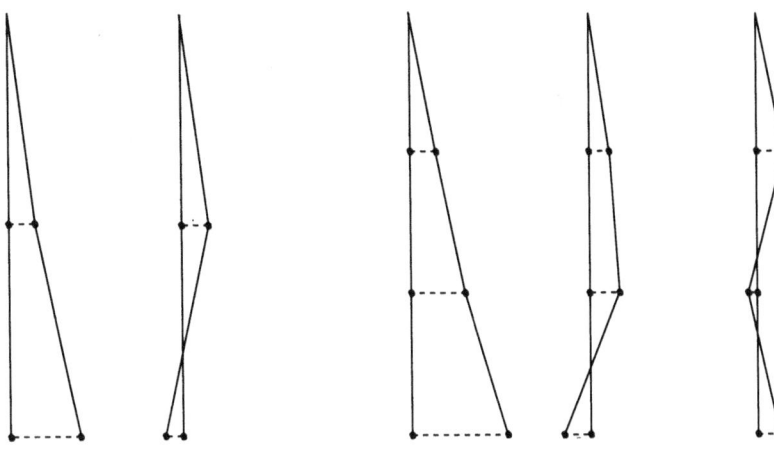

The two modes of a string loaded by two weights

The three modes of a string loaded by three weights

Figure 6.2 Modes of a string's movement when loaded by two or three weights

had to Mersenne a century earlier. He considered, rather, modes to be discrete motions which a flexible body was capable of assuming.

Soon entering into this research along with Bernoulli was probably the most brilliant and unquestionably the most prolific scientist in the eighteenth century, Leonhard Euler (1702–83), known to musicians for his magnum opus of speculative *musica theorica*, the *Tentamen novae theoriae musicae* published in 1739. Euler and Bernoulli poured out a torrent of research on the physics of flexible and rigid bodies, opening the way for unprecedented advances in the understanding of vibrational mechanics.[66] One finding relevant to music theory emerged from this research. In a study of the transverse vibrations of a rigid bar made in 1742, Bernoulli found that the initial vibrational modes of some flexible systems were not harmonic. That is to say, the frequencies of the upper modes did not necessarily relate in integral proportions to the frequency of the fundamental mode. Bernoulli's calculations for the first five modes of a vibrating rod are shown in Table 6.1.[67]

Table 6.1 Modes of a vibrating rod

Mode	Frequency	Ratio to fundamental
1	6,345	1
2	17,627	2.78
3	34,545	5.44
4	57,105	9
5	86,308	11.36

[66] Cannon and Dostrovsky cover the history of this research in detail in their excellent survey. *Ibid.*, 53–109.

[67] "De sonis multafariis quos laminae elasticae diversimode edunt disquisitiones mechanico-geometricae experimentis acusticis illustratae et confirmatae," *Commentarii Academiae Scientiarum Imperialis Petropolitanae* 13 (1741–43), 167–96. Also cited in Truesdell, "The Rational Mechanics," 198.

Only the frequency of the fourth mode stands in integral proportion to the fundamental. Similar inharmonic modes resulted no matter how the clamping conditions of the rod changed (clamped on both ends, on one end only, pinned in the middle, and so forth). Again, there was no mention that such modes could coexist, although by now such a possibility had occurred to Bernoulli.

Attention soon turned back to the vibrating string. Drawing upon their understanding of the dangling chain and elastic rods and bars, Euler and Bernoulli were able to show that Taylor's assumption was false; the motion of a vibrating string is much more complex than a simple sinusoid. Describing this motion mathematically was another problem, though. Fortunately such a description was now possible with the help of a newly developed tool in calculus: partial differential equations.

The first scientist fully to develop and apply partial differential calculus was d'Alembert, in a prize essay on wind entered in a competition at the Berlin Academy in 1746.[68] D'Alembert imaginatively approached the problem by analyzing wind as an "atmospheric tide."[69] His findings, while completely abstract, were nonetheless of momentous importance for mathematics. In his paper we encounter for the first time the partial differential equation "as we understand it today."[70]

D'Alembert's success with his study of wind soon led him to consider the vibrating string. Although these phenomena may appear unrelated, an accurate mathematical description of the vibrating string, like that of wind, requires the use of partial differentials. In order to determine the position of a point y on the vibrating string illustrated in Figure 6.3, one must determine it with respect to the x axis, as well as time t. Its amplitude will then be represented by a function of two independent variables x and t such that $y = f(x, t)$. In two pioneering papers of 1747, d'Alembert derived a solution which could precisely determine y with respect to x and t. This is d'Alembert's famous wave equation:[71]

$$\frac{\partial^2 y}{\partial t^2} = C^2 \frac{\partial^2 y}{\partial x^2}$$

As shown here, y is the displacement of a point on the x axis, over or under point x at time t. C represents the constant of string tension. D'Alembert's discovery was important, as Hankins has pointed out, "because it opened the way for the study of oscillations propagated in continuous media."[72] Field equations, as they are called today, have proved to be among the most powerful mathematical tools in modern physics.

[68] *Réflexions sur la cause générale des vents* (Paris, 1747).
[69] Steven B. Engelsman, "D'Alembert et les équations aux dérivées partielles," *Dix-Huitième Siècle* 16 (1984), 27.
[70] S. S. Demidov, "Création et développement de la théorie des équations différentielles aux dérivées partielles dans les travaux de J. d'Alembert," *Revue d'histoire des sciences* 35/1 (January 1982), 15.
[71] "Recherches sur la courbe que forme une corde tendue mise en vibration," *Histoire de l'Académie royale des sciences et belles lettres de Berlin* 3 (1747), 214–49; "Suite des recherches . . ." Ibid., 220–49.
[72] Thomas Hankins, *Jean d'Alembert, Science and the Enlightenment* (Oxford, 1970), 48.

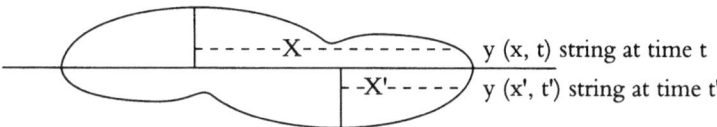

Figure 6.3 A vibrating string at time t and t'

In his paper, d'Alembert attempted to show how his wave equation could account for the transverse vibrations of any shaped string. According to his reasoning, such a system needed but one function to show its displacement from equilibrium at any moment. The function would be determined by the form of the stretched string just before being released. For a number of misconceived reasons, though, d'Alembert believed that the displacement function could be of only certain restricted sorts. In a rebuttal to d'Alembert's paper, Euler argued that d'Alembert's restrictions were unnecessarily severe. He countered with his own equation, which he claimed was valid for any shape of string. Not to be left out, Daniel Bernoulli followed with a third solution differing fundamentally from both d'Alembert's and Euler's.

THE "VIBRATING STRING" CONTROVERSY

And thus began the great "vibrating string" controversy. It turned into the most noisy and vituperative scientific dispute of the mid-century, drawing into battle all the leading geometers of Europe, which is to say, d'Alembert, Euler, Daniel Bernoulli, and later, Joseph Lagrange and Pierre Laplace.[73] (Even Diderot joined in the fray.) We may wonder what all the fuss was about. After all, was it not possible to test competing theories concerning the vibrating string through straightforward empirical analysis? Such, alas, was not the case. As an object of scientific inquiry, the vibrating string lies in the domain of both physics and mathematics; it can be fruitfully analyzed from a variety of perspectives.

For d'Alembert and Euler, the vibrating string was interesting on account of the mathematical problems it posed. Consequently, their research centred on general mathematical questions and methodology, and more specifically over the definition of an "analytic function" and how restricted this definition ought to be. Bernoulli, on the other hand, was more interested in explaining the physical behavior of the string itself than the abstract mathematical problems that engaged d'Alembert and Euler. Basing his work upon a careful empirical analysis of the vibrating string (much as Mersenne had done), Bernoulli concluded that its motion must be analyzed by a standing wave, and the only wave that conforms to this stipulation is one of Taylor's sines. In order to produce the irregular curvatures that Euler and

---

[73] A concise analysis of the vibrating string controversy, especially as concerns the methodological arguments, is by J. R. Ravetz, "Vibrating Strings and Arbitrary Functions," *The Logic of Personal Knowledge: Essays Presented to Michael Polanyi* (London, 1961), 71–88. Truesdell thoroughly covers the technical side of the controversy in "The Rational Mechanics," 237–50. Also worthy of mention is Piero Delsedime's article, "La disputa delle corde vibranti ed una lettera inedita di Lagrange a Daniel Bernoulli," *Physis* 13 (1971), 117–46.

d'Alembert attempted to represent by their various species of "functions," Bernoulli proposed a trigonometric expansion series.[74] In other words, the graph of any string undergoing periodic motion could be composed through the addition of infinitely many harmonically related sines (or, as he called them, "trochoids") with suitably adjusted amplitudes:

$$y = \alpha \sin\frac{\pi x}{a} + \beta \sin\frac{2\pi x}{a} + \gamma \sin\frac{3\pi x}{a} \ldots$$

These sines were nothing less than the upper modes of vibration he had discovered while investigating the dangling chain. By this theory, he believed he could account for all the harmonic overtones heard in a vibrating string. Thus, Bernoulli was arguing that overtones and the formula for the vibrating string, two subjects which had up to that point been considered as unrelated, were indeed related in the most fundamental way. Unfortunately, while this theory is essentially correct, there was no known general principle by which it could be proven. A rigorous mathematical proof would not be formally set down until the nineteenth century with the work of Fourier.[75] Thus, Bernoulli had recourse only to heuristic arguments of physical plausibility. For just these very reasons, however, Euler and d'Alembert rejected Bernoulli's solution.[76]

These difficulties notwithstanding, Bernoulli launched a scathing verbal attack upon Rameau. He argued that the *corps sonore*, as defined by Rameau, was a fiction. Many of the elastic bodies and air columns he studied did not emit the complete and strictly harmonic series of partials Rameau claimed. The inharmonic modes of vibrating rods and bars could coexist just as easily as could harmonic modes. On this basis, he concluded that

every *corps sonore* contains potentially an infinity of sounds and an infinity of corresponding ways of making its regular vibrations. Finally in each different kind of vibration the bendings of the parts of the *corps sonore* occur differently.[77]

Parodying an experiment undertaken by Rameau, Bernoulli found:

If you take an iron rod by the middle and strike it, you will hear at the same time a mixture of confused sounds which would be found by an experienced musician to be extremely unharmonious.[78]

---

74 "Réflexions et éclaircissemens sur les nouvelles vibrations des cordes exposées dans les mémoires de 1747 & 1748," *Histoire de l'Académie royale . . . de Berlin* 9 (1753), 147–72; "Sur le mêlange de plusieurs especes de vibrations simples isochrones, qui peuvent coexister dans une même système de corps," *Ibid.*, 173–95.

75 Fourier was to show that the solutions of Bernoulli and Euler were essentially in agreement once their respective terminologies and analytic perspectives were properly sorted out.

76 In the lengthy *Encyclopédie* article "fondamental," d'Alembert rebutted Bernoulli's theory with this objection: if vibrations truly could coexist, there would be no way for the smaller vibrations (higher frequencies) to be harmonic. For a string to produce an octave, d'Alembert pointed out, the middle node must precisely bisect the string and be absolutely stationary. Yet this is an ideal which is never achieved under normal circumstances owing to the distortions caused by the fundamental mode.

77 "Réflexions et éclaircissemens," 151.

78 *Ibid.*, 152–53.

Rameau, presumably an experienced musician, had of course come to quite a different conclusion, although one wonders whether his conclusion was based on real empirical evidence as much as wishful self-delusion. He stated in the sixth "experiment" of the *Génération harmonique* that if one struck a pair of tongs (*une pincette*), the resultant clang would quickly settle down and produce a harmonious sound.

Hang up some tongs by a slender thread, each end of which you apply to an ear. Strike it; you will perceive at first only a confusion of sounds, which will prevent you from discerning any of them. But as the highest ones gradually abate and as the sound diminishes in strength, the lowest sound of the whole body begins to seize the ear . . . along with which is distinguished its 12th and major 17th.[79]

Bernoulli would have none of this. Inharmonic partials were as natural as the perfect twelfth and major seventeenth, "from which one sees that the harmony of sounds heard in a *corps sonore* at the same time is not essential to it and *ought not to serve as a principle for systems of music*" (emphasis mine).[80] Bernoulli would often repeat this point in his writings. The idea that under normal circumstances every sonorous body emits harmonic overtones, let alone harmonic overtones delimited by the fifth partial, seemed absolutely preposterous to him.[81]

Euler apparently agreed with Bernoulli. In a letter to Rameau in 1752, Euler gently suggested to the composer, "I admit also that many sounds of musical instruments actually contain their octave, 12th, 15th, and 17th, although it seems to me that this mixture is not the rule and that there are also pure sounds."[82] Elsewhere Euler was more categorical. In a letter to Lagrange in 1759, he wrote,

As for musical tone, I am in perfect agreement with you, Sir, that the consonant sounds M. Rameau claims to hear in a single string derive from other vibrating bodies. And I do not see why this phenomenon ought to be regarded as the principle of music more than the true proportions which are their foundations.[83]

Euler refers here to a passage in Lagrange's *Recherches sur la nature et la propagation du son* that appeared in 1759. There Lagrange had attributed the càuse of overtones to sympathetic resonance:

But I confess that after much reflection, I have not been able to resolve this subject [overtones] satisfactorily. Having examined the oscillations of a stretched string with all the attention of which I am capable, I have found them always to be simple and singular in their motion throughout the length of the string, whence it appears to me impossible to conceive how different sounds could be generated at the same time. . . I am thus inclined

---

79 *Génération harmonique*, 17-18.
80 "Réflexions et éclaircissemens," 153.
81 In later writings, Rameau acknowledged that not all vibrating systems will emit a stable family of harmonic partials (*Observations*, 33; *CTW* III, 283). But he still insisted that this was due to imperfections of the vibrating object. In order that a vibrating system be able to sustain a true musical pitch (i.e. to be a true *corps sonore*), Rameau believed that it must sound its third and fifth partials (the perfect twelfth and major seventeenth). Otherwise the result would be just noise.
82 Letter dated September 13, 1752; reprinted in *CTW* V, 147.
83 Letter to Lagrange dated October 23, 1759; in *Correspondance de Leonhard Euler* in *Euleri Opera Omnia*, Series 4, vol. V, 425.

to believe that these sounds are produced by other bodies which resonate to the sound of the principal, just as one sees with [several] strings. Giving some credence to this conjecture [is the fact that] this *mélange* of harmonic sounds is audible only in a harpsichord or other instruments possessing several strings.[84]

In order to verify his conjecture, Lagrange suggests that someone "with an extremely fine ear" and "well experienced in hearing music" listen to a single vibrating string with no surrounding strings which might resonate sympathetically.[85] Lagrange obviously never seems to have undertaken this experiment himself.

Unlike Euler, Lagrange did not reject Rameau's theory on account of its suspect acoustical premise. On the contrary, he believed that it was still valid, but only because its principle was based upon a more fundamental acoustical truth: the coincidence theory of consonance. Lagrange believed the *corps sonore* to be the principle of harmony only because it was composed of intervals whose frequency ratios were the simplest. Lagrange concluded that Rameau's theory was at heart really based upon the same principle as Euler's.[86]

Throughout the entire vibrating string controversy, the only scientist who accepted *verbatim* Rameau's description of the *corps sonore* was d'Alembert. We are led to wonder, then, how d'Alembert reconciled Rameau's *corps sonore* with his research into the vibrating string. Surprisingly, the answer is that he did not. D'Alembert believed his wave equation accounted for the shape and motion of a string set into vibration, but he never claimed that it also accounted for harmonic overtones. In fact, d'Alembert saw the phenomenon of overtones, much as did his seventeenth-century predecessors, as an entirely separate issue. He did not believe it was his business as a mathematician to explain something in the domain of the physicist. Writing in 1761, he admitted:

One may object, perhaps, that it is impossible to explain by my theory why a string struck in various ways always renders much the same sound, since its vibrations, according to my theory, can be very irregular in many cases. I agree, but I am persuaded that the solution to this question does not pertain to analysis, which has accomplished all that could be expected of it. It is up to physics to handle the rest.[87]

The actual sounds produced by the *corps sonore* were clearly of no concern to d'Alembert in his calculations. It was not that he refused to recognize the empirical evidence for overtones, but rather that he simply did not believe it to be relevant to his particular concern, which was mathematical. Thus, he could admit that "the real movement of the string given by experience is very different from that which one finds by calculation," yet nonetheless insist upon the verity of his mathematical equations.[88]

---

84 Joseph-Louis Lagrange, *Oeuvres*, ed. M. Serret and L. Lalanne (Paris, 1867–92), I, 146–47.
85 *Ibid.*, 147.
86 *Ibid.*, 147–48. Lagrange admitted that in other respects, Rameau's theory was original and brilliant: "But this author will always have the merit of knowing he was the one to have deduced with the most extreme simplicity the majority of the laws of harmony that were made known through much scattered and blind experience."
87 "Recherches sur les vibrations des cordes sonores" in d'Alembert, *Opuscules Mathématiques*, 8 vols. (Paris, 1761), I, 40.
88 *Ibid.*, 41.

D'Alembert's faith that the true geometer need not – indeed, ought not – be overly concerned with accommodating all empirical evidence may strike the reader as somewhat paradoxical. Yet it was an attitude characteristic of d'Alembert's scientific epistemology, and indeed, much eighteenth-century science in general. In solving any problem, a scientist must invariably delimit the domain he investigates. This means knowing what to exclude from consideration as much as what to include. For eighteenth-century science, a certain amount of mathematical abstraction and disregard for physical evidence proved highly productive; by analyzing physical phenomena as a Cartesian problem of matter and impact, and quantifying such concepts as mass and force, the scientist may operate with a rigorous mathematical methodology without recourse to experimentation. It was with just such a methodology, Clifford Truesdell has pointed out, that the greatest strides were made in the eighteenth century in hydrodynamics, statics, astronomy, and optics, sciences for which he has coined the term "rational mechanics."[89] D'Alembert's research on the vibrating string is a case in point. Although the wave equation is not adequate by itself for describing the empirical phenomenon of the vibrating string, it proved to be a powerful mathematical tool with applications far beyond what d'Alembert could have envisioned.

Once d'Alembert had intellectually separated his mathematics from empirical phenomena, he could easily accept Rameau's description of the *corps sonore* as accurate. Indeed, what better witness is there for an acoustical phenomenon than the ear of a great musician?

Moreover, M. Rameau, possessing an ear upon which we can rely in this matter, tells us in the *Génération harmonique*, p. 17, that if one strikes some tongs, one will perceive first a confusion of sounds that cannot be distinguished, but as the highest sounds begin to die away insensibly as the resonance diminishes, a most pure sound of the entire body begins to seize the ear along with which is distinguished its 12th and its 17th.[90]

Empiricism and calculation each had an independently valid epistemological basis. If they seemed mutually inconsistent, that was only because our knowledge was so limited. D'Alembert had no doubt that there was some scientific explanation for overtones that would prove congruent with his calculations, but he did not pretend to offer one. In almost positivist fashion, he restricted himself to one clearly definable subject. He refused to erect ad hoc hypotheses (as he accused Bernoulli and Mairan of doing) to account for a poorly understood, even if well-confirmed, physical observation. D'Alembert believed it essential for a scientist to recognize the limits of his knowledge.[91] Thus it was that he chastised Bernoulli:

---

89 Clifford Truesdell, "A Program Toward Rediscovering the Rational Mechanics of the Age of Reason," *Archive for the History of Exact Sciences* 1 (1960). Nor is this characteristic only of eighteenth-century science. Recent historians of science have recognized that a good deal of the methodology historically followed by scientists is non-empirical, and even anti-empirical, contrary to the picture traditionally drawn by positivist historians. See Larry Laudon, *Progress and Its Problems* (Berkeley, 1977), especially 45–69.
90 *Encyclopédie*, s.v. "fondamental."
91 For a more detailed discussion of d'Alembert's scientific epistemology, see Ronald Grimsley, *Jean d'Alembert 1717–83* (Oxford, 1963), 246–68; and Hankins, *D'Alembert*, 104–31.

Let us recognize, then, that all these [overtones] are an enigma inexplicable by us. In effect, can one flatter himself to explain them by regarding the movement of the points of the string as composed of many others, by supposing fictitious anti-nodes and mobile nodes? There would be nothing, it seems to me, which could not be explained by so arbitrary a method.[92]

D'Alembert's criticism of Bernoulli underscores the excesses to which his own rationalist arrogance at times carried him. If his bias towards mathematical abstraction could lead him to brilliant insights, so, too, at other times could his disdain of experimental physics lead him astray.[93] He accuses Bernoulli of proposing an unfounded hypothesis for which d'Alembert the geometer can find no mathematical justification. Bernoulli's justification, of course, was entirely empirical. Long before, Sauveur had shown that a vibrating string did indeed contain various nodal points that were for all practical purposes stationary. It was precisely the experimental evidence that was Bernoulli's strongest defense. D'Alembert's unwillingness to appreciate this kind of evidence was certainly in Bernoulli's mind when he wrote to Euler several years earlier complaining about d'Alembert's research:

[D'Alembert] gave not the slightest attention to my experiments to verify how closely my physical hypothesis agrees with nature and whether my mathematical calculations satisfy the hypotheses of the physicist.[94]

What then of Bernoulli's conclusion that the *corps sonore* cannot serve as a foundation for harmony on account of its frequently inharmonic overtones? This conclusion, d'Alembert feels, is too "precipitous," since "in general, vibrating bodies generate very audibly the 12th and the 17th as M. Daniel Bernoulli himself has agreed."[95] If there are exceptions, d'Alembert insists, they are extremely rare, and "without doubt stem from some structure peculiar to the body which prevents it from truly being regarded as a *corps sonore*." He follows up Bernoulli's example of the tongs: "The sound of tongs, for example, may contain many discordant sounds. But also the sound of tongs is scarcely a harmonious and musical sound. It is more a dumb noise than a tone."[96] D'Alembert then goes on to reiterate that in any case, Rameau had confirmed that a pair of tongs will indeed sound an upper twelfth and seventeenth above its fundamental frequency after its other partials have died away.

92 "Recherches sur les vibrations des cordes sonores," 61.
93 We will see a clear example of this rationalist arrogance in Chapter 9 when we examine in detail d'Alembert's interpretation of Rameau's theory in his Elémens de musique.
94 Letter dated September 7, 1745. In Ph. H. Fuss, *Correspondance mathématique et physique de quelques célèbres géomètres du XVIIIème siècle* (St. Petersburg, 1843), 584. Yet Bernoulli could also be critical of Euler's mathematical abstractions. In a passage that ironically recalls d'Alembert's criticism of Rameau's rationalist excesses, Bernoulli wrote: "I do not the less value the calculations of Messrs. d'Alembert and Euler, which certainly include what is most profound and most sublime in all of analysis, but which show at the same time that an abstract analysis, if heeded without any synthetic examination of the proposed question, is more likely to surprise than enlighten us. It seems to me that paying attention to the nature of the vibrations of strings suffices to foresee without any calculation all that these great geometers have found by the most thorough and abstract calculations that the analytic mind has yet conceived" ("Réflexions et éclaircissemens," 148).
95 *Encyclopédie*, s.v. "fondamental."
96 *Ibid.*

It is ironic that Bernoulli's trigonometric expansion series offers one of the strongest scientific justifications for Rameau's principle conceived in the eighteenth century. Bernoulli showed that the only vibrations which a vibrating string can sustain without suffering decomposition are those harmonically related. Given, too, that the higher modes tend to decay more quickly than the lower modes, Rameau's claim that the vibrating string emits harmonic overtones delimited by the fifth partial is not altogether unreasonable. It is only when one analyzes more complex elastic bodies capable of sustaining multiple transverse waves (such as bells and rods) that one encounters conspicuously inharmonic modes of vibration. Had Rameau been satisfied to restrict his definition of the *corps sonore* to a vibrating string, then, perhaps he would have found in Bernoulli an ally instead of an antagonist.

As it turned out, it was d'Alembert who was on the composer's side. For the third time in his life, Rameau found himself relying upon a scientific colleague for support and protection. And as with Castel and Mairan in earlier years, this support came at a critical time. Just when the very scientific foundation of Rameau's principle of the *corps sonore* was being attacked by Bernoulli and Euler, arguably the most influential scientist in France came to the composer's defense.[97] It is true, of course, that d'Alembert did not provide a mathematical explanation of his own for the *corps sonore*, the correct explanation ironically being available to Daniel Bernoulli. The essential point is that a respected scientist corroborated Rameau's empirical description of the *corps sonore* as well as its invocation as the principle of harmony. For Rameau, who above all else wished to set music theory upon a firm scientific footing, the value of d'Alembert's support can scarcely be overestimated.

It must not be thought that d'Alembert's role with respect to Rameau's theory was merely one of corroborater, though. He also served as an advisor and critic, helping the composer to clear his theory of unnecessary and obviously bogus acoustical and mathematical baggage, including Mairan's atomistic hypothesis. The cleansing effect of d'Alembert's criticism is manifest in Rameau's next major treatise published after the *Génération harmonique*, the *Démonstration du principe de l'harmonie* of 1750. Here some more historical background is necessary.

THE *DEMONSTRATION DU PRINCIPE DE L'HARMONIE*

On November 19, 1749, Rameau read before a session of the Académie Royale des Sciences a "Mémoire ou l'on expose les fondemens du système de musique théorique et pratique." As Albert Cohen has documented, it was long considered the proper domain of the Académie to review and pass judgment upon musical questions pertaining to tuning systems, instrument design, pedagogical methods,

---

[97] By the early 1750s, d'Alembert was one of the most powerful figures in the Académie Royale des Sciences in addition to having influential connections among the aristocracy and philosophes. Inevitably his judgment carried with it a good deal of weight. Not the least significant manifestation of his power – and vanity – was his successful effort to block dissemination of Bernoulli's and Euler's work on the vibrating string in the pages of the Académie's *Mémoires* and the *Encyclopédie* (Truesdell, "The Rational Mechanics," 245).

and harmonic theories.[98] As the most prestigious scientific institution in continental Europe, the official approbation of the Académie was obviously highly coveted. This was precisely Rameau's goal with his "Mémoire."[99]

There are actually two different copies of the "Mémoire" surviving in manuscript. A lengthy copy described by Jacobi is found in the "Dossier Rameau" in the archives of the Académie Royale des Sciences.[100] The text of this manuscript is heavily rewritten and corrected. With minor variation, it corresponds to the text of the *Démonstration du principe de l'harmonie* published in 1750. But there is a second, much shorter version of the "Mémoire" that has gone unnoticed by historians in the archives of the Paris Opéra.[101] Unlike the "Académie Mémoire," this copy of the text is clean and without correction.[102]

I think that the "Opéra Mémoire" (as I shall refer to it) is the actual text Rameau read before the Académie. It is virtually identical to the longer "Académie Mémoire" up to the point where Rameau begins discussing technical matters of his theory (which is to say, up to about page 19 of the *Démonstration*). The "Opéra Mémoire" presumes no practical knowledge of music and concerns general philosophical, historical, and scientific issues related to Rameau's discovery of the *corps sonore*. In both content and length, it would have been an appropriate text to read before an audience of Académie members.

Rameau begins his lecture as he did in many of his other writings, by criticizing the ancients for failing to identify the *vrais fondements* of music. Relying solely upon experience, they allowed themselves to be misled into positing the simplest interval ratios (octave, perfect fifth, and perfect fourth) as the principle of their music. Of course, the condition of the "moderns" is no better, Rameau adds. Musicians, too, have relied upon experience and authority for their rules of music, without having looked carefully into nature to see if she might offer a more certain means. Rameau, of course, took it upon himself to seek a more firm basis in nature using the methods so gloriously applied by his scientific audience. Rameau then recounts the "method" of Cartesian introspection by which he arrived at his principle of the *corps sonore*. (I have quoted part of this section on page 12 above.) In the remainder of the "Opéra Mémoire" he elaborates – although he provides no technical details – how the *corps sonore* furnishes just the natural and scientific basis for which he was searching. Anyone as wise and knowledgeable as the members of the Académie,

---

98 Cohen, *Music in the French Royal Academy of Sciences*.
99 The "Mémoire" was not Rameau's first contact with the Académie; some thirteen years earlier he had dedicated and submitted his *Génération harmonique* to the Académie in order to secure similar approval. Despite the support of Mairan at that time, though, Rameau's hopes for an official approbation went unfulfilled.
100 *CTW* III, xliii–xlv; VI, 191–93.
101 *F–Po* Ms. B 24 (8) fols. 119–128v.
102 The manuscript is found in a collection of musical writings copied out by François-Paul Boisgelou (1697–1764), an aristocrat and amateur music theorist and scientist. According to Laborde, Boisgelou was a fervent admirer of Rameau's music theory, although critical of a number of scientific arguments made by the composer, arguments that Boisgelou attempted to improve in his own writings (Jean Benjamin de Laborde, *Essai sur la musique ancienne et moderne*, 4 vols. [Paris, 1780], IV, 587).

he continues obsequiously, must surely appreciate and recognize what a great discovery the *corps sonore* is. Rameau closes his lecture by again asking the scientists to grant his theory their official seal of approval, and reminding those remaining skeptics that his theory may be seen to be vindicated in his own "practical applications" – presumably meaning his operas – that today enjoy such public approval.[103]

This, then, is the lecture Rameau read before the Académie on November 19, 1749. Evidently he had earlier distributed supporting material for "a new music system by Mons. Rameau."[104] These notes could well have consisted of technical details that were later incorporated into the "Académie Mémoire" that was subsequently published as the *Démonstration* in 1750.[105] But Rameau evidently felt it unnecessary, and probably inappropriate, to explicate technical details of his theory in a public lecture.

There is much more to be said about both the contents as well as the rhetoric of the *Démonstration*, and we will return to this document in the next two chapters. For now it is appropriate to emphasize that no publication of Rameau's was as blatantly a *scientific* text as the *Démonstration*. Even the *Génération harmonique,* for all its experimental apparatus, was still largely a practical work, containing as it does a lengthy chapter on the rules of composition (Chapter 18). There is nothing in the *Démonstration*, however, that can be considered as remotely "practical." The entire aim of the text is to "demonstrate" how the *corps sonore* is the unique principle of music. Significantly, Rameau does this without a single bit of musical notation. Once he gets beyond the methodological prolegomenon by which the *corps sonore* was "discovered," he proceeds to generate in quasi-geometric fashion subsequent musical materials: melodic half steps, the diatonic tetrachord, the triple progression, cadences, the major mode, dissonance, the minor mode, and the chromatic and enharmonic genres – again, all without any musical notation. This was accomplished with such terseness and precision that even those without any knowledge of music theory or ability to read musical notation could follow and understand his arguments without problem.[106]

---

103 The "Opéra Mémoire" closes with this comment: "Voilà, messieurs, tout ce que je pouvais vous dire des fondemens de mon système sans entrer dans des détails de pratique . . . et il me semble que, si les musiciens n'étoient pas satisfaits de ma théorie, qu'ils ne sont pas en état d'entendre. Le public étoit content de l'application que j'en ai fait jusqu'à présent dans la pratique" (fol. 128v).
104 Cohen, *Music in the French Royal Academy of Sciences*, 83.
105 This hypothesis explains well, incidentally, why the "Académie Mémoire" is written by two different hands. The first fourteen pages of the manuscript are in a clean and polished script and represent most of the original lecture found in the "Opéra Mémoire." The text thereafter, in Rameau's unmistakably spindly handwriting, represents his later emendations and elaborations. This part of the text seems to have been in constant revision up to the point when it was finally set by the printer.
106 Interestingly, the only other major theoretical publication of Rameau with no musical notation was his practical treatise on accompaniment, the *Dissertation* of 1732. His reasons for excluding musical notation there were quite different, though, than in the *Démonstration*, and had to do with its intended readership. He aimed the former work at beginning students who wished to learn to accompany and compose skillfully "even without knowing how to read music." Rameau's "new method" of accompaniment, as we saw in Chapter 3, was designed precisely to avoid using musical notation, a goal he soon thereafter abandoned owing to its impracticality.

As was customary, a committee of Académie members was appointed to review the submitted "Mémoire." D'Alembert and Mairan were among those selected. This marked d'Alembert's first exposure to Rameau's theory. Indeed, it was probably his first exposure to any music theory of a sophisticated nature. Yet despite this handicap, he was able to read and master Rameau's "Mémoire," and, indeed, he became an enthusiastic supporter of the composer's ideas. As head of the reviewing committee, it was d'Alembert's duty to write a summary for the Académie. He accomplished this task brilliantly. In a remarkable document, he effectively presented the content of Rameau's expanded "Mémoire" in clear and lucid prose.[107] After some forty-five pages of quite technical narrative, he concluded with the flattering salute we have quoted in Chapter 1, pp. 6–7.

Rameau soon thereafter published his "Mémoire" – proudly bound with the committee report – as the *Démonstration du principe de l'harmonie*. In the interim, though, he had made a number of changes in the text, not the least significant being its new title. Erwin Jacobi has pointed out that the original manuscript of the "Académie Mémoire" was significantly revised upon publication; numerous passages and whole pages were crossed out or covered with revisions pasted over the original manuscript.[108] He has suggested that it was Rameau who made these changes. According to Jacobi's reconstruction of events, after the original "Académie Mémoire" had been read and approved by the committee, the composer surreptitiously inserted these alterations in order to introduce material – such as the title – to which they would have undoubtedly objected. And indeed, there is much evidence for this; in latter years, when the relations between Rameau and d'Alembert had distinctly soured, d'Alembert would chastize Rameau for having presumed that his theory was "demonstrated," let alone that the Académie would have sanctioned such a claim.[109]

Yet not all of Rameau's changes were of this kind. It is just as reasonable to assume that many of the alterations were made at the request of the Académie. Indeed, based upon my own examination of the "Académie Mémoire," it is evident that many of the changes actually clarify or correct material found in the original. A good example is Rameau's sympathetic resonance theory of the minor triad.

REVISIONS OF ACOUSTICAL GENERATION: THE MINOR TRIAD

By 1750 it was recognized by most informed scientists that Mairan's atomistic hypothesis was untenable. D'Alembert, for instance, was able to expose a number of fallacies in his *Encyclopédie* article "fondamental." For one thing, d'Alembert pointed out, if individual air particles behave by purely mechanistic interaction, as Mairan claimed, they must follow strictly defined laws of motion and impact.

---

[107] Printed as the "Extrait des registres" and appended to the *Démonstration*.
[108] *CTW* III, xliii–xlv.
[109] See Chapter 9, pp. 262–63.

There is no reason, though, why the oscillations of one particle should activate only those particles whose natural frequency differs by integral divisions or multiples. And having recently written the most important study of dynamics since Newton – the *Traité de dynamique* of 1744 – d'Alembert was quite familiar with the behavior of colliding rigid bodies. There was no physical law he knew that could possibly support Mairan's hypothesis. More damaging to Mairan's thesis, though, was d'Alembert's demonstration of the longitudinal propagation of sound with the wave equation.[110] Axiomatic to a longitudinal wave theory is the presumption that air is a homogeneous mass that responds uniformly to all displacement forces, contrary to Mairan's hypothesis that air is composed of heterogeneous particles. It seems plausible, then, that it was d'Alembert who informed Rameau of the dubiousness of Mairan's theory soon after he had submitted his completed "Mémoire." At the point in the "Académie Mémoire" where Rameau speaks of the minor triad, a sympathetic resonance theory similar to the one proposed in the *Génération harmonique* is crossed out.[111] Pasted over this material is a new explanation of the minor triad that firmly renounces the sympathetic resonance theory.[112] In its place, Rameau offers a "modified sympathetic resonance" theory. Essentially, Rameau admits strings tuned a twelfth and seventeenth below a sounding string do not resonate sympathetically as a whole, but rather only in aliquot parts corresponding to the frequency of the sounding string. This would produce a series of unisons. Rameau then lamely claims that this experiment still demonstrates the source of the minor triad, even though the triad is never acoustically sounded.

Needless to say, the modified sympathetic resonance theory is an even weaker acoustical justification than the original theory. How can Rameau claim that such sympathetic resonance is the acoustic origin of the minor triad when that triad is not even heard? Rameau's answer to this is weak indeed:

One cannot suppose the resonance of these multiples in their totality in order to form a harmonious whole without deviating from the first laws of nature... But does it not suffice to find in this proposition the indication of the perfect [minor] chord which can be

---

110 Clifford Truesdell, "The Theory of Aerial Sound 1687–1788," in *Euleri Opera Omnia*, Series 2, Vol. XIII, xxxvii.
111 A section in the "Opéra Mémoire" that is found in neither the "Académie Mémoire" nor the *Démonstration* confirms that Rameau's initial idea was to retain the original resonance theory: "I looked once again outside myself and considered the phenomenon of the *corps sonore*, seeing if it could not offer me the sound that I was lacking. And this time I succeeded. I perceived the taut strings vibrating and even making the other strings resonate. I looked at this phenomenon more closely, and saw to my great satisfaction the fifth above and below the fundamental sound vibrating. At last, I told myself, all the sounds that were missing are found, and the sufficient explanation for my predilection for these fifths whose truth I sensed through experience" (fol. 123v).
112 "Académie Mémoire," fol. 27. The passage in question begins on p. 64 of the *Démonstration*: "pour former un accord parfait où le *genre mineur* ait lieu. . . ." One wonders, incidentally, how Mairan reacted to all this criticism considering he was on the very reviewing committee for a work that repudiated his own scientific theory. Mairan never got along well with d'Alembert, whom he believed to be an arrogant young upstart. The two had earlier engaged in a polemic concerning the utility of philosophical systems for science. Nonetheless, by 1750 it was clear that an atomistic hypothesis of sound propagation offered to the physicist more problems than it solved, a conclusion Mairan himself was eventually forced to concede.

formed from it? Nature offers nothing useless, and we see most often that she is content to give to art simple indications to put it on its way.[113]

This argument is hardly convincing. One could have tuned just about any two strings below a sounding string so long as each had at least one upper partial that corresponded to the fundamental of the higher string. By his own reasoning, nature no more indicates the minor triad than it does the diminished-seventh chord.[114]

But even granting Rameau this point, there is a second problem with far more serious musical consequences. (This is a problem with the original "sympathetic resonance" theory, too.) What is to be the fundamental of the minor triad? If a chord's generator is to be the same as its fundamental, then the upper fifth of a minor triad must assume this role. Not only is this counter-intuitive, though, it also wreaks havoc with his rules governing the progression of the fundamental bass. Rameau concedes that by one's musical judgment, the lowest sound of the minor triad is the fundamental. Even though the C in Example 6.1 "theoretically" generates the lower twelfth F and seventeenth A♭, the ear takes the F to be the true fundamental of the chord. The reason is that the ear assigns acoustical priority to the harmonic proportion of the major triad. Rameau explains this in his *Génération harmonique* as follows:

Since it is necessary to consider that the harmonic proportion is the only one whose tones strike the ear in the resonance of the *corps sonore*, this [proportion] is consequently the only one by which we ought to be guided such that everything ought to be subordinate to it. Thus since the lowest and predominating sound of a *corps sonore* is always, in the judgment of the ear, the fundamental sound, it is necessary to suppose that it will be the same with the arithmetic proportion.[115]

Rameau is thus forced to sever the connection he had earlier made between chord generation and root attribution; but since it is precisely the point of his theory that these should be identical, he finds himself in an untenable position. Of course he is in an untenable position only by virtue of having implicitly adopted the arithmetic series to define the minor triad, much as Zarlino had done 150 years earlier. Precisely because of this conflict, Rameau had rejected the arithmetic series as the source of the minor triad in his *Traité*.[116] But caught up as he was with the notion of acoustical generation now, Rameau finds himself slipping willy-nilly into Zarlino's dualism.

Rameau is acutely aware of his problem, for after acknowledging the problems with his original sympathetic resonance theory of the minor triad in his *Démonstration*, and suggesting the "modified sympathetic resonance" theory, he goes on

---

113 *Démonstration*, 65.
114 Rousseau found this aspect of Rameau's theory particularly absurd. "The strings [tuned to the lower 12th and 17th], according to [Rameau], vibrate and tremble through their whole length, but do not sound. This seems to me to be a most strange physics. It is as if one said that the sun shines but one sees nothing." *Oeuvres complètes*, 12 vols. (Paris 1872), vol. 6: *Essai sur l'origine des langues*, Chapter 19.
115 *Génération harmonique*, 36–37.
116 Book 1, Chapter 4.

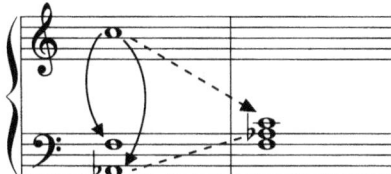

Example 6.1 Generation of the minor triad through the "sympathetic resonance" theory

to offer an entirely new and incompatible explanation of its origin. Rameau begins by reasserting the primacy of the *corps sonore*. A sounding tone emits only higher harmonic partials. This is the "pure and simple operation of nature" and "the foundation of all harmony and all succession."[117] It is to this principle that we must look for the origin of the minor mode:

> What does nature intend? She wishes that the principle which she has once established give the law everywhere, that everything relate to it, everything submit to it, everything be subordinate to it – harmony, melody, order, mode, genre, effect, in short, everything. So, as regards these unions of multiples [Rameau means here the modified sympathetic resonance theory], one can only conclude that the principle forcing them to combine in this way reserves for itself, yet further, so to speak, the right to determine the variation that the new genre can bring, which the multiples indicate in what has already been produced.[118]

Rameau's new solution is to posit the notion of "co-generation." An A minor triad is formed by the third partial of A, and the fifth partial C. These two fundamentals together generate an upper E. This is somewhat akin to the "phonic" explanation of the minor mode propounded in the nineteenth century by Arthur von Oettingen, and, in a modified fashion, by Hermann Helmholtz. I do not think it is quite accurate to say, as does Shirlaw, that Rameau was directly anticipating Helmholtz, for Rameau's explanation was based upon quite different principles than Helmholtz's.[119]

Rameau's argument runs as follows: The major mode of C is determined by the major seventeenth C–E generated by the root C. The true foundation of harmony, though, is the perfect fifth, C–G, for the fifth "as is now known, constitutes the harmony and determines the proportion upon which all the fundamental succession of the mode depends."[120] This is confirmed by the triple geometric progression of

---

117 *Démonstration*, 62 and 64.
118 *Ibid.*, 67.
119 Shirlaw, *Theory of Harmony*, 236. Helmholtz was not concerned with chord roots as Rameau was. Helmholtz analyzed a chord with respect to the harmoniousness of its constituent pitches, determined by the relative concordance of their respective upper partials. The fundamental of a chord was the pitch whose upper partials were maximally coincidental. Rameau had a more musical but less scientifically rigorous notion of a fundamental. In his theory, the harmonic root of the minor triad was always the prime, whereas the mediant could equally well be taken as a "fundamental" in Helmholtz's theory depending on the inversion and spacing of the triad (Hermann Helmholtz, *On the Sensations of Tone*, trans. and ed. Alexander S. Ellis [London, 1885], 294–95). There was a theorist from Rameau's own day who did anticipate something of Helmholtz's ideas, though – Pierre Estève. We will briefly look at a few of Estève's ideas in Chapter 8.
120 *Démonstration*, 71.

the fundamental bass which consists of a chain of fifths (a topic we will consider in detail in the next chapter). In the *Traité* and *Génération harmonique,* the third is assigned the task of defining the genre of the mode. Rameau, however, modifies this observation in the *Démonstration*. Instead of the genre being determined by the kind of third found directly above the root, it is now determined exclusively by the position of the major third within the fifth. This may sound like a mere semantic change; shifting upwards the position of the major third, after all, will still produce a minor third above the fundamental. But Rameau is really emphasizing an important distinction.

The only third which is acoustically generated by a *corps sonore* is the major third. Consequently, if the different modes are to have an acoustically generated origin, then it is the major third which determines the genre, and the perfect fifth which determines the mode. Genre is thus defined by the position the major third holds within the fifth. Taking the major third C–E as an example, we can place it within the perfect fifth span C–G, or within the perfect fifth span A–E. In the latter case, it shares with A the role of generator. A is subordinate to C as concerns the genre of the mode, although it is fundamental in regards to the tonic of the mode (see Example 6.2). As a subordinate generator, Rameau means that the fundamental A "is forced to follow, in all cases, the law of the first generator" (which is C).[121] In other words, A minor shares its scale with C major, and is strongly controlled by its harmonies and progressions. He calls this the "grande communauté de sons" and the "entrelacement" of modes. This is a verity which any sensitive musician will affirm; the mediant of the minor mode does indeed exert a strong pull upon the tonic. But in respect to the determination of the mode, Rameau adds, A assumes for itself its rightful role as fundamental by virtue of its fifth relation to E.[122]

The most obvious problem with this theory is that we have two generators. Shirlaw has claimed, "here we find not one fundamental note, but two; the note regarded by Rameau himself, and by the vast majority of musicians since his time, as the real fundamental note of the minor harmony appears as an added and foreign tone, derived from no one knows where."[123] But this is not the quandary Shirlaw

---

[121] *Ibid.*, 72.

[122] *Démonstration*, 62–84. The co-generative theory of the minor triad – one of Rameau's most important and original theories – also seems to have been a last-minute addition to the manuscript. (How else can one account for two contradictory accounts of the minor triad in the same treatise?) As with the first discussion of the minor triad in the "Académie Mémoire," this second discussion is also heavily rewritten. Indeed, entire pages have been pasted over with new material. But exactly how much all of this is new or simply a rewording of the original manuscript is impossible to say without being able to remove the scraps of paper for a comparison of texts. Unfortunately, both Erwin Jacobi and I were refused permission by the authorities of the *Académie* to make such a comparison (*CTW* VI, xviii).

There is another possible scenario, though. The "co-generative" theory is present in the *Extrait* written by d'Alembert. This raises the possibility that it might have been d'Alembert who suggested the idea to the impressionable Rameau. This was a purely acoustical idea that d'Alembert the physicist could easily have conceived. And it is telling that in all his published theoretical writings, d'Alembert repeated this theory, even when Rameau dropped it! We will return to d'Alembert's ideas on this topic in Chapter 9.

[123] Shirlaw, *Theory of Harmony*, 237.

Example 6.2 Generation of the minor triad through the theory of co-generation

makes it out to be. Rameau is quite explicit as to where the added tone comes from: it is the fundamental of the relative major mode that so intertwines itself in the minor mode that it acts in essence as a co-generator.[124] Unfortunately for Rameau, he never articulated this distinction very clearly in the *Démonstration*, mixed up as his discussion was with the "modified sympathetic resonance" theory of the minor mode. For the reader of Rameau's text, the result was a confusing and contradictory explanation of the minor mode.[125]

In most ways, though, the *Démonstration* marks a major improvement in reasoning over the *Génération harmonique*, particularly in its abandonment of Mairan's atomistic hypothesis. Now Rameau could claim that overtones were intrinsic to the *corps sonore* itself, and not the result of some mechanical collision of air particles taking place outside of it. This was indeed a more attractive proposition for Rameau from a philosophical viewpoint. The *corps sonore* was the unique source for all these harmonic partials. Every vibrating string thus contains in itself the germ of all music.

The *corps sonore* – which I rightfully call the fundamental sound – this single source, generator, and master of all music, this immediate cause of all its effects, the *corps sonore* I say, does not resonate without producing at the same time all the continuous proportions from which are born harmony, melody, modes, and genres, and even the least rules necessary to practice.[126]

Ironically, this brought Rameau back to much the same ontological position he had articulated in the *Traité de l'harmonie* some twenty-eight years before.

Rameau did not offer in any of his later writings a physical explanation of the *corps sonore*. As we have seen, buoyed by d'Alembert's corroboration, he obviously felt no need to offer one. Writing in 1752, he could confidently assert:

124 The theory of "co-generation" was applied systematically by a contemporary of Rameau's, the Swiss theorist Jean-Adam Serre. In his *Essais sur les principes de l'harmonie* (Paris, 1753), Serre severely criticized Rameau for not accepting the full implications of his theory of co-generation by failing to recognize that two separate and equal generators formed the minor mode. In his harmonic analyses, Serre would indicate this co-generation by placing two notes for the fundamental bass below a minor triad – its prime and mediant. Serre expanded this idea to include double and even triple fundamentals for dissonant chords, an idea d'Alembert also suggested. Even disregarding the question of how a musician is to make sense of a double or triple root, Serre's theory would make utterly useless the various species of fundamental bass motion Rameau identifies, since he provides no criteria by which one may prioritize the various roots.
125 We should note again that Rameau never returned to the "co-generative" theory of the minor triad after this, citing only the "modified sympathetic resonance" theory. His reason was clear: he wished to emphasize that there was but *one* origin, and hence *one* fundamental for harmony commensurate with the fundamental sound of the *corps sonore*.
126 *Démonstration*, 19–20.

As soon as the *corps sonore* vibrates, it divides itself into aliquot parts and produces as a consequence different sounds. Can we know at present what is the principle of this division? It is one of those first causes the understanding of which is above our faculties, and for which the true philosophes today search.[127]

As d'Alembert had argued, it was enough for the scientist (and musician) simply to recognize and accept the *corps sonore* as an empirical reality without having to provide any kind of formal explanation. With the *corps sonore* established as a legitimate – even if ill-understood – scientific observation, Rameau now had a seemingly unshakable empirical foundation upon which to build his system of harmony. In the following chapter we shall examine what further consequences Rameau's adoption of the *corps sonore* as his new principle of harmony would have for the rest of his theory.

[127] *Nouvelles réflexions de M. Rameau sur sa démonstration du principe de l'harmonie* (Paris, 1752), 3; *CTW* V, 100.

7

MODE AND MODULATION

We have seen how the fundamental bass was foreshadowed in many ways in the seventeenth century. Ideas such as the generative fundamental, chordal inversion, the cadential parsing of phrases, and the concatenation of dissonance were ones for which Rameau could find precedents – however scattered they may have been throughout the speculative and practical music literature. Such was not the case for the concept of key, though. In all of his publications, we see Rameau groping to find words and models that could elucidate critical features of the nascent tonal key system. In the *Traité* he made some progress toward this end. But he was unable to work out a more complete and systematic notion of tonality, encumbered as he was by older modal conceptions that proved incompatible with these tonal intuitions. The real maturation of Rameau's tonal theory would take place only in his writings postdating the *Traité*, not coincidentally after he had adopted the *corps sonore* as the new principle of harmony.

The tonal features that we will see increasingly dominating Rameau's attention involve the content and behavior of harmonies within a key, and, on a higher structural level, the relationship of keys to one another. In the *Traité,* as we have seen in Chapter 5, Rameau's attention was focused for the most part upon the mechanics of the fundamental bass. While the cadential models he posited could account for local chordal successions, they failed to provide any broader understanding to how a key was delimited and expressed. There was a term theorists of Rameau's day used to describe such a feature: "modulation." But the word came to be used by Rameau in a sense quite different from what his contemporaries understood by it, and, for that matter, different from how we understand it today. To see what these differences are, and hence just where the challenges lay for Rameau, we need first to review the older notion of modulation. We will then delve into his discussion of mode found in the *Génération harmonique* and the *Démonstration*. While Rameau's arguments there are dense, they constitute the heart of his mature music theory. However abstract they may seem, the problems he addresses are critical ones that have formed the crux of almost every sophisticated theory of tonality since.

SEVENTEENTH-CENTURY THEORIES OF "MODULATION"

Modulation was a term widely used in the seventeenth century to designate in the broadest sense the expression of a mode. A "mode" was defined, it will be recalled, not as a collection of pitches (akin to our modern scale) but rather as characteristic intervallic and melodic patterns. In the Renaissance modal system, these characteristic intervals and patterns made up the *species, repercussio, differentiae,* and *ambitus* of a mode.

Of course by the beginning of the eighteenth century, most musicians had to worry about only two modes – the major and minor. With the exception of a few pockets of conservatism in ecclesiastical circles, the modal system had largely died out by Rameau's day.[1] On the other hand, musicians did have to know how to transpose these two modes – a novel and baffling concept for most of them. Hence at the turn of the century we find dozens of transposition primers published in order to aid musicians in this challenging new skill, and to help them learn the many key signatures associated with these transpositions.[2] Despite the evolution in tonal language, though, most theorists in the generation immediately preceding Rameau still thought of a mode in much the same way their Renaissance predecessors did: as comprising characteristic intervallic and melodic features. The art of "modulation" was commensurate with the proper articulation and expression of these salient modal features, as Masson succinctly puts it: "the manner of beginning, conducting, and concluding a piece of music through pitches and notes appropriate to each mode or key."[3]

There were of course many new features of musical practice that Baroque musicians had to consider with respect to modulation to which received modal theory offered little guidance. Certainly the most critical of these was harmony, or more accurately, chordal succession. One could no longer speak of a mode only in terms of its characteristic intervallic and melodic patterns; it was also necessary in Baroque practice to consider the characteristic chordal constituents and progressions exhibited in the thorough bass. Still, this did not alter in any fundamental way the traditional ontological conception of mode.

In Chapter 3 we have already looked at one of the most ubiquitous practical guides by which Baroque musicians codified and taught basic chordal vocabulary and syntax: the *règle de l'octave*. We recall that the *règle* originated as a rule of thumb for harmonizing an unfigured diatonic bass line. The progression codified by Campion (given in Example 3.1) provided an easy and generally reliable guide for the beginning accompanist and composer as long as the bass line was not too

---

[1] For a review of modal theory in the seventeenth and eighteenth centuries, see Joel Lester, *Between Modes and Keys: German Theory 1592 – 1802* (Stuyvesant, N.Y., 1989).

[2] One of the most popular was Alexandre Frere, *Transpositions de musique, réduites au naturel par le secours de la modulation* (Paris, 1706). Even Rameau felt obliged to add a guide on transposition in the supplement of his *Traité* (incorporated into Chapter 25 of Book 2).

[3] *Nouveau Traité*, 9.

complicated. At the same time, since the *règle* was considered to be a paradigmatic harmonization of a mode, theorists recognized that it was itself a quintessential *expression* of that mode. Hence the *règle* could serve as a basis for a composer or improviser wishing to "modulate" harmonically within a mode.

Francesco Gasparini prescribed the *règle de l'octave* for just this purpose in his influential keyboard treatise of 1708. In a chapter on "modulazione," the student encounters a series of partially-harmonized scale progressions in twenty-one major and minor keys.[4] Gasparini includes the partial *règle* not as a mechanical prescription for realizing an unfigured bass (although he certainly recognizes it can fulfill this function), but as a model for improvisation, or, as he puts it, "to provide assurance in the technique of modulating through all the keys." By learning how to concatenate the *règle de l'octave* in various keys, and further by varying it with "diminutions, embellishments, and adornments" (as Chapter 10 of Gasparini's treatise is entitled), the performer has a palette of musical ideas upon which to draw. By the middle of the eighteenth century, it is as a modulatory model for the free fantasy (and not as a prescription for unfigured bass realizations) that the *règle de l'octave* was most often advocated.[5]

RAMEAU'S THEORY OF MODULATION (I)

When Rameau speaks of modulation in the *Traité*, he has the *règle de l'octave* very much in mind. "Modulation," he tells us, "immediately reveals the key in use and consequently the place a certain note occupies in this key, the chord it should bear, and the fundamental sound which may be implied, supposed, or borrowed there."[6] He elaborates upon this definition in four lengthy and important chapters of Book 3 in which he quotes the *règle*, and analyzes its harmonies and fundamental bass in detail (see Example 7.1).[7] Rameau does not use the designation *règle de l'octave*, however; he calls the progression simply the "general example of the octave ascending as well as descending." In line with the mechanistic model of the fundamental bass propounded in Book 2, we see how Rameau analyzes the progression exclusively in terms of consonant triads and dissonant seventh chords connected by the fundamental fifth progression. In m. 2, where the *règle* suggests a root succession of an ascending second (C to D), Rameau interpolates a fundamental bass A.[8] The primary scale degrees of the key articulated by the *règle de l'octave* are the tonic and dominant, both of which are the only ones to take

---

4 Francesco Gasparini, *L'armonico pratico al cimbalo* (Venice, 1708); translated by Frank Stillings as *The Practical Harmonist at the Harpsichord* (New Haven, 1963), Chapter 8, "Remarks on How Best to Master Accompaniment in Every Key: How to Modulate Well, Anticipate, and Pass Properly from One Key to Another."

5 I have discussed this important – but little recognized – use of the *règle* in my article "The *Règle de l'octave* in Thorough-Bass Theory and Practice," *Acta Musicologica* 64/2 (Fall, 1992), 91–117.

6 *Traité*, 135; Gossett, 148–49.

7 *Ibid.*, Book 3, Chapters 9–12.

8 Note that no added-sixth chord is indicated in the fundamental bass, even though one is suggested on the ascending fourth scale. However, in a second quotation of the *règle* found in Book 4, Rameau does analyze the chord in this manner (*Traité*, 382–83; Gossett, 396–97).

Example 7.1 *Traité*, 213

"perfect chords" (i.e. 5/3 triads). All other scale degrees take some variety of sixth chord, representing either an inversion of a consonant triad, or an inversion of a dissonant seventh (dominant) chord. The point Rameau wishes to draw from his analysis is that the variety of chords traditionally taught as indigenous to each scale degree in a mode (i.e. the *règle*) are products of the fundamental bass.

It will be recalled that Rameau had earlier insisted that consonant triads occur only on tonics, and therefore any tonic can be reciprocally defined by the presence of a consonant triad. Technically, then, the fundamental bass analysis Rameau gives to Example 7.1 establishes G as tonic three times in the *règle de l'octave*. But we must also remember Rameau's further stipulation that a tonic is defined by the *cadence parfaite*, necessitating a *dominante-tonique* chord resolving to a consonant triad.[9] (Presumably an imperfect cadence can also fulfill this role.) Hence, the G major triads in m. 3 and 5 cannot be true tonics, since neither one is preceded by a *dominante-tonique*.

M. 6 is another matter. Here the G major triad is preceded by what seems to be a bona-fide *dominante-tonique* with the introduction of the chromatic F♯ in the alto voice, creating a chord of the "small sixth" (6/4/3). "All notes which, descending," Rameau tells us, "precede a note bearing the perfect chord should bear the chord of the small sixth."[10] The G chord in m. 6, then, must indeed be a tonic, since it is preceded by such a chord, and it thus "may always be regarded as a tonic note."[11] But Rameau contradicts himself several pages later when speaking of this same chord. He writes: "the dominant might appear to be a tonic note, its real nature being revealed only by means of the note which follows it."[12] In other words, with the introduction of the "chord of the tritone" on F, we know that we are [still?] in the mode of C. The question of whether a true change of key has occurred thus arises. And here we encounter the second meaning of modulation with which we are familiar today – modulation as key change.

When Rameau speaks of leaving a key in the *Traité*, he most commonly uses the expressions "changement du ton" or "passer d'un ton à l'autre." In a few

---

[9] *Traité*, 146; Gossett, 160. [10] *Traité*, 209; Gossett, 229.
[11] *Traité*, 205; Gossett, 225. [12] *Traité*, 214; Gossett, 233.

places, however, he uses the term "modulation" to suggest a change of keys.[13] Some historians have drawn a rigid distinction between these two senses of modulation, suggesting that there is a fundamental incommensurability between the two.[14] In the older meaning of modulation, one remains *within* a mode by playing appropriate notes, chords, and progressions, while in the latter meaning one digresses *outside* the mode. But the distinction was never so clear-cut in the eighteenth century. For Baroque musicians, a key change need not have entailed the strong tonal rupture that is suggested by a simplistic Roman-numeral analysis. One could change a *ton* and still remain, so to speak, in the original mode.[15] Movement to keys built upon closely related scale degrees, in other words, was as much an idiomatic and proper part of "modulation" (*within* a key) as was the articulation of diatonic melodic progressions (*of* a key).[16]

For eighteenth-century musicians, the most closely related keys were those whose tonics were diatonic in the original key, or as Rameau put it, were "formed from notes found within the octave of the original key."[17] There are five such keys in any mode. In major modes, they are the second through sixth scale degrees, while for minor modes, they are the third through seventh scale degrees. As Rameau notes with delight, these scale degrees relate to the tonic by basically the same intervals that guide the fundamental bass. In other words, the largely consonant intervals that connect the roots of most adjacent chords also help define those key areas that stand in closest "rapport" with the tonic.[18]

In Chapter 23 of Book 3, Rameau lays down some guidelines as to how these keys can be employed in a good "modulation." He advises first that the tonic key be established well at the beginning: "No matter in what key we begin, we should modulate in this key for at least three or four measures."[19] We should then pass to the dominant, and onwards to other related keys, making sure that such "modulations" (that is each articulation of a new key) are appropriate to the original key, not tarrying too long in any one, nor returning too often to the same key, and

---

13 For example in the title of Chapter 23 in Book 3: "On how to pass from one Key to another; i.e., on how to Modulate" (*Traité*, 248; Gossett, 267). In the *Génération harmonique,* Rameau proposed the term *transposer* to refer to the changing of mode (*Génération harmonique*, 79).

14 E.g. William S. Mitchell, "Modulation in C. P. E. Bach's *Versuch*," in *Studies in Eighteenth-Century Music: A Tribute to Karl Geiringer,* ed. H. Y. C. Robbins Landon (London, 1970), 333–34.

15 This is why Alexandre Frere, when he wished to speak of a true change of mode, used the seemingly oxymoronic term "modulations transposées." *Transpositions de musique*, 11.

16 For a good discussion of this topic, see Cynthia Verba's article "Rameau's Views on Modulation and Their Background in French Theory," *Journal of the American Musicological Society* 31/3 (1978), 467–79.

17 *Traité*, 250; Gossett, 268.

18 But Rameau cannot push the homology of key changes and the fundamental bass too far. Although keys will occasionally connect by descending seconds, this is forbidden to the fundamental bass. Also, we do not find in key relationships the preponderance of falling fifths as we do in the fundamental bass. Thus while tempted in Chapter 23 to draw a strong connection between key change and fundamental bass motion, Rameau ultimately refrains from proposing this as an axiom in his theory. Interestingly, it is Schenkerian theorists who are more prone to conflate hierarchical levels by equating the "foreground" syntax of voice-leading with more background "tonicizations."

19 *Traité*, 248; Gossett, 267.

Example 7.2 *Traité*, 252

finally making sure we firmly restate the original key at the end. In the following chapter, Rameau illustrates one possible series of modulations in the music given in Example 7.2. We see that all of the five primary diatonic scale degrees of C major (i.e. D, E, F, G, and A) are articulated by various combinations of perfect and irregular cadences (although a few "keys" are touched on without any cadential confirmation). There is also a very brief movement to B♭ – the flat seventh.[20] We may recall here another analysis by Rameau, already looked at in Chapter 5, that was to offer an illustration of "perfect" modulation: Lully's monologue from *Armide*. Lully's music touches on all the primary diatonic keys related to the tonic E minor in judicious proportion. Far from these modulations weakening the sense of tonic, they in fact reaffirm it.

We can now begin to see how the notion of modulation as key change is hardly a radical change in meaning; rather, it is a natural evolution from the older notion. The diatonic scale degrees that constitute the appropriate chords and harmonic successions needed for a good modulation are the same ones that constitute appropriate key changes. The difference is really one of hierarchy. When Rameau looked at Example 7.2, he would say that there are six independent modulations, meaning that there are six keys affirmed *through* a modulation. It is really only a small shift in nuance to speak of a modulation "in" a key and modulation "to" a key. Rameau could thus define modulation in the *Code de musique* simply as "the art of conducting a melody and its harmony as much in the same key as from one key to another."[21] Theorists throughout the eighteenth century continued to use the term

---

20 Rameau offers a narration of another potential series of modulations in his *Nouveau système*, 42.
21 *Code de musique pratique*, 135.

"modulation" in both senses, without seeing any fundamental incompatibility between the two.[22]

RAMEAU'S THEORY OF MODULATION (II)

For all that "key changes" were seen as an acceptable component of good modulation, theorists came to recognize that not all key changes were of equal tonal weight. In Example 7.2, the "modulations" to B♭ in measure 19 and to A minor five measures later (among others) are obviously weak ones given that they lack any cadential confirmation using a characteristic dissonance. In the *Traité*, Rameau made some feeble attempts at distinguishing degrees of "modulation" based upon the closeness of the new key to the original tonic, and the degree of confirmation for the new key.[23] But it was only with the *Génération harmonique* and his practical composition treatises, "L'Art de la basse fondamentale" and the *Code de musique pratique*, that Rameau worked out a clearer distinction between the main tonic and more transient tonics.

In the *Génération harmonique*, Rameau introduces the concept of "implied" tonic (*censée tonique*).[24] Any diatonic triad can be made into a tonic if it is approached by a fundamental fifth progression and confirmed by a leading tone, thus establishing the new key. If, however, the triad is not confirmed by a leading tone, but still approached by a fifth (thus imitating one of the primary cadence types), then the chord is *censée tonique*. Rameau is thereby suggesting that there are differing degrees of modulation. He moves further in this direction in his composition manuscript, "L'Art de la basse fondamentale." There he reaffirms the five diatonic keys which stand in closest rapport with the tonic.[25] Now, however, he views all modulations as hierarchically subsidiary to the original tonic key. There is only one *tonique principale* (or *véritable tonique* as he sometimes calls it).[26] Rameau also offers two new and weaker categories of modulation. A *tonique passagère* is a diatonic triad that is approached by some fundamental bass progression other than a perfect fifth, while the *tonique étrangère* is a non-diatonic triad whose root belongs to the principal key.

A concrete illustration of Rameau's ideas on subsidiary tonics is found in Gianotti's *Guide du compositeur* (see Example 7.3).[27] Using for now the fundamental bass with only consonant triads, Rameau categorizes the various chords according to their relationship to the main tonic. (The topics of dissonance and chordal

22 See e.g. Rousseau, *Dictionnaire de musique*, s.v. "modulation."
23 See his comments on p. 262 of the *Traité* (Gossett, 281).
24 *Génération harmonique*, 173.
25 "L'Art de la basse fondamentale," fol. 27.
26 *Ibid.*, fol. 28, fol. 44v. In the *Code de musique pratique* of 1760, Rameau called the main tonic the "Ton régnant" (pp. 43–44).
27 Pietro Gianotti, *Le Guide du compositeur* (Paris, 1759). The reader is reminded to consult Appendix 2 for a history of Gianotti's *Guide*. The section in question is from Chapter 8, Part 1 of the *Guide*: "De la possibilité de passer d'une tonique à une autre par tous les intervalles consonnans, & des toniques étrangères ou passagères dans le ton qui existe" (pp. 41–44). The corresponding chapter in Rameau's "Art" is Chapter 13, Part I: "Du passage d'une tonique a une autre des notes sensées toniques, et des toniques etrangères ou passagères" (fols. 27r–29r).

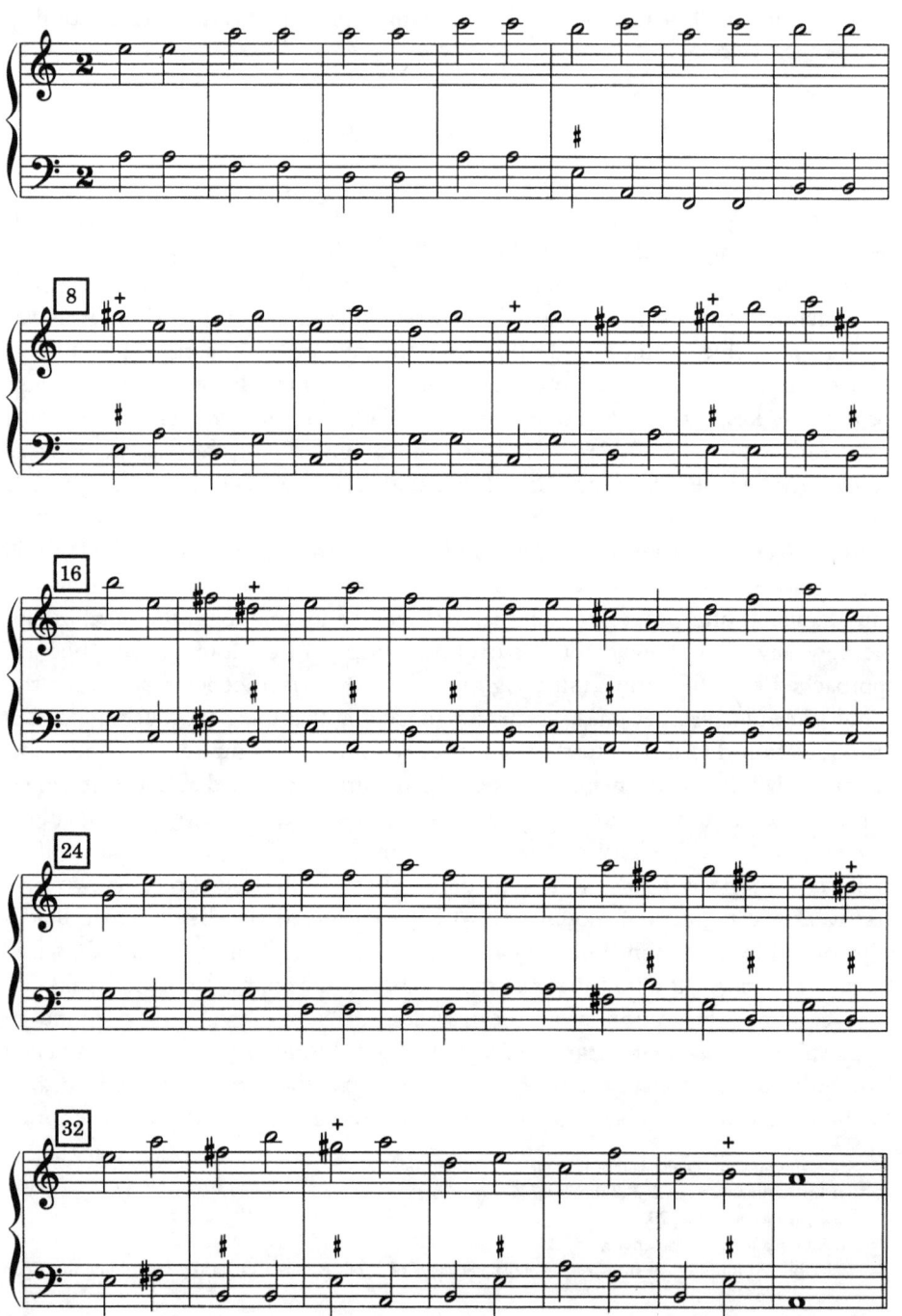

Example 7.3 Gianotti's *Guide*, Ex. 13, Plate 5

inversion are not discussed until much later.) To begin with, we can see that there are a number of modulations in this progression to the primary scale degrees of A minor, even lacking the characteristic dissonant seventh of a dominant modifier. Based upon criteria laid out in the previous chapters, key areas can be identified at mm. 10 (C major), 15 (A minor), 16 (G major), 18 (E minor), 19 (D minor), 24 (C major), 30 (E minor), and 34 (A minor). Each of these represents a new tonic, although A minor remains the "principal" tonic of the whole piece. The G major triad in m. 25 – a *dominante-tonique* of the key of C major – is *censée tonique* since it is approached by a fifth progression and takes place on a strong beat (suggesting an imperfect cadence) but lacks the confirmation of a leading tone. As examples of lesser degrees of tonic confirmation, Rameau calls the F major triad and D minor triad in mm. 2–3 *toniques passagères* since they are all consonant and diatonic, yet are not approached with the fundamental fifth in the bass, nor confirmed by the leading tone (*Guide*, p. 43). The D major chord in m. 13, on the other hand, is a *tonique étrangère* since it contains an accidental non-diatonic to the principal key of A minor.

These are remarkable distinctions, indicating a clear awareness of tonal hierarchy not seen again until the nineteenth century. I should add that Rameau was neither always very clear nor consistent in his use of these terms. He causes further confusion by ambiguously introducing terms such as "imaginée tonique" (p. 48), "réputée tonique" (p. 130), "modulation étrangère" (p. 173), and "toniques successives" (p. 218).[28] Nonetheless, his essential thesis is clear: all chords and key changes form a hierarchy of tonal relations that are subordinate to one tonic key, and together constitute a single "modulation."[29]

Even with this more nuanced view of key change, there still remained for Rameau the problem of accounting for the principal chords and key areas that constituted a good "modulation." As we have seen, the fundamental fifth progression that he posited as the primary motion of the fundamental bass was quite successful in accounting for localized cadential motion. Likewise, his differentiation between implied, passing, and foreign tonics offered a welcome clarification of chord hierarchy. What was needed now was an explanation that could unify both these ideas. Simply put, Rameau needed to demonstrate how a single mode could be both a cause and an expression of tonal coherence. His initial conception of mode, as we have seen, was dependent upon seventeenth-century theory, even if updated with harmonic garb. But beginning with the *Nouveau système* of 1726, and

---

[28] The notion of "implied" tonic was picked up by a number of subsequent theorists, particularly by Jean-Laurent de Bethizy, *Exposition de la théorie et de la pratique de la musique* (Paris, 1754). Some historians have asserted that Rameau got the idea of "reputed" tonics from Bethizy, since the *Code* – the only published work of Rameau that had hitherto been known to have discussed the topic in any detail – was published after Bethizy's *Exposition*. But as we have seen, Rameau was teaching this idea much earlier.

[29] It is supremely ironic that the twentieth-century theorist who holds a conception of modulation most resembling Rameau's is Schenker. For Schenker, key changes did not constitute moves outside the original tonic but rather temporary tonicizations of keys that were ultimately subsumed on a more background level as scale degrees within the tonic key. Cynthia Verba is the first historian of whom I am aware to note this connection: "Rameau's Views on Modulation and Their Background," 467–79.

especially in the *Génération harmonique* of 1737, Rameau revamped his definition of mode, severing most of the connections to these received conceptions.

THE GEOMETRIC TRIPLE PROGRESSION

We have seen in Chapter 6 how Castel was responsible for bringing to Rameau's attention Sauveur's acoustical research. There was evidently a second piece of scientific information conveyed by Castel, which, while perhaps less sensational, proved to be equally catalytic: the *geometric progression*.[30] A geometric progression is any numerical series expanded by a common multiple, or, as Rameau defined it, "a series of terms that all have the same quotient."[31] There are three particular geometric progressions that will interest Rameau. They come from the three fundamental partials that are generated by the *corps sonore*: the octave (2), the perfect twelfth (3), and the major seventeenth (5). The geometric expansion of each of these terms produces, respectively, the "double geometric progression" (1–2–4–8–16, etc.); the "triple geometric progression" (1–3–9–27–81, etc.); and the "quintuple geometric progression" (1–5–25–125–625, etc.).

Rameau was attracted to these geometric progressions because they concisely modeled the most important movements of the fundamental bass. Since the ratios between any two adjacent terms within a geometric progression are identical, the ascending triple geometric progression models a succession of ascending fifths C–G–D, etc. (presuming, of course, octave reductions). The quintuple geometric progression models a succession of major thirds C–E–G♯, etc., while the double geometric progression (1–2–4–8, etc.) models a succession of octaves.[32]

Of course all these progressions are not generated directly by the *corps sonore* as the harmonic and arithmetic progressions are. But Rameau argues that they can still be considered as emanating from the *corps sonore* since the individual ratios comprising each series are present as a simultaneity, and thus suggest the possibility of expanding these ratios into a linear progression. Here is Rameau's explanation in the *Génération harmonique*:

Once this principle is well understood, one sees how only the intervals of the octave, fifth and major third can be made to succeed one another at first. Then, as the ratios of these intervals are recognized, it is easy to imagine progressions determined by each of these ratios, in order to see what their product will be and to derive from this product the advantages that can be expected from it.[33]

Rameau became fascinated by these geometric progressions. In a "Table of progressions" contained in the *Nouveau système*, he determines the triple progression to the twenty-eighth term (a "C quadruple sharp") and the quintuple progression to

---

30 As mentioned on p. 110 above, Castel claimed he had imparted some mathematical ideas to Rameau in the course of their earlier conversations. Rameau introduced the idea of a geometric progression along with other new mathematical terms in the "Préliminaires de mathématique" of the *Nouveau système*, 8–17.
31 *Ibid.*, 11.
32 *Ibid.*, 13.
33 *Génération harmonique*, 42.

the seventh term (also a "C quadruple sharp").³⁴ Because these geometric progressions involve justly tuned ratios, the higher terms suffer increasing discrepancies of a comma (81/80) from their enharmonic equivalents. (The C quadruple sharp derived from Rameau's triple progression, for instance, is shown to be seven full commas flatter than an E natural.) Rameau indicates these comma discrepancies with ciphers in his table, and calculates exactly the resulting interval ratios. (These differences were incidentally one of the primary catalysts for Rameau embracing equal temperament in the *Génération harmonique*.) We thus see how Rameau once again attempts – as he did in the *Traité* – to show how the progression of the fundamental bass is related to the generation of chords. Now that the *corps sonore* validates the third and fifth partials as primary, it was logical, he argued, that their ratios become the basis of a geometric expansion series.

There were several consequences that Rameau drew from his new geometric series that would be critical in his reformulation of mode. Most important, the triple geometric progression suggests the importance of fifth relations to the tonic. We know from Rameau's convoluted discussion of cadence in the *Traité* that he considered the fifth to be the interval that constituted the fundamental progression of the bass. The geometric progression helped to crystallize in Rameau's mind this interval as a *continuous* series, and moreover one that was valid in either direction. The fifth *below* the tonic was as much a part of the expanded triple geometric progressions as was the dominant *above* the tonic. Much to his delight, Rameau discovers that by bringing in this lower term – which he christened the *sous-dominante* – he had stumbled upon a harmonic relationship that enjoyed both empirical and theoretical confirmation.

THE SUBDOMINANT

If Rameau was actually not the first theorist to have recognized the tonal significance of the subdominant, he was certainly the first to designate it by that name and examine its function in a systematic way. In 1717, an obscure Scottish pedagogue, Alexander Bayne, had already listed the fourth scale degree along with the dominant and tonic as "the three most principal and fundamental notes wherein the harmony chiefly depends."³⁵ Bayne's justification for this was his own *règle de l'octave* (named the "Stated form of a Bass in all the usual keys"), which utilized "perfect" chords on scale degrees 1, 4, and 5. Most other theorists did not accept this harmonization of the scale, though. The fourth scale degree was almost universally harmonized in ascending as a "chord of the small sixth" (6/5), while in descending it became the chord of the tritone (6/4♯/2).

The reason for the lack of value accorded the fourth scale degree by most theorists was that it simply was not considered to be one of the *nottes essentielles* of a mode. For French theorists of the seventeenth century, these essential notes were

---
34 *Nouveau système*, 24.
35 A[lexander] B[ayne], *An Introduction to the Knowledge and Practice of the Thoro-Bass* (Edinburgh, 1717), 7.

those defined by Zarlino as comprising the *harmonia perfetta*: the final, dominant, and mediant. They represented pitches appropriate for a melody to emphasize and upon which to cadence. As a cadence point, the fourth scale degree was considered less fundamental than either the dominant or mediant.[36] As a modulatory goal, the fourth scale degree was considered equally irregular in Baroque music, at least in comparison to the other primary scale degrees.[37] When designated at all by French theorists, the fourth-scale degree was referred to as the *soudominante* (not to be confused with Rameau's *sous-dominante*).[38] It was the scale degree directly below the dominant, just as the leading tone was below the tonic and so sometimes referred to as the *soutonique*.

In the *Traité*, as we have just seen, Rameau had not yet worked out his mature conception of mode involving the subdominant. In this work, the filiations to a more conservative seventeenth-century theoretical tradition are obvious by his references to the subdominant simply as "la quatriéme notte." When he discussed the fundamental chord types in his argument with Montéclair, he itemized, besides the tonic, the simple dominant on the second scale degree, the *dominante-tonique*, and the diminished-seventh chord on the leading tone in minor.[39] But he did observe a number of special qualities about the fourth scale degree that set it apart from the other (non-dominant) ones. For example, he distinguished it as one of the only scale degrees other than the tonic and dominant that may habitually receive a consonant triad.[40] Elsewhere, he recommended the fourth scale degree as the optimal key to move to in a chromatic progression.[41] And finally, Rameau did at times suggest that the added-sixth chord on the fourth scale degree might be a kind of fundamental chord, as we recall from his convoluted discussion of the irregular cadence and analyses such as Example 3.3 and Example 5.5.

With the discovery of the geometric progression, Rameau came to recognize a greater importance for the subdominant, or perhaps more properly, he found a formal validation of it. Along with the dominant, it becomes one of the terms of a triple progression that defines the tonic. Most crucially, any three triads related by the triple geometric progression (1–3–9) comprise and reciprocally constitute a mode. Whereas Rameau's earlier definition of a mode concerned the melodic ordering of tones within an octave,[42] his new definition emphasized mode as a *harmonic relationship* determined by the triple geometric progression.[43] "Mode in music is nothing but the prescribed order between sounds by the triple proportion, whether together or separately, which is to say, whether in harmony or melody."[44]

---

36 German theorists termed cadences on the fourth scale degree *clausulae peregrinae* (Mattheson) or *auserordentlich* (Heinichen).
37 A conclusion affirmed by Elmar Seidel, "Über eine besondere Art Bachs, die Tonart der IV. Stufe zu Verwenden," *Musiktheorie* 1/2 (1986), 139–52.
38 E.g. Jean-François Dandrieu, *Principes de l'accompagnement du clavecin* (Paris, 1719), Plate VI.
39 *CTW* VI, 57. See also Example 3.2.
40 *Traité*, 232; Gossett, 252. As we have just seen, in later writings Rameau considerably expanded the number of scale degrees that could receive triads by invoking his new categories of "implied" and "passing" tonics.
41 *Traité*, 286; Gossett, 304. 42 *Traité*, 143; Gossett, 157.
43 *Génération harmonique*, 64. 44 *Démonstration*, 34.

Mode and modulation

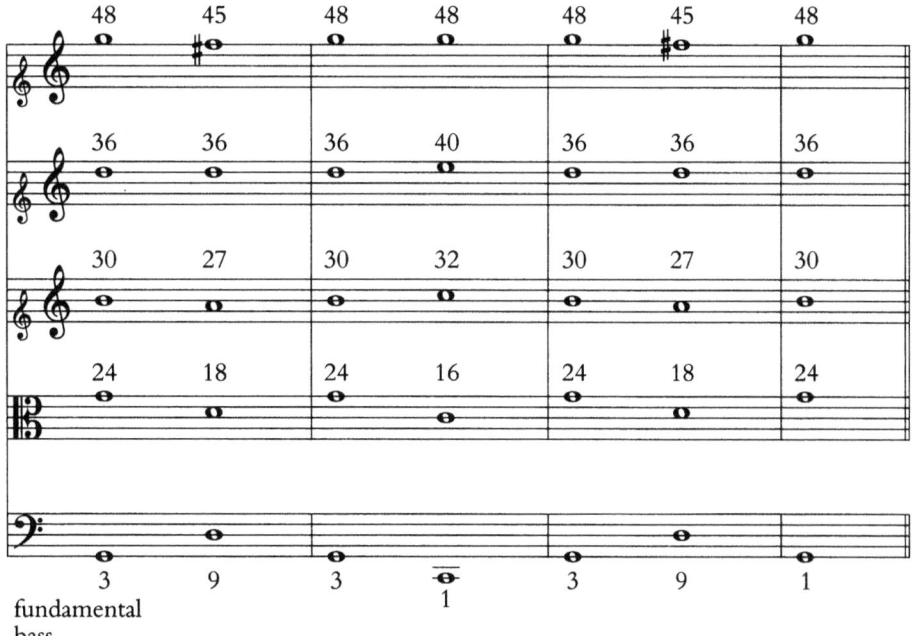

Example 7.4 Rameau's generation of semitones and whole tones

Rameau arrived at this radical redefinition of mode by rethinking how the diatonic scale – the ostensible progenitor of mode – could be generated by the three terms of the triple geometric progression. He first notes that the simple alteration of the fundamental bass by a perfect fifth automatically produces a number of diatonic successions in the upper voices. In other words, the progression 1–3 (C–G) can generate the major semitone B–C, the major whole tone C–D, and the minor whole tone D–E. In the same way, the progression 3–9 (G–D) can generate F♯–G, G–A, and A–B (see Example 7.4).[45]

Much to his delight, he also discovers that these very same semitones and whole tones correspond to the ancient Greek tetrachord. By joining the two tetrachords built upon B and E conjunctly, Rameau believes he has discovered the origin of the Greek diatonic modal system. It is none other than the fundamental bass determined by the geometric triple progression (see Example 7.5). "It is astounding," he marvels, "that the Ancients thus discovered one of the first consequences of the principle without having actually recognized this principle."[46] He concludes that

---

[45] *Nouveau système*, 33.

[46] *Génération harmonique*, 60. The historical basis of Rameau's arguments is obviously precarious, although, given the general state of knowledge of ancient Greek music at the time, not entirely ludicrous. Beginning in the late 1720s, much information was being conveyed to French readers concerning Greek music theory in the *Histoire* of the Académie Royale des Inscriptions et Belles Lettres, particularly by the polyglot historian Pierre-Jean Burette. Burette argued that Greek musicians did not practice harmony as the "moderns" do, but sang only monophony or primitive kinds of organum. Still, the various kinds of proportions and genres that Burette described concerning Greek music theory may well have been one of the catalysts for Rameau's discussions of these same topics in the *Génération harmonique*.

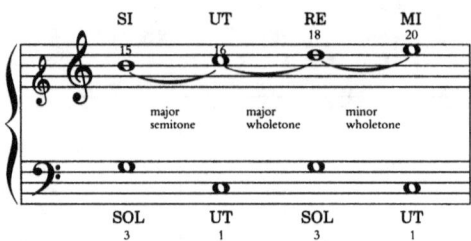

Example 7.5 *Génération harmonique*, Plate 5

this fact proves how far the ear can take us, but, when not guided by reason, also lead us astray.[47]

The fundamental bass progression of the perfect fifth, Rameau observes, must clearly be the origin of diatonic melody. By combining the two adjacent tetrachords given above, it is possible to construct all the notes of a diatonic scale. The three notes of the fundamental bass that comprise these two tetrachords can be rearranged as follows, taking C as the first term, and G and D as 3 and 9, respectively (see Plate 7.1). G thus assumes the function of tonic, D the dominant, and C the subdominant.[48] Rameau has dropped the term *dominante-tonique* in the *Nouveau système* since the relation of a "dominant" to the tonic is now determined in the context of the triple progression (although in his later publications, such as the *Code*, he retains the designation).

We can see in Plate 7.1 how Rameau is able to harmonize the complete G major scale using only the geometric triple progression 1–3–9. Notice, however, how he has avoided connecting the sixth and seventh scale degrees of the scale, since such a connection would require the support of non-adjacent terms from the geometric progression: 1–9. This succession, resulting in a fundamental bass motion of a whole step (C to D), is prohibited in Rameau's theory. His immediate reason for proscribing the use of non-adjacent geometric terms in the generation of mode is that such a progression will generate consonances that are a comma too large. This is also why musicians instinctively have difficulties in singing three whole tones in succession, he claims. Rameau's more global argument is that the fundamental progression of the perfect fifth must be in all cases represented so to maintain *liaison* (common tones) in the generation of the diatonic scale. Regardless of this discrepancy, though, Rameau triumphantly concludes that he has shown mode to arise from the triple progression of the fundamental fifth originating in the resonance of the *corps sonore*. How wrong it is for musicians to think that it is the diatonic system that is the true foundation of music when it is in reality but a consequence of harmony!

Appealing as his new definition of mode appears to be, it causes a number of problems. First, the triple progression by itself cannot determine which note is

---

[47] Rameau would further develop his ideas about ancient music and its origins in his later writings. We will look at some of these arguments in Chapter 10.
[48] *Nouveau système*, 38.

Plate 7.1 *Génération harmonique*, Plate 6

tonic, for every term is related by an identical ratio to any adjacent term. In order to distinguish the central tonic from its surrounding dominants, we need something that uniquely defines the tonic. Since the tonic itself cannot be altered as a perfect consonance, this alteration must occur within the dominants by means of some characteristic dissonance.[49] These dissonances are the familiar ones we have encountered already in the second Book of the *Traité*: the seventh on the *dominante-tonique*, and the added sixth on the subdominant. In the *Génération harmonique*, Rameau is no longer hesitant about labeling the added sixth a fundamental dissonance. He delights in the seemingly endless number of symmetries it creates with the dominant. The same minor third is added above and below the harmonic and arithmetic proportions, respectively, and both resolve to the same note: the determining third of the mode. In the case of the dominant, the added sound is the fundamental of the subdominant, while for the subdominant the added sound is the fifth of the dominant (see Example 7.6).

Of course in practice the dissonance added to the subdominant is found *above* the triad, creating an added sixth. But this is only because the fundamental of the subdominant should be found in the bass to reflect its subordination to the harmonic proportion of the dominant.[50] The fact that this chord of the added sixth is identical to the inversion of a dominant on D, far from being the embarrassing discrepancy it was in the *Traité*, now becomes a rich new musical resource. It can be interpreted as assuming either function, depending upon the context of the bass.[51]

---

49 *Génération harmonique*, 108.
50 *Génération harmonique*, 113.
51 Ibid., 115.

Example 7.6 Characteristic dissonances added to the dominant and subdominant

This "double employment" (*double emploi*) will be shortly called into service when Rameau tries anew to generate the scale with his fundamental bass.

In the *Génération harmonique*, Rameau uses the added sixth on the subdominant to retackle an issue with which he had such problems in the *Traité*: the "irregular" cadence. Confident now that the subdominant scale degree as well as the added-sixth chord are both fundamental structures, he has no fears in assigning this cadence equal status with the perfect. Indeed, to emphasize its symmetrical relation to the perfect cadence, he renames it "imperfect" (*imparfaite*).[52] Now we have two fundamental cadence types governed by fifth motion that approach the tonic from opposite directions: the perfect and imperfect cadences.[53]

A second problem that arises with the new definition of mode concerns its generation. By taking the triple progression 1–3–9 as the model of a mode, it would seem that the subdominant (term 1) is the generator. This makes no tonal sense, though, since Rameau obviously wants the central tonic to be the generator from which the dominants radiate outward in opposite directions. Alas, the *corps sonore* cannot generate the fourth scale degree. Thus Rameau must abandon the Platonic axiom of the *Traité* that unity is both source and generator. "The major system cannot begin on unity or any other number that doubles it since its fourth cannot be found in these numbers."[54] Instead, Rameau must posit the term 3 as generator of the triple progression (or, as he does in the *Démonstration*, the term 9).

A number of observers have considered this to be one of the most significant failings of Rameau's theory. Shirlaw, for instance, finds the problems of reconciling the generation of the geometric progression (which is one-directional) with the tri-functional modal system (which is symmetrical) to be almost fatal.[55] For partly this reason, d'Alembert called the use of geometric progressions a "ridiculous abuse of geometry" and "illusory."[56] But I do not think Rameau's problems with the geometric progression are quite as grievous as his critics make them out to be; both Shirlaw and d'Alembert misconstrue the nature of these numbers. The geometric progression is not the generative series the harmonic or arithmetic proportions are. Rather, it is an enchainment of ratios that remain invariant, whether ascending or descending. The actual number taken as a base is really besides the point, which is

---

52 This is the original name that Nivers had given to the cadence where a bass ascends a perfect fifth. In the *Traité*, Rameau had reserved the term *cadence imparfaite* to designate any cadence whose harmonies were inverted (*Traité*, 257; Gossett, 279).
53 Evidently unconcerned about any inconsistencies, Rameau reverts in the *Code de musique pratique* to calling this cadence *irrégulière* (p. 38).
54 *Nouveau système*, 36.
55 Matthew Shirlaw, *The Theory of Harmony*, (London, 1917), 140–41.
56 *Elémens de musique* (1762), xii.

Table de la progreſſion Triple & Soutriple.

$$\left\{\begin{array}{c} \text{folb. réb. lab. mib.ſib.fa. ut.ſol. ré. la. mi ſi. fax.} \\ 729\ 243.\ 81.\ 27.\ 9.\ 3.\ 1.\ \frac{1}{3}\ \frac{1}{9}\ \frac{1}{27}\frac{1}{81}\frac{1}{243}\frac{1}{729} \\ \text{Arithméthique.} \qquad ♭ \qquad \text{Harmonique.} \end{array}\right\}$$

Plate 7.2 *Génération harmonique*, 43

why Rameau felt free to have 3, 9, or 27 represent the tonic as he saw fit. In his discussion of mode, Rameau chose numbers other than the prime to represent tonic only so as to avoid the use of fractions (⅓–1–3). But ontologically the tonic was not a numerical term; it was an actual sound.[57]

Rameau was clearly fascinated by the symmetrical features of his new geometric definition of mode. Through the geometric progression, he could model both a descending and ascending series of proportions, each of which is projected by the multiples and divisions of the arithmetic and harmonic series, respectively. With the *tonique*, nature generates harmonic and arithmetic series in opposite directions, from which are derived the dominant and subdominant functions, respectively. These two terms serve as the "limit" of the mode. Each radiates out from the tonic center in opposite directions, yet each is ultimately drawn back to that center. The modal universe Rameau now describes is no longer the rigorously mechanistic, directed chain of dominants found in the *Traité*. Instead we seem to have a more dynamic and entropic model of chord relationships. The function of the mode can now be understood as a kind of solar system, where the tonic represents a large body like the sun drawing smaller planets from all directions towards its own center. It was not a coincidence, I think, that the illustration Rameau uses to display this relationship in the *Génération harmonique* (reproduced as Plate 7.2) replicates so strikingly textbook illustrations of a heliocentric solar system. As I hope to show now, there were important changes taking place in contemporaneous understandings of celestial mechanics that display surprising parallels with Rameau's theoretical revisions of mode. I suspect that this scientific information was appropriated by our attentive composer ever on the alert for interesting and useful ideas related to his theory.

NEWTONIAN GRAVITY AND TONAL ATTRACTION

We have seen in Chapter 5 how a mechanistic philosophy underlay Rameau's initial conception of tonal motion. Following the fundamental premise of the mechanistic philosophy that the only real causative agent in nature could be matter impacting upon matter, Rameau found in the seventh chord just such a motive

---

[57] In Chapter 10 we will see Rameau attacking this problem anew, armed with occasionalist arguments.

agent. Through the percussive force of its dissonance, each seventh chord was impelled to move by a fundamental fifth progression until some final consonant resolution was reached.

Mechanistic explanations of all phenomena, as I suggested, were much in vogue in the seventeenth century. As Fontenelle put it, they were considered the only acceptable kind of explanations for the "moderns." Yet the mechanistic philosophy was not uniformly triumphant. Numerous natural phenomena proved recalcitrant to mechanistic explanations, particularly in the biological sciences. Nowhere were the weaknesses of Descartes's mechanistic views shown to be more spectacularly deficient than in his theory of vortices.

Vortices (*tourbillons*) were the ethereal particles Descartes hypothesized as filling the universe, and which swirled around all astral bodies in regular circular motions. It was by means of these vortices that Descartes was able to offer a purely mechanistic explanation of all planetary and lunar orbits. While there were a number of empirical difficulties posed by the theory of vortices, it was indubitably a mechanistic explanation, and one easy to conceive.[58] (One of the aims of Fontenelle's *Dialogues*, from which we quoted in Chapter 5, was to popularize the notion of vortices.)

Newton, of course, rejected Descartes's theory of vortices. In his *Philosophiae naturalis principia mathematica* of 1686, he offered an alternative theory involving universal "attraction" or "gravitation." In Newton's theory, planets orbit around the sun not because they are propelled and restrained by whirling vortices, rather because they are kept in place by an unseen force called gravity. And this force – contrary to Descartes's opinion – could indeed operate over a void. What is gravity? Newton never offered an answer. It was not necessary in his view to proffer a mechanical explanation as to gravity's nature. In a classic illustration of his positivistic restraint from speculation, Newton was satisfied to observe the effects of gravity and deduce from them his inverse-square law of attraction:

But hitherto I have not been able to discover the cause of those properties of gravity from phenomena, and I feign no hypotheses; for whatever is not deduced from the phenomena is to be called a hypothesis, and hypotheses, whether metaphysical or physical, whether of occult qualities or mechanical, have no place in experimental philosophy. In this philosophy particular propositions are inferred from the phenomena and afterward rendered general by induction. . . And to us it is enough that gravity does really exist and act according to the laws which we have explained, and abundantly serves to account for all the motions of the celestial bodies and of our sea.[59]

---

[58] Rameau's early Cartesian sympathies might well have led him to entitle one of the harpsichord pieces contained in his second book of *Pièces de clavecin* (1724) "Les Tourbillons."

[59] Isaac Newton, *Philosophiae naturalis principia mathematica*, 2 vols. (London, 1686), vol. II, General Scholium, 547. Newton's statement that he will "feign no hypotheses" (*hypotheses non fingo*) does not mean, incidentally, that he eschews the proposing of any causal explanation altogether. Here he is only referring to the perniciousness of positing a mechanical explanation without having sufficient knowledge of the phenomena to justify such an explanation. As many Newtonian scholars have pointed out, though, in many other places Newton is not at all hesitant in proffering explanatory hypotheses.

The notion of gravity was quickly attacked by Cartesians, who saw in it nothing but the discredited "occult forces" of Aristotelian physics. How was it possible, they demanded, that two bodies could act upon one another through a vacuum without some kind of mechanistic causation? We know today that the Cartesian accusation was more accurate than they may have realized; much of the inspiration for Newton's conception of gravity came from hermetic and alchemic teachings disseminated in England during the seventeenth century with which he was actively (if somewhat clandestinely) involved.[60] A belief in hidden forces and attractions permeating all of nature was a common denominator in hermetic thought. In any case, it was not because of any hermetic or alchemic parentage that Newton's ideas came to be accepted, but rather, on account of the ever-accumulating empirical evidence that corroborated the inverse-square law. Scientists in the eighteenth century were eventually compelled to accept that some force like gravity did exist, even if no one could explain just what it was.

French scientists, as we might expect, were slower to adopt the Newtonian program in the eighteenth century owing to their fidelity to Descartes. The acceptance of Newtonian physics on the continent was a slow and contentious process, prepared as we saw in the last chapter by the *Opticks*. Ironically, it was a non-scientist who did more than anyone else to lead the way: Voltaire. Beginning with his "English Letters" of 1734, and continuing with his important *Eléments de la philosophie de Neuton* of 1738, Voltaire was almost single-handedly responsible for introducing and promoting the new Newtonian cosmology to his fellow countrymen.[61]

To be sure, there were French scientists before Voltaire (Mairan being one) who were acquainted with much of Newton's work and incorporated parts of it into their own research. The importance of Voltaire was that he made many of the ideas of Newton's cosmology accessible and even palatable to the non-scientific, Cartesian-bred French reading public. His role was not so different from Fontenelle's a generation earlier in popularizing Descartes's cosmology. While Newton's theory continued to encounter opposition in France, a large number of French scientists and lay public began to convert to Newtonian science. This conversion entailed two distinct aspects. First, there was the increasing popularity of "experimental physics" patterned after Newton's *Opticks*. Secondly, there was a widespread application of the theory of gravity to a variety of subjects. While gravity proved not to be quite the universal principle the continental Newtonians had hoped, subjects like chemistry and electricity all benefited from being unshackled from a mechanistic paradigm. Among non-scientists, we find the concept of "attraction" invoked to explain everything from headaches and gout to the passions of love and economic policies of the state.

By the 1730s, Rameau was friendly with a number of Newtonians who, I believe, helped bring the composer's attention to numerous Newtonian ideas.

---

60 John Henry, "Newton, Matter, and Magic," *Let Newton Be! A New Perspective on His Life and Works*, ed. John Fauvel (Oxford, 1988), 127–45.
61 R. L. Walters, "Voltaire, Newton, & the Reading Public," *The Triumph of Culture: 18th Century Perspectives*, ed. Paul Fritz and David Williams (Toronto, 1972), 133.

188   Rameau and Musical Thought in the Enlightenment

Rameau was at this time in the service of the philanthropist and aristocrat La Pouplinière, through whose household a host of luminaries paraded on a regular basis. It is easy to imagine Rameau, always on the lookout for new ideas that might relate to his music theory, eagerly following the latest intellectual concepts (like Newtonian physics) that must have been bantered around the dinner table and salon.[62] We have already noted the distinctly new Newtonian accent to Rameau's *Génération harmonique* with its self-conscious use of experimentation and observation patterned upon Newton's *Opticks*. As we have seen in the last chapter, this work was written with the help of the physicist Mairan, one of the first French scientists to familiarize himself with Newton's work. At this same time, Rameau was also in close touch with Voltaire, with whom he collaborated in 1733 in an aborted operatic production, *Samson*. This was incidentally just one year before the publication of Voltaire's "English Letters".[63]

I believe that several important aspects of Rameau's theory as conveyed in the *Génération harmonique* can be attributed to his acquaintance with Newtonian ideas,

Plate 7.3 Voltaire and Rameau engraved by C. de Tersan.

62 Even if Graham Sadler is correct that Rameau only entered into La Pouplinière's service around 1736 – and Sadler can only hypothesize this based upon circumstantial evidence – this would not alter the fact that Rameau had many an opportunity as a celebrated artistic figure in Paris to meet and mingle with *hommes de lettres* who would have been conversant with the latest ideas, fashions, and discoveries from abroad. Graham Sadler, "Patrons and Pasquinades: Rameau in the 1730s," *Proceedings of the Royal Musical Association* 113/2 (1988), 316.

63 For more information on Rameau's collaboration with Voltaire, see Cuthbert Girdlestone, *Jean-Philippe Rameau: His Life and Work*, 2nd edition (New York, 1969), 194–96.

in addition to the obvious use of "experimentation." Above all, there is a heightened sensitivity by Rameau to the general question of "modulation" entailing the *functional* relation of individual harmonies to the tonic. This constitutes a far less mechanical way of thinking about harmonic relations. No more is the dissonant seventh described as a "collision" of sounds as it was in the *Traité*. Rameau's description in the *Génération harmonique* is much more entropic in flavor, with notions of a non-tonic harmony "returning to its source," "drawing towards the center," and so forth.

Consider first this representative description of gravity as contained in one of the many popularizers of Newtonian science from the eighteenth century:

Gravity, my young friends, is that universal disposition of matter which inclines or carries the lesser part; this is called weight or gravitation in the lesser body, but attraction in the greater, because it draws, as it were, the lesser body towards it. Thus, all bodies in or near the earth's surface have a tendency, or seeming inclination, to descend towards its middle part or centre.[64]

Rameau's description of tonal attraction is very much like this popular characterization of gravity. The tonic, Rameau tells us in evocatively Newtonian language,

must be seen as the centre of the mode, towards which is drawn all our desires (*auquel tendent tous nous souhaits*). It is effectively the middle term of the proportion to which the extremes are so tied (*liés*) that they cannot stray from it for a moment. If [the progression] passes to one of them, it must return back right away (*y retourner sur le champ*).[65]

Why are the dominant terms drawn to the tonic term? Partly because they each possess a characteristic dissonance borrowed from the other which tends to pull them back; these dissonances act as counter-weights that help to restore a kind of equilibrium:

The mutual assistance lent by the dominant and subdominant connect them (*les lient*) to the principal sound such that they cannot stray from it. The harmonic sound of one, whose harmonic succession it has already determined, obliges the other to submit to it, and consequently to return to the principal sound.[66]

In the process of "de-mechanizing" his fundamental bass, Rameau modifies numerous other tenets of his theory. He allows much more freedom in the kinds of intervals by which the fundamental bass may progress, expands the number of cadence types available, and refines his notion of "modulation" to allow non-seventh dissonances and consonant triads on non-tonic scale degrees, all of which can be hierarchically arranged around the tonic. He also emphasizes the notion of *liaison* – the connection (preparation) of dissonance. While he finds he cannot make this into a hard and fast rule, he observes that preparing the dissonant seventh in

---

64 *The Newtonian System of Philosophy; Explained by Familiar Objects, in an Entertaining Manner for the Use of Young Ladies and Gentlemen by Tom Telescope*, revised edition (London, 1798), 8.
65 *Génération harmonique*, 109.
66 *Ibid.*, 112.

a previous chord as a consonance does soften the percussive impact of an unprepared dissonance. (The added sixth, being an apparent consonance, needs less preparation.)

All these changes point to a more entropic notion of tonality that has its parallel in Newton's theory of gravity. Both gravity and tonal attraction are unseen forces that operate over distances. (One is almost surprised Rameau never drew the analogy between his geometric progression and the inverse-square law of attraction!) And just as Newtonian theory shifted attention away from the *impact* of matter to the *attraction* of matter, so too did Rameau begin to define tonal motion less by the concatenation of dissonant dominant chords above the fundamental bass than by the attractive quality of the tonic. One could almost reduce this to a simplified formula: in the *Traité* Rameau was concerned mainly with the function of "dominants," while in the *Génération harmonique* he was concerned with the function of the tonic. In other words, whereas the primary tonal forces described in the *Traité* originate in dominant harmonies by means of the percussive agitation of dissonance, in the *Génération harmonique* the primary tonal force resides with the tonic by means of its power to generate, coordinate, and draw all dominant subfunctions.

Admittedly it is risky to push the analogy with Newton's theory of gravity too far. Many of these revisions were begun first in the *Nouveau système* of 1726, long before Rameau would have been likely to hear anything concerning Newton's theory.[67] And nowhere in his writings does Rameau ever explicitly acknowledge the influence of Newton, something our insecure philosophe would ordinarily have been eager to do in order to add credibility to his writings. Nor did Rameau ever abandon his fidelity to the Cartesian method, as the quotations from the *Démonstration* cited in Chapter 1 make clear. But we have seen that there clearly was a self-conscious adoption of Newtonian experimental methods in the *Génération harmonique*, and there is no reason to doubt that along with this Rameau also incorporated elements of Newton's most celebrated discovery: gravity. Whether this was done intentionally by Rameau as a specific Newtonian conversion I cannot say for sure. Perhaps it was Rameau's indirect absorption of ideas and notions through his contacts with Newtonians like Voltaire and Mairan, combined with his own maturation as a theorist, that together helped leaven his rigidly mechanistic model of the fundamental bass. In any case, if Rameau was not explicit in calling attention to the Newtonian character of his theory, we recall from Chapter 1 that others were not so hesitant. More than once the fundamental bass was compared to Newton's theory of gravity.[68]

CASTEL'S CRITIQUE

One observer who had no illusions about where Rameau's new ideas concerning mode and tonal attraction came from was his erstwhile champion and fellow

---

[67] Although not in the *Traité*. There the tonal authority of the tonic chord in determining a mode was only vaguely suggested. When Rameau spoke of the *tonique* in the *Traité* as a "centre harmonique," he was referring to the fundamental of the chord in relation to its general constituents, not the tonic of the mode in relation to its scale degrees.

[68] See also d'Alembert's comparison recorded in Chapter 2, p. 40.

Cartesian, Father Castel. In a series of articles and letters dating between 1735 and 1737 – just when Rameau was preparing his *Génération harmonique* for publication – Castel voiced harsh words for the changes he was observing in his friend's thinking. The enthusiasm that he had expressed for the *Traité* over a decade earlier had in the meanwhile chilled considerably.

The first rumblings of discontent with Rameau's theory were contained in one of a series of lengthy articles Castel had published in 1735 elaborating his synaesthetic theories.[69] In the course of discussing analogies he saw between the three primary colors and the sounds comprising the *corps sonore*, Castel dropped a few disparaging remarks on the side concerning the prolixity of Rameau's *Traité*, and its author's dependence upon Kircher and Zarlino for the notion of the *basse fondamentale*. Unable to allow any criticism to pass by unanswered, the hypersensitive Rameau responded to Castel's comments with his own open letter.[70] There he indignantly defended the originality of his ideas and pointedly reminded Castel of his earlier approbation. Castel responded in turn with another letter, itemizing twenty-nine specific points of disagreement.[71] (It is from this last letter that we learn Castel had been in recent touch with the composer, discussing with him numerous theoretical ideas that were about to appear in the *Génération harmonique*; Rameau had evidently showed Castel some preliminary sketches of the work and asked him for help in drafting a complete text.)

Castel's new-found hostility to Rameau can be attributed to several factors. There is first of all the very simple explanation that Castel must have been jealous of Rameau's increasing success on both the theoretical and the operatic fronts. (The conservative Jesuit priest never could bring himself to approve of Rameau's stage productions.) Further, by the mid 1730s, Castel was working out an elaborate theory of synaesthesia to justify his ocular harpsichord, and was vexed by the skeptical reactions it was receiving. It must have been galling for the Jesuit to see his erstwhile protégé beginning to receive acclaim from the same scientific and musical communities who were now ridiculing his own efforts. Moreover, many of the ideas Rameau was employing in his revisions (including both the *corps sonore* and the geometric progression) were ones which Castel had communicated to Rameau much earlier, and which the ungrateful composer failed to acknowledge. Perhaps, too, Castel now perceived himself as something of Rameau's rival. In 1732 he announced his intention to publish a "new method" for learning music that presumably was to compete with Rameau's publications.[72]

Surely the most important reason for Castel's hostility, though, was the conspicuously Newtonian hue Rameau's theory was taking. While Rameau had

---

[69] "Suite et seconde partie des nouvelles expériences d'Optique et d'Acoustique," *Journal de Trévoux* (August, 1735), 1,619–66; *CTW* VI, 70–85.
[70] "Lettre de M. Rameau au R. P. Castel," *Journal de Trévoux* (July, 1736), 1,691–1,709; *CTW* VI, 86–92.
[71] "Remarques du P. Castel sur la Lettre de M. Rameau," *Journal de Trévoux* (September, 1736), 1,999–2,026; *CTW* VI, 93–102.
[72] *Mercure de France* (May, 1732), 841–56. Several manuscripts by Castel on musical subjects – including a method of composition – today lie in the Bibliothèque Royale in Brussels. Obviously Castel never consummated his plan by publishing it (Donald S. Schier, *Louis Bertrand Castel: Anti-Newtonian Scientist* [Cedar Rapids, Iowa, 1941], 214).

not yet published the *Génération harmonique* when the polemical exchange transpired, he must have already had most of the basic ideas contained therein worked out, and communicated them personally to Castel. Rameau's change of allegiance was certain to nettle the unrepentant Cartesian physicist.[73] Castel must also have been alarmed that Rameau was about to adopt Mairan's atomistic theory of sound propagation, considering how closely modeled it was upon Newton's optical theories.[74]

An important theme underlying Castel's criticism is that Rameau's many new explanations of the fundamental bass are not mechanistically consistent. Concerning Rameau's analysis of *supposition*, for instance, Castel could not accept that a note C fixed in the bass against which an upper dominant-seventh chord on G is sounded could itself be considered an added dissonance. "Is not the true character of a base and foundation to be solid and immovable?" Castel demands; ". . . One easily sees how all the basses presumed fundamental by M. Rameau are much less than that."[75] He then goes on to offer this analysis:

Because in every impact (*choc*) there is an action (*coup*) and reaction (*contrecoup*), percussion and repercussion. F is the only real dissonance because it alone is incommensurable and minor. . . F is the active dissonance, the others are passive dissonances. F collides with G–B–D, and in return is hit and reflected; [it is] repulsed with such force that C becomes an immovable barrier (*appui*) against [the chord] G–B–D.[76]

Castel's criticisms were not only of a metaphysical nature, though. When the *Génération harmonique* was finally published, Castel wrote a strongly negative review, detailing a number of concrete objections. After repeating his earlier general criticism that Rameau's ideas were not geometrically rigorous and relied too much upon experience and Newtonian ideas, Castel went on to condemn Rameau's interpretation of mode and the fundamental bass as being circular and obscure.[77] The added-sixth chord on the subdominant he considered to be an "error in modulation" since it could not be generated in any harmonic series by the *corps sonore*. What was of value in the fundamental bass, he repeated once again, was either taken from his own ideas or those of his fellow Jesuit and scientist/music theorist, Athanasius Kircher.

---

[73] Ibid., 142. Castel's hostility to Newton would be vented in a huge 500-page attack entitled *Le Vrai Système de physique generale de M. Isaac Newton exposé et analysé en parallèle avec celui de Descartes* (Paris, 1743). This was one of the last major defenses of Cartesian physics to be published in the eighteenth century. While Castel was forced to concede the superiority of much in Newton's theories, he tried valiantly to defend the Cartesian cosmology from the Newtonians, and criticized Newton wherever possible for propounding unfounded hypotheses, occult forces, and meaningless experiments.

[74] Mairan was incidentally one of the most vocal critics of Castel's optical ideas in the Académie, and as *Secrétaire perpétuel* was able to block the Jesuit priest's bid for membership. Anne-Marie Chouillet-Roche, "Le Clavecin oculaire du Père Castel," *Dix-Huitième Siècle* 8 (1976), 162.

[75] *Journal de Trévoux* (August, 1735), 1,637–39; *CTW* VI, 76.

[76] Ibid.

[77] *Journal de Trévoux* (December, 1737), 2,163; *CTW* VI, 146.

Rameau was obviously stung by Castel's unrelenting attacks, and he responded a second time with a letter published in a rival journal.[78] He disputed, naturally, that Kircher had anticipated anything in his theory. And he wondered aloud about the motives behind Castel's sudden change of heart, considering how full of praise Castel had been some ten years earlier. As for the specific problems Castel noted concerning the relation of mode to the fundamental bass and the derivation of the subdominant, we can only concur. Rameau's arguments were weak here indeed. He implicitly conceded as much given that these arguments were the ones most heavily revised in his subsequent publications.

Castel's attacks otherwise had little resonance, except perhaps to provoke bemusement among a few readers. Voltaire, long nettled by Castel's anti-Newtonian propaganda, took gleeful note of the battle between "Orpheus-Rameau" and "Euclide-Castel."[79] In an open letter written to Rameau in 1738, Voltaire proclaimed his support for Rameau, and attempted to assuage the sensitive composer's wounded ego. Fighting Castel, he wrote, "is like fighting with Bellerophon. Think, Sir, of your rash undertaking. You limit yourself to calculating sounds and to giving us excellent music for the ears, while dealing with a man who makes music for the eyes . . ." Advising Rameau against responding any more to Castel's attacks, Voltaire concludes: "He will perhaps write another letter to reassure the world about your music, for he has already written many pamphlets to enlighten and reassure the world. Follow the world, Monsieur, and don't answer back."[80]

THE GENERATION OF MODE

No attentive reader of the *Génération harmonique* can miss the "vicious circle" to which Castel referred concerning Rameau's derivation of mode. We have already articulated the crux of the problem: it is impossible to reconcile the fundamental bass motion of a perfect fifth delimited by the triple geometric progression with the orthodox diatonic ordering of a scale. There is simply no way of connecting the sixth and seventh scale degrees without either breaking the prescribed fifth motion of the fundamental bass, or trespassing the boundary of the triple progression.

According to Rameau, shortly before he was to turn his manuscript of the *Génération harmonique* over to be published, a new idea suddenly occurred to him that was to answer this dilemma. "It is as much in favor of my new system as against the theory of the ancients and the moderns, and obliged me to retrace my steps."[81] Rameau's "new idea," it seems, was the *double emploi* or "double employment." We have seen that the origin of the *double emploi* lay in a characteristic

---

[78] *Le Pour et Contre* 14 (1738), 73–96, 141–43; *CTW* VI, 171–79.
[79] *CTW* III, xvii.
[80] *CTW* VI, 180–83. Voltaire's support for Rameau was motivated not only by his antipathy towards Castel but by his own literary designs as well. It was exactly at this time, when Rameau's quarrel with Castel broke out, that Voltaire was trying to rekindle Rameau's interest in their unfinished collaboration, *Samson*: Cuthbert Girdlestone, "Voltaire, Rameau, et *Samson*," *Recherches sur la musique française classique* 6 (1966), 133–43.
[81] *CTW* VI, 90.

dissonance symmetrically added to the subdominant that was to parallel the dissonance added to the dominant.[82] In Chapter 11 of the *Génération harmonique*, Rameau returns to this chord in an attempt to resolve the vicious circle Castel had complained of. The diatonic succession between scale degrees 6 and 7 that had hitherto appeared unbridgeable using the fundamental fifth progression can indeed by linked by applying the *double emploi* at scale degree 6. As Rameau indicates in his fundamental bass in Example 7.7, the chord is interpreted in two ways.

As the chord succeeding the tonic harmonizing D, it is heard as a true subdominant (the fifth progression 3–1 notated by a cursor on the lower C). But as the chord preceding the *dominante-tonique* harmonizing the leading tone F♯, we reinterpret it as a seventh on the *sutonique* A (represented by the term 27). The ear, Rameau explains, is evidently able to recognize a change of function in the course of the progression:

> In this double employment, the ear hears at 27 the same harmony that it wished to find above 1, following 3. As this same harmony . . . offers a combination similar to that which connects the dominant 9 to the principal sound 3, the ear is sufficiently affected by it to adopt the fundamental succession from 27 to 9 in the same way [that it does] 9 to 3. This is especially so as 3, which would be expected after 1 [but is] represented by 27, is delayed for only a moment.[83]

Obviously the incorporation of a fourth term appears to contradict Rameau's earlier assertion that any mode is delimited by the terms of the triple geometric progression. The *double emploi* suggests that D (9) becomes the new principal sound in the mode by virtue of its being the middle term of the geometric proportion 3–9–27. And Rameau admits that this is indeed the case. The upper tetrachord of a scale is heard as belonging to the dominant mode. This is why musicians instinctively feel a pause at scale degree 5 when ascending the scale. Nevertheless, the identity of the original mode is not thereby effaced. Because the fourth term displays such similitude to the subdominant, it is not perceived as independent.[84]

Example 7.7 *Génération harmonique*, Plate 15

---

82 Rameau actually used the term *double emploi* in the *Dissertation* of 1732 (p. 33). But he did not explore any theoretical implications in regard to mode there. Several fundamental-bass analyses from the *Traité* and *Nouveau système* also suggest the idea of *double emploi* (see e.g. Example 3.3), although again he did not discuss any of the theory behind it.

83 *Génération harmonique*, 129–30.

84 In a later publication Rameau calls the *sutonique* dominant an "associate" of the first generator (subdominant term) (*Nouvelles réflexions*, 21; *CTW* V, 109.)

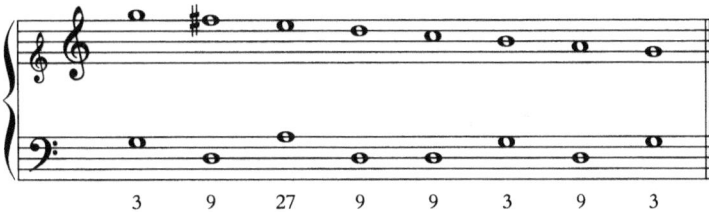

Example 7.8 *Génération harmonique*, Plate 16

Here we must recall Rameau's hierarchical view of modulation in order to understand how a "foreground" move into the dominant mode in the upper tetrachord does not in fact constitute a true change of key. The dominant chord lacking confirmation by its own (secondary) leading tone is *censée tonique*. But as the most-closely related – and dependent – function to the tonic, it can never displace the tonic completely. The addition of the fourth term thus does not really violate Rameau's prescript that a mode is bounded by the geometric triple progression 1–3–9.

This hierarchical distinction also becomes important in the descending version of the scale, where an even stronger modulation to the dominant is articulated (see Example 7.8). No *double emploi* is needed in this harmonization, nor any subdominant terms. Thus, the three terms used to harmonize the descending scale comprise the triple progression of the dominant – not the tonic! Rameau argues that term 3, not 9, is still the tonic, since the "dominant" (term 27) lacks the necessary leading tone.[85] Further, the *dominante-tonique* used to harmonize the descending fourth scale degree is sufficient to suggest the subdominant. (We will recall that he had earlier described this chord as an amalgamation of subdominant and dominant notes.) To the extent that the upper tetrachord is still heard as a modulation in the dominant, it is only *censée tonique*. This is again why musicians know instinctively to pause at the dominant as if it is a kind of caesura. With the arrival of the fourth scale degree harmonized by a full *dominante-tonique*, we know we have returned to the original tonic key.

In the *Démonstration*, Rameau tried anew to clarify the paradoxical "bi-modal" character of the major scale with a slightly altered analysis of its fundamental bass (see Plate 7.4). Rameau now emphasizes the natural repose of the fifth scale degree by notating an imperfect (plagal) cadence. This scale degree is then repeated with a new dominant harmony, allowing the upper tetrachord to proceed using the fundamental fifth progression in the bass. The implied modulation to the dominant

---

[85] Notice how Rameau has altered the normative harmonization of the *règle de l'octave* by repressing the secondary leading tone above scale degree 6 here. Presumably the presence of so strong an articulation of the dominant would be too much of a modulation for Rameau to tolerate. However in an earlier publication he had suggested that the sixth scale degree might take a "chord of the small sixth" (raised sixth) in both ascending *and* descending versions of the *règle* precisely so that the dominant receives the same degree of confirmation with its own leading tone as had the tonic with scale degree 2. "Lettre de M. à M. sur la musique," *Mercure de France* (September, 1731), 2,138–39; *CTW* VI, 61.

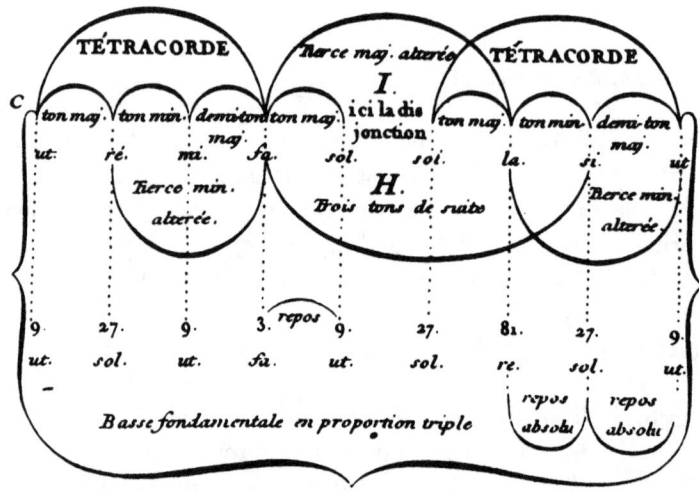

Plate 7.4 *Démonstration*, Plate C

(by means of the fourth term 81 used under scale-degree 6) is negated by the final perfect cadence employing the seventh of the *dominante-tonique*.[86]

Rameau's insight that this upper tetrachord of the scale is more in the "dominant" sphere than the lower half, and moreover one metrically delineated in most scalar melodies by a repose on the dominant note, has been affirmed by subsequent musicians.[87] Unfortunately, it does prove to be a problem for the theorist seeking to confine mode within the rigid confines of the geometric triple progression.

If the problems posed by the major scale are perplexing, the problems posed by the minor scale prove to be outright intractable to Rameau. The problem does not lie in the ascending minor scale. As seen in Example 7.9, the sixth and seventh scale degrees are both raised to conform to the fundamental bass of the major scale, thus allowing the use of the *double emploi*. The difficulty, rather, lies in the descending minor scale. Because the sixth and seventh scale degrees of the minor scale are normally lowered when descending (creating the so-called "melodic minor" scale), the fundamental bass used in an ascending format cannot be used in retrograde, even allowing for modulation or the use of double employment.[88]

---

[86] *Démonstration*, 53–54.

[87] A twentieth-century music theorist whose observations about the tonal dynamics of the ascending and descending major scale are surprisingly similar to Rameau's is Victor Zuckerkandl, *Sound and Symbol: Music and the External World* (Princeton, 1973), 95ff.

[88] *Génération harmonique*, 134. Rameau was not the first French theorist to prescribe the "melodic minor" scale. Delair, Clérambault, and Campion all taught it as the normative progression for the minor mode.

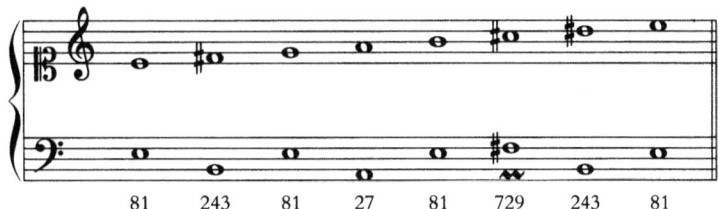

Example 7.9. *Génération harmonique*, Plate 17

Rameau attempts to solve the puzzle by proposing the fundamental bass shown in Example 7.10. Two problems are apparent. First, the descending seventh is harmonized with a minor dominant, contradicting all other modal inflections of this function. Rameau can only say the chord is here minor since it acts in this tetrachord as the principal sound of the mode, and thus must reflect its quality. (The term 243 is the geometric mean of 81 and 729.) Secondly, Rameau must justify the diminished fifth supporting C in descending. He argues that this dissonance is acceptable since it really suggests the subdominant, thus the chord can be interpreted with the *double emploi*.[89] But this is not how Rameau had originally defined the term. Properly speaking, the *double emploi* always acts as an intermediary between a tonic and its upper dominant. In the example under consideration, the fundamental bass can only be an F♯, since it is flanked on both sides by B. C is still left unaccounted for in such an analysis. These irregularities lead Rameau to confess at the end of his discussion that the minor mode possesses many "singularities" on account of its "imperfect" origin.[90] In the *Démonstration*, Rameau mentions one other solution (although he does not illustrate it): one may treat the seventh scale degree (here D) as a passing note ("pour le goût du chant"), thus allowing the tonic to connect directly with the sixth scale degree supported by the subdominant.[91]

All the fuss Rameau makes about coordinating the diatonic scale with the geometric triple progression may strike us today as a bit incomprehensible – the music theorist's attempt to square the circle. Yet, as Castel's critique suggested, there were profound theoretical implications to the problem. Rameau's success or failure in solving it had the utmost consequences as to the validity of his theory. If harmony was indeed the source of all music, including mode, then Rameau felt

---

[89] *Génération harmonique*, 136. Shirlaw completely misunderstands this argument. Somehow he gets the impression that Rameau justifies the diminished fifth as representing a tempered perfect fifth (Shirlaw, *Theory of Harmony*, 226). Nowhere, however, does Rameau speak of temperament with such an application in mind.

[90] *Génération harmonique*, 136.

[91] *Démonstration*, 77. It is interesting to note, I think, that Rameau was not the only theorist to entangle himself in this problem. The difficulties of harmonizing the upper tetrachord of a descending scale are implicit in Schenkerian theory. See *Der freie Satz*, tr. Ernst Oster as *Free Composition*, 2 vols. (New York, 1979). In the *Urlinie* models sketched in *Der freie Satz* that descend the full octave (the "eight-line"), Schenker in many cases notates the seventh and sixth scale degrees as passing tones without harmonic support, creating an "unsupported stretch" or "empty run" (*Leerlauf*). (See Figure 18 of *Der freie Satz*.) No doubt the problem of finding a good counterpoint to accompany this upper tetrachord that can be reconciled with the basic triadic unfolding that defines the tonic mode in the background helps to explain why the eight-line is such a problematic and rare phenomenon in Schenkerian analysis.

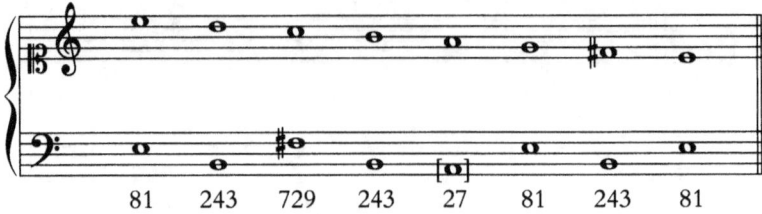

Example 7.10 *Génération harmonique*, Plate 18

he had to show in what consistent way the scale – the melodic articulation of a mode – was generated from harmony, and not the other way around. Only by doing so did Rameau believe he could justify his claim that melody was subordinate to harmony. There was also a pedagogical issue of secondary importance, too. Specifically, Rameau wished to demonstrate the superiority of the fundamental bass as a means of learning thorough-bass over the tried-and-true *règle de l'octave*. If Rameau could show that the *règle* was itself only a product of the fundamental bass, then it was logical that thorough-bass pedagogy should be based upon the latter source. This was precisely the motivation driving Rameau's scathing attacks upon the *règle* in his debate with Montéclair, described in Chapter 3.[92]

Because of the difficulties Rameau encountered in generating the minor mode as a *parallel* of the major mode, in his later writings he tested a new idea wherein the minor mode was derived as the *relative* of a major mode (although this is not the term he used). Actually, this was not entirely a new idea. Both in the *Nouveau système* and the *Génération harmonique* he laid out the minor scale as a relative to – and hence derivative of – the major scale.[93] And we recall from Chapter 6 how in the *Démonstration* Rameau suggested (possibly with d'Alembert's coaching) that a minor triad could be understood as co-generated by its mediant ("relative major"). By extending this notion to the full mode, it was possible to see the minor mode as co-generated by the relative major. There is a "grande communauté" of sounds between the two.[94] Each of the geometric terms of the minor mode on A (called now by Rameau the *adjoints*) are related to the geometric terms of the major mode on C, just in the way that the chord of A minor is derived from the chord of C major.[95] We can display their derivative relationship in the following way:

F – C – G
d – a – e

The five most closely related keys to a tonic are seen to be derivable from a single triple geometric progression. (Rameau refers to this as the *entrelacement* of keys.)

[92] While it is not the place here to pursue this question, we may note that the subject of reconciling the major and minor scales with the fundamental bass became one of the most frequent topics debated by French theorists in the generations following Rameau. D'Alembert, Serre, Bethizy, Rousseau, Roussier, and Blainville all argued about it and offered their own myriad solutions to the riddle. For more background on this problem, see my article "The *règle de l'octave* in Thorough-Bass Theory and Practice."
[93] *Nouveau système*, 34–35; *Génération harmonique*, 142.
[94] *Démonstration*, 72.
[95] Ibid., 83.

He concludes that the minor mode is "subordinate" to the major mode, and ultimately a product of art. The major mode alone is generated by the *corps sonore*; it alone is the *maître de l'harmonie*.

In his last writings, Rameau thus moved away from an explanation in which the minor mode was generated independently of the major mode, to a position where the minor mode is entangled in – and dependent upon – the major mode for its meaning.[96] I think this is another sensitive insight of Rameau into tonal behavior, even though it was one he found difficult to reconcile with the older – but not entirely discarded – theory of arithmetic generation.

THE CHROMATIC AND ENHARMONIC GENRES

Rameau grouped all non-diatonic harmonic successions that did not follow the basic fifth progression of the fundamental bass as kinds of chromatic and enharmonic genres. These "genres" are generated much the same way the diatonic "genre" is – through the temporalization of intervals contained in the *corps sonore*. Just as the perfect twelfths resonating above and below the *corps sonore* suggest to Rameau the triple progression of fifths, so too do the major seventeenths suggest a "quintuple" progression of major thirds (1–5–25) from which are generated chromatic and enharmonic intervals. Actually, it is more than the major third that is needed; a minor third by parallelism (presumably related to the arithmetic series) must also be included. By moving the fundamental bass either up or down a major or minor third, four possible chromatic semitone relationships are created in the soprano (see Example 7.11). Each of these chromatic (minor) semitones is theoretically smaller than the diatonic (major) semitone created by the fundamental progression of fifths (15 : 16 versus 24 : 25).[97] A consequence of this is that the minor semitone is less natural to sing. Rameau observes that when it is introduced in a song after a major semitone, singers commonly soften it with an upper-neighbor appoggiatura (the *coulé*) or a trill (*cadence*).[98] This may be seen in Example 7.12. The greatest use of the chromatic genre, though, is to change modes. In

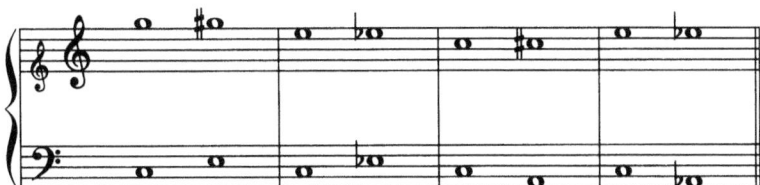

Example 7.11 *Génération harmonique*, Plate 19

---

96 Ideas developed further in the *Code de musique pratique*, 43–46 and the *Nouvelles réflexions sur le principe sonore*. We will return once more to Rameau's revisions of his theory concerning the minor mode in Chapter 10.

97 In his discussion of chromaticism in the *Traité* (Book 3, Chapter 34), Rameau tries, but ultimately is unable, to derive all chromatic half steps from the fundamental fifth progression in the bass.

98 *Génération harmonique*, 147.

Example 7.12, the chromatic semitone announces a new leading tone of a dominant on A, pointing to D as the new key.

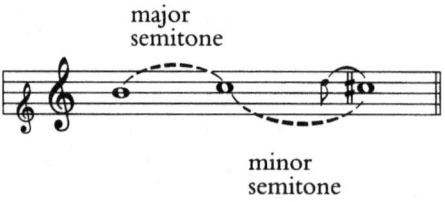

Example 7.12 *Génération harmonique*, Plate 20

Another means of changing modes by virtue of the quintuple geometric progression is the "interrupted cadence" (*cadence interrompue*) that Rameau introduces in the *Génération harmonique*.[99] He defines this new cadence as "a fundamental succession in which the dominant, instead of passing to the fundamental sound, descends a third to another dominant" (see Example 7.13).[100] The "interrupted cadence" is a kind of deceptive cadence that violates the expected fifth progression in the fundamental bass. This is why Rameau introduces it at the same time as the "broken cadence" (*cadence rompue*). Both the "interrupted" and "broken" cadence *suppose* the perfect cadence.[101] Together with the *cadence parfaite* and *cadence imparfaite*, we now have a total of four cadences – two that resolve regularly by fifths, and two that resolve irregularly, one to another dominant a third lower, and the other to a "feigned" tonic on the sixth scale degree.[102]

The "enharmonic" species is created by connecting the extremes of the quintuple geometric progression (1–5–25) in the fundamental bass. In Example 7.14, we see that this fundamental bass progression is a diminished fourth B♭–F♯, creating an enharmonic relation B♭–A♯ in the soprano. Rameau refers to this as a diminished "quarter tone" (*quart de ton*), even though the relationship (125 : 128) represents only the difference between a major and minor semitone. Of course such

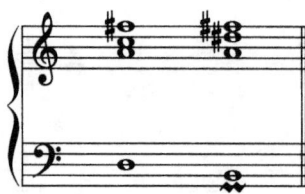

Example 7.13 The "interrupted cadence"

---

[99] Rameau does speak of the interrupted cadence in the *Nouveau système* (*Nouveau système*, 41), but without describing or analyzing its behavior.
[100] *Génération harmonique*, 157.
[101] *Observations*, 49.
[102] *Code de musique pratique*, 61.

enharmonic connections are only practical using some kind of temperament. Rameau thus finds himself forced to specify his views on temperament, views that until the *Génération harmonique* were far from clear.

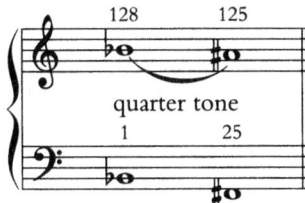

Example 7.14 An enharmonic "quarter tone"

We recall from Chapter 4 that in the *Traité*, Rameau generated all consonant intervals through arithmetic divisions of a monochord string, resulting in an initial series of just (superparticular) ratios. Not all diatonic consonances, however, were of such simple ratios. Indeed, while Rameau never lays out in the *Traité* any tuning system, he ends up with a traditional syntonic/diatonic tuning for the diatonic scale using major and minor whole tones (8 : 9 and 9 : 10), as well as a chromatic scale with three different sized semitones (15 : 16, 24 : 25, and 25 : 27).[103] The resultant matrix of intervals produces a whole palate of different-sized consonances and dissonances that in more remote keys would produce horrendous results. Some kind of temperament was clearly called for.

Rameau used the *Nouveau système* of 1727 finally to articulate a theory of temperament. In the twenty-fourth and last chapter of the book, he admits the need for some kind of temperament in order for any effective "modulation" to be carried out. There he recommends an irregular temperament, in which as many major thirds are kept as pure as possible, achieved largely through the tempering of perfect fifths by a quarter comma (Rameau believed that perfect fifths could suffer greater deviation than major thirds, since, he claimed, two strings tuned to a tempered perfect fifth could resonate sympathetically together, whereas no two strings tuned to a tempered major third could.[104]) As one moved into keys with larger numbers of sharps or flats (or, as he called them, "less utilized modulations"), more and more intervals became increasingly out of tune in comparison to the justly tuned major thirds belonging to the more common keys.[105] But since Rameau never specified how this irregular temperament was to be carried out in full, we cannot know for sure exactly which of these intervals were altered the most.[106]

With the publication of the *Génération harmonique* in 1737, Rameau's ideas concerning tuning and temperament had taken a decisive turn. Whether as a

---

[103] *Traité*, Book 1, Chapter 5.   [104] *Nouveau système*, 107.   [105] *Ibid.*, 110.
[106] J. Murray Barbour offered one possible reconstruction of Rameau's temperament, but admitted that Rameau's instructions were too "vague" to offer any certainty on the matter: *Tuning and Temperament: A Historical Survey* (East Lansing, Mich.,1953), 135.

consequence of his own compositional experience, or of internal developments in his theory related to his advocacy of the geometric progression and enharmonic genres, or perhaps of both, Rameau had now abandoned his meantone temperament proposal as a "mistake" and came out fully in favor of equal temperament. In the lengthy seventh chapter of the *Génération harmonique* (pp. 75–104), he justifies his position in some detail. He first begins by offering several "propositions" in which empirical evidence of practice and arguments of practicality are offered on behalf of equal temperament (much as he had earlier in the same treatise offered empirical experiments to establish the *corps sonore*): there are no distinctions between major and minor semitones on a keyboard; the ear cannot distinguish a minor third from an augmented second; most singers and string players will naturally temper a justly tuned interval to conform to the harmonies of the music, etc. Moreover, equal temperament is essential for preserving the unity of a mode (lest modulatory passages sound intervals that are too discordant). Finally, as he will show in later chapters, equal temperament is required in order to perform any enharmonic passage with success. Equal temperament is clearly an alteration demanded by both the ear and reason.[107]

Of course in advocating equal temperament, Rameau might seem to be betraying the simple numerical ratios he has established through the naturally resonating harmonic series in the *corps sonore*. If all intervals other than the octave can – and indeed, must – be altered in practice, what is left of the natural basis for harmony and mode that he has claimed? In fact, he insists, everything is left. Nature has only given us the intervals contained in the *corps sonore*: the perfect twelfth and major seventeenth. It is our job to take these intervals and apply them to music. To the extent that octave reductions and minor temperings of these intervals are necessary in order to employ harmony, it only goes to show how it is the fundamental bass – the product of the *corps sonore* – which is the true guiding force of the musician. His reasoning is as follows. If you take a chromatic semitone such as C–C♯, and compare it on an equally tempered keyboard to the diatonic semitone B♯–C♯, you will not notice any difference.[108] But as soon as a bass is added to each progression (in this case, C–A, and G♯–C♯), we notice an immediate difference between the semitones. This difference, Rameau tells us, may not

---

107 *Génération harmonique*, 78. Rameau's advocacy of equal temperament in the *Génération harmonique* caused a minor spat, which, as another illustration of his growing sensitivity when it came to criticism of his theory, is reported here. In 1740, a member of the Lyons Académie named Louis Bollioud-Mermet read a paper in which he claimed Rameau's method for tuning a keyboard in equal temperament was too imprecise and thereby "determined nothing" – a fault Bollioud-Mermet planned to remedy with a method of his own invention. Bollioud-Mermet's criticism was justified, as Rameau's described method for tempering fifths in the *Génération harmonique* was completely informal. Nonetheless, Rameau could never let a criticism go by unanswered, particularly one from an Académie scientist. As soon as Rameau got wind of Bollioud-Mermet's criticism, he shot off an indignant letter to the Lyons Académie defending his ideas, and railing against the institution for allowing such slanderous accusations to be aired (the letter is transcribed in *CTW* VI, 186–87). While Rameau's attention quickly turned elsewhere, his immediate and irate response offers a foretaste of the vituperative exchanges he was to engage himself in with the Encyclopedists in another decade.
108 I have excerpted this particular example from a longer progression that Rameau analyzes in some detail (*Génération harmonique*, 82–86).

Example 7.15 The diminished-seventh chord as composite of subdominant and dominant elements

acoustically be present in the melody itself, but we will nonetheless sense a dramatic contrast between them on account of their different fundamental basses. All this is proof, Rameau believes, that the fundamental bass is the true "compass" of the ear. Temperament is a practical necessity of music that on the surface may seem to sully the perfection of nature's intervals. But it really only shows the dependence of the ear upon harmony for determining the true function and relationship of melodic pitches to one another.

Undoubtedly the most useful application of the enharmonic genre, Rameau tells us, occurs with the diminished-seventh chord. He points out that the notes of this chord, found as we recall from Chapters 3 and 4 on the leading tone of a minor mode, are a combination (*réunion*) of dominant and subdominant features. In Example 7.15, the diminished-seventh chord on the leading tone of the mode in E minor is composed of the bottom third of the subdominant A minor triad (A–C), and the upper third of the dominant triad (D♯–F♯).[109] In line with his new-found fascination with symmetry, Rameau no longer derives this solely as a dominant seventh with a borrowed fundamental bass. He will now most typically analyze the chord with a fundamental bass on the leading tone.[110]

An important function for the diminished-seventh chord is its role as a pivot chord in modulation. Any one of the four notes of this chord can be respelled and in turn act as the leading tone of a new key, thus allowing the chord to act as a pivot in modulation by minor thirds. Such enharmonic respellings, Rameau notes, can produce dramatic and beautiful effects when tastefully employed by the composer.[111]

The enharmonic genre can also modify the diatonic and chromatic genres, respectively, to create hybrid genres. As illustrated in Plate 7.5, the "diatonic-enharmonic" genre involves the fusion of two intersecting diatonic semitones (such as B♭–A and A–G♯). A particularly striking example of this very enharmonic relationship can be found in one of Rameau's own harpsichord pieces, entitled (not coincidentally) "L'Enharmonique" (see m. 15 of Example 7.16).[112] The same diatonic semitones illustrated in the *Démonstration* are here connected in the move from G minor to A major (indicated with circles). "The effect expressed in [Example 7.16] may not perhaps be to everyone's taste right away," Rameau warns the performer in his preface to the collection:

---

109 *Génération harmonique*, 151.
110 See e.g. Example 9.10 and Example 9.12.
111 In the manuscript of the "Opéra Mémoire" (mentioned in Chapter 6), Rameau suggested giving such an enharmonic modulation the name of *entraharmonique* (fol. 125r). For reasons we do not know, he decided against including this term when he finally revised the "Mémoire" for publication.
112 From the *Pièces de clavecin; Nouvelles suites* (Paris, 1731).

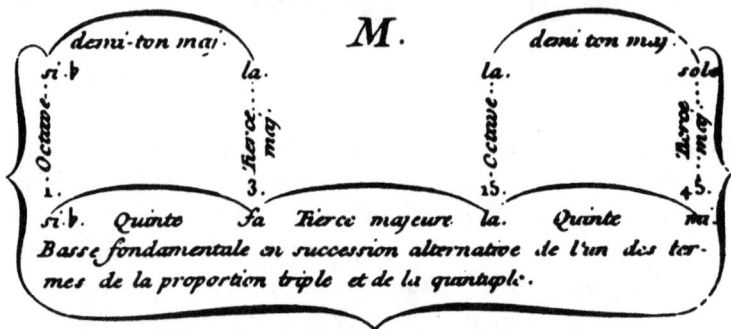

Plate 7.5 *Démonstration*, Plate M

One can nonetheless become accustomed to it after a little application and even come to sense all of its beauty once one has overcome the initial aversion, which in this case might result from lack of familiarity. The harmony which creates this effect has by no means been thrown in haphazardly; it is based upon reason and has the sanction of nature herself.[113]

After a further sequencing of this progression, we reach a dramatic climax with the arrival of a double appoggiatura over a diminished-seventh chord in m. 54 (see Example 7.17). This is the only point in the piece where Rameau employs a fermata. The D♭ of the diminished-seventh chord here has been respelled enharmonically from the C♯ in the previous measure, thus preparing the key shift from D minor to F minor. Rameau referred to this particular passage as "thrilling" (*saissant*) and recommended that the performer bring out its beauty "through a

Example 7.16 "L'Enharmonique," mm. 12–18

[113] *Ibid.*, "Remarques sur les pièces de ce livre, & sur les differens genres de musique."

Example 7.17 "L'Enharmonique," mm. 52–56

softening of the touch and by suspending the appoggiaturas (*coulez*) more and more as one approaches it."[114]

A "chromatic-enharmonic" genre is illustrated by Rameau in Plate 7.6. Here two chromatic semitones (E♭–E and E–E♯ – both modal inflections of a triad) are linked by an enharmonic quarter tone. Lest we think this is merely an abstract theoretical concoction, though, Rameau hastens to add that he had employed just such an enharmonic progression in the famous "Trio of the Fates" from his first opera, *Hippolyte et Aricie* (1733). (See Example 7.18.) Underscoring the dramatic text ("Où cours-tu malheureux? Tremble, frémis d'effroi!") is a breathtaking modulatory sequence altering chromatic and enharmonic shifts in the upper voices. By means of an enharmonic respelling of applied dominants, Rameau is able to bring about a descending chromatic modulation from F♯ minor through F minor, E minor, E♭ minor, and finally D minor. The music, Rameau ruefully reported, proved beyond the capabilities of all but a few singers at the Opéra and had to be omitted from production.[115] But he decided to leave it in the score for the benefit of connoisseurs, and expressed his hopes that musicians would soon learn to appreciate such enharmonic subtleties.

Plate 7.6 *Démonstration*, Plate N

114 *Ibid.* 115 *Démonstration*, 94.

In all these examples, Rameau insisted that the ear recognizes a profound difference between the enharmonically respelled notes, even if they are performed with equal temperament:

Example 7.18 *Hippolyte et Aricie*, Act II, Scene V
Where are you running unhappy one? Tremble, shudder with fright!

[The ear] feels in this lack of relation (*rapport*) the harshness which [the enharmonic genre] causes; we are struck by the quarter-tone without realizing it; we are revolted by it because it is unnatural and because our ear cannot appreciate it. Nonetheless, the common harmony by which this passage is carried out from one mode to the other modifies the harshness. The moment of surprise passes like a flash and soon this surprise turns into admiration when we find ourselves transported from one hemisphere to another, so to speak, without having had time to think about it.[116]

Rameau was singularly proud of his insights into such chromatic and enharmonic practices. It is true that the ancient Greeks calculated the ratios of these various genres. But clearly they did not understand the true harmonic origin of them:

What are we to think of the Ancients who were acquainted only with the products of these different genres, when the effects which they attribute to them do not depend at all on their products, seeing that it – I refer to the quarter tone – is inappreciable by the ear.[117]

With the discovery of the chromatic and enharmonic genres, Rameau had essentially completed his theoretical system. Now he believed he had all the harmonic vocabulary and rules governing their use he needed in order to account for tonal practice. While he would continue to refine his arguments over the remaining years, his basic theoretical system was now firmly in place. This system is summarized in Figure 7.1.

The resonating *corps sonore* generates through its aliquot divisions a harmonic series of upper partials sounding the major triad (1, ⅓, ⅕). All even partials produce octave compounds that are perceived by the ear to be identical, and hence replications of simpler ratios. Through the sympathetic resonance of strings tuned as aliquant multiples of the *corps sonore*, an arithmetic series is suggested, one which produces the minor triad (1, 3, 5). As the two perfect fifths – octave reductions of the perfect twelfths – are the closest terms emanating from the fundamental, we can further infer from the *corps sonore* the concatenation of perfect fifths modeled as a triple geometric progression (1, 3, 9). These upper and lower fifths model the primary fundamental bass motion of all music, and together serve to define the mode and diatonic scale, from which are derived the dominant and subdominant functions, respectively. In the merging of elements of both dominant terms (1 and 9), one discovers the source of dissonance (the dominant seventh, subdominant added-sixth chord, and diminished seventh). A potential fourth term added to the triple progression is another source of dissonance available to harmonize the upper tetrachord of the mode through the *double emploi*. Just as the upper and lower perfect twelfths constitute the triple geometric progression, the upper and lower major seventeenths relate to the *principe* in a quintuple geometric progression (1, 5, 25). When activated as a fundamental bass succession, the chords connected by this progression create chromatic and enharmonic intervals, depending upon whether adjacent or extreme terms are connected.

We need not rehearse here once again the many obvious problems – both empirical and logical – that plagued this system. They were not enough to counter its

[116] *Génération harmonique*, 153.   [117] *Démonstration*, 101.

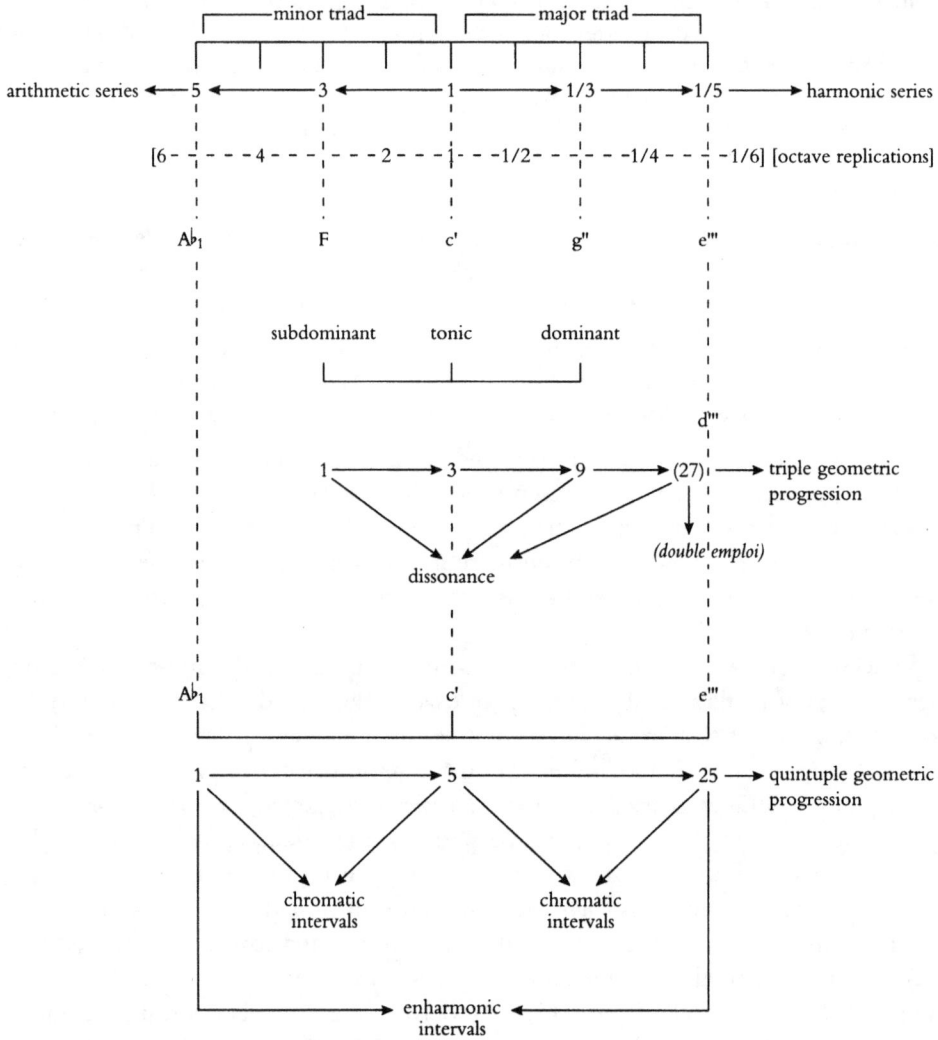

Figure 7.1 Summary of Rameau's derivations from the *corps sonore*

equally obvious virtues. Through his keen musical intuitions, as well as a redoubtable determination to account in as economic a way as possible for the material of musical practice, Rameau forged a unified and symmetrical theoretical system through a pluralistic methodology of synthesis, deduction, analogy, and, admittedly on occasion, spurious logic. Nonetheless, in its breadth and elegance, the result must be seen as a stunning achievement and victory for Rameau, one by which he was able to arrive at some of his most profound and lasting insights into the nature of tonality. Confident he had at last discovered in the *corps sonore* the natural principle of music so long hidden to musicians, it now remained for Rameau to persuade others of this fact.

8

RAMEAU AND THE PHILOSOPHES

The years between 1749 and 1752 mark the apex of Rameau's musical career. It was during this period that his fondest hopes for recognition and acceptance of his music theory seemed to have been realized. His system of the fundamental bass was endorsed by the leading scientific academy in Europe, redacted by one of its most influential members, and praised and taught in the pages of the *Encyclopédie*. It is a testament to Rameau's increased stature that before 1750, only three theoretical works were published in France that in any substantial way made use of the fundamental bass, whereas between just 1752 and 1754, eight such works appeared in quick succession.[1] On top of this, we must not overlook that Rameau's operas and ballets were enjoying unprecedented success. In 1749 alone, no less than six of his works could be heard at the Opéra – a record for any composer – and the number might have gone higher had it not been for the intercession of Madame Pompadour.[2] It would seem that our elderly composer-theorist, now sixty-seven years of age, had cause for satisfaction and contentment. But such was not to be the case.

Having tenaciously struggled for so long to achieve this success, Rameau was rapidly to lose many of his gains over the following years. For reasons that were partly due to changing intellectual and musical tastes, but also his own obstinate personality, Rameau alienated one by one most of his former supporters. Scarcely had the first volume of the *Encyclopédie* appeared in print when Rameau petulantly accused the editors of incompetence and infidelity to his theory. At the same time, his operas were being dragged into the boisterous *Querelle des Bouffons* that erupted after a visiting troop of Italian players had performed in Paris in 1752. In addition to all this, Rameau began to suggest certain scientific consequences of the *corps*

---

[1] The three works published before 1752 are by Charles-Antoine Vion, *La musique pratique et théorique* (Paris, 1742); Charles Levens, *Abrégé des règles de l'harmonie pour apprendre la composition* (Bordeaux, 1743); and Charles-Henri Blainville, *Harmonie théorico-pratique* (Paris, 1746). The eight works published between 1752 and 1754 are by Jean Le Rond d'Alembert, *Elémens de musique théorique et pratique* (Paris, 1752); Jacques Lacombe, *Dictionnaire portatif des Beaux-Arts* (Paris, 1752); Michel Corrette, *Le Maitre de clavecin pour l'accompagnement* (Paris, 1753); Claude de la Porte, *Traité théorique et pratique de l'accompagnement du clavecin* (Paris, 1753); Jean-Edmé Gallimard, *Arithmétique des musiciens* (Paris, 1754); Jean-Laurent de Bethizy, *Exposition de la théorie et de la pratique de la musique* (Paris, 1754); M. Dubugrarre, *Méthode plus courte et plus facile que l'ancienne pour l'accompagnement du clavecin* (Paris, 1754); and Francesco Geminiani, *L'art de bien accompagner du clavecin* (Paris, 1754).
[2] The works were *Les Fêtes de l'Hymen et de l'Amour, Zais, Pygmalion, Les Surprises de l'Amour, Nais*, and *Zoroastre*.

sonore that would astound and exasperate scientists like d'Alembert. If Rameau's scientific pretenses had been indulged and even countenanced by scientists up to this point, his newest pronouncements could enjoy no such sanction. With all of these developments transpiring at the same time, and exacerbated by the stubborn egos involved, the stage was set for a tempestuous battle.

It is somewhat pathetic in retrospect finding Rameau engaging in polemical duels with the likes of d'Alembert and Rousseau. Yet the popular depiction of Rameau the "embittered and doting monomaniac" and "obvious crank" haplessly fulminating "with the zeal and perseverance of the Old Testament prophet" at targets intellectually better armed than he obscures the fact that Rameau was still making important theoretical arguments.[3] To be sure, Rameau's last writings tax the patience of the reader with their endless rhapsodic praise to the powers of the *corps sonore*; in listening to his diatribes against d'Alembert, we can only scratch our heads in wonderment that Rameau would insist upon pushing his points with such relentlessness that he ensured the enmity of a man whose friendship and support he had every reason to nurture and protect. But when we move beyond all the hysteria and reverie, Rameau was still developing his theory in interesting and profitable ways. He never lost sight of the musical issues involved. It is telling in this regard that at the same time as he was trying to reduce his theory to the most tightly synthesized and abstracted scientific system premised upon the *corps sonore,* to say nothing of speculating broadly about the metaphysical consequences therefrom, Rameau was working on his most empirically sober and detailed treatise on composition and accompaniment – the *Code de musique pratique* of 1760. To the end of his life, the practical composer and pedagogue never parted company from the speculative theorist.

RAMEAU AND THE ENCYCLOPEDISTS

The history of Rameau's stormy relationship with the young philosophes associated with the founding of the *Encyclopédie* – Diderot, d'Alembert, and Rousseau – has been often told, and there is no need here to report any but the most basic facts.[4] All of the philosophes were sincere admirers of Rameau's music and theory, at least at the beginning. They saw in Rameau an innovative reformer of the French opera, whose music had successfully displaced the increasingly stale formulas of

---

[3] The pejorative characterizations are to be found in James Doolittle, "A Would-Be Philosophe, Jean-Philippe Rameau," *Publication of the Modern Language Association* 74 (1959), 239, 246, and 241, respectively.

[4] A recently published study offering much insight, particularly in its analysis of the aesthetic issues involved, is Cynthia Verba's *Music and the French Enlightenment: Reconstruction of a Dialogue* (Oxford, 1992). Her work supplements Alfred Richard Oliver, *The Encylopedists as Critics of Music* (New York, 1947). Another book with much useful information is Béatrice Didier, *La Musique des Lumières: Diderot – L'Encyclopédie – Rousseau* (Paris, 1985). Jean-Jacques Robrieux's lengthy article ("Jean-Philippe Rameau et l'opinion philosophique en France au dix-huitième siècle," *Studies on Voltaire and the Eighteenth Century* 238 [1985], 269–395) unfortunately cannot be recommended, consisting as it does of a mish-mash of outdated scholarship, discredited stereotypes, and shallow analyses of the intellectual-musical issues involved.

Lully's *tragédie en musique*. His recitatives were considered more lyrical than Lully's, his orchestral scoring more colorful. Rameau's daring use of dissonance gave his music an unprecedented depth of expression that proved to be highly effective in depicting and underscoring a panoramic range of human passions. With the *Querelle des Bouffons* yet to be fought, Diderot could celebrate in his risqué parody *Les Bijoux indiscrets* of 1747 the triumph of the composer "Utremifasollasiutututut" (Rameau) over poor "Utmiutsol" (Lully) in the fictitious land of Banza.[5] Several years later, in his Preliminary Discourse, d'Alembert would describe Rameau as a "manly, courageous, and fruitful genius," on whose account "foreigners who could not bear our 'symphonies' are beginning to enjoy them, and the French at last appear to be persuaded that Lully left much to be done in this branch of the arts." D'Alembert continued:

In carrying the practice of his art to such a high degree of perfection, M. Rameau has become simultaneously the model and the object of jealousy of a large number of artists, who deprecate him at the same time as they are trying to imitate him.

D'Alembert concludes his panegyric of Rameau – incidentally, one of the longest in the *Discourse* – with these words:

I readily take the opportunity of celebrating this artist-philosopher in a Discourse directed principally to the praise of great men. His merit, which he has forced our century to acknowledge, will be well known only when time has made envy hold its tongue; and his name, which is dear to the most enlightened part of our nation, cannot offend anyone here.[6]

It should be noted that even after the commencement of the *Querelle des Bouffons*, all the philosophes, with the exception of Rousseau, maintained a sincere respect for Rameau, even as they were lambasting French operatic traditions in favor of the Italian style.[7] One of the most important partisans in the "Coin de la Reine," Baron von Grimm, repeatedly singled out Rameau for praise in his important pamphlets, "Lettre sur Omphale" and "Le Petit prophète de Boehmischbroda," of 1753.[8] So, too, would Diderot praise Rameau in his contribution to the *Querelle*, "Au Petit prophète de Boehmischbroda et au grand prophète Monet." But it was not difficult for the public to see the obvious inconsistencies of dismissing French operatic practice, yet at the same time sparing its leading composer. Rousseau's open attack upon Rameau in his "Lettre sur la musique française" of 1754 must have seemed to many – as it certainly did to Rameau – a display of the philosophes' true colors. Nonetheless, Diderot and Grimm were sincere in their admiration for

---

5 Diderot, *Les Bijoux indiscrets* (Paris, 1747), in *Oeuvres complètes de Diderot*, 26 vols. (Paris, 1975–), III, 70.
6 *Preliminary Discourse*, 100.
7 The "Bouffon quarrel" was one of several lively pamphlet wars over the respective merits of French and Italian opera to take place in France during the eighteenth century. The quarrel received its name from the troupe of traveling Italian players who visited Paris in 1752 to perform Pergolesi's *La serva padrona*. A concise account of the Encyclopedists' role in the quarrel is found in Oliver, *The Encyclopedists as Critics*, 89–100. See also Louisette Richbourg, *Contribution à l'histoire de la querelle des Bouffons* (Paris, 1937).
8 The "Petit prophète" is partially translated in Oliver Strunk, *Source Readings in the History of Music* (New York, 1950), 619–35.

Rameau the composer. If the French opera at one time needed Rameau to reform it, so then did French opera of a later time stand in need of a new reformer, a "new Rameau."

The Encyclopedists were more than mere partisans of Rameau's music, though; they were the first influential group of intellectuals to recognize the philosophical implications of his music theory. (Rameau's earlier scientific supporters, Castel and Mairan, wielded little of the weight the Encyclopedists did in the early 1750s.) They believed Rameau's theory to be the most complete and logical systematization of music yet offered. As their enthusiastic commendations recorded in Chapter 1 testify, they were thereby convinced that they had found in Rameau the "Newton of Music" whose theory could be added to the arsenal of weapons in their philosophical campaign. It is little wonder that one of the goals Diderot set for his Encyclopedia project was to promote the composer's theory.

Shared admiration did not translate into uniform acceptance, however. Diderot, Rousseau, and d'Alembert each had differing agendas that colored their reception of the composer's ideas, and these differences come out clearly in their respective redactions and commentaries: Diderot's early essays on aesthetics and psychology, Rousseau's *Encyclopédie* articles and polemical writings on opera and language, and d'Alembert's *Elémens de musique*. While it is beyond the domain of this study to offer a comprehensive analysis of the musical aesthetics and theories of each of these men, it will be appropriate in this chapter to look at the respective writings and activities of Diderot and Rousseau insofar as they impinge upon Rameau's ideas. Because d'Alembert's relationship with Rameau was ultimately the most complex and consequential among the Encyclopedists, and because his quarrel with Rameau can serve as a useful summary for most of the issues that have arisen over the course of the present study, I will consider his writings separately in the next chapter.

DIDEROT AND THE *DEMONSTRATION*

We do not know under what circumstance Rameau and Diderot first met.[9] But it seems to have been sometime around 1748 when the young writer was just beginning the *Encyclopédie* project. Diderot was always interested in music. One of his first publications, the *Mémoires sur différents sujets de mathématiques* of 1748, addressed some acoustical and aesthetic questions relevant to music.[10] In the same work he also proposed a number of novel musical inventions, including a method for determining exact pitch, a primitive metronome device called a "chronomètre," and a mechanical organ "upon which one can play any piece of music without knowing music."[11] Despite such obvious fascination with musical topics, however, it does not

---

9 For background on Diderot's friendship with Rameau, see Béatrice Durand-Sendrail, "Diderot et Rameau: Archéologie d'une Polémique," *Diderot Studies* 24 (1991), 85–104; and Lucette Perol, "Diderot et Rameau," *Rameau en Auvergne MCMLXXXIII*, ed. Jean-Louis Jam (Clermont-Ferrand, 1986), 109–19.

10 Denis Diderot, "Mémoires sur différents sujets de mathématiques," *Oeuvres complètes*, II, 221–338.

11 Diderot's lifelong fascination with music has finally begun to receive the attention it deserves from scholars. Catalytic was a ground-breaking article by Paul Henry Lang, written with his customary erudition:"Diderot

seem that Diderot at this time understood very much concerning the practice or theory of music. Only in his later years did he remedy this deficiency, particularly in his collaboration with Bemetzrieder. In the acoustical essay just mentioned, Diderot did discuss a few questions relating to tuning and harmonic overtones, but nothing concerning the technicalities of the fundamental bass. Elsewhere in the same publication, he confessed that he was an "ignoramus" concerning music.

As with Condillac and d'Alembert, though, Diderot could still admire the concision of Rameau's theory even without understanding its details. He called the *Génération harmonique* an "admirable system of composition," and expressed the wish that "someone will draw it from the obscurities in which it is enveloped and place it within the reach of all the world, less for the glory of its inventor, than for the progress of the science of sounds."[12] Diderot obviously saw his *Encyclopédie* as the forum most perfectly suited for this task.

Music as both a theoretical science and practical art held an honored position in the Encyclopedia's grand "Système figuré des connoissances humaines." Diderot was determined that Rameau's ideas would be presented fully and accurately in its pages. Not surprisingly, then, he approached Rameau about writing the articles on music, an offer the composer evidently refused.[13] That Rameau declined to write the articles may have been due to self-doubts about his literary ability, or perhaps an ego that refused to stoop to the level of mere *collaborateur*.[14] Whatever the reason may have been, Diderot turned the job over to Rousseau, at the time the philosophe with the most musical experience and knowledge. Rousseau set to work right away on the articles, completing them, he claimed, within a three-month period at the beginning of 1749.[15]

Matters were proceeding less smoothly for Diderot, however. On account of several controversial tracts he had earlier published anonymously, he was arrested in the summer of 1749 and confined to the Royal prison at Vincennes.[16] (His

---

as Musician," *Diderot Studies* 10 (1969), 95–107. Also of value is Jean Mayer's fine introduction to the volume of Diderot's musical writings in *Oeuvres complètes*, XIX, ix–xxii. A recent symposium concerning Diderot's views on art (fourteen of the papers deal explicitly with music) has been published as *Diderot: Les Beaux-arts et la musique*, Actes du colloque international tenue à Aix-en-Provence (Aix-en-Provence, 1986). Finally the chapters on Diderot in the books by Didier and Verba cited above can be highly recommended.

12 *Oeuvres complètes*, II, 265.
13 Our only evidence for this is a bitter remark made long after the fact by Rameau. In an open letter denouncing what he perceived to be the Encyclopedists' misrepresentation of his theory, Rameau scolded, "You could have avoided these errors by sending me your manuscripts that I offered to examine after having excused myself from undertaking the whole enterprise" ("Réponse de M. Rameau à MM. les editeurs de l'Encyclopédie sur leur dernier avertissement" [Paris, 1757], 53; *CTW* V, 360). Although Rameau is usually not the most reliable source for the historian, especially in his polemical writings, his account here is probably true. In the late 1740s, Rameau's relationship with the philosophes was quite cordial; there is no reason why Diderot would not have initially offered the job to the famous theoretician following his own expressed wish to secure the most "eminent authorities" as contributors to the *Encyclopédie*.
14 This second possibility is suggested by Oliver, *The Encyclopedists as Critics*, 102.
15 We will consider Rousseau's articles in more detail at the end of this chapter (pp. 247–51).
16 A drama narrated in Arthur Wilson, *Diderot: The Testing Years* (New York, 1957), 103–16.

detention was not so onerous, though, that he could not receive visitors or continue his own writings.) In order to secure his release, Diderot wrote a letter of "confession" to the Police commissioner, Berryer, in which he described some of his more recent activities. Striving to present himself in the most virtuous manner, Diderot disclosed: "I was always ready to lend my pen and give my time to those who had need of it for useful activities."[17] One of those who profited from Diderot's altruism seems to have been Rameau. According to Diderot's letter, he had recently produced an "exposition du système de musique de M. Rameau." Raynal confirms something along these lines, describing Diderot in 1749 as

> an intimate friend of M. Rameau, whose discoveries he is shortly going to publish. This sublime and profound musician has given us works some time ago which he failed to endow with sufficient clarity and elegance. M. Diderot will rework these ideas, and he is most capable of setting them forth to excellent advantage.[18]

Later on, Raynal added, "Our very illustrious and celebrated musician, M. Rameau, claims to have discovered the principle of harmony. M. Diderot has lent him his pen in order to set forth this important discovery to its best advantage."[19]

What text could Diderot and Raynal have been referring to? The only theoretical work Rameau produced during this period was the *Démonstration du principe de l'harmonie* of 1750. While it is unlikely that Diderot had much to do with any technical details of Rameau's theory as presented in the *Démonstration* given his general ignorance of music theory during this time, the philosophical prolegomenon that prefaces this text is another matter altogether.

We recall from Chapter 6 that the original draft of the *Démonstration* was a "Mémoire où l'on expose les fondemens du système de musique théorique et pratique de M. Rameau." Two copies of the "Mémoire" exist in manuscript – a short and clean copy in the archives of the Opéra, and a second, longer, and much revised copy now housed in the archives of the Académie Royale des Sciences.[20] I suggested that many of the corrections and revisions to be found in this latter manuscript were made under the supervision and coaching of d'Alembert, who later would incorporate these very revisions in his review of the "Mémoire" and his *Elémens de musique théorique et pratique*. The shorter version of this "Mémoire" has a somewhat different history. As I also suggested in Chapter 6, this copy was the original lecture delivered to the Académie audience. In it, we find little technical discussion of music theory, but rather a phenomenological essay on method and the *corps sonore* that is written in a style far more polished than any Rameau had ever produced before. Moreover, a number of new ideas make their appearance there, suggesting that Rameau was once again up to his old habits of collecting and

---

17 Letter dated August 10, 1749; *Correspondance de Diderot*, ed. Georges Roth and Jean Varloot, 16 vols. (Paris, 1954), I, 86.
18 Friedrich Melchior von Grimm *et al.*, *Correspondance littéraire, philosophique, et critique*, ed. Maurice Tourneux, 16 vols. (Paris, 1877–82), I, 202.
19 *Ibid.*, I, 313.
20 See Chapter 6, pp. 160–62.

incorporating new ideas into his theory. From whence came these ideas? The answer seems to point unequivocally in the direction of Diderot.

There are several plausible reasons why Diderot would have been willing, indeed eager, to help the composer in the composition of this "Mémoire." First, as we have already seen, like all the other philosophes at this time, Diderot sincerely admired Rameau's theory of music, even if he could not appreciate its technical details. It would have been a strategic move for Diderot, just then getting ready to issue the first volume of the *Encyclopédie*, to gain the alliance of so influential a public figure as Rameau. Helping the composer work out his theory would have been the perfect opportunity to do this. Secondly, Diderot was familiar with many of the members and organization of the Académie Royale des Sciences, having just been turned down for membership in February of that year. Possibly he was motivated to coach Rameau in his bid for membership (for which purpose the "Mémoire" was to serve). Thirdly, and most importantly, Diderot must have recognized how the subject matter of Rameau's theory related to certain philosophical ideas with which he was avidly engaged at the time. All this evidence suggests strongly, then, that the Opéra "Mémoire," whose full title corresponds closely to the title Diderot indicated in his confessional letter ("Exposition du système de M. Rameau"), was guided by Diderot's hand.[21]

RAMEAU'S SENSATIONALIST CONVERSION

We recall from Chapter 1 how warmly the philosophes received Locke's sensationalist empirical psychology. The thesis that knowledge was derived mainly through the senses was one strongly appealing to those holding both empiricist and mechanist ideologies. (It was quite easy to reconcile Descartes's mechanistic metaphysics with sensationalism simply by stripping away the former of innate ideas and God – something many of the philosophes were only too happy to do.[22]) By the 1740s, a number of French writers pushed the sensationalist philosophy to extremes much further than Locke ever did by reducing man the sentient being to virtually nothing more than a passive automaton, or as La Mettrie put it in his notorious materialist tract of 1748: *L'homme machine* – Man the Machine.

Diderot became one of the most enthusiastic proponents of the sensationalist epistemology. In his *Lettre sur les aveugles à l'usage de ceux qui voient* ("Letter on the Blind for the Use of Those Who See") of 1749 – one of the works, incidentally, that helped land its author in jail – Diderot addressed questions central to the sensationalist epistemology: what kinds of knowledge are dependent upon the sense of sight, and what would the effects be of a blind person suddenly being

---

21 It may also be of significance, as Jacobi has pointed out, that the publisher for Rameau's *Démonstration* was Durand, the same house that brought out Diderot's *Mémoires* and the *Encyclopédie*. Durand was on especially friendly terms with Diderot, consenting in 1750 to stand as godfather to Diderot's son (*CTW* III, p. XLII).
22 Aram Vartanian, *Diderot and Descartes: A Study of Scientific Naturalism in the Enlightenment* (Princeton, 1953), 203ff.

granted this sensory capability? Such questions were loaded ones, as they led our intrepid editor to consider a host of related psychological, pedagogical, and theological issues that were judged scandalous by the authorities.[23]

Diderot pondered a widely reported story of a blind boy who had his cataracts removed and was able to see for the first time. What were his first impressions, Diderot wondered? What images would first strike his eye, and what sense would they make to him? I think when Diderot first discussed Rameau's theory with the author, he would have recognized right away how sound could be experienced in similar sensationalist ways, and he coached our impressionable composer along these lines. Tellingly, one year later Diderot published a follow-up to his first letter on the blind, but this time dealing with the deaf and dumb: *Lettre sur les sourds et muets à l'usage de ceux qui entendent et qui parlent* ("Letter on the Deaf and Mute for the Benefit of Those who Hear and Speak"). Of course the subject of deafness raises a set of problems different from those of blindness, problems that led Diderot to ponder questions of language, gesture, and music. Nonetheless, the same epistemological question can be posed for music as for visual impressions: What kinds of sensations do musical sounds make upon an untutored listener and how does one learn to interpret them? One of the many images Diderot describes in this *Lettre* is an automaton (mechanical man) whose soul receives sensory impressions much as if its mind were a bell outfitted with many little hammers each attached to threads:

If several of the little threads are pulled at the same instant, the bell will be struck by several hammers, and the little figure will hear several sounds at once. Now, suppose that among all these strings there are some that are being pulled continuously; just as our only proof of the noise that is made in Paris by day is the silence we are aware of at night, so there will be sensations inside us that will often elude us precisely because they are always there – such as the sensation of our existence.[24]

Diderot thought that the proportions suggested by the resonating *corps sonore* are inculcated in our minds through constant repetition, without our being aware of them. He further speculated that the way musicians learned to recognize and apply these proportions was a mirror of the way the human mind acquired all knowledge: as the accumulation (memory) and comparison (judgment) of sensory impressions.

It would be easy for me to extend this comparison and to add that the sounds given out by the bell do not fade immediately; that they possess duration; that they form harmonies with the sounds that follow them; that the little listening figure compares them and forms an opinion as to whether they are concords or discords; that our memory at any given moment, the power of recall that we need in order to form opinions and to express them, is represented by the vibrations of the bell, our power of judgment by the formation of concords, and

---

23 For a good analysis of the *Lettre*, see D. J. Adams, *Diderot, Dialogue and Debate* (Liverpool, 1986), 116–39. Along with such speculative questions, the philosophes were also interested in practical problems of pedagogy for the blind. Never one to ignore some idea in vogue, Rameau subtitled his *Code de musique* of 1760, *Méthodes pour apprendre la musique même à des aveugles*.

24 From *Diderot's Selected Writings*, trans. Derek Coltman, ed. Lester G. Crocker (New York, 1966), 32–33.

our discourse by their sequence; and that it is not without good reason that we describe some people's brains as being "cracked."[25]

With tongue firmly in cheek, Diderot goes on to draw a fanciful analogy between Rameau's theory of *liaison* and the common elements that must be shared for sentences to connect to one another with any logic.

Rameau seemed to have learned his lesson well. In the "Mémoire," Rameau articulates ideas wherein I think we can detect the telltale signs of Diderot guiding our composer towards a more overt "sensationalist" interpretation of his theory. Above all, Rameau's rhetoric is different. Rather than employing the clumsy and impersonal scientific discourse of the *Génération harmonique*, Rameau speaks directly to the reader in the first person to report his many sensory perceptions and thoughts: "Je sentai," "J'imaginai," "Je regardai autour de moi," "J'examinai," and "Je m'appercus."[26] In language reminiscent of Diderot's *Lettre*, Rameau recounts the method by which he would have us believe he had arrived at his principle of harmony.

Beginning with the Cartesian experiment reported in Chapter 1, Rameau examines carefully the musical intervals he sang to himself after clearing his mind of all habits and memories, much as a child might. The intervals he sang were the perfect fifth and major third, suggesting these were the most primitive and fundamental intervals. But this experiment does not satisfy Rameau, for he felt that despite his best efforts, habit and experience still may have suggested these intervals to him, try as he might to avoid this. He concludes forlornly, "I have no right to attribute the melodies I sang to principles other than those arising from habitude, unexamined conventions (*convenances*), and other such arbitrary laws."[27]

A new idea then occurs to Rameau that departed radically from his previous Cartesian epistemology. Rather than seek certain principles about music by introspection or mathematical demonstration, he asks, why not see what nature herself suggests to our attentive senses? Rameau tries this by imagining himself as a deafmute who hears a sound for the first time, and whose mind was to be a kind of acoustical tabula rasa. We will pick up at the end of the passage already quoted on page 12:

I then placed myself as well as I could into the state of a man who had neither sung nor heard singing, promising myself even to resort to extraneous experiments whenever I suspected that habit . . . might influence me despite myself. . . That done, I began to look around me

---

25 *Ibid.*, 33.
26 Anne-Marie Chouillet has analyzed the rhetoric of Rameau's theoretical writings, and has statistically documented an increase in "sensationalist" vocabulary in Rameau's later treatises. Whereas terms suggesting *perceptual* faculties such as "sentir" and "sensibilité" are found only four times in the *Traité*, there are twenty-two occurrences in the much shorter *Observations sur notre instinct pour la musique* of 1754. Conversely, the term "goût," suggestive of a rationalist judgment internal to the mind, is mentioned twenty-five times in the *Traité*, but only four times in the *Observations* (Anne-Marie Chouillet, "Le Concept de beauté dans les écrits théoriques de Rameau," *Rameau en Auvergne MCMLXXXIII* ed. Jean-Louis Jam [Clermont-Ferrand, 1986], 91).
27 "Académie Mémoire," fol. 6. This section was omitted from publication in the *Démonstration*, but is transcribed by Jacobi in *CTW* VI, 192.

and search in nature for what I could not draw from myself, neither as clearly nor as surely as I would have desired. My search was not long. The first sound which struck my ear was like a flash of light. I perceived right away that it was not one [sound], rather the impression it made upon me was composite.[28]

Rameau's "flash of light" was of course the *corps sonore*. Here is one of the most pure and ubiquitous phenomenological stimuli offered by nature. As Rameau will make quite clear over the following pages, the *corps sonore* must be the source from which humans have learned to draw their musics. Over and over Rameau will stress the importance of his discovery of the *corps sonore* as a *sensory* experience, and how it alone constitutes the principle of music for which he had so long searched:

Suddenly there arose in me the suspicion that the harmonics, which I (and others like me) had always heard in fundamental sounds, might after all be the true cause of the predilection that I felt for certain sounds after intoning some others, and for which I had searched in vain for a satisfactory reason in myself. It was a fact that needed to be verified, and I undertook to examine it, entirely ready to abandon this path if it failed.[29]

How could this natural phenomenon be the principle of music if it had not been recognized until now? The answer must be that repeated exposure to it has dulled our sensitivity. Like the hammers incessantly striking the bell of Diderot's automaton, we are constantly hearing sounds (including those of our own voice) that resonate the upper partials of the twelfth and seventeenth, but scarcely know this fact. Nonetheless, these proportions must have been etched subconsciously into the minds of ancient musicians who accepted them as fundamental consonances.

Musicians soon learned to construct more elaborate music using these intervals, reflecting upon, comparing, and combining the proportions they perceived in the *corps sonore*: the perfect twelfth and major seventeenth, or their octave equivalents, the perfect fifth and major third. In Rameau's ethnological reconstruction, this is how harmony was born, and from harmony, the diatonic succession of the tetrachord, the full scale, and finally, all melody. Musicians in advanced civilizations soon discovered other resources latent in these proportions: dissonance, modulation, and various species of chromatic and enharmonic genres. Rameau's conclusion is simple. Since all music seems to be an elaboration of the basic proportions contained in the *corps sonore*, this natural phenomenon is the unique source and generator of music.

PYGMALION: THE ANIMATED STATUE AS LOCKEAN ALLEGORY

It was not only in his theoretical writings, though, that sensationalist ideas may be seen to have influenced Rameau. We can find Locke's psychology treated in one of Rameau's most splendid stage works, the opera-ballet *Pygmalion*. But before looking

---

[28] "Académie Mémoire," fols. 6–7. This passage is contained without change in the *Démonstration*, 11–12.
[29] "Opéra Mémoire," fols. 121v–122r.

at this work, we must first digress for a moment and consider the philosophical writings of the Abbé Condillac. Condillac was one of the most avid disciples of Locke's empiricist psychology among the philosophes. In two important treatises, the *Essai sur l'origine des connaissances humaines* of 1746, and the *Traité des sensations* of 1754, Condillac laid out a comprehensive theory of knowledge based entirely upon sensationalist premises. To model how sensory knowledge is acquired, he proposed in his *Traité* that we imagine a marble statue. By endowing this statue with sensory capabilities one by one, Condillac is able to show the extent and limits of knowledge related to each sense, and how cumulatively they constitute the psychological whole of human experience.

The use of a statue to model psychological experiences was one long predating Condillac. Descartes, Molyneux and Bouffon had all suggested something along these lines before Condillac's *Traité*. But there was a much older source for the story of an animated statue in the famous Pygmalion legend of Ovid. Throughout the seventeenth and eighteenth centuries, writers and poets adapted the Pygmalion legend in a variety of literary genres.[30] One of the most famous stage adaptations of the Pygmalion story in France was made by Houdar de La Motte in 1700.[31] In La Motte's version, the sculptor Pygmalion chisels a statue of a woman so beautiful that he is overcome with passion and love. Of course the statue cannot reciprocate this love, and the distraught artist is left to curse his fate. Moved by the depths of his anguish, Venus intervenes and brings the statue to life, whereupon Pygmalion and his now-human creation – named "Galatea" in many versions – are united in love.

The Pygmalion story was popular in French artistic and literary circles throughout the Enlightenment.[32] Michel de La Barre had set a version to music in 1709, André-François Boureau-Deslandes set it in prose in 1741, and Rousseau penned a libretto on the story in 1770. It is not surprising that Rameau would eventually set the legend. The occasion came in 1748 – not coincidentally, I think, at just the time sensationalist theories were in such vogue. Ballot de Sovot, a member of La Pouplinière's circle, provided a libretto based upon de La Motte's story sufficiently rich with sensationalist references and images to appeal to the most sophisticated of Rameau's listeners. The *Acte de ballet* that Rameau composed using Sovot's text is widely considered to be one of his best. It was certainly one of his most popular compositions during his lifetime, receiving numerous performances even through the Bouffon quarrel.[33]

As we find Pygmalion in Scene 3 (Example 8.1), the distraught artist, alone with his statue, pleads with the gods to still his unfulfillable longings. After closing his lament in G major ("Reconnais à mes feux l'ouvrage de ton fils: Lui seul pouvait

---

30 For the literary history of the Pygmalion legend, see Annegret Dinter, *Der Pygmalion-Stoff in der europäischen Literatur* (Heidelberg, 1979), Chapter 5.
31 "La Sculpture," or the "Cinquiéme Entrée" of *Le Triomphe des Arts, Oeuvres de Monsieur Houdar de la Motte*, 6 vols. (Paris, 1754), VI, 186–94.
32 J. L. Carr, "Pygmalion and the *Philosophes*," *Journal of the Warburg and Courtauld Institutes* 23 (1960), 239–54.
33 Cuthbert Girdlestone, *Jean-Philippe Rameau: His Life and Work*, 2nd edition (New York, 1969), 467.

Example 8.1. *Pygmalion*, Scene 3

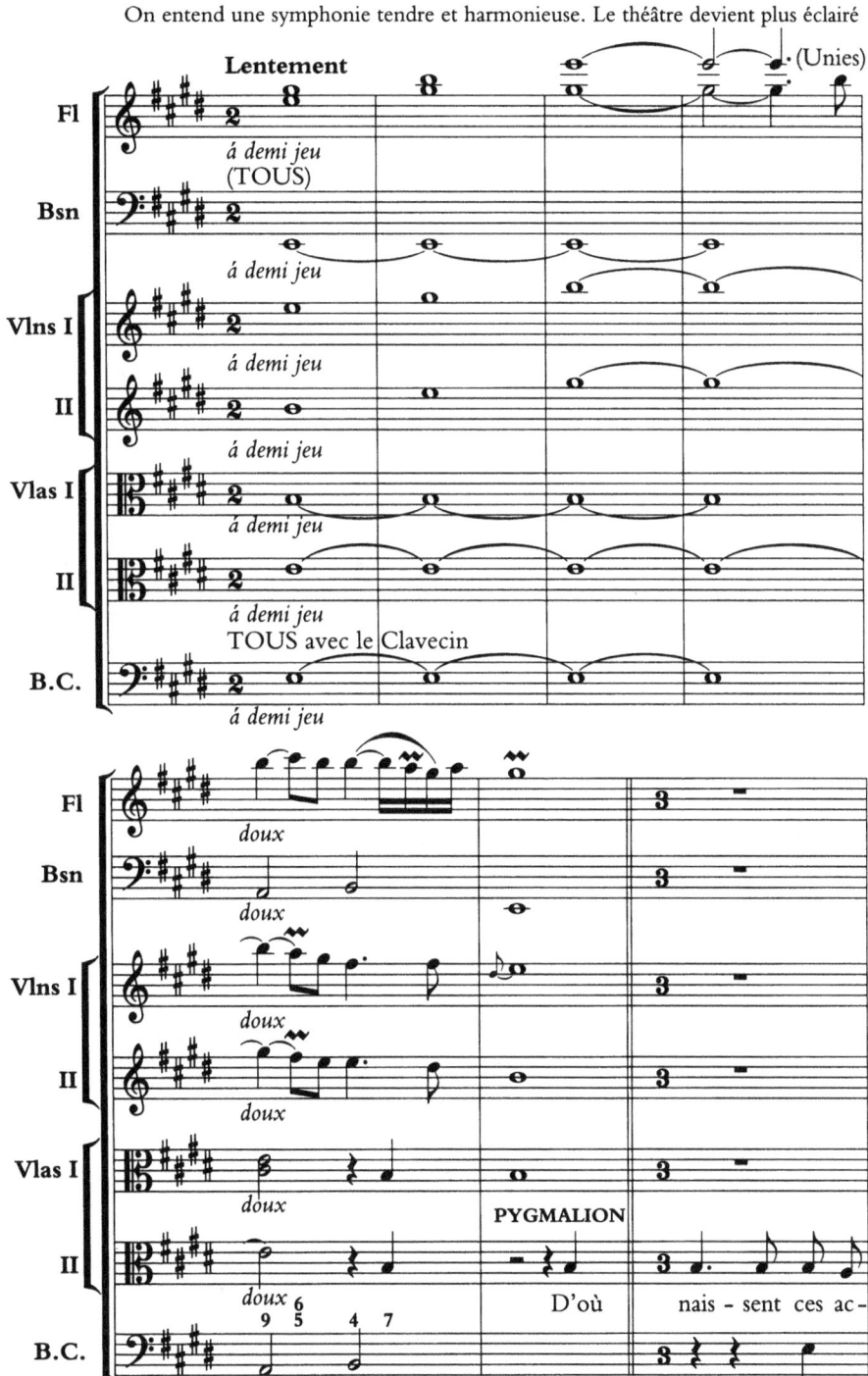

Pygmalion: Whence come these harmonies? These concordant sounds? A dazzling brightness fills this place. What a marvel! What god? By what power has a dream ravished my senses? Can I possibly be mistaken, o divine influence? Protector of mortals, mighty gods, benign gods?

The Statue: What do I see: Where am I? And what am I thinking? Whereby do I have the power to move?

Pygmalion: O heavens!

rassembler tant de charmes"), Pygmalion hears a lush E major sonority. (The libretto notes: "On entend une symphonie tendre et harmonieuse.") The striking chromatic change of tonality and new orchestral colors together help underscore the symbolic change under way in the story, and were singled out by Grimm for particular praise in his *Lettre sur Omphale*. "D'où naissent ces accords?" Pygmalion asks in breathless awe – "Quels sons harmonieux?" He need not have looked far: the source of these harmonies was indicated by Rameau's orchestration. The "delicate and harmonious" E major triad is dispositioned by Rameau following the initial proportions of the *corps sonore*. Over the three following measures, the violins and flutes slowly unfold the upper partials as if Rameau were composing out the *corps sonore* itself. It is little wonder that Pygmalion soon recognizes the power of this harmony: "une vive clarté se répand dans ces lieux."[34]

It is at this point that the statue begins to awake – stirred, as it were, by these sounds.[35] Pygmalion observes the statue moving and asks in Cartesian innocence, "Par quelle intelligence un songe a-t-il séduit mes sens? Je ne m'abuse point, o divine influence?" His eyes do not deceive. The statue is indeed awakening. Her first tentative steps are accompanied by a descending tetrachord in the flutes. The first question asked by the now-awakened statue were suitably philosophical ones that would have pleased Diderot: "Que vois-je? Où suis-je? Et qu'est-ce que je pense? D'où me viennent ces mouvements?" Lest the relevance of the *corps sonore* to all this activity be missed, Rameau quotes it again in Scene 5, where the chorus sings the praises of love – the power that animated Pygmalion's statue to begin with – set again with a resplendent major triad dispositioned according to the exact harmonic proportions of the *corps sonore* (see Example 8.2). Rameau was particularly pleased by the result of this scoring, and made many proud references to it in his theoretical writings.[36] The answer to Pygmalion's question ("d'où naissent ces accords?") is implicitly provided by Rameau's scoring: the chords he heard came

---

[34] Those lines of Pygmalion that make such obvious references to the music are not to be found in de La Motte's original libretto. I think it is quite possible that de Sovot added these lines at Rameau's request, precisely so that the sensationalist basis of the *corps sonore* could be so dramatically underscored.

[35] One is reminded of Shakespeare's words: "Music, awake her: strike! 'Tis Time; descend, be stone no more" (*The Winter's Tale* V/3). The power of music to awaken the dead or inanimate material such as a statue of marble is a theme that can be found throughout mythology and literary history, from Orpheus and the Don Juan legend, through to Shelley's *Frankenstein*. Dinter (*Der Pygmalion-Stoff*) offers an exhaustive bibliography of such literature.

[36] See, e.g., *Démonstration*, 29. *Pygmalion* was not the only work in which Rameau self-consciously scored the *corps sonore*, though. In his very last opera, *Les Boréades* of 1764, Rameau used an identical scoring in the strings for the scenery change music in Act 5, Scene 5.

Example 8.2 *Pygmalion*, Scene 5

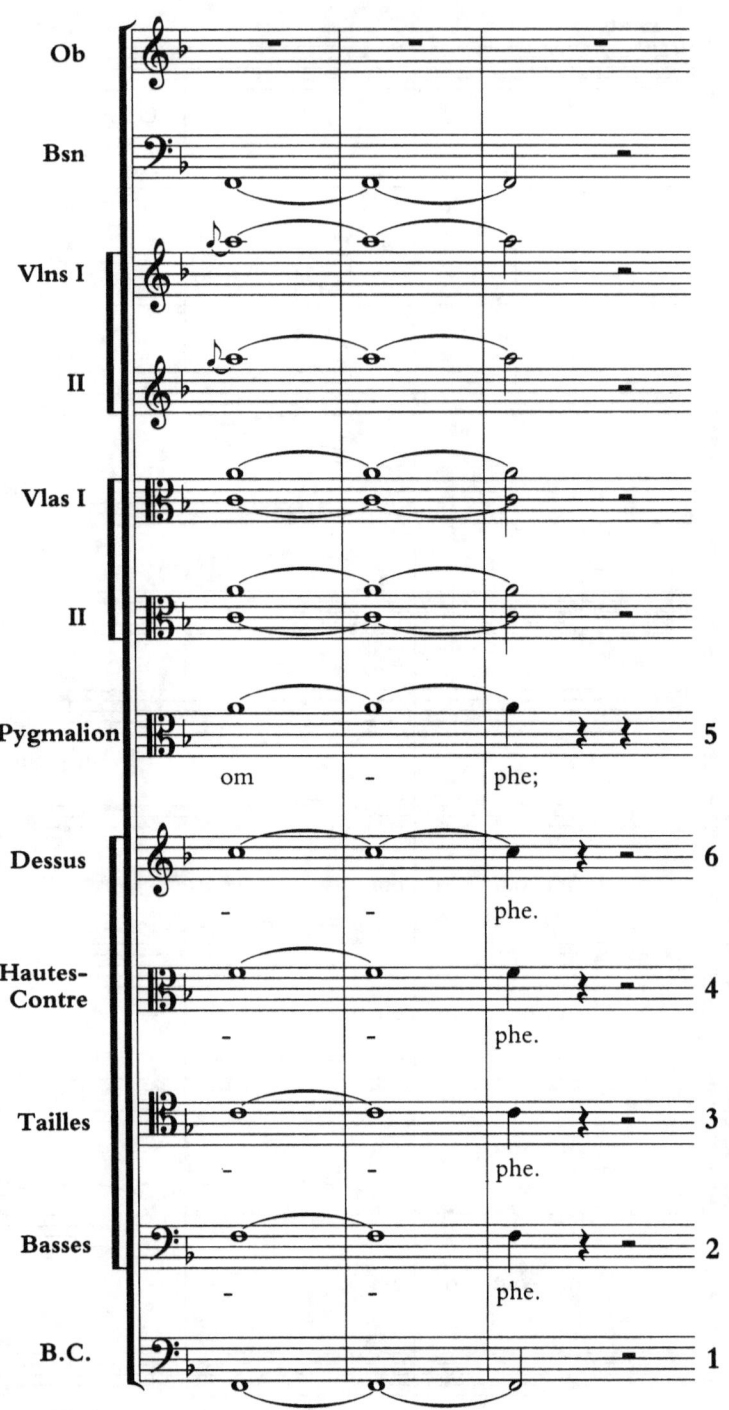

Love is triumphant!

from nature herself. The dramatic effect of this passage could thus be attributed to our instinctive recognition of the proportions contained in the *corps sonore*.[37] By reinforcing the partials naturally generated by every *corps sonore* through instrumentation, Rameau was thus able to convey in his Pygmalion setting a double sensationalist message. The same musical proportions that helped to animate Pygmalion's statue are those that animated the consciousness of early man, and from which he learns to extract in order to sing and compose his own music. Pygmalion, in short, was a musical allegory of Lockean sensationalist psychology.[38]

THE *NOUVELLES REFLEXIONS*

In all his theoretical writings after the *Démonstration*, Rameau continued to emphasize the sensationalist implications of the *corps sonore*. This is apparent in his follow-up to the *Démonstration*, the *Nouvelles réflexions de M. Rameau sur sa démonstration du principe de l'harmonie* of 1752. As the title might forewarn, the text is a desultory compilation of scattered thoughts, revisions, and rebuttals. Its primary purpose, though, seems to have been to extend the sensationalist thesis first laid down in

---

37 *Erreurs sur la musique*, 33–34.
38 It may not be a coincidence that the very first steps taken by the statue are accompanied by a diatonic tetrachord in the flutes. Could this be a not-so-veiled reference to the Greek tetrachord that Rameau believed to be among the first musical constructs drawn by man from the *corps sonore*?

   Christian Berger has argued that *Pygmalion* was something of a test piece for Rameau to try out a number of his theoretical ideas ("Ein 'Tableau' des 'Principe de l'Harmonie': *Pygmalion* von Jean-Philippe Rameau," *Rameau Colloque International*, 371–84). Berger cites as examples the scoring of the *corps sonore* quoted in Example 8.2, as well as the seemingly systematic key plan Rameau chooses for the Ballet pieces and irregular means of dissonance resolution. (Oddly, though, he fails to mention what I think is the most obvious extra-musical element in the work: the explicit references to Locke's sensationalist psychology described above.) In any case, I think Berger has overdrawn his thesis. With the obvious exception of the quotation of the *corps sonore* seen in Example 8.2, I am not convinced that the musical design and harmonic vocabulary of *Pygmalion* were conceived by Rameau with such didactic purposes in mind – no more, at least, than in any of his other compositions. With the possible exception of the enharmonic passages discussed in Chapter 7, Rameau did not compose his music as theoretical experiments; it was music that drove the theory, never the other way around. This is not to say, of course, that the musical elements and rules detailed in his theoretical writings cannot find confirmation in his music. It would be extraordinary, indeed, if this were not the case. An interesting – if somewhat desultory – inventory of correspondences between Rameau's theory and his musical practice can be found in Chapter 8 of Paul-Marie Masson's *L'Opéra de Rameau* (Paris, 1930), 423–549.

the *Démonstration*. In the very first sentence of the *Nouvelles réflexions*, Rameau informs us that "this principle [the *corps sonore*] is effectively drawn from nature herself and palpable to three of our senses." To those who might think that the *corps sonore* was only a philosophical conjecture or hypothesis, Rameau countered emphatically, "it is not a question of either conjecture or hypothesis. And anything that is antecedent [to this principle] is absolutely useless for attaining any knowledge of the theory and practice of the arts to which it serves as a guide."[39] The three senses by which the *corps sonore* could be known were hearing, sight, and touch (the last two because we may observe a string breaking into aliquot divisions while vibrating, and may feel these divisions by lightly touching their nodal points). But it is by hearing that the proportions of the *corps sonore* are most immediately and accurately perceived. Rameau came across an aphorism of Cicero at this time that seemed to encapsulate this idea perfectly: "Superbissimum auris judicium" – the judgment of the ear is superior.[40] This virtually became Rameau's personal motto after 1752.

Rameau found the sensory evidence of the *corps sonore* so persuasive that he soon began to wonder if the other fine arts might not be related to music by virtue of their reliance upon common harmonic proportions. The example he cites is architecture. From the findings of the architect Charles Briseux, Rameau was delighted to learn that many of the monuments of Greek and Roman antiquity were constructed following simple numerical ratios and proportions.[41]

Charles Etienne Briseux (1660–1754) was an architect of modest success who toward the end of his life undertook a concerted study of ancient architecture. In analyzing the designs of hundreds of classical buildings, edifices, monuments, floor plans, columns, obelisks, porticos, and the like, he discovered that they seemed most commonly to be laid out according to simple arithmetic, harmonic, and geometric proportions. It was through the employment of these proportions, Briseux argued, that ancient architecture conveyed such beauty, and, conversely, why much "modern" architecture did not.[42]

Briseux was of course not the first to have subordinated architecture to numerical proportions. The idea was a venerable one in architectural theory that can be traced back to Vitruvius. With a strong revival of Vitruvian theory in France in the seventeenth century, the dependence of architectural design upon simple numerical proportions became a lively subject of debate between Claude Perrault

---

[39] *Nouvelles réflexions*, Preface.
[40] Ibid., 51. This was a widely cited aphorism of empirical musical aesthetics in the eighteenth century. Rameau could have picked up the phrase from Brossard's *Dictionaire* (s.v."temperamento"), Charles Batteux's treatise (*Les Beaux-arts réduits à un même principe* [Paris, 1746], 275), or Castel's review of the *Génération harmonique* (*CTW* VI, 146).
[41] *Nouvelles réflexions*, 49.
[42] The research of Briseux was published in a beautifully printed treatise whose lengthy title aptly conveys its thesis: *Traité du Beau essentiel dans les Arts appliqué particulièrement à l'Architecture, et démontré phisiquement et par l'expérience; avec un Traité des proportions harmoniques, et l'on fait voir que c'est de ces seules proportions que les edifices généralement approuvés, empruntent leur beauté réelle et invariable* (Paris, 1752).

and François Blondel.⁴³ But Briseux pursued the correlation between architecture and numerical proportion with a particular rationalist ardor and didactic rigor. So convinced was Briseux of the indispensability of these proportions for architecture, that when some design he discovered did not follow them as closely as he thought proper – as with many by Perrault – he would revise the design in his text! This rationalist zeal earned him the scorn and ridicule of several contemporaneous architectural theorists, including Marc-Antoine Laugier.⁴⁴

What most set Briseux apart from his Vitruvian predecessors, though, was the novel explanation he gave as to why ancient architects employed simple numerical proportions in their designs with such consistency. He rejected the Pythagorean notion that prime numerical relations possess an innate simplicity that naturally appeals to us. Nor did he accept Alberti's anthropomorphic hypothesis in which architectural proportions are derived from the proportions to which the parts of the human body are ideally related. The real reason, Briseux was convinced, must be more empirically consistent and sensible than that. And what better fits the bill than the natural phenomenon of Rameau's *corps sonore*? Briseux states his thesis succinctly in the title of his third chapter: "Où l'on fait voir que les grands architectes ont réglé les principaux corps de leurs édifices sur les principes de l'harmonie" ("Wherein it is demonstrated that great architects have disposed the main bodies of their edifices according to the principles of harmony").⁴⁵ Citing the evidence of Rameau's discoveries, Briseux concurred that the *corps sonore* is the one natural phenomenon that conveys proportions directly to the mind in the most direct and uncomplicated manner. These proportions are thus so thoroughly inculcated, he concludes, that architects would have wanted to replicate them in their designs. And in fact, Briseux shows in his text how many indigenous musical ratios did indeed correlate to the classical architectural orders. Plate. 8.1 reproduces one of Briseux's many designs based upon the harmonic and geometric proportions found in music. The principle of architecture is thus found in music, or, to be precise, in the *corps sonore*.⁴⁶

---

43 Emil Kaufmann, "Die Architekturtheorie der französischen Klassik und des Klassizismus," *Repertorium für Kunstwissenschaft* 44 (1924), 197–237. For a richly illustrated narration of the Perrault–Blondel quarrel and its historical and theoretical roots, see Antoine Picon, *Claude Perrault 1613–1688 ou la curiosité d'un classique* (Paris, 1988), 115–56.

44 Marc-Antoine Laugier, *Essai sur l'Architecture*, 2nd edition (Paris, 1755), 260ff. Laugier (1713–69) is a fascinating figure whose work in architecture intersects with Rameau's theory in many ways. He was a partisan of French artistic taste, and defended Rameau and French opera in a pamphlet he issued during the Bouffon quarrel. In his *Essai*, Laugier proposed to detail his discovery of the fundamental "principle" of architecture – one that was at once natural, demonstrable, and historical. This principle was not, however, the numerical proportions prized by Briseux but rather a Rousseauian ethnographic principle: the "tiny rustic hut" (*petite cabane rustique*) in which primitive man first lived. From the expediencies of material, function, and simplicity that constrained the earliest dwellings of primitive man arose the classical architectural categories of solidity, commodity, and beauty. The closer modern architecture conformed to these basic natural laws, Laugier argued, the more beautiful it would be. Divergent as Laugier's writings may be from Rameau, he shared the composer's belief in the essential unity of his art, the existence of a single natural principle guiding it, and the reliance upon an ethnographic hypothesis to reconstruct its origins.

45 *Traité du beau*, 79.

46 For Briseux's discussion of Rameau's principle, see *Ibid.*, 41–45. Actually Briseux was not the first to find the principles of architecture in music. René Ouvrard, the seventeenth-century music theorist we have already

Plate 8.1 Briseux's *Traité du beau*, Plate 32. The text reads as follows: "The length AB is divided into 20 equal parts. Each of the pairs of columns marked E comprises 2 parts, separated by 3 parts at D, and 6 parts at C. These three different distances are dispositioned according to the harmonic proportion 2, 3, 6, which in music produces the fifth and its octave.

The columns F are placed at the edge of the pilaster such that their bases are set back slightly. The width between GH is divided into 5 parts, 4 of which correspond to the height IK. Thus this height is to the width GH as 4 is to 5, which is the ratio of the major third. The 3 parts LM, MN, NO are in the harmonic proportion 2, 3, 6, which produces the fifth and its octave. Finally, the principal masses of the pedestal are in the arithmetic proportion 1, 3, 5."

Rameau was obviously delighted to find confirmation of his hypothesis that the *corps sonore* must be the principle of all arts, or at least of those arts that are in some way based upon proportions, symmetry, and balance for their aesthetic beauty.[47]

If, on the other hand, we discover in considering the infinite number of ratios that are common to the arts and that arouse in us the sentiment of beauty, that they are similar everywhere, are we not justified in concluding that they are based upon one and the same principle? And that if we would find this principle today to have been discovered and proved as stemming directly from harmony and as sensible as we could wish in our perceptions, does this not convince us beyond any doubt?[48]

Rameau was counting upon his readers to answer his rhetorical questions affirmatively. After all, if the *corps sonore* could not yet be explained scientifically, at least the sensory evidence of its existence should be convincing.

All this constitutes an extraordinary evolution in Rameau's theory. The *corps sonore* was now an object quite different from that in the *Génération harmonique*, to say nothing of the monochord in the *Traité*. In many ways, its changing ontology reflects the general trajectory of Enlightenment thought in the eighteenth century. From a rigorous Cartesian first principle in the *Traité* established through geometric deduction, to a phenomenon of nature revealed by experimental science, the *corps sonore* was now a purely Lockean sense impression.[49] Given its manifestly irrefutable empirical validation, as well as its new status as a sensory principle, Rameau felt confident that he had not only found the true principle of music, but also the principle of all the arts. Soon, he was to go even further and claim that the *corps sonore* is the principle of all geometric sciences, which, after all, also have their origin in harmonic ratios and proportions.[50]

---

encountered in Chapter 3, published a little book in 1679 in which he proposed the source of architectural beauty to lie in the ratios of musical harmony: René Ouvrard, *Architecture harmonique ou application de la doctrine des proportions de la musique à l'architecture* (Paris, 1679). But for Ouvrard, as well as for other Vitruvius-influenced architectural theorists such as Blondel, the rationale for these musical ratios lay in Pythagorean theory, not in acoustics or sensationalist epistemologies. For more on Ouvrard and the correlations between music and architecture in the seventeenth century, see Philippe Vendrix, "Proportions harmoniques et proportions architecturales dans la théorie française des XVIIe et XVIIIe siècles," *International Review of the Aesthetics and Sociology of Music* 20 (1989), 3–10.

47 Whether this was a conclusion Briseux arrived at on his own cannot be known. Knowing the aggressive way in which Rameau promoted his own theories, it is not difficult to imagine Rameau, upon learning of Briseux's research, coaxing and cajoling him toward the conclusion that music must be the source and cause of the harmonic proportions found in ancient architecture.

48 *Nouvelles réflexions*, 62–63.

49 Charles Lalo has made the fascinating suggestion that the actual chronology of Rameau's treatises follows almost the reverse ordering one might expect from a purely inductive process. If I interpret Lalo correctly, he suggests the following scenario. An empirical scientist might begin with a detailed analysis of musical practice (*Code de musique pratique*, 1760). From such analysis, he might come to recognize an inclination for harmony in man (*Observations sur notre instinct*, 1754), and from there investigate the possible sensory origins of this inclination in nature (*Nouvelles réflexions*, 1752). Our investigator might arrive at a unifying principle of harmony (*Démonstration*, 1750), which is then investigated using experiments (*Génération harmonique*, 1737). These experiments would point to a single acoustical principle of harmony in the *corps sonore* (*Nouveau système*, 1726), which can then be abstracted into a numerical principle (*Traité*, 1722). Charles Lalo, *Eléments d'une esthétique musicale scientifique* (Paris, 1939), 80–81.

50 Rameau first broached this idea in the *Démonstration*, vi–vii, but was to pursue it most vigorously in his last writings, as we will shortly see.

THE AESTHETICS OF *RAPPORT*

Rameau's speculations concerning the origins of the arts and sciences, however disputed they would be by d'Alembert, were not so extravagant when seen in historical context. He was able to call for support upon two related tenets of French neoclassical thought with rich historical traditions: Batteux's thesis of art as the imitation of nature, and Diderot's aesthetic of *rapport*.

1. In his important treatise on aesthetics of 1746, *Les Beaux-arts réduits à un même principe*, Charles Batteux reiterated the widely accepted Aristotelian thesis that the primary aim of art was the imitation of nature. Batteux did not mean by this the servile copying of nature, though, but rather the portrayal of an idealized nature – *la belle nature*. Nature was too bountiful and diverse in his view to be copied literally. The artist needed instead to be able to focus selectively and with discrimination upon nature, and discern an abstracted ideal that he then express in an "entirely natural whole, one that would be more perfect than nature herself."[51]

What in nature was available for the musician to imitate? Again drawing from Aristotle, Batteux answered that it was the essential passions: grief, joy, rage, love, and so forth. This was done not by literal mimesis (representation) but by an idealized ("artificial" was his actual term) portrayal of human passions. Through the employment of certain stock melodic figures, rhythmic gestures, and harmonic progressions, the composer is ostensibly able to convey in music the most perfect expression of some emotion. Of course for Batteux, as for all neoclassicists, some text or clearly defined dramatic motivation was helpful in order to define the particular passion desired, since Baroque musicians and theorists could never agree upon any uniform canon of rhetorical figures.

By the middle of the eighteenth century, theorists were looking elsewhere than the traditional rhetorical figures in order to identify the source of music's expressive powers. One such source was melody. Rousseau argued emphatically in his writings that it was only by means of a vocally conceived melody that music derives its expressive powers. In his article "chant" written for volume 3 of the *Encyclopédie* (issued in November, 1753), he explains this idea:

It is by the different sounds of the voice that men have first had to express their different sensations. Nature has given them first the sounds of the voice in order to convey outwardly the sentiments of sadness, joy, pleasure which they were experiencing inside . . . The sounds are thus innate in man: he knows how to sing; he was struck by noises, [through which] all his sensations and all his instinct lead him to imitation.[52]

In his *Lettre sur la musique française* of 1753, Rousseau elaborated upon this idea in regard to national operatic styles. Italian composers, he argued, were naturally disposed to write more beautiful and unconstrained melodies than the French on account of their more sonorous language and uninhibited constitution. Logically,

---

[51] Batteux, *Les Beaux-arts*, 45.
[52] *Encyclopédie*, s.v. "chant."

then, Italian opera was superior to French opera since it was more suited to expressing human passions.[53]

Rameau certainly agreed that the primary function of music is to express emotions. In the *Génération harmonique*, after all, he had already announced succinctly: "The aim [of music] is to please and excite in us the various passions."[54] And in the *Code de musique pratique* published thirteen years later, he reiterates this thesis: "In a word, the expression of thought, sentiment, and passions ought to be the true aim of music."[55] However, he did not believe such passions could be aroused simply by the employment of stock rhetorical figures. Nor, on the other hand, did he agree with Rousseau that melody was the means by which such passions were expressed. For Rameau, it was only by means of harmony – the product of the natural *corps sonore* – that musical expression could take place. In the *Observations sur notre instinct pour la musique* of 1754, Rameau's major statement of his aesthetic views, he writes:

It is to harmony alone that there belongs the arousal of the passions; melody draws its force only from that source, from which it emanates directly; and as to the differences of low and high, etc., which are only the surface modifications of melody, they therefore add to it almost nothing, as will be demonstrated by striking examples in the course of this work, in which the principle is verified by our instinct, and that instinct by its principle, which is to say, where cause is verified by the experienced effect, and that effect by its cause.[56]

There was nothing in nature, Rameau points out repeatedly in this work, that suggests melody to us, whereas in almost every vibrating object (*corps sonore*) she sings to us the harmonic partials of the perfect twelfth and major seventeenth. As for Rousseau's argument that historical evidence confirms that melody came before harmony, and thus harmony was only an artifice of a corrupted society, Rameau counters with arguments showing how the earliest known melodies (Greek tetrachords and Chinese pentatonic scales) were in fact generated by harmony via the triple geometric progression.[57] The first musical ideas suggested by our voice, Rameau argued, were not the primitive vocal inflections Rousseau claimed. Prior to these stood necessarily and ontologically the acoustical sound of the human voice that (Rameau claims) is a composite of overtones – the natural *corps sonore*.[58]

---

53 Rousseau developed in more detail his arguments concerning the origins of musical expression in an essay that was never published during his life: the *Essai sur l'origine des langues*. Robert Wokler and Marie-Elisabeth Duchez have independently shown that Rousseau's *Essai* was originally drafted as a response to Rameau's music theory: Robert Wokler, "Rameau, Rousseau, and the *Essai sur l'origine des langues*," *Studies on Voltaire and the Eighteenth Century* 117 (1974), 179–238; Marie-Elisabeth Duchez, "'Principe de la mélodie' et 'Origine des langues': Un brouillon inédit de Jean-Jacques Rousseau sur l'origine de la mélodie," *Revue de musicologie* 60 (1974), 33–86.
54 *Génération harmonique*, 30. Similar sentiments are expressed in Rameau's famous letter of 1727 to Houdar de la Motte, cited in Chapter 2, p. 34.
55 *Code de musique pratique*, 170.
56 *Observations sur notre instinct pour la musique* (Paris, 1754), vi–vii; trans. Edward A. Lippman in *Musical Aesthetics: A Historical Reader*, 3 vols. (New York, 1986), I, 340.
57 *Observations*, 29–30.
58 *Code de musique pratique*, 18, 165.

Of course Rameau did not advise the composer to copy the *corps sonore* literally in music (unless presumably it was to achieve a deliberate and extraordinary effect, as in his *Pygmalion* setting cited in Example 8.2). Instead, the composer should take the material afforded by the *corps sonore,* that is, the various proportions it conveys, and deploy them "artificially," as Batteux would say. (Most intervals of nature, it will be recalled, need to be tempered in order to be practicable to musicians.) The composer's task was thus much like that of an experimental scientist, testing various applications, modifications, and combinations of these proportions in musical settings in order to arrive at the most perfect and beautiful result. Music, simply put, copies nature not because it mimics primitive vocal inflections through melody – an origin that Rameau would hardly have accepted as "natural" – but rather through the employment of the proportions generated in the *corps sonore*.[59]

2. A second tradition of aesthetic thought drawn upon by Rameau that enjoyed equal classical pedigree was the equation of beauty with the qualities of order, proportion, and relationship (*rapport*). As articulated by aestheticians such as Jean-Pierre Crousaz and Yves-Marie André, beauty could be judged by the criteria of *rapport* between diverse elements.[60] All artists seek to attain such *rapport* in their creations: the painter with lines and colors, the poet with ideas and words, and the musician with notes. The true genius, Crousaz notes, is the artist who can create the richest relationships and diversity without losing the critical sense of unity.[61] Conversely, *bon goût* is the ability by which the discerning viewer (or reader or listener) can apperceive these relationships.

The notion of *rapport* as a key component to beauty can of course be traced back to Plato. We have already noted how indispensable Briseux found the notion of *rapport* to the aesthetics of architecture. But the idea enjoyed renewed vigor among British empirical aestheticians in the eighteenth century. Lord Shaftesbury, Francis Hutcheson, and David Hume had cumulatively broken the rationalist stranglehold of neoclassical mimetic theory by legitimizing the subjective tastes and sentiments of the viewer (reader/listener).[62] Beauty became less an intrinsic ideal embodied in the art work and governed by strict rules of propriety, than a subjective response of pleasure aroused within the perceiving subject. And what in the work of art provokes pleasure? For British empiricists, it is the numerous relationships we perceive in the material deployed by the artist. The most beautiful work of art is the one that employs the most interesting and varied relationships.

---

59 Michel Baridon develops this thesis with intelligence in his article "Le Concept de nature dans l'esthétique de Rameau," *Rameau Colloque International,* 445–59.
60 Jean-Pierre Crousaz, *Traité du beau* (Amsterdam, 1715); Yves-Marie André, *Essai sur le beau* (Paris, 1741).
61 *Traité du beau,* 34.
62 Ernst Cassirer has traced this development in eighteenth-century aesthetic thought with particular acumen (*The Philosophy of the Enlightenment,* trans. Fritz C.A. Koelln and James P. Pettegrove [Boston, 1955], 297–331).

A number of French writers, including the Abbé Du Bos, adopted and developed with enthusiasm many of the ideas of British empirical aesthetics.[63] (It was largely on account of Du Bos's work that the concepts of *sentiment* and *sensibilité* became common currency in French discussions of aesthetics in the eighteenth century.) But it remained for Diderot, who was one of the most avid readers of British thought among the philosophes, to articulate in his earliest philosophical essays a fully sensationalist aesthetic of *rapport*.[64]

In his early essays, Diderot argued that no mind possesses innate ideas of beauty, order, or perfection by which it can judge an art work. (The influence of Condillac here is unmistakable.) Everything that we know we learn through accumulated sensory impressions.[65] The mind does possess the capacity to remember and compare these various sensory impressions, though. What we call beautiful is but a response of the mind to particularly interesting and unified relationships. In his acoustical "Mémoires" of 1749, Diderot explains himself as follows:

> The perception of relationships (*rapport*) is the unique basis of our admiration and our pleasures. And it is from here that one must begin in order to explain the most delicate phenomena that are offered to us by the sciences and arts . . . This principle ought to serve as the basis of a philosophical essay on taste if one could find someone possessing enough knowledge capable of making a general application of that to which it pertains.[66]

Diderot apparently took up his own challenge. In a lengthy article on beauty ("beau") contained in volume two of the *Encyclopédie,* Diderot develops a comprehensive psychology of beauty that is based entirely upon the subjective judgment of *rapport*. His conclusion there is unambiguous:

> I therefore term "beautiful" independently of my existence, everything that contains the power of awakening the notion of relation in my mind; and I term "beautiful" in direct relation to myself everything that does awaken that notion.[67]

Diderot does not thereby infer that there is only one standard of beauty. On the contrary, since experience and perception vary from person to person, one's judgment of *rapport* must consequently be subjective; there will always be a potentially infinite number of possible relationships to be apperceived by any person.

Diderot finds music, among all the arts, to be the one in which "relationships" are most immediately and powerfully conveyed by the contrasts it deploys between

63 *Réflexions critiques sur la poësie et sur la peinture* (Paris, 1719).
64 The relevant writings of Diderot are the "Mémoires sur différents sujets de mathématiques," the two letters on the blind and deaf, and the article "beau" in vol. II of the *Encyclopédie*. Diderot's aesthetic ideas have been thoroughly analyzed in the magnificent study by Jacques Chouillet, *La Formation des idées esthétiques de Diderot* (Paris, 1973). Also of value is Lester Crocker, *Diderot's Chaotic Order* (Princeton, 1974); Pierre Saint-Amand, *Diderot: Le Labyrinthe de la relation* (Paris, 1984); and Xenia Baumeister, *Diderots Ästhetik der Rapports* (Frankfurt, 1985). One should keep in mind that the aesthetic of *rapport* discerned here applies mainly to Diderot's early writings, and not to the much more complex and richly ambiguous naturalist aesthetic expressed in works such as *Le Neveu de Rameau*.
65 Baumeister, *Diderots Ästhetik der Rapports*, 25–26.
66 "Mémoires," 104.
67 *Diderot's Selected Writings*, 54.

high and low, slow and fast, loud and soft, and so forth. Most important for Diderot is the simplicity found in the ratios of all consonances. The perception of these simple ratios in a unified ensemble, he argues, is at the heart of all musical pleasure. Diderot side-stepped the difficult problem of explaining how the mind can perceive proportions through auditory stimulus. He speculated that the mind might possess the capacity of "natural trigonometry" wherein it can intuitively recognize proportions, much as we can estimate the distance of some object without knowing any geometry.[68] In any case, the history of music since Pythagoras proves that musicians have been "secretly guided" by the perceptions of relationships, even if theorists have not always recognized this fact correctly.[69]

As we saw earlier, Diderot and Rameau were working on the musical "Mémoire" sometime in 1749, shortly after Diderot has published his similarly named mathematical "Mémoires."[70] It is not a coincidence, I think, that it was just at this time Rameau began arguing that the specific and restrictive *proportions* generated by the *corps sonore* (the perfect twelfth and major seventeenth) were the true foundations of his theory of music. Throughout the "Mémoire" and subsequent *Démonstration*, Rameau speaks repeatedly of the *rapport* of these intervals and the possibility of deriving all musical material from them, whether harmonies, scales, modes, or genres. (Recall Rameau's statement quoted on p. 167.) In his *Observations,* he attributed the pleasure we receive from perceiving these auditory relationships to a natural instinct given to us by nature:

Where is the philosopher, where is the man, who with a modicum of common sense will not recognize as due to Nature, to his pure instinct, this agreeable feeling he experiences in hearing certain relationships (*rapport*) of tones?[71]

Du Bos had claimed man possesses a "sixth instinct" by which he can apperceive beauty before reason can explain why. Rameau suggests one reason why this happens, at least in the case of music: We instinctively respond to music with pleasure since this music corresponds to the ratios inculcated in our mind by the *corps sonore*.

It was not a very large leap in reasoning for Rameau to suggest that these naturally generated proportions may also be of significance to the other arts and sciences which rely upon the notion of *rapport* in some way. Diderot himself had suggested something along just these lines:

Musical pleasure lay in the perception of the relationships of tones. But this origin is not unique to musical pleasure. Pleasure in general lay in the perception of proportion. This principle is applicable to poetry, painting, architecture, morality, and all the arts and sciences. A beautiful machine, a beautiful painting, a beautiful portico please us only on account of the relationships that we have discerned. Cannot one even say that they possess a liveliness like a beautiful concert (*une belle vie comme d'un beau concert*)?[72]

---

68 "Mémoires," 106.
69 *Ibid.*, 86 and 105.
70 Wilson, *Diderot: The Testing Years,* 88.
71 *Observations,* 16–17; translated in Lippman, *Musical Aesthetics,* I, 345.
72 "Mémoires," 104.

I hope it is now clear how Rameau could eventually view the *corps sonore* as the principle of all the arts and sciences. It was at once an empirical phenomenon of nature and an aesthetic ideal of perfect *rapport*. Since the *corps sonore* was undoubtedly one of the first and most ubiquitous sensory stimuli of nature that primitive man would have experienced, Rameau did not see how one could but conclude that it was the auditory source by which humans developed a *sensibilité* to the beauties of *rapport*, and from which they learned to extrapolate for the benefit of all arts and sciences:

> It was to the sense of hearing alone that was reserved the discovery of a phenomenon from which has been developed a principle whose universality can scarcely be contested. By recognizing this in harmony, are we not also tacitly granting to it the same authority over all the other sciences? Because, after all, where proportions command, harmony should reign. Our instinct speaks to us each day by the applications we make of these harmonies to things that have some kind of rapport between them, while reason ventures to consent. Always deaf to the voice of nature (who nonetheless has chosen sound to make herself heard the most clearly), the geometer claims at present to determine compass in hand harmonic ratios (*rapports*), when on the contrary, it is these ratios that determine the angles of this compass.[73]

One cannot say that Rameau ever developed a very sophisticated, let alone original, theory of aesthetics with his *corps sonore*. But there were seeds of a radically new aesthetic doctrine contained in his writings that would germinate in the next generation. By defining the heart of musical expression as one of pure tone relationships rooted in harmony, Rameau laid the groundwork for the development of an aesthetic of musical autonomy that would break once and for all with the Aristotelian dictum that music was an imitative art. Rameau never took this decisive step, and no doubt would not have wanted to if pushed. It is significant, though, that one of those who did in the next generation – Michel-Paul Guy de Chabanon – was a partisan of Rameau's theory.[74] The fundamental bass offered an ideal tool for explicating a fully empirical and autonomous rhetoric of music that was independent of the spoken language. Endowing the *corps sonore* with ideas drawn from French neoclassical aesthetic theory, as well as the newer sensationalist psychology, Rameau was able to find double validity for his principle of harmony, and inspiration to extend his principle ever more boldly to other domains. If the philosophes would soon be fighting Rameau concerning his imperialist ambitions, we must not forget that it was they who gave him the weapons he used in the first place.

RAMEAU AND HIS CRITICS

It was obvious to observers that Rameau did not suffer criticism of his theory kindly. He was never so touchy when it came to criticisms of his operas. But

---

[73] "Nouvelles réflexions sur le principe sonore," appended to the *Code de musique pratique*, 213.
[74] We recall Chabanon from Chapter 2 as one of Rameau's eulogists in 1764. Fifteen years later he published one of the first aesthetic treatises proclaiming the autonomy of musical expression: *Observations sur la musique et principalement sur la metaphysique de l'art* (Paris, 1779). Chabanon's treatise was especially influential in Germany, where it was known through Johann Hiller's translation, *Ueber die Musik und deren Wirkungen* (Leipzig, 1781).

whoever might have been impertinent enough to suggest even the slightest deficiency in the fundamental bass or *corps sonore* was sure to receive a stern rebuke from the irascible composer, as Montéclair, Castel, and Louis Bollioud-Mermet all could have testified.[75] Not surprisingly, with the increased attention accorded Rameau's ideas beginning around 1750 by the Académie and Encyclopedists, his theory was subjected to increased scrutiny and criticism by a number of music theorists, scientists, and philosophers. Throughout this decade, Rameau found himself attacked on many fronts concerning a variety of issues. And he did his best to respond to them all. The *Nouvelles réflexions* of 1752 contains rebuttals to three such critics.

The first was his old nemesis, Father Castel, who was still dissatisfied with Rameau's explanation concerning mode. As we saw in Chapter 7, in both the *Génération harmonique* and *Démonstration*, Rameau had spent considerable effort discussing this very topic. Castel evidently urged Rameau to clarify his thoughts even further on the matter.[76] In response, Rameau reformulated his definition of mode and offered a number of new thoughts on the subject. (The most important of these have already been discussed in Chapter 7.) Castel was apparently satisfied with Rameau's clarifications, for his review was the warmest in tone since the one accorded the *Traité* some thirty years earlier.[77]

A second provocation for Rameau was the appearance of an anonymous *Prospectus* announcing the imminent appearance of a new treatise on music.[78] The author of the *Prospectus* outlines plans for an ambitious treatise dealing with the history, theory, and practice of music. But he also takes the opportunity to criticize parts of Rameau's theory. While there is no attribution in the text, I think the author was almost certainly Charles Henri Blainville (1710–77).

Blainville was a talented historian of music and competent theorist, if a mediocre composer. His knowledge of Rameau's theory seems to have been of long standing; with the publication of his first music treatise in 1746, he became one of the first French theorists to adopt and apply the fundamental bass, even if in a

---

75 For the polemics with Montéclair, Castel, and Bollioud-Mermet, see Chapters 3 and 7 above.

76 Castel's review of the *Nouvelles réflexions* is reproduced in *CTW* V, 152.

77 The cordial tone of Castel's review (indeed, in places it is quite complimentary) suggests that the two elderly men had patched up their earlier row. One cause may have been the advent of the Bouffon quarrel, in which Castel took up a decidedly pro-French position (Donald S. Schier, *Louis Bertrand Castel: Anti-Newtonian Scientist* [Cedar Rapids, Iowa, 1946], 49). But another reason can be surmised; Castel's optical theories had not been well received by scientists. Further, in 1752, Castel was getting ready to unveil the first prototype of his ocular harpsichord. No doubt he was apprehensive about its reception and he may well have been hoping to gain Rameau's support by his favorable review. Once Rameau had finally distanced himself from the overtly Newtonian experimental method he tested in the *Génération harmonique*, Castel must have realized that he really would not be able to find any musician whose views were more compatible with his than Rameau, or whose ideas lent better support to his optical theories. Castel found in the composer's demonstration of the triune make-up of the *corps sonore* confirmation of his thesis that there were but three fundamental colors. He happily quoted Rameau's criticism of Newton for basing his color spectrum upon the seven-note diatonic scale (see p. 145 above), calling it, naturally, "an important observation" (*CTW* V, 161). Now it was the scientist relying upon the composer! For his part, Rameau made a number of respectful comments concerning Castel's ocular harpsichord (e.g. in his *Erreurs sur la musique*, 47; *CTW* V, 220).

78 *Prospectus d'un traité général de musique où l'on prétend rendre raison de tout ce qui appartient à cet art* (Soissons, 1752).

somewhat superficial manner.[79] Blainville was also actively involved with theoretical problems at the time the *Prospectus* was issued.[80] There is a bulky cache of lengthy manuscripts by Blainville now in the Bibliothèque Nationale that look like the drafts of the very treatise described in the *Prospectus*.[81] While Blainville never brought out the promised treatise, much of this material (particularly related to historical questions) was eventually published in 1767.[82]

Blainville takes great pains to praise Rameau throughout the *Prospectus*.[83] Eager to show off his historical erudition, he places Rameau at the head of a long list of distinguished theorists of music that can be traced back to antiquity. He refers to the *Traité de l'harmonie* as a *chef-d'œuvre*, and hails the fundamental bass as a brilliant discovery. But regrettably, he continues, Rameau expressed his ideas in an obscure and sterile manner. Blainville singles out two problems in particular: (1) The geometric proportions Rameau proposed in the *Démonstration* can only produce out-of-tune intervals; and (2) Rameau was too restrictive concerning the intervals by which the fundamental bass may move. (Blainville thought that the minor third should be given as much weight as the major third.) He promises to correct both these failings in his own treatise, clarify other obscurities with helpful tables, simplified explanations (e.g. omitting the unnecessary and contorted theories of supposition and borrowed roots), and devote more space to compositional issues.[84]

As might be expected, Rameau was none too happy to hear these criticisms, or that our anonymous critic thought there was a need for an alternative composition treatise to his own! In a supplement added to the *Nouvelles réflexions* just before it was to go into print, Rameau answered some of the charges of Blainville. While agreeing that the extremes of his geometric proportion are out of tune with one another, he takes this as proof for the need of temperament. In any case, he argues, the ear really cannot distinguish comma differences.[85] Rameau never appears to have addressed Blainville's second major criticism (concerning the movement of the fundamental bass), although he might easily have referred back to the arithmetic proportion described in his *Démonstration* that offers a theoretical grounding of the minor third on a par with the major third.[86]

---

79 *Harmonie théorico-pratique* (Paris, 1746).
80 In 1751 Blainville submitted to the Académie Royale des Sciences an *Essay sur un troisième mode* for their evaluation and approval, along with a "Symphony" in which this mode is utilized. Blainville's "third mode" turns out to be nothing but a phrygian mode on E, for which he tried to find a normative diatonic harmonization along the lines of the *règle de l'octave*. Although Rameau never commented upon Blainville's "discovery," the other philosophes found it curious enough to mention it in their musical writings.
81 *F-Pn* Ms. fr. n.a. 6,326–6,328.
82 Charles-Henri Blainville, *Histoire générale critique et philologique de la musique* (Paris, 1767).
83 The relevant portions are printed in *CTW* V, xxiv–xxxi.
84 Blainville did indeed fulfill all of these promises in his *Histoire générale*, which, despite its title, contained much concerning music theory. The only area where Blainville seemed to cut back any was in the section on compositional pedagogy. The disorganized notes he left behind show that he struggled mightily to put his ideas in order (see particularly Ms. fr. n.a. 6,328). But evidently the challenge proved too taxing.
85 *Nouvelles réflexions*, 45.
86 A more detailed and direct rebuttal of Blainville's *Prospectus* was written, of all people, by Rameau's younger brother, Claude. In a pamphlet entitled *Lettre de M. R. le C. à M. * * * published in 1752, Claude Rameau

A third critic to whom Rameau responded in his *Nouvelles réflexions* was a physicist from Montpellier named Pierre Estève. Like many other scientists of his day, Estève was greatly interested in musical questions. After reading Rameau's *Démonstration*, Estève issued a pamphlet to voice his opinions concerning several of Rameau's ideas.[87] It turns out that Estève was an adherent to Mairan's theory of atomistic sound propagation. He could not understand first of all why Rameau limited his definition of the *corps sonore* to vibrating systems resonating their third and fifth harmonic partials, when according to Mairan's theory, other partials such as the seventh should also be heard.

Another aspect of Estève's pamphlet is worth mentioning here, although it is not something Rameau ever responded to in detail. Estève suggested a novel theory of consonance that anticipates one articulated by Helmholtz over a hundred years later, explaining it as the greater concordance of harmonic partials shared by any two tones (or chords). Conversely, dissonance was the product of clashing partials, or as he colorfully put it, "le combat des harmoniques."[88] Estève offered a number of tables in which he calculates the degrees of overtone concordance between differing intervals. Rameau's only response was to refer back to the fourth "expériment" of the *Génération harmonique* in which he showed how the overtones of a sounding organ pipe can blend with the fundamental sound to seem like a unison, even if those overtones are reinforced with other stops.[89] If we actually could hear the partials of every sounding tone "in combat," Rameau continued, then we would only hear an unbearable "cacophony." (However, Rameau did not explain clearly how this fact was to be reconciled with his earlier insistence that the third and fifth partials in every musical tone were audible to skilled listeners. Presumably he would have argued something to the effect that in combination, tones make heard only their fundamental frequencies, while in isolation, a tone's "compound nature" can be made perceptible by experiments like those detailed in the *Génération harmonique*.)

One final question Estève raised concerned the identity of octaves. Estève disputed Rameau's claim that all octaves sounded above the fundamental in any *corps sonore* are inaudible. Since even partials had just as independent a generative basis as did odd partials (according to Mairan's theory), Estève argued that Rameau's thesis of octave identity was opinion, not demonstration.[90] Rameau did not really answer Estève's arguments in the *Nouvelles réflexions* except to reiterate his conviction that any octave is inaudible in the *corps sonore*. It was in his next publication that Rameau addressed this problem in depth.

    defended his brother's honor from the "scurrilous" and "groundless" attacks of the anonymous author of the *Prospectus*. (It does not seem that Claude Rameau knew that Blainville was the author, either.) For a transcription and analysis of this letter, see Paul-Marie Masson, "Une polémique musicale de Claude Rameau en faveur de son frère (1752)," *Revue de Musicologie* 21 (1937), 39–47.

87 *Nouvelle découverte du principe de l'harmonie, avec un examen de ce que M. Rameau a publié sous le titre de Démonstration de ce principe* (Paris, 1751).
88 Ibid., 47.
89 *Nouvelles réflexions*, 68–69.
90 *Nouvelle découverte*, 33.

EULER AND THE IDENTITY OF OCTAVES

We recall from Chapter 6 how Rameau had written to Euler in April of 1752, sending him a copy of his just-published *Nouvelles réflexions*, and asking for the scientist's approbation "which is too precious to me to neglect obtaining." (The letter sent to Euler is virtually identical to the one he wrote to Johann Bernoulli a week earlier.[91]) Euler mailed off a reply to Rameau's letter in September of the same year. But rather than receiving the endorsement he was expecting, Rameau got a politely worded rebuff from the scientist. We have already quoted Euler's skeptical circumscription of Rameau's *corps sonore* in Chapter 6 (on p. 155). A second issue Euler raised concerned the question of octaves.[92] Euler did not accept that any two intervals related by octave compounding or inversion could be considered identical. Their degree of consonance (*agrément*), according to Euler, will necessarily be different.[93]

It was clear why Euler could not accept Rameau's ideas concerning the octave. Like his seventeenth-century scientific predecessors, Mersenne and Descartes, Euler subscribed to the mathematical coincidence theory of consonance. In his *Tentamen novae theoriae musicae* of 1739, Euler used the coincidence theory to grade in a strictly quantitative ranking any and all chordal combinations through a somewhat elaborate and clumsy formula.[94] Just as Mersenne could not accept that the perfect fifth (2 : 3) was more consonant than the perfect twelfth (1 : 3) since the latter's ratio was simpler, Euler could not accept that intervals or chords compounded or inverted by an octave could be considered identical. In his letter to Rameau, Euler tried to be as diplomatic as possible, emphasizing points of agreement in their theories. But Rameau was not to be so easily assuaged. He recognized immediately the gravity of Euler's thesis in regard to the validity of his own theory. In December of 1752, Rameau published an open letter to Euler in the *Mercure* concerning the subject of octave identity, which he then issued in pamphlet form the following spring: *Extrait d'une réponse de M. Rameau à M. Euler sur l'identité des octaves*.[95]

Rameau begins his *Extrait* by repeating his conviction that in the resonance of the *corps sonore* one hears only the perfect twelfth and major seventeenth. All the

---

[91] *CTW* V, 145–46.
[92] From a few other remarks in Euler's letter, it appears that he was responding to some specific issues Rameau had apparently raised in another earlier letter. In the published catalogue of the exhibition marking the bicentennial of Rameau's death held at the Bibliothèque Nationale in 1964, there is an unelaborated reference to a letter of Rameau written to Euler on April 30, 1752 supposedly in the archives of the Academy of Sciences in St. Petersburg (Item 363, p. 72). But I have been unable to find any further information concerning this letter.
[93] *CTW* V, 147. "Agreeableness" for Euler was synonymous with "perfection" for Mersenne and Descartes. Subjective "agreeableness" (*douceur* or *excellence*) as defined by seventeenth-century theorists had no place in Euler's theory.
[94] For a more expansive analysis of Euler's music theory, see Hermann R. Busch, *Leonard Eulers Beitrag zur Musiktheorie* (Regensburg, 1970). See also the excellent introduction by Ferdinand Rudio to the *Tentamen* in Euler's *Opera Omnia* (Leipzig, etc., 1912–) Series 3, vol. I, vii–xxv.
[95] *CTW* V, 167–88. Perhaps insecure in attacking a scientist of Euler's stature so directly, Rameau wrote the *Extrait* in the third person as if to distance himself from its arguments.

octaves that are sounded above the fundamental are "mute" and "confounded" with the fundamental, even though they might be observed vibrating sympathetically in neighboring strings.[96] Rameau uses the term "identity" for the first time here to describe this phenomenon. The "identity of octaves" is an "occult sentiment" whose cause is not known, but acknowledged by all musicians.

In his *Traité*, we will recall that Rameau had recourse largely to empirical practice in order to justify the inversional replication of intervals and chords; he could offer no rational explanation that was congruent with his canonist precepts. With his adoption of a sensationalist epistemology, however, Rameau could point to perceptual evidence confirming the thesis of octave identity. In the resonance of the *corps sonore*, he reiterated, one cannot perceive octaves sounding above the fundamental sound. The ear thus offers all the proof needed. It does not matter what the scientist may show with his calculations if the senses contradict it.

As I have said, Rameau did not abandon any of his older arguments concerning octave identity in his *Extrait*. We find reported the same empirical evidence of musical practice recounted in his earlier writings: musicians rarely identify intervals greater than an octave as compounds but rather tend to reduce them to their simplest form. Likewise in thorough-bass practice, musicians invert chords freely, yet accept that the resulting harmonies are related. Why do musicians accept such octave duplications and inversions so readily? Rameau answers that it is both practical and natural to do so. Even nature herself uses the axiom of octave identity to generate musical intervals. The minor whole tone D–E (9 : 10), for instance, is found through the comparison between the ninth and tenth partials, the latter being an octave replication of the fifth partial (major seventeenth).[97] If the ancients had understood the principle of octave identity as clearly as musicians today did, Rameau speculated, they certainly never would have chosen to generate their musical system from the octave.[98] Quite simply, Rameau concludes, octave identity is an essential axiom to make the naturally generated series of pitches practical for musicians to use. Otherwise it would be a "chaos of sounds."[99] And if someone (like Euler) can acknowledge this truth, but still is reluctant to use so strong a term as "identity," Rameau allows that "one may substitute some other term as one sees fit that, while saying less, says enough."[100]

The polemic with Euler – if we can really call it that, since Euler never responded to Rameau's pamphlet – is another example of the irrational and self-destructive behavior of the composer to engage in arguments with those whose friendship and

---

[96] *Extrait*, 3.
[97] Ibid., 10–11. By bringing into consideration partials higher than the fifth (major seventeenth), Rameau seems dangerously close to undermining his more restricted principle of the *corps sonore*. But Rameau is not referring to sounding upper partials indigenous to the *corps sonore* here. Rather, he is referring to the harmonic series generated artificially through monochord divisions or the natural trumpet series.
[98] Ibid., 15, 25.
[99] Ibid., 34.
[100] Ibid., 39.

support he should have had most reason to value. While Rameau was always testy when it came to his theory, as we have seen, until the 1750s he had enough sense to consolidate his alliances when he went on the attack. In his last years, however, he abandoned this sensible strategy and lashed out at any and all who he perceived to veer from the sacred truth of the *corps sonore*. It is of the greatest irony that the philosophe whose behavior Rameau's most closely mirrors was to be his arch-enemy: Rousseau. But these were events still in the future. At the beginning of the decade Rameau was still held in high esteem by the Encyclopedists. To fend off any possible animosity, Diderot and d'Alembert were doing their utmost to make certain that Rousseau was accurately and fairly representing the composer's system of the fundamental bass in his music articles.

ROUSSEAU'S ARTICLES FOR THE *ENCYCLOPEDIE*

As we noted earlier, Rousseau became responsible for the music articles in the *Encyclopédie* after Rameau declined to write them. Rousseau was undoubtedly the logical choice after Rameau, being the most musically engaged of the philosophes. His first published work, the *Dissertation sur la musique moderne* of 1743, was based upon an original system of notational reform he had proposed to the Académie Royale des Sciences in 1742.[101] He was also active as a composer, writing *Les Muses galantes* in 1743 and parts of *Les Fêtes de Ramire* in 1745. When Rameau heard the former work at its first performance, he was unmerciful in his criticism, calling it a *mélange* of poor French tunes and plagiarized Italian ones.[102] Nonetheless, at least in 1749, Rousseau still conceded admiration for Rameau's music, however bitter he may have been about the elder composer's criticism. Rousseau was evidently quite familiar with Rameau's theory of harmony; he read the *Traité de l'harmonie* during a convalescence and relied upon it to learn composition.[103] In the posthumously published *Leçons de musique* of 1742–43, Rousseau demonstrated that he had patiently and thoroughly worked out the compositional ramifications of the fundamental bass early on.[104]

According to Rousseau's own testimony, he wrote the music articles in great haste, "and consequently very ill in the three months ... given me."[105] (It seems Rousseau

---

[101] *Oeuvres complètes de Jean-Jacques Rousseau*, 12 vols. (Paris, 1872), VI, 260–321. The works on music are all contained in vols. VI and VII. Still the indispensable reference for Rousseau's musical activities is that by Albert Jansen, *Jean-Jacques Rousseau als Musiker* (Berlin, 1884). Maurice Cranston's study, *Jean-Jacques: The Early Life and Work of Jean-Jacques Rousseau 1712–1754* (London, 1983), while not devoted to music, brings together much recent scholarship relevant to Rousseau's musical activities in his formative years.

[102] *Erreurs sur la musique dans l'Encyclopédie*, 41–42.

[103] Rousseau, *Confessions* (London, 1925), 141, 163. Also see the *Correspondance complète de Jean-Jacques Rousseau*, ed. R. A. Leigh, 36 vols. (Geneva, 1965), I, 272.

[104] Julien Tiersot, "Les Leçons de musique de Jean-Jacques Rousseau," *Sammelbände der Internationalen Musikgesellschaft* 14 (1912–13), 267.

[105] Rousseau, *Confessions*, 276. This would have been early in 1749, as evidenced by a letter of Rousseau to Madame de Warens dated January 1749 reporting that he was totally preoccupied with writing the music articles. *Correspondance complète de Rousseau*, II, 112–13.

was one of the few contributors who had met Diderot's deadline.) Nevertheless, he had tried as best he could to present Rameau's theory accurately and fairly.[106] In most all of his articles of the early volumes, including those on "accord," "accompaniment," "basse fondamentale," "cadence," "consonance," "dissonance," "dominante," and "échelle," Rousseau follows Rameau's theory of the fundamental bass.

Even Rameau's principle of the *corps sonore* is mentioned with respect. Virtually all of the major ideas present in the *Génération harmonique* and *Démonstration* – whether it be the "modified sympathetic resonance" theory of the minor mode, the theory of supposition, or the *double emploi* – are present in Rousseau's various articles. Where Rousseau is non-committal, d'Alembert usually added a few remarks (in his role as co-editor) to report Rameau's opinion of a subject – a practice that Rousseau came to resent greatly. (The articles "cadence," "compositeur," and "dissonance" contain such supplements by d'Alembert.) All in all, though, Rousseau's articles were quite respectful towards the composer. Consider this compliment found in the article "accompagnement":

> It is to M. Rameau, who by the invention of a new notation and the perfection of fingerings, has also suggested to us the means of facilitating accompaniment. It is to him, I say, that we are indebted for a new method that remedies all the drawbacks of those that we have relied upon until now. He is the first to have revealed the fundamental bass by which he has discovered for us the true foundations of an art that had appeared entirely arbitrary.

For all Rousseau's later well-known disagreements with Rameau's ideas, there is little to be found in the first volumes of the *Encyclopédie* that any objective reader could interpret as disrespectful or critical towards his theory – unless, of course, that reader was Rameau.

THE ENCYCLOPEDIST QUARREL

To understand why Rameau eventually reacted with such vehemence to Rousseau's generally innocuous articles, we must recall that in 1753 Rousseau had launched the Bouffon quarrel with the publication of his incendiary *Lettre sur la musique française*. While there was no explicit discussion of Rameau's theory in the *Lettre*, Rousseau's provocative denunciation of French operatic practice did touch on a central tenet of Rameau's thought, to wit, that melody was subordinate to harmony.[107] Citing the famous monologue from *Armide* that Rameau had earlier used to illustrate his fundamental bass in the *Nouveau système* (see Plate 5.1 above), Rousseau attempted to show how the affections of the text were vitiated if not entirely contradicted by Lully's faulty setting. Had Lully been more sensitive to the

---

106 However, he was not so dissatisfied that he would not extract over one third of these articles without substantial alteration to include in his *Dictionnaire de musique* published some twenty years later. Thomas W. Hunt, "The *Dictionnaire de musique* of Jean-Jacques Rousseau" (Ph.D. dissertation, North Texas State University, 1967), Appendix 6, 522–29.

107 Rousseau's *Lettre* has been discussed so repeatedly by scholars that there is no need to examine it here. A particularly succinct analysis of its content and context in Rousseau's intellectual development may be found in Cynthia Verba's recent study, *Music in the French Enlightenment,* particularly in Chapters 2 and 3.

text, Rousseau argued, he would have set the monologue with a far more natural melody, one that was not so constrained by the harmony.

Rameau first countered Rousseau's *Lettre* with the *Observations sur notre instinict pour la musique* of 1754. Defending Lully's setting line by line from Rousseau's attacks, Rameau showed how the harmonies underlying Lully's melody offered an appropriate and emotive setting of the text. Three kinds of expressive harmonic techniques were singled out by Rameau: (1) modulation to the dominant and subdominant poles, engendering moods of liveliness and sorrow, respectively (pp. 57–61); (2) chromaticism produced by the quintuple progression, engendering feelings of pathos and pain (pp. 63–68); and (3) changes of mode from minor to major, engendering an emotional shift from despair to triumph (pp. 91–93). Rameau tried to show how Lully's monologue, through its subtle exploitation of these harmonic devices, vindicated his thesis that harmony is the true source of musical expression, and melody only a product therefrom.[108] Rousseau had argued that melody attains its particular force by mimesis of vocal inflections, and particularly by the contours of its lines. To confute this theory, Rameau took a few measures of Lully's recitative and cast it in alternatively ascending and descending melodic lines using dominant and subdominant modulations, respectively. In Rameau's judgment, a change of melodic direction could not alter the expressiveness of the music if the harmony remained unaltered, proving that the affection of the music depends upon the modulation of the harmony, not upon the contour of the melody.

Not satisfied with this rebuttal, Rameau decided the following year to go on the offensive. In 1755, after the first four volumes of the *Encyclopédie* had been issued, Rameau anonymously published a pamphlet criticizing six of Rousseau's articles.[109] The articles in question were "accompagnement," "accord," "cadence," "choeur," "chromatique," and "dissonance." The following year, Rameau came out with a second pamphlet in response to an article found in the fifth volume, "enharmonique."[110] Rameau's pamphlets were certainly disproportionate in both tone and length to Rousseau's articles. (The article "enharmonique," for example, which prompted a thirty-five-page diatribe from Rameau, was only two columns in length!) Despite d'Alembert's best efforts at editing and adding to Rousseau's articles, Rameau found just about everything concerning his theory as presented in the *Encyclopédie* to be wanting. For the most part, he complains about trivial aspects of wording or critical innuendos that he reads into Rousseau's prose. He feels his theory is misrepresented or not taken sufficiently into account (e.g. in Rousseau's interpretation of supposition in the article "accord"). Many of his arguments were more substantial, though. Concerning the article "accompagnement,"

---

108 A detailed analysis of Rameau's arguments is given by Cynthia Verba in her article "The Development of Rameau's Thoughts on Modulation and Chromaticism," *Journal of the American Musicological Society* 26/1 (1973), 69–97.
109 *Erreurs sur la musique dans l'Encyclopédie*; *CTW* V, 198–261.
110 *Suite des Erreurs sur la musique dans l'Encyclopédie* (Paris, 1756); *CTW* V, 311–330.

for instance, Rameau defends his recommendation that a good accompaniment should be harmonically replete so as to represent the *corps sonore* (p. 18). He reiterates his well-known thesis that melody derives its expressiveness only through harmonic support by showing how the single melodic interval of the tritone (C–F♯) can be harmonized in nine differing settings (pp. 52–56).[111] Each setting has its own unique character, Rameau notes, determined entirely by the differing harmonies placed underneath. But in the overwhelming percentage of space in both pamphlets, Rameau inveighs against the Italian operatic practice and aesthetic ideals Rousseau holds so dear. The two pamphlets can thus be seen as yet another contribution to the burgeoning war of words sparked by the Bouffon visit and Rousseau's *Lettre*.

While there is little new to Rameau's arguments, an increased acerbity is noticeable in his fulminations against Rousseau, whom he refers to derisively throughout as "le musicien." To offer one illustration of the sardonic tone of Rameau's prose, I quote the opening paragraph of the second pamphlet:

Here the erudition of M. Rousseau shines brightly to enlighten us regarding the enharmonic genre. He noticed a few Greek words concerning this genre whose light dazzled him, and he thought we would likewise be dazzled.[112]

The same sarcastic tone is maintained throughout the pamphlet. Grimm was no doubt voicing the opinion of all the Encyclopedists when he commented, in his privately circulated newsletter:

It would not be difficult perhaps to find fault with many things in the musical articles [of the Encyclopedia]. They are probably neither refined nor thorough enough. But this is not the reproach they receive in the insipid pamphlet to which I refer. One thing for sure is that neither M. Rameau nor anyone else could have done any better.[113]

Rousseau responded to Rameau's attacks with an essay of his own, although it was never published in his lifetime.[114] Rousseau also made explicit many of his disagreements with Rameau when he revised his Encyclopedia entries for his own music dictionary published in 1767.

Interesting and important as Rousseau's development as a musical thinker is, it is a development that no more concerned Rameau. Most of Rousseau's arguments with Rameau were driven by his own ideological agenda, and reflect his maturing thoughts on language, education, society, and politics – an agenda Rameau was fully incapable of recognizing or appreciating. For his part, Rousseau was blind to the systematic *desiderata* of Rameau's theory and deaf to its musical subtleties. It is

---

111 Rameau made somewhat the same demonstration in the *Nouveau système* where he illustrated how the interval of the perfect fifth (G–C) could be assigned no less than twenty different fundamental basses (*Nouveau système*, 48).
112 *Suite des Erreurs*, 1–2; *CTW* V, 311–12.
113 Grimm et al., *Correspondance littéraire*, III, 129.
114 "Examen de deux principes avancés par M. Rameau, dans sa Brochure intitulée: Erreurs sur la musique dans l'Encyclopédie" (c. 1755); reprinted in *CTW* V, 266–85.

no wonder, then, that their respective arguments failed so obviously to engage the other in any direct way. In any event, by 1756, Rameau had a new target upon which to focus the attention of his wrath: d'Alembert. For the few remaining years of his life, it would be against his former expositor and friend d'Alembert that Rameau would ceaselessly campaign. That the relationship between these two former allies could become so bitter and hostile in so short a time indicates that deeper forces were at work. As we consider carefully the events and issues that precipitated their break, we will see exposed in the clearest manifestations yet most of the fundamental epistemological tensions engendered by Rameau's efforts to apply scientific language and methods to his theory of music. Thus an examination of the d'Alembert–Rameau quarrel will serve as a fitting culmination and conclusion to our study.

9

D'ALEMBERT

There is a supreme irony to the quarrel between d'Alembert and Rameau. By any measure, d'Alembert tried to be a faithful exegete of Rameau's theory; none of the composer's scientific or philosophical collaborators ever worked harder to navigate his labyrinthine prose, or labored so selflessly in aiding the composer to refine and propagate his theory. The *Elémens de musique théorique et pratique suivant les principes de M. Rameau* stands as a testament to d'Alembert's real talent for rendering otherwise abstruse notions into organized and clear language. Yet this reduction came at a price. The qualities of synthesis and precision that make the *Elémens* such an accessible work also entail drawbacks. By reducing, reorganizing, and generally simplifying Rameau's theory, d'Alembert also distorted it. As I will show over the course of this chapter, many of the theoretical explanations in the *Elémens* differ in critical ways from those Rameau articulated in the *Génération harmonique* and the *Démonstration* – the two principal works upon which d'Alembert drew. Likewise, the composition primer that constitutes Book 2 of the *Elémens* pales in comparison to the richly illustrated and nuanced advice Rameau offers in his two major composition treatises: "L'Art de la basse fondamentale," and the *Code de musique pratique*. Despite the initial gratitude expressed by Rameau for d'Alembert's efforts, it was inevitable that the real differences separating the two would eventually come out in the open. This indeed happened with the advent of the Encyclopedist quarrel recorded in the previous chapter. D'Alembert and Rameau entered into their own personal but nonetheless highly public debate that quickly exceeded the former in its intensity and rancor.

Many of the issues of their disagreement were technical ones, involving problems we have already encountered in previous chapters: the generation of dissonant harmonies, definitions of mode and key, and rules governing the motion of the fundamental bass. Thus by analyzing their arguments, we will have a chance to hear Rameau's last and most mature thoughts on questions with which he had wrestled for almost a half century. But the issues separating Rameau and d'Alembert were not just of a technical nature. There were deep-seated epistemological differences between the two men. By teasing out these differences, we shall be able to draw together and encapsulate most of the fundamental problems of scientific language, method, and validation that we have seen were engendered by Rameau's theoretical enterprise.

There is one final dividend we will gain from this analysis. As d'Alembert's *Elémens* became the primary means by which Rameau's theory was disseminated both at home and in Germany (in the guise of Marpurg's translation), a study of its fidelity to Rameau's thought will be useful for understanding the problematic *Rezeptionsgeschichte* of the *basse fondamentale* in the later eighteenth century. While we await another study to trace this history in detail, I am convinced that many of the most popular misconceptions about Rameau's theory can be traced to d'Alembert's little book. As we will shortly see, the *Elémens* in some ways tells us as much about d'Alembert's scientific epistemology as it does about Rameau's music theory.

THE *ELEMENS DE MUSIQUE*

We have seen that d'Alembert's first contact with Rameau's theory came in late 1749. Charged by the Académie des Sciences to review the "Mémoire" Rameau had submitted, d'Alembert drafted a lengthy summary of the composer's paper. This résumé, it seems, was favorably received, for soon thereafter, he reports, "at the request of several friends who were little versed in music, but who wished to inform themselves of the discoveries and principles of this illustrious artist," he expanded his review into a comprehensive overview of the composer's entire theoretical system.[1] The result was of course the *Elémens de musique théorique et pratique suivant les principes de M. Rameau*.[2] During the composition of his text, it seems that d'Alembert consulted with Rameau. In the one extant letter we have of d'Alembert written to Rameau, he asks the elder composer for advice: "I beg of you to examine [my manuscript] carefully, and to add your remarks in writing so that I may profit from them."[3] Rameau was happy to oblige.[4]

While composing his *Elémens,* d'Alembert also began to take a more active interest in supervising Rousseau's music articles for the *Encyclopédie*. We have a letter of Rousseau written to d'Alembert in which we read that Rousseau had returned a batch of corrected articles beginning with the letter C (including important entries on "cadence," "chiffres," "chromatique," and "consonance"). Evidently d'Alembert, in his capacity as coeditor, had requested several changes. "I have come around to all your opinions," Rousseau replied,

---

[1] Elémens (1752), v.

[2] D'Alembert mentions at one point that the *Elémens* was written fifteen months before it was published ("Lettre de l'Auteur ⋆ des Elémens de musique," *Journal Oeconomique* [Nov., 1752], 114; *CTW* VI, 257). Since the *privilège du Roi* for the *Elémens* was February 21, 1752, this would place the date of its completion around December 1750.

[3] CTW VI, 233. The letter is undated, but Jacobi places it at the end of 1750 (*CTW* III, lvi). It could probably have not been much later, since by the beginning of 1751, d'Alembert was totally preoccupied writing the Preliminary Discourse to the *Encyclopédie*, by his own account an exhausting and time-consuming task.

[4] In a later document, d'Alembert reported that Rameau had examined a complete draft of the *Elémens*, making no changes in the first half, but offering him useful criticism (*avis utiles*) in the second. Rameau penned these suggestions in the margins of the manuscript, all of which d'Alembert claimed he followed ("Lettre de l'Auteur ⋆ des Elémens de musique," 113; *CTW* VI, 257). Rameau also gave to d'Alembert a manuscript copy of an uncompleted composition treatise around this time to help in the writing of Part 2 of the *Elémens*. (See Appendix 2.)

Plate 9.1 An engraving of Jean Le Rond d'Alembert; engraver unknown

and I approve of the changes you have judged fit to make. I have, however, reinstated one or two sentences that you suppressed, because in following the guidelines that you yourself established, it seemed to me that the original remarks were much to the point, neither betraying anger nor containing anything wounding. However, it is my wish that you should be absolute master, and I submit everything to your judgment and your wisdom.[5]

This is a very interesting admission by Rousseau, for it reveals that by this time d'Alembert felt himself competent enough to edit theory articles of a highly sophisticated nature. (The articles "cadence" and "chiffres" were especially detailed.) We cannot be certain about all the changes d'Alembert requested. But it seems they were done to soften any criticism – direct or implied – of Rameau. Both d'Alembert and Diderot were anxious about the reception of the Encyclopedia project (the first volume of which was to be issued two days after Rousseau's letter of June 26), and they naturally would have wished to forestall any criticism, especially coming from an artist with the prestige of Rameau.

D'Alembert was not just cynically trying to curry favor with Rameau on behalf of the Encyclopedia project, though. His praise for Rameau found in the Preliminary Discourse (quoted on pp. 5–6) is testament to a real respect for Rameau's theoretical accomplishments. D'Alembert was not one to be extravagant in his praise of others, either; he had enough integrity to exclude those figures he felt to be unworthy of mention in his Discourse, even though several of them – for instance the president of the French Academy, Renault – held positions of great influence.[6]

Let us now look at the contents of d'Alembert's little résumé. As the title indicates, d'Alembert treats both the theory and practice of music based upon Rameau's principles. These topics are addressed in the first and second books of the *Elémens*, respectively. Book 1, which contains "the theory of harmony," serves to establish the "elements" of musical practice: intervals, chords, scales, cadences, and modes. D'Alembert tells us that everything is presented and explained in as clear a manner as possible, "which supposes . . . no knowledge of music other than the syllables ut, re, mi, fa, sol, la, si, ut."[7] The second Book, which contains "the principal rules of composition," serves as a primer in composition. Here the fundamental bass is introduced and used to teach the student how to write basic harmonic progressions, rules for treating dissonance, and the harmonization of melodic lines. D'Alembert does not claim his work is exhaustive; numerous "elements" and rules of lesser importance are not included so as not to encumber the text with too much detail. The *Elémens*, "if I may express myself so, is really only a *rudiment* of music designed to expound for beginners the fundamental principles and not the details."[8]

The sources for d'Alembert's text are not difficult to trace. The majority of material contained in Book 1 is derived from Rameau's *Démonstration*. (Indeed, in places d'Alembert has extracted passages *verbatim*.) In the following concordance, I have correlated d'Alembert's chapters with the specific pages in Rameau's

---

5 Letter dated June 26, 1751. *Correspondance complète de Jean-Jacques Rousseau*, ed. R. A. Leigh, 36 vols. (Geneva, 1965), II, 159.
6 Ronald Grimsley, *Jean d'Alembert 1717–83* (Oxford, 1963), 79.
7 *Elémens* (1752), vii.
8 Ibid., x.

Démonstration, and in a few instances, those relevant chapters from his *Nouveau système* and *Génération harmonique* (abbreviated NS and GH, respectively).

Elémens (chapter)		*Démonstration* (page numbers)
1	Preliminary and Fundamental Experiments	
	a The *corps sonore*	12–14; 19–21
	b The Minor Triad	21–22
	c Octave Identity	16–18
2	Origins of the Two Modes	22–24
3	On the Succession of Fifths	30–33
4	On Mode in General	33–35
5	Formation of the Greek Diatonic Scale	46–47; 75
6	Formation of the Modern Diatonic Scale	34–35; 47–57
7	On Temperament	104–110
8	On Cadences [Perfect and Imperfect]	36–38
9	On the Minor Mode	62–72
10	On the Diatonic Scale of the Minor Mode	72–80
11	On Dissonance	84–87
12	On the Double Employment of Dissonance	50–52
13	Uses and Rules of Double Employment	(*GH*, Ch. 9)
14	On the Different Kinds of Seventh Chords	(*GH*, Ch. 9)
15	On the Preparation of Dissonances	(*GH*, Ch. 10/1)
16	On the Rule for Resolving Dissonances	(*GH*, Ch. 10/2)
17	On the Broken and Interrupted Cadences	88 (*GH*, Ch. 15)
18	On the Chromatic Genre	90–91
19	On the Enharmonic Genre	92–93
20	On the Diatonic-Enharmonic Genre	93–94
21	On the Chromatic-Enharmonic Genre	95
22	That Melody is Born of Harmony	(*NS*, Ch. 8)

D'Alembert's talent for synthesis and systematization is readily apparent in his chapter organization. Dispensing with virtually all of Rameau's phenomenological and mathematical preliminaries, he establishes right away the basic musical elements and axioms of Rameau's theory (Chapters 1–3), and moves from there to deduce in methodical fashion ever more complex tonal material: cadences, scales, modes, dissonance, and genres. Rameau was never able to attain such clear organization. His prose was invariably more desultory. Thus, to give one example, Rameau introduces the diatonic scale on pages 33–35 of the *Démonstration,* only to digress into a discussion of cadence and the geometric progression before returning to his subject some twelve pages later. Admittedly all these topics are interdependent in Rameau's theory and must be understood as a whole. Nonetheless, his digressions often become confusing to the reader.

The second Book of d'Alembert's *Elémens* (containing the "rules of composition") was another story altogether. For this section – the most difficult and time-consuming for him to write – d'Alembert had to rely entirely upon one section: Chapter 18 of the *Génération harmonique*.[9] (The *Démonstration*, it will be recalled, contained no practical material dealing with the rules of composition.) Chapter 18 is the longest in the *Génération harmonique,* and contains "a summary of the rules of composition." Rameau is typically discursive and disorganized in his presentation. He does not present any systematic pedagogy of composition; rather, he makes numerous observations and prescriptions in quite random order. D'Alembert's success in managing this morass of detail must be counted as one of his most outstanding accomplishments. He was able to synthesize just five basic rules governing the succession of the fundamental bass and the preparation of dissonance, augmented by three secondary rules. From there, d'Alembert went on to discuss a number of consequences, elaborations and licenses to these rules. Included among these "licenses" are broken and interrupted cadences, and chords of supposition, suspension, and the diminished seventh.

Perhaps the most striking feature of the second Book is its inferential structure. Every rule is justified by one of the fundamental principles or elements that had been established in the first Book. (This is indicated with a numerical reference to the specific article in Book 1 to which the reader of Book 2 may turn.) D'Alembert was quite proud of this deductive structuring. He wrote in the introduction that "these rules are founded on the principles presented in the first book. . . Those who will have read the first book will find in each rule of the second a reference to the place in the first book wherein is given the justification of that rule."[10] These rules of composition, d'Alembert believed, "derived evidently" from the first part.[11] Thus, an idealized deductive structuring of Rameau's theory is attained. Book 1 establishes all the material of the theory, while Book 2 details how this material is utilized in practice by the musician – put into musical time, if you will.

When the *Elémens* appeared in June 1752, it was immediately hailed as a triumph. Although it was published anonymously (a common practice of the day), there was no doubt in the public's mind as to the author. Diderot, Condillac, and Grimm all praised it, as was to be expected. But so did all the French periodicals, including that implacable foe of the *Encyclopédie,* the Jesuit *Journal de Trévoux*.[12] Rousseau himself was forced to acknowledge its merits, even though he might easily have

[9] *Ibid.,* 86–87; *CTW* VI, 263.
[10] *Elémens* (1752), viii.
[11] *Ibid.,* 112.
[12] For a reprint of these reviews, see *CTW* VI, 235–93. The only critical review of the *Elémens* was published in a relatively minor journal, the *Journal Oeconomique,* by a partisan student of Rameau who was preparing to bring out his own résumé of the master's theory, Jean-Laurent de Bethizy. Bethizy's criticisms prompted a surprisingly lengthy reply from d'Alembert (over fifty-six pages), in which he rebutted point by point every one of Bethizy's objections.

Jacobi suggests that the *Journal Oeconomique* was the only periodical willing to carry a review critical of the powerful d'Alembert (*CTW* III, liv). But this is doubtful. Conservative journalists such as Berthier, Castel, and Fréron showed little reluctance in taking on the Encyclopedists in other matters. When Rameau eventually came out critically against the *Encyclopédie,* they took obvious delight in amply reporting the composer's profound indignation. See John Pappas, "Berthier's *Journal de Trévoux* and the Philosophes," *Studies on Voltaire and the Eighteenth Century* 3 (1957), 221.

ÉLÉMENS DE MUSIQUE,

THÉORIQUE ET PRATIQUE,

SUIVANT

LES PRINCIPES DE M. RAMEAU.

A PARIS,

Chez { DAVID l'aîné, rue S. Jacques, à la Plume d'Or.
LE BRETON, Imprimeur ordinaire du Roi, au bas de la rue de la Harpe.
DURAND, rue S. Jacques, à S. Landry, & au Griffon.

M. DCCLII.

AVEC APPROBATION ET PRIVILEGE DU ROI.

Plate 9.2 Title page to the first edition of d'Alembert's *Elémens de musique* (1752)

interpreted the *Elémens* as a disparaging comment upon his own articles. (Presumably his articles were to serve the same purpose as d'Alembert's book, that is, to present Rameau's theory in a "clear and methodical" manner.[13])

13 Here was Rousseau's first reaction to d'Alembert's book: "The theoretical works of M. Rameau have the singularity of having become famous without having been read. And this will likely remain the case since a

Perhaps the most satisfied reader, though, was the composer himself. In a glowing letter sent to the *Mercure,* Rameau profusely thanked and praised the young geometrician for his efforts:

> The illustrious man to whom my gratitude is addressed has looked into my works not for faults to reprove but for truths to analyze, to simplify, to make better known, clearer and as a result more useful to a large number [of people] by this sort of distinctness, order, and precision that characterizes his works. He has not disdained even to get within the reach of children through the strength of this genius that bends, masters, and modifies at his will all the matters that he treats. Finally, he has given me personally the comfort of seeing added to the solidity of my principles a simplicity to which I believed them susceptible, but which I could have given them only with much more difficulty, and perhaps less successfully than he.[14]

One wonders, though, whether Rameau was applauding the intrinsic adequacy of the *Elémens* as much as expressing gratitude to its author for granting him the recognition and approbation he had so long desired to receive from scientists.

FRIENDSHIP WITH RAMEAU: TENSION AND RUPTURE

As we saw in Chapter 8, the *Encyclopédie* had reached only the first four volumes (up to the letter C) before Rameau felt compelled to issue a pamphlet censoring Rousseau's music articles. His main motive, it will be recalled, was less the content of the music articles themselves than the *Lettre* on French music Rousseau had just independently published, and which had launched the Bouffon quarrel. The *Encyclopédie* articles seemed more of a pretext for Rameau to rebut Rousseau's defiantly anti-French manifesto, and chide the editors for associating themselves with an author who possessed such an obvious lack of musical talent and taste. Still, there were a number of specific arguments in Rousseau's articles with which Rameau took issue. Even d'Alembert's additions and clarifications of Rousseau's articles failed to placate Rameau, who interpreted them as thinly disguised apologies for Rousseau's incompetence. Striving to be as charitable as he could, Rameau emphasized that however deferential d'Alembert tried to be, his remarks were woefully insufficient in the face of such egregious distortions of his own theory.[15]

D'Alembert must have been as surprised as he was annoyed at Rameau's petulant display of bad manners and ingratitude. Still, he probably would have just as soon let Rameau's attacks go unanswered had he not also felt responsible for the welfare

---

   philosophe has taken the trouble to summarize the ideas of this author. It is certain that this summary will make obsolete the original, and with such compensation that one will have no cause for regret" ("Lettre à M. Grimm," in *Oeuvres complètes de Jean-Jacques Rousseau,* 12 vols. [Paris, 1872], VI, 245). In his later paranoia, Rousseau would in fact accuse d'Alembert of having plagiarized his articles in the *Elémens* ("Rousseau Juge de Jean-Jacques," *Ibid.*, IX, 114).

14 *CTW* VI, 238; translated in Robert M. Isherwood, "The Conciliatory Partisan of Musical Liberty: Jean Le Rond d'Alembert, 1717–1783," in *French Musical Thought, 1600–1800,* ed. Georgia Cowart (Ann Arbor, 1989), 99.
15 *Erreurs,* 94, 102; *CTW* V, 244, 248.

of the *Encyclopédie* project. Thus, in his capacity as coeditor, d'Alembert felt called upon to reply to Rameau's unwelcome criticisms. In an "Avertissement des éditeurs" prefacing the sixth volume of the *Encyclopédie*, which appeared in 1756, d'Alembert called the author of the pamphlet to order and reaffirmed his faith in Rousseau's musical competence:

M. Rousseau, who in addition to his ample knowledge and taste in music, possesses the talent of thinking and expressing himself with clearness (which musicians cannot always do), is much too capable of defending himself for us to presume to do so for him here.[16]

D'Alembert then expresses his incredulity – no doubt sincere – that Rameau could be the author of a pamphlet attacking so rudely the very people who were trying their best to champion his theory:

Everything causes us to think otherwise: the little response this criticism caused among the public, the rude imputations – as unreasonable as they are inappropriate – which the artist could not possibly make against the two learned men who have always paid him the most sincere homage, and whose advice he did not refrain from seeking concerning his own works; the inconsiderate way in which M. Rousseau is treated in this pamphlet, although he always named the musician in question with praise and respect, even in the small number of places where he felt it necessary to disagree with him; finally, the most unusual opinions maintained in this article, that do not stand in its favor, among others, that geometry is based upon music, that one may compare music to any science whatsoever, that an ocular harpsichord demonstrating the correspondence between harmony and colors merits approval, and so on for the rest. If these are the truths that we are accused of ignoring, of neglecting or of concealing, we will merit the stigma of this reproach for a long time.[17]

D'Alembert's rebuttal hints at one of the issues that was to accelerate their eventual falling out: by this time, Rameau was beginning to make claims for the scientific and metaphysical primacy of the *corps sonore*. It will be recalled how Rameau had surreptitiously changed upon publication the title of the "Mémoire" he had submitted to the Académie to that of *Démonstration*. D'Alembert apparently allowed Rameau this indulgence at the time, not taking seriously the composer's scientific pretension. But as Rameau continued to insist ever more emphatically that he had indeed "demonstrated" the truth of his principle of harmony (testified, he thought, by the Académie approbation and the philosophes' earlier support), d'Alembert was forced to call Rameau to order. Rameau's theory, d'Alembert granted, was the most logical and coherent system yet known, but it could hardly be said to have been "demonstrated" in any scientific sense. Rather than retreating, though, Rameau became increasingly bold in his claims.

---

16 "Avertissement des éditeurs," *Encyclopédie* VI, 1–2; *CTW* V, 289. Rousseau actually did respond to Rameau's attack in an essay that was never published in his own lifetime: "Examen de deux principes avancés par M. Rameau, dans sa Brochure intitulée: Erreurs sur la musique dans L'Encyclopédie" (c. 1755); reprinted in *CTW* V, 266–85. Jacobi suggests that d'Alembert may have requested that Rousseau not publish this response so as not to further anger Rameau (*CTW* V, xxxviii). Although firm in its tone, d'Alembert's "Avertissement" still seems to hold out the possibility of reconciliation with the composer.
17 *Ibid.*, 290.

Rameau responded to d'Alembert's "Avertissement" with the customary pamphlet – this time using his name on the title page.[18] The tone of Rameau's remarks in this pamphlet are notably more shrill. He spares no efforts to disparage the efforts of the Encyclopedists, or to cast aspersions upon their motives. (One gets the impression Rameau was now being coached by anti-Encyclopedists like Fréron and Berthier.) In a virtual line-by-line rebuttal, Rameau defends himself from the criticism of d'Alembert's "Avertissement." He begins by reminding the editors that it was against Rousseau that his earlier pamphlets were directed, not themselves. Since they insist now upon entering into this dispute out of whatever misguided sense of loyalty, he will respond in turn. Rameau then complains that the editors misinterpreted his remarks, took them out of context, and omitted his many qualifications. He claimed to have only suggested that there *might* be something to Castel's color–sound analogy. Nowhere did he *directly* state that geometry is premised upon music. But he quickly adds that the very evidence that the Académie endorsed strongly suggests there is a strong correspondence between the two disciplines in any case! Indeed, Rameau would proceed to push this last point even further. Taking up ideas he had first suggested in the *Nouvelles réflexions* of 1752, Rameau asserted that "if it be true that geometry is based upon proportions and if the *corps sonore* produces them . . . it is then natural to conclude that science must have an intimate connection to music. I see only this last conclusion from which one can infer that geometry is founded on music."[19] Rameau continued to elaborate in this fashion over the remaining twenty pages of the pamphlet. He marvels again and again at the wonder that is the *corps sonore*, its indisputable perceptual basis in nature, and its capacity to provide all the proportions that together define the geometric arts and sciences:

The single resonance of the whole [*corps sonore*] produces at the same instant roots, tree, branches, proportions, progressions, division, addition, multiplication, squares, cubes, etc. What principles from a single source! What idea cannot one form from it? To which ideas are we not led? . . . One cannot repeat such facts of experience too often, so I hope this short recapitulation will perhaps make more of an impression than appears to have been made until now.[20]

Rameau ends his pamphlet with a dig at d'Alembert's *Elémens* – the first direct criticism of this work he made – by noting that the author's rules concerning the progression of the fundamental bass in relation to the harmonic and arithmetic proportions are faulty.

Rameau probably did not realize that by attacking d'Alembert, he was engaging in combat a personality every bit as pugnacious and intolerant of criticism as he was himself. D'Alembert was by far the most irascible of the Encyclopedists. Throughout his life he was involved in a number of drawn-out controversies, usually of his own creation. D'Alembert could not suffer criticism without responding in kind,

---

18   "Réponse de M. Rameau à MM. les éditeurs de l'Encyclopédie sur leur dernier Avertissement" (Paris, 1757); *CTW* V, 336–61.
19   *Ibid.*, 33.
20   *Ibid.*, 51.

whether it came from his scientific rivals Clairaut and Euler, or from critics of the *Encyclopédie* such as Fréron or Berthier. He wore out the patience of the censor Malesherbes by too frequently requesting the suppression of critical writings.[21] Consequently, when Rameau attacked the *Encyclopédie*, d'Alembert took it as a personal insult and felt the need to respond.[22]

In the seventh volume of the *Encyclopédie* (issued in 1757), d'Alembert forcefully answered Rameau's pamphlet in two lengthy articles: "fondamental" and "gamme." In the first of these articles, d'Alembert comments critically upon several scientific questions related to Rameau's theory. In probably the strongest rebuke directed at Rameau, d'Alembert criticized "those musicians who employ in their writings calculation on top of calculation, and believe that all this apparatus is necessary to their art." Such pretence, he continues, conveys a "false scientific air that could only fool the ignorant" and constitutes a "ridiculous abuse of geometry in music." As for the idea that geometry has its origin in music, d'Alembert asks incredulously:

What will we say about what has been suggested lately, that geometry is founded upon the resonance of the *corps sonore*, because geometry, it is said, is founded upon proportions, and that the *corps sonore* generates them all? Geometricians would not be grateful if we take seriously such assertions. We will permit ourselves only to say here that the consideration of proportions and progressions is entirely useless to the theory of the musical art. I believe I have sufficiently proven this in my *Elémens de musique* where I have given, it seems to me, a theory of harmony sufficiently well deduced according to the principles of M. Rameau without having used proportions or progressions.[23]

In the second article, Rameau is taken to task again for asserting that his theory has been "demonstrated." The conclusions Rameau draws from his theory, d'Alembert insists, cannot ever possess the "evidence of Euclid's theorems"; they can only be placed "in the class of probabilities."

We can see quite plainly that the good will toward Rameau that characterized d'Alembert's earlier writings is no longer in evidence. For his part, Rameau forgot the gratitude he had once felt for d'Alembert. D'Alembert quickly superseded Rousseau as Rameau's most hated adversary. In the "Lettre à M. d'Alembert sur

---

21 Grimsley, *D'Alembert*, 64–65.
22 The history of the d'Alembert–Rameau controversy is retold in several sources: James Doolittle, "A Would-Be Philosophe, Jean-Philippe Rameau," *Publication of the Modern Language Association* 74 (1959), 233–48; Richard Oliver, *The Encyclopedists as Critics of Music* (New York, 1947), 101–12; Jonathan Bernard, "The Principle and the Elements: Rameau's Controversy with d'Alembert," *Journal of Music Theory* 24/1 (1980), 37–62; Marie-Elisabeth Duchez, "D'Alembert diffuseur de la théorie harmonique de Rameau: déduction scientifique et simplification musicale," *Jean d'Alembert, Savant et philosophe: Portrait à plusieurs voix*, ed Monqiue Emery and Pierre Monzani (Paris, 1989), 475–95; Françoise Escal, "Musique et science: d'Alembert contre Rameau, *International Review of the Aesthetics and Sociology of Music* 14/2 (1983), 167–89; Thomas Christensen, "Science and Music Theory in the Enlightenment: D'Alembert's Critique of Rameau" (Ph.D. Dissertation, Yale University, 1985); and most recently, Cynthia Verba, *Music and the French Enlightenment: Reconstruction of a Dialogue* (New York, 1992), especially Chapter 4: "Music as Science: Contributions of D'Alembert." Jacobi has scattered throughout his editorial annotations of his edition of Rameau's theoretical writings a number of relevant facts: *CTW* IV, xiii–xiv, xlii–xlvi; V, xxxv–xliv; and VI, xxx–xxxv.
23 *Encyclopédie*, s.v. "fondamental."

ses opinions en musique, insérées dans les articles Fondamental et Gamme de l'Encyclopédie," published and bound with the *Code de musique pratique* of 1760, Rameau attempted to rebut the criticism contained in d'Alembert's articles.[24] He began by accusing d'Alembert of having declared an "open war" on him. Referring back to various historical and logical arguments he had just enunciated in his *Nouvelles réflexions sur le principe sonore* (also appended to the *Code*), Rameau reasserts the scientific basis of his theory and the primacy of the *corps sonore*. Rameau reminds d'Alembert that the Académie had earlier endorsed his theory as being "more geometric" than any previous theory, so his present retraction is both hypocritical and treacherous. If d'Alembert cannot bring himself to recognize the obvious dependence of geometry upon the basic and ubiquitous experience of the *corps sonore,* then this is only a sign of the stubborn ego of the geometrician. It was obvious to Rameau that d'Alembert's motives were political, and had nothing to do with a desire to reach the truth of the matter: "If I am *fooling others*" – Rameau is here responding to d'Alembert's claim that the mathematical calculations of Rameau's theory can only serve to "fool the ignorant" – "at least I offer the means to discover the truth. But you, sir, sow confusion everywhere. You deny, you criticize, you raise doubts, and explain nothing under the pretence that we *would not be grateful* to you to do so" – another reference to d'Alembert's earlier remark that "geometricians would not be grateful if we take seriously" Rameau's claims concerning the primacy of the *corps sonore*.[25] Once again, d'Alembert was prompted to respond to Rameau's attacks. A final slew of letters was exchanged between the two, all of them published in the *Mercure de France*.[26]

In 1762, d'Alembert came out with a new edition of the *Elémens,* "revised, corrected, and considerably augmented," as the title page announced.[27] The subtitle is not an exaggeration. Numerous passages of the first edition are completely altered or eliminated. In their place d'Alembert introduces much new material now openly critical of Rameau. Undoubtedly the most important part of the revised *Elémens,* though, is its lengthy *Discours préliminaire* (not to be confused with the *Discours préliminaire* of the *Encyclopédie*) – a wide-ranging essay in which d'Alembert crisply summarizes his theoretical and epistemological differences with Rameau.

After publication of the revised *Elémens,* d'Alembert no longer engaged in polemics with Rameau. The elderly composer would continue to attack "le géometre" in his writings.[28] But his words fell upon deaf ears. D'Alembert ended his final

24 *CTW* IV, 267–80.
25 "Lettre à M. d'Alembert," 13.
26 The series of letters is as follows: d'Alembert: "Lettre de M. d'Alembert à M. Rameau" (April, 1761); Rameau: "Réponse de M. Rameau à la Lettre de M. d'Alembert, qu'on vient de lire" (April, 1761); Rameau: "Suite de la Réponse" (July, 1761); and d'Alembert: "Réponse à une Lettre imprimée de M. Rameau" (March, 1762). The last letter was reprinted with the revised edition of the *Elémens* in 1762. All the letters are to be found in *CTW* V, 367–85; and VI, 478–88.
27 *Elémens de musique théorique et pratique suivant les principes de M. Rameau, éclaircis, développés & simplifiés; Nouvelle édition revue, corrigée & considérablement augmentée* (Lyons, 1762).
28 Rameau pursued his "Controverse" with d'Alembert in a half dozen letters and "anonymous" commentaries published in various Parisian periodicals: *CTW* IV, 313–24; VI, 439–55; as well as a final installment missed

letter to Rameau with these trenchant words: "I flatter myself, Sir, that I have sufficiently satisfied your criticisms, at least those that I understood. But I also flatter myself that I have given you sufficient proof of affability and attachment to you by answering once; and I believe thereby that I have earned the right to keep silence henceforth."[29]

PHYSICO-MATHEMATICS AND THE EMPIRICAL DEDUCTIVE METHOD

What could fuel such animosity? If d'Alembert's motives for rebuking Rameau were only out of solidarity for his fellow Encyclopedists, after 1757 no such motive could be imputed. For it was just after the seventh volume of the *Encyclopédie* was published that d'Alembert resigned from his position as coeditor.[30] Obviously, there were deeper philosophical issues involved. While we have already seen that much of d'Alembert's anger was rooted in his antipathy towards Rameau's increasingly imperialist claims on behalf of the *corps sonore*, their differences were more complicated than that. If we see only a scenario in which d'Alembert plays the sober scientist rebuking the naive composer for making unfounded and outrageous scientific claims on behalf of his theory, we will miss the much richer substance of their arguments.

We may begin by reminding ourselves of d'Alembert's peculiar epistemology, one informed by his work in that hybrid domain of physics and mathematics called "rational mechanics," or as one said in his own day, "physico-mathematics." In reading the Preliminary Discourse to the *Encyclopédie*, one comes away with the impression that d'Alembert was an enthusiastic champion of empirical philosophy. There he propounds Locke's sensationalist psychology with seeming conviction, and cites approvingly Newton's science as its premier model and vindication. But as a scientist of rational mechanics, d'Alembert also knew the value of mathematical and geometric deduction. Thus his epistemology also contains strongly rationalist doctrines. His ideal method for attaining sure knowledge of some phenomenon as described in the Discourse was essentially a trope of Newton's analytic-synthetic method (discussed in Chapter 2): We must begin – as Locke taught us – with the

---

by Jacobi and reprinted with commentary by Philippe Lescot: "Conclusion sur l'origine des sciences: un texte méconnu de Jean-Philippe Rameau," *Rameau Colloque International*, 409–24. In these letters, Rameau repeats over and over his claims concerning the primacy of the *corps sonore* as the principle of all the sciences, and castigates d'Alembert for failing to acknowledge this truth.

29 *Elémens* (1762), 231.
30 The catalyst for d'Alembert's resignation was his lengthy article "Geneva," in which he inadvertently caused a scandal by praising the Genevan clergy for espousing a kind of Deistic Socinianism. This was a compliment the conservative Swiss Calvinists would hardly have received with favor. In addition, d'Alembert indiscreetly urged – evidently with Voltaire's coaxing – the Genevan authorities to allow a theater within the city limits, presumably in order to leaven its moral austerity. This unwelcome advice caused a torrent of criticism to rain down upon the Encyclopedists. It was all too much for the sensitive d'Alembert to bear, and he tendered his resignation to Diderot shortly thereafter, earning the latter's bitterness for "desertion." For further information on the "Geneva" scandal, see Grimsley, *D'Alembert*, 56–77.

data presented to our senses; through careful analysis, we break down the objects of our sense impressions into smaller and ever more abstract components; having reached the most primitive constituents (preferably ones that can be quantified), we can reassemble the parts into a whole system again thus attaining a perfect understanding of their connection.[31] D'Alembert thought that with such a method, it was possible to derive a few principles – perhaps even a single principle – which can be said to govern any particular system.[32] This is exactly what he claimed to have accomplished in his *Traité de dynamique* of 1743. In that landmark study, d'Alembert essentially reduced mechanics to equations of impenetrable matter and impact. From this very Cartesian basis, he derived three laws which cover, respectively, inertia, the compounding of motion, and equilibrium. All physical motion, d'Alembert believed, could be described as some combination of these three conditions, from which is derived a general principle of mechanics, known today as "d'Alembert's principle."[33] D'Alembert made some extravagant claims on behalf of his principle, most – although by no means all – of which have proven to be unfounded. Nonetheless, it pointed to the ideal he held for all knowledge: the simplification and reduction of complex situations from which the most general principles may be drawn.

But as we saw in Chapter 6 when considering d'Alembert's position in the "vibrating string" controversy, d'Alembert sometimes placed a bit too much faith in mathematical deduction. He often displayed astonishing disregard for experimental evidence in favor of highly abstract mathematical calculations. How could d'Alembert reconcile his Lockean precepts with such conspicuously non-empirical methods? Simply because he believed that mathematics was ultimately a surer means for attaining the truth. As we saw in his arguments with Bernoulli, d'Alembert believed that experimental evidence was simply too unreliable and imprecise. Empiricism was fine as a principle of psychology and a general epistemological heuristic, but when it came down to real scientific knowledge, only mathematics offered certainty. In some cases, d'Alembert claimed, one needed only to begin with a single well-formulated empirical experiment or observation to deduce using mathematics the whole of that particular science:

The physico-mathematical sciences, by applying mathematical calculations to experiment, sometimes deduce from a single and unique observation a large number of inferences that remain close to geometrical truths by virtue of their certitude. Thus, a single experiment on the reflection of light produces all of Catoptrics, or the science of the properties of mirrors. A single experiment on the refraction of light produces the mathematical explanation of the rainbow, the theory of colors, and all of Dioptrics, or the science of concave

---

31 Jean Le Rond d'Alembert, *Preliminary Discourse to the Encyclopedia of Diderot*, trans. Richard N. Schwab (Indianapolis, 1963), 6.
32 *Ibid.*, 22.
33 One gets a sense of d'Alembert's ambitious program from the full title of his treatise: *Traité de dynamique dans lequel les loix de l'équilibre & du mouvement des corps sont réduites au plus petit nombre possible & démontrées d'une manière nouvelle, & où l'on donne un principe général pour trouver le mouvement de plusieurs corps qui agissent les uns sur les autres d'une manière quelconque* (Paris, 1743).

and convex lenses. From a single experiment on the pressure of fluids, we derive all the laws of their equilibrium and their movement. Finally, a single experiment on the acceleration of falling bodies opens up the laws of their descent down inclined planes and the laws of the movements of pendulums.[34]

D'Alembert, of course, could not entirely discount empirical evidence from his science. Its role seemed limited, though, only to the initial stages of method. He believed that as long as one *began* with an experimental or observational basis, the empiricist desideratum was thereby satisfied.

D'Alembert thus betrays a closer kinship to the Cartesian ideal than his empirical pieties expressed in the *Preliminary Discourse* would suggest.[35] As I have already pointed out in the first chapter of this study, such Cartesian sympathies were by no means rare among the philosophes. Unmistakable traits of Cartesian science can also be detected well into the mid century in the writings of such scientists as Mairan, Castel, and Condorcet. But even granting the intellectual syncretism of the Enlightenment, d'Alembert's rationalist epistemology was extreme – and recognized as such by his contemporaries. Diderot, in particular, found this aspect of his colleague's philosophy distasteful. Even fellow mathematicians such as Euler, Lagrange, and Condorcet, who presumably could most sympathize with the deductive ideals of d'Alembert's methodology, never accepted his extreme mechanistic assumptions, his zeal for abstraction and simplification, or his arrogant disregard of experimental evidence, and they said so quite openly.

Clearly d'Alembert was not unaware of his isolated position; there was rarely a time when he was not engaged in heated polemics with one of his scientific colleagues.[36] One can detect in d'Alembert's scientific writings a certain defensiveness and even defiance in the tone with which he argues his mechanistic philosophy. But although he must have felt embattled, d'Alembert was by no means willing to abandon his rationalist stance.

And from at least one unexpected source he found welcome confirmation of his position: the music theory of Rameau.

MUSIC THEORY AS SCIENTIFIC PROPAGANDA

When d'Alembert first read Rameau's "Mémoire" in the fall of 1749, he must have been immediately struck by the affinities between the composer's avowed empirical-deductive ideals and his own goals in rational mechanics. We recall that d'Alembert had referred in his *Preliminary Discourse* with obvious approval to those "physico-mathematical" sciences that "sometimes deduce from a single and unique

---

[34] *Preliminary Discourse*, 24.
[35] D'Alembert's scientific philosophy has received the attention of several historians within the last few years. Most notable is Thomas Hankins, *Jean d'Alembert, Science and the Enlightenment* (Oxford, 1970). More recent assessments can be found in a collection of essays commemorating the bicentennial of d'Alembert's death in a special issue of the French history journal, *Dix-Huitième Siècle* 16 (1984), 7–203.
[36] D'Alembert's stormy relations with his scientific colleagues are chronicled in detail by Hankins, *Jean d'Alembert*, 28–65.

observation a large number of inferences that remain close to geometrical truths by virtue of their certitude." In his Encyclopedia article "physico-mathématique," d'Alembert included music as one of these sciences. Was there a "single and unique observation" in music similar to the ones he had cited for catoptrics, hydrodynamics, and his own mechanics? Indeed there was: Rameau's *corps sonore*. D'Alembert made this clear in the Preface to his *Elémens*, where he insisted his sole purpose in writing the work was "to show how one may deduce from a single experiment the laws of harmony which artists had arrived at only, so to speak, by groping."[37] The Preface to the second edition of the *Elémens* published in 1762 was even more explicit:

In the resonance of the *corps sonore*, [Rameau] found the most probable origin of harmony, and the cause of that pleasure which we receive from it. He developed this principle, and showed how the different phenomena of music were produced by it; he reduced all harmony to a small number of simple and fundamental chords, of which the others are only combinations or inversions.[38]

The result was a true scientific system fully in accord with d'Alembert's ideal. "[Rameau] reduced the principal facts [of music] to a thoroughly consistent and methodical system . . . deduced from a single experiment, and . . . established upon this simple foundation the most common rules of musical art."[39] In one of d'Alembert's most revealing passages, he indicates clearly the source of Rameau's method as he understood it:

The illustrious artist of whom we speak was for us the *Descartes of music*. It seems to me one can hope to make progress in the theory of this science *only by following the method which he has traced*.[40]

Most of d'Alembert's biographers have been content to describe the *Elémens* as a simple popularization of Rameau's theory.[41] In this view, it is but one instance of that ubiquitous genre of eighteenth-century didactic popularizers. And undeniably the *Elémens* did serve this purpose; more than any other work, it helped to disseminate Rameau's ideas throughout Europe in the eighteenth century, with translations in English, German, and Italian. It was certainly d'Alembert's single most successful publication, going through six separate editions in his lifetime. But if the *Elémens* was merely a popularization, the question naturally arises why d'Alembert would have written it. Why would he have invested the considerable time and energy such an enterprise must have required on a subject of which he had no previous knowledge, moreover during one of the most busy and stressful periods of his life, that immediately preceding the publication of the first volume of the *Encyclopédie*? Surely something must have motivated d'Alembert more than a suddenly inspired enthusiasm for music theory or aspirations to become Rameau's Boswell.

37 *Elémens* (1752), vi.
38 *Elémens* (1762), vi–vii.
39 *Ibid.*, viii.
40 *Elémens de philosophie* (1762), in *Oeuvres philosophiques, historiques, et littéraires de d'Alembert*, 5 vols. (Paris, 1821–22), I, 331. (The emphasis is mine.)
41 E.g. Grimsley, *D'Alembert*, 140.

The answer, as I have suggested elsewhere, is that the *Elémens* represented more than popularization – it was propaganda.[42] By reformulating Rameau's brilliant but ineptly articulated theory into a more rigorous scientific model, d'Alembert was able to provide both a vindication of, as well as an advertisement for, his own peculiar scientific epistemology. Rameau's theory was far more digestible to the average reader than d'Alembert's dry mathematics, and it shared little of its controversy. It was the perfect means to illustrate the merits of his professed empirical-deductive methodology. D'Alembert was simply following a tried-and-true strategy used by all the philosophes – but put to use with particular mastery by Voltaire – in which one employs the most innocuous literary genre in order to disseminate covertly some controversial or otherwise opaque idea.[43]

In his redaction, d'Alembert strove to portray the empirical-deductive structuring of Rameau's theory as clearly as possible. After defining certain preliminary terms, he proposes three *expériences préliminaires & fondamentales* that serve as empirical axioms. These are the acoustical experiments and observations that establish, respectively, the major triad, the minor triad, and the identity of octaves. Now this may seem to contradict d'Alembert's earlier affirmation that in the *corps sonore*, Rameau had found the "probable origin of harmony." In fact, though, d'Alembert concedes that the *corps sonore* is not a sufficient basis. By itself, the *corps sonore* can only directly establish the major triad. In order to establish the minor triad and the thesis of octave identity, d'Alembert finds it necessary to introduce two additional "observations." This admission by no means weakens the theory, though.

In those sciences which are called physico-mathematical (among which may perhaps be placed the science of sounds), there are some [elements] which depend only upon one single experiment, one single principle. There are others which necessarily suppose more, whose combination is indispensable in forming an exact and complete system, and music perhaps is among this last kind.[44]

Consequently, music is still a physico-mathematical science, but lacking the perfection of d'Alembert's own mechanics since the latter could be reduced to a single axiomatic principle. D'Alembert thought it probable that the means would eventually be found to reduce these primary observations to only one. But until that time, he was convinced that these three were hypostatic to Rameau's theory.[45]

For all that d'Alembert's *Elémens* was a model of clarity and synthesis, it was less successful as a pedagogical text. Indeed its very strengths in logical consistency and

---

42 I have elaborated this thesis in more detail in my article "Music Theory as Scientific Propaganda: The Case of D'Alembert's *Elémens de musique*," *Journal of the History of Ideas* 50 (1989), 409–27.
43 In the article cited in the previous footnote, I proposed that the model for d'Alembert's *Elémens* was the similarly named popularization of Newton's theories by Voltaire: *Eléments de la philosophie de Neuton, mis à la portée de tout le monde* (Amsterdam, 1738).
44 *Elémens* (1762), xvii.
45 We will soon see how in the second edition of the *Elémens*, d'Alembert found a means to reduce the number of his preliminary observations to but two by combining the derivations of both the major and minor mode through the principle of co-generation.

simplicity were also its major defects. D'Alembert's scientific ideal, it will be recalled, was always to reduce and simplify. While Ockham's razor served d'Alembert well in rational mechanics, the result was disastrous when applied to Rameau's theory. Accepting music as a "physico-mathematical" science, d'Alembert held a strict test of admissibility for his system. If any part of Rameau's theory could not be rigorously deduced from the initial axioms, it was jettisoned or relegated to the status of an anomalous "license" granted on behalf of "bon goût." To rectify these perceived flaws, d'Alembert attempted to draw new deductions and find new explanations that he believed to be more logically consistent than those of Rameau. But what d'Alembert viewed as specious or inconsistent in Rameau's system frequently turned out to be a musically perspicacious insight. By eliminating these from the *Elémens,* and substituting arguments of his own that were not musically substantiated, d'Alembert ended up with an impoverished – and in important respects, distorted – picture of Rameau's thought, even if it was "clarified, developed, and simplified" as he claimed in the subtitle to the second edition. Rameau's theoretical explanations, for all their inconsistencies, verbiage, and logical fallacies, were invariably more insightful. The result, as Marie Duchez has rightly concluded, was a mess. She points to:

> the simplification that d'Alembert often applies to a musical thought whose complexity or multiple compositional possibilities he could not always penetrate. This complexity, these musical possibilities, could not be attained by his deductive rigor and logical demands. He logically analyzes the Ramist system, then he confronts his analysis with the music in a synthetic contact. But his confrontation is not one of an active musician, of a producer or even a performer of music, but rather a passive auditor. In fact, d'Alembert often treats the musical facts upon which he reasons as if they are abstract entities of a mathematized physical theory, without aurally realizing their musical implications. He does not think musically and the concretely musical consequences of his deductions escape him.[46]

It must be remembered that Rameau's theory was ultimately an empirical one in that it was rooted in his rich experience as a composer and performer. The Cartesian deductive structuring was one imposed only afterwards – and quite clumsily at that. That this is so is evident from his continued difficulties over some fifty years in connecting all of his ideas within a single, comprehensive, and logically connected system. In this respect, d'Alembert's criticisms were absolutely justified. Rameau was simply too inept a logician ever to reconcile harmonic practice within the confines of his narrowly conceived rationalist system, try as he might. D'Alembert, however, was not in a position to appreciate the real empirical underpinnings of Rameau's theory. Indeed, given his philosophical prejudices as well as his lack of experience with music, it would have been virtually impossible for him to do so. It was inevitable, then, that his interpretation of Rameau's theory would prove wanting.

---

[46] Duchez, "D'Alembert," 484.

D'ALEMBERT'S CRITIQUE OF RAMEAU

Having considered d'Alembert's epistemological biases concerning Rameau's theory, we are now in a better position to examine in some detail their dispute on various theoretical issues. While I obviously cannot itemize every point of difference between the two, in the following survey I will discuss four topics that I believe encompass the most important aspects of their disagreements: (1) the generative limits of the *corps sonore*; (2) geometric progressions and mode; (3) the fundamental bass; and (4) the rules of composition.

(1) The generative limits of the *corps sonore*

The issue upon which d'Alembert most sharply differed with Rameau concerned the latter's ontological claims on behalf of the *corps sonore*. Rameau, it will be recalled, began to assert ever more emphatically in his last writings that the *corps sonore* offered the most universal and palpable experience by which man could learn of ratios and proportions. He concluded from this that this acoustical phenomenon must be the principle of not only music, but also all the arts and science that rely to some extent upon the idea of proportion. D'Alembert's impatience with Rameau's argument here can be more clearly understood against the background of his Cartesian prejudices.

As we saw in Chapter 6, d'Alembert did not reject the empirical qualities Rameau attributed to the *corps sonore*. He believed – or at least he granted the truth of Rameau's testimony – that most vibrating systems do emit a series of harmonic overtones delimited by the sixth partial, with the even partials blending to such an extent that they are scarcely audible. What d'Alembert could not accept was the inference Rameau drew from this experience. The *corps sonore* was not the universal principle of the arts and sciences Rameau suggested it was simply because this latter inference was predicated upon it being understood as a sensory stimulus. For d'Alembert, as we have seen, nothing that was perceived by the senses could have the same kind of ontological value that a mathematical or mechanical axiom could. Proportions for d'Alembert were mathematical and geometrical abstractions that ultimately have no need of substantiation in hearing. He did not doubt that we may get an idea of proportions via the senses. But even if this is so, sight and touch are better indicators for this purpose than hearing:

> The *corps sonore* does not and cannot convey to us by itself any idea of proportion . . . When one hears these octaves and their multiples [resonating in the *corps sonore*], the sense of hearing can in no way convey to us the notion of ratio or proportion that can be acquired by sight or touch. In order to acquire a clear idea of proportions and ratios, it is necessary to compare an object using these last two senses; the perception of sounds contributes absolutely nothing to this, adds nothing, and is totally irrelevant. In a word, if all men were deaf, there would be no difference in regard to ratios, proportions, and geometry.[47]

[47] *Elémens* (1762), 213–14.

D'Alembert granted the senses of sight and touch more value than hearing because, for a geometrician, they were more valuable for measuring distances between objects. Rameau argued, contrariwise, that the ear was a much more sensitive judge. Only the ear can recognize immediately the ratios of an interval by the quality of its consonance. Change the ratios by the slightest amount and a just interval will sound out of tune. No other sense is so discriminating. In any other sense but hearing, Rameau elsewhere added, proportions are only an image: "movement, action, the animation of *rapports* and its analogies are all only a kind of acoustic."[48]

It may seem paradoxical, given d'Alembert's austere positivism, that he could still accept the *corps sonore* as the "probable" principle of music. Yet there is no contradiction when we understand the extreme generative restrictions that he placed upon the *corps sonore* in his version of Rameau's theory. For d'Alembert, the *corps sonore* was primarily an acoustical phenomenon. Its interpretation thus was to be guided by strictly generative criteria. When so treated, the *corps sonore* could indeed serve as a true scientific principle. But, as we will now see, this was a quite different use of the *corps sonore* than that made by Rameau, who was much more inclined to draw from it an increased authority for one's aural judgment. The resulting differences are apparent in how each man treated the question of the minor triad.

We recall from Chapter 6 how Rameau expended much effort in his *Démonstration* explaining the origins of the minor triad. In that work he not only abandoned his earlier "sympathetic resonance" theory of the minor triad in favor of a "modified sympathetic resonance" theory, but also offered a second, entirely new, derivation of the minor triad based upon the notion of "co-generation." All of these changes, I suggested, may well have come about on account of d'Alembert, whose standards of consistency and economy would have made him naturally predisposed toward the theory of co-generation.

In his 1752 edition of the *Elémens* and his Encyclopedia article "fondamental," d'Alembert included Rameau's "modified sympathetic resonance" theory of the minor triad along with the newer theory of co-generation, perhaps out of deference to the composer. With the publication of the revised edition of the *Elémens* in 1762, though, d'Alembert evidently felt he had to choose between one or the other. The "modified sympathetic resonance" theory of the minor mode was entirely jettisoned in favor of the theory of co-generation. The later explanation, d'Alembert explains, "appears to me more direct and simple." Most importantly, "it presupposes no other experiment than that of [the *corps sonore*] . . . since it preserves C as the fundamental sound in both modes without being obliged, like M. Rameau, to change [the fundamental] into F."[49]

What prompted d'Alembert's change of mind? The answer seems to be that he had decided the theory of co-generation is a more efficient acoustical explanation. Both the major and minor triads could be accounted for through the verifiable principle of harmonic resonance in the *corps sonore*. Moreover, the explanation

[48] *Code de musique pratique*, 190.
[49] *Elémens* (1762), 24.

fulfilled one of d'Alembert's most cherished goals: to simplify and reduce any theory to as few principles as possible. By having recourse to only one *expérience* (a single resonating *corps sonore*) instead of Rameau's two *expériences*, d'Alembert had taken music theory one more step towards becoming a truly scientific system. This sentiment is perfectly reflected in a statement from his Preliminary Discourse:

> Indeed, the more one reduces the number of principles of a science, the more one gives them scope, and since the object of a science is necessarily fixed, the principles applied to that object will be so much the more fertile as they are fewer in number.[50]

Rameau naturally never doubted for a minute that the *corps sonore* was also the single generative principle of music – including of course the minor triad. But holding a far less restrictive conception of the *corps sonore* than d'Alembert, he felt himself more at liberty in extrapolating musical material from it through a variety of differing strategies. Thus, we have seen how Rameau tested a number of derivations for the minor triad: triadic parallelism, sympathetic resonance theory, modified sympathetic resonance theory, and co-generation. (In Chapter 10 we will encounter yet another strategy involving the *entrelacement* of the minor triad with its relative major.) No matter what his explanation was, though, Rameau always insisted that the source of the minor triad was the same as for the major triad; it was to be deduced *somehow* from the resonance of a single *corps sonore*. From this point of view, the co-generative theory of the minor triad that d'Alembert came to advocate was perhaps the least congenial to Rameau, since it suggested a double generator. The theory may have represented a single "physical principle" as far as d'Alembert was concerned, but to Rameau it was a fractured and highly problematic musical explanation. The distinction is a subtle but critical one in understanding the different epistemological positions of the two men. For Rameau, the retention of a single generative *fundamental* was more critical in his derivation of the major and minor triads than was the retention of a single acoustical principle of generation. For d'Alembert, however, the opposite was the case. D'Alembert could not ultimately appreciate the *musical* issues of mode and the *basse fondamentale* that drove Rameau to reject the theory of co-generation.

A further extension of d'Alembert's acoustically based theory of co-generation can be seen in his discussion of dissonance. We have followed Rameau in the previous chapters as he has struggled to find a consistent source for dissonance. In the *Traité* he proffered the dominant-seventh chord as just such a source. But in practice, there were many kinds of seventh chords whose origins could not be accounted for in a strictly generative fashion. While Rameau eventually gave up trying to account for each and every seventh chord, d'Alembert believed each seventh had to have a definitive generative explanation. This is why he was unwilling to group together all seventh chords as one type like Rameau. In the revised edition of the *Elémens*, d'Alembert thought that the theory of co-generation might be one explanation as to the source for some of these dissonant harmonies. The note B of the major

---

50 Preliminary Discourse, 22.

seventh chord shown in Example 9.1, for instance, can be considered to be generated by the third of the chord's mediant (E), as well as by the dominant note (G).[51] Likewise, the G♯ of a C augmented triad could arise from the resonance of the mediant E. Even the note of *supposition* in a ninth or eleventh chord might be accounted for as a co-generator along with the "true" fundamental bass.[52]

Example 9.1 Co-generation of dissonance

Of course the theory of co-generation was not capable of accommodating all dissonant chords. But the theory was able to account for most of the five basic seventh chords that d'Alembert identified in common practice (see Example 9.2). (The dominant-seventh chord and diminished-seventh chord, it will be recalled, were explained by Rameau as composites of subdominant and dominant harmonies – origins that are basically akin to the theory of co-generation.)

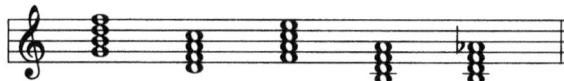

Example 9.2 D'Alembert's five basic seventh chords

D'Alembert's rigorously acoustical conception of harmony led him to draw two different – and in a sense contradictory – conclusions. On the one hand, since a wide number of commonly used dissonant chords could not be explained by acoustical generation, d'Alembert was skeptical about subsuming all harmony within the fundamental bass and the *corps sonore*.[53] The ease – and for d'Alembert, the license – with which Rameau assigned roots to his many chords suggested to d'Alembert

---

51 *Elémens* (1762), 90.
52 D'Alembert's "co-generative" theory of dissonance would be thoroughly developed by Helmholtz some one hundred years later. In fact, d'Alembert may have been a major influence upon Helmholtz. There are several citations of the revised *Elémens* in *On the Sensations of Tone* (trans. Alexander Ellis; New York, 1954). Helmholtz at one point describes d'Alembert's book as "an extremely clear and masterly performance, such as was to be expected from a sharp and exact thinker, who was at the same time one of the great physicists and mathematicians of his time" (*Ibid.*, 232). As would be imagined, Helmholtz cites with particular approval the co-generative theory of the minor triad (believing erroneously that this represented Rameau's preferred theory, too). Helmholtz usually grouped d'Alembert and Rameau together, without realizing how they differed upon important theoretical questions. Like many historians and theorists of the nineteenth century, when Helmholtz made reference to "Rameau's theory," he was often actually referring to d'Alembert's interpretation.
53 For that matter, d'Alembert even wondered whether certain chords – including the augmented-sixth chord – ought properly to be included in practice since their theoretical basis was so problematic (s.v. "fondamental"). Rameau responded to this idea by parodying Rousseau's attacks on French music, and claimed such an assertion made as much sense "as if I imagined, for example, to prove to you that you do not exist, and if you do exist, it is all the worse for you" ("Lettre à M. d'Alembert," 6–7) .

that music theory had a long way to go before it could be considered a truly axiomatized science. On the other hand, since there did exist a large number of dissonant chords that musicians made use of – regardless of whether there might be a generative origin for them or not – d'Alembert logically thought that there might exist other chords that musicians had not yet discovered:

I believe that the majority of musicians, some blinded by tradition, others on account of systems, have not drawn from harmony all that they might, and that they have excluded an infinite number of chords that might on many occasion produce good effects.[54]

Example 9.3 D'Alembert's five additional dissonant chords

D'Alembert listed the five chords in Example 9.3 as possibilities. "Why," he demanded to know, "are these chords proscribed from harmony, which, with the exception of the last, contain only one or two dissonances?" He granted that all five chords did not sound uniformly pleasant. But might this not be a prejudice due to our exposure to a limited and conservative musical practice? None of these harmonies contains any more dissonance than do the chords of Example 9.2. And most of them (thought d'Alembert) may be easily accounted for through the theory of co-generation. To drive his point home, d'Alembert then thought up another nine possible combinations (shown in Example 9.4) that contain only one or two dissonances. (For d'Alembert, the augmented fifth in most of these harmonies did not represent a true dissonance since it was acoustically enharmonic to the minor sixth.) Just as Euler had, d'Alembert offers his list of chords as an example of the harmonic riches that await the adventuresome composer not bound by the shackles of convention.

Example 9.4 D'Alembert's nine "new" chords

Rameau naturally found d'Alembert's ideas ludicrous. Many of d'Alembert's discoveries were of course not new, and constituted only enharmonic respellings or inversions of familiar constructs.[55] Others contain dissonant clashes that make them unlikely harmonic choices. Just because an augmented fifth was enharmonic to the minor sixth, Rameau scoffed, it did not mean the one could be substituted for the other. For Rameau, the perfect fifth takes priority in chord structuring and root designation; the augmented fifth, by virtue of clashing with the perfect fifth generated by the fundamental, could never be mistaken for a consonance. D'Alembert, not understanding the tonal function of the fifth, argued that if

---

[54] *Encyclopédie*, s.v. "fondamental."
[55] An observation noted by Jean-Adam Serre in his *Observations sur les principes de l'harmonie* (Geneva, 1763), 30.

Rameau's reasoning was valid, a major triad should also sound dissonant, since the fifth partial of its mediant (major seventeenth) is dissonant with the perfect fifth of the triad. Again, d'Alembert's analysis is rigidly mechanistic in contrast to Rameau's. He understands no tonal distinction between the perfect fifth generated from the fundamental and a major third generated from the mediant.

By pointing out the apparent impossibility of finding a consistent generative source for many chords, d'Alembert was not thereby abandoning the fundamental bass as principle of harmony. He made it quite clear that he still considered the fundamental bass the "probable" source of harmony, but that there existed exceptions to it in practice, as shown by his "new" list of chords. D'Alembert hoped that theorists might discover a means to reconcile these anomalies by refining or expanding Rameau's system in some yet undiscovered way. Of course there was also the possibility that an entirely new principle of harmony might be found that would replace the fundamental bass – Tartini's *terza suono* was one possible candidate. Then again, it might be discovered that there is no single principle of harmony after all. In an essay written in 1777, long after the last embers of his row with Rameau had died out, d'Alembert reflected upon his chordal inventions:

These new chords united and combined with the old [chords] will lead perhaps to some general principle that will serve as the base of the true theory which we still await, or they will convince us that there is no theory of music to be hoped for, which would be much the same thing for the progress of science. Because a question is resolved when one is assured that a solution is impossible.[56]

The essential conflict in the two men's arguments was rooted in their respective notions of scientific rigor. D'Alembert assumed that every note of a chord was to be generated from some fundamental as an upper partial. If a chord could not be derived *directly* from the resonance of a single *corps sonore* (that is, as a consequence of the fundamental and its third and fifth harmonic partials) – and there was only one chord that could be so generated: the major triad – it would need to be analyzed as a composite of partials originating from multiple generators. Rameau always wished to maintain a *single* generator for his principle, that is, a single fundamental for each chord. He was thus forced to be looser in his extraction from the *corps sonore* than d'Alembert the physicist would ever allow. If a chord could not be given a fundamental bass by strictly generative criteria (such as was the case for the minor triad and d'Alembert's list of seventh chords), Rameau would improvise some explanation to justify the fundamental he wanted. The notion of double or triple generators conflicted with the musical sense he made of the fundamental bass, and thus was not an acceptable alternative, however plausible it may have been according to strictly acoustical criteria. In any case, the question of chordal "generation" from a fundamental was now a moot question for Rameau. He no longer believed that chords were to be generated artificially from a fundamental unity

---

56 "Réflexions sur la théorie de la musique," [1777], *Oeuvres et correspondance inédites de d'Alembert*, ed. Charles Henry (Paris, 1887), 141.

as he did in the *Traité*. He was now convinced that they originated as a composite of proportions drawn from the single source that is the *corps sonore*. Consequently, the relation of a chord's constituent tones to its fundamental was not so much the issue as was the intervallic structure of the chord itself and the relation of the intervals to the ratios contained in the *corps sonore*.

(2) Geometric progressions and mode

D'Alembert never took very well to Rameau's use of geometric progressions. The value of abstract concepts borrowed from mathematics and geometry, he argued, "is not only useless, but even, if we may say so, illusory when applied to the theory of music." Music theorists who utilize such concepts stand guilty of a "ridiculous abuse of geometry," which lends "a false air of science that can impress only the ignorant, and will only render their treatises more obscure and less instructive."[57] Consequently, when d'Alembert composed his *Elémens,* he dispensed with all the geometric progressions Rameau had employed in the *Démonstration*. D'Alembert did not object to assigning numerical labels to musical elements; this was implicit in his acceptance of music as a "physico-mathematical" science. He objected, rather, to the unnecessary complications Rameau introduced into his theory by insisting upon using geometric proportions when simple ratios should have sufficed. He explained this distinction as follows:

> One may even dispense with the theory of geometric proportions in those instances when a consideration of geometric ratios (*rapports*) is useful, which is to say, in the comparison of sounds between themselves. The notion of ratio is less complex than proportion, and thus sufficient for the objective proposed. And you may observe in effect, Sir, that in my *Elémens* I had need only of the theory of ratios without having recourse to those of proportion for the reason that I sought to simplify the theory as much as it was possible for me, and to borrow from arithmetic only the most indispensable notions.[58]

Here is a perfect example of d'Alembert's penchant towards simplification. As a firm advocate of Ockham's razor, he saw the geometric proportion as an unnecessary complication of a notion that could be expressed more clearly by ratios.[59] Following the precepts of his work in rational mechanics, he wished to decompose musical elements into their simplest parts. The relationship between two tones was just such a reduction. Since any proportion is only a composite of ratios, he saw no advantage in describing something as a compound when it was possible to reduce this compound to its elements, exactly as stipulated by Condillac's rules of analysis.[60]

---

57 *Elémens* (1762), xii, xxx.
58 *Elémens* (1762), 216
59 D'Alembert defined a "geometric proportion" as "an equality between two geometric ratios; a geometric ratio is the manner in which one quantity contains in itself another. Thus, the idea of a proportion contains at least three quantities, while the idea of ratio contains only two" (*Ibid.*).
60 One wonders whether d'Alembert may have saved the notion of "ratio" from criticism even as he was rejecting the use of "proportions" in a theory of art out of consideration for his fellow editor, Diderot. We saw in the last chapter how Diderot had espoused an aesthetic theory based on the idea of *rapport*.

But d'Alembert's reduction came at a cost. While a proportion may indeed be a composite of simple ratios, it was an insight of no small musical significance for Rameau to have recognized in these ratios a closed system of mode consisting of three chords – one exhaustively and concisely modeled by the geometric triple progression. The theorist so intent upon decomposing an object into minutiae here loses the insights offered to the observer willing to take a step back for a *vue d'ensemble*. (D'Alembert's scientific work was often criticized on account of its similar myopic and obsessively reductionist character.) By reducing his definition of mode to one of concatenated ratios rather than an interlocking proportion, d'Alembert is unable to convey the tonal unity Rameau succeeds at capturing with his geometric triple progression. For d'Alembert, mode becomes determined only by the fundamental fifth motion of the bass, whereas for Rameau it is a *bounded* motion delimited by three terms. Consider how d'Alembert revises Rameau's definition of mode:

Le mode en musique n'est autre chose que l'ordre prescrit entre les sons tant ensemble qu'en particulier c'est-à-dire, tant en harmonie qu'en mélodie, par la proportion triple. *Démonstration*, 34	Le mode en musique n'est autre chose que l'ordre prescrit entre les sons tant en harmonie qu'en mélodie, par la progression des quintes. *Elémens* (1752), 25

Without the boundaries of the geometric triple progression, d'Alembert's mode could – and indeed does – contain far more than Rameau's three fundamentals. Thereby, though, he weakens the sense of tonic identity. Moreover, the fundamental dissonances Rameau posits for the dominant and subdominant terms – each borrowed reciprocally from the other – remain unexplained. We can see the problems this gets d'Alembert into by considering his analysis of the *règle de l'octave*. In the first edition of the *Elémens*, d'Alembert was content to repeat the fundamental bass analyses Rameau had offered in the *Démonstration*. Rameau's analysis of the ascending major and minor scales, given as Examples 7.10 and 7.11, were cited by d'Alembert without alteration. For the problems involved in the descending version of the minor scale, he concurred with a suggestion Rameau had elsewhere made – that the seventh scale degree might be analyzed as a "note de passage" without a fundamental bass.[61] (To recapitulate the problem: the seventh and sixth scale degrees cannot be connected in a descending minor scale using the same harmonies in ascending because of the chromatic changes; no other harmonization can be found that does not violate either the fundamental fifth motion of the bass, or the boundary of the triple geometric progression.)

Not content with this solution, though, d'Alembert reconsidered the problem anew in the second revised edition of the *Elémens* in 1762. Why not, he asks, raise the sixth scale degree, thus allowing the fundamental bass progression given in

---

61 *Elémens* (1752), 60–61, 62.

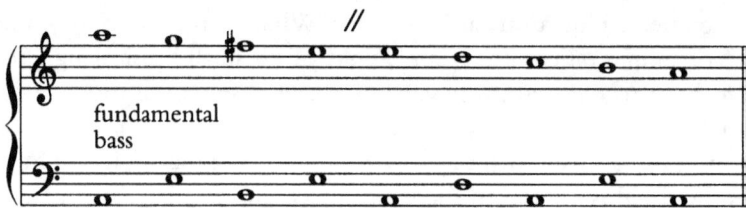

Example 9.5 D'Alembert's revised harmonization of the descending minor scale

Example 9.5?[62] This would essentially retrograde the ascending minor scale, with the exception that the seventh scale degree is lowered. (Although should this lack of symmetry bother the reader, d'Alembert asserted that the seventh scale degree might also be raised when descending [!] "as is proved by an infinity of examples with which all musical literature is filled."[63])

D'Alembert's choice to raise scale-degree 6 is entirely consistent with his strictly generative conception of the fundamental bass. A diminished fifth cannot be generated by the *corps sonore*, thus $\hat{6}$ must be raised if B is its fundamental. It was clearly of secondary importance to d'Alembert that in practice $\hat{6}$ was normally lowered when descending to $\hat{5}$. Rameau had no qualms in assigning B as the fundamental bass to F on account of the *double emploi* it suggests (with the subdominant).[64] In any event, he knew well enough that the descending seventh and sixth scale degrees were normally naturalized in practice.

One amusing consequence of this squabble was that many musicians and musical amateurs who read d'Alembert's revised *Elémens* tried their hand at solving the problem of the descending minor scale.[65] Some of these solutions came from reputable musicians (such as the theorist Ducharger). Other solutions come from individuals of more questionable musical competence. A Monsieur Desmoulins from "Hautes Bruyères," for instance, wrote to d'Alembert that the descending minor scale should be considered a "mode mixte," much as was the major mode in ascending (along the lines of Example 7.10). By beginning with an F major triad and ending with a D minor triad, it was possible to harmonize the A minor scale (including its lowered sixth degree) as shown in Example 9.6.[66]

Example 9.6 Desmoulins's "mixed-mode" harmonization of the scale

62 *Elémens* (1762), 71, 219–20.
63 Ibid., 73.
64 "Lettre à M. d'Alembert," 10.
65 Among d'Alembert's papers in the Institut de France, there are numerous unsolicited letters addressed to d'Alembert containing proposed bass progressions for the descending minor scale (F–Pi Ms 2466).
66 Letter dated March 9, 1768, *Ibid.*, fols. 66–67.

Strangely enough, d'Alembert seemed persuaded by Desmoulins's bizarre solution. In 1777, he repeated this harmonization as a potential solution, adding to it two other "mixed mode" solutions, one for the minor and one for the major scale (see Example 9.7).[67] It is obvious that d'Alembert had lost whatever musical common sense he once possessed. It is true that the fundamental basses of these solutions move strictly by fifths. But by what criterion any one of them establishes the respective modes of A minor and C major is difficult to perceive.[68] These solutions are a direct consequence of d'Alembert's definition of mode we have just considered. Without the bounded functional relationships afforded by the geometric triple progression, his fundamental bass tumbles on in a series of undirected fifths as in Example 9.7. Again, it seems that d'Alembert was drawn to an answer that was technically consistent, although it was of obvious musical deficiency in comparison to Rameau's.

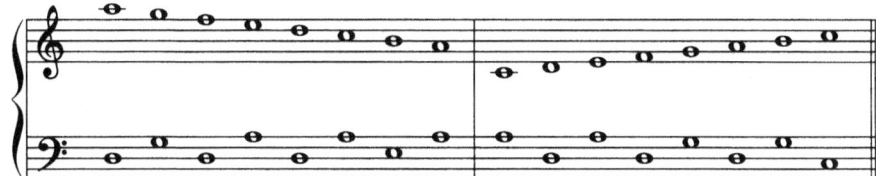

Example 9.7 D'Alembert's mixed-mode harmonizations of scales

I do not want to exaggerate this point. Rameau's theory of the triple geometric progression is not without its own problems of consistency and logic, as our discussion in Chapter 7 revealed. And d'Alembert was surely justified in calling Rameau to order for his loose invocation of mathematical terms and excessive scientific pretensions. But at least Rameau had a single, coherent definition of a mode. The geometric triple progression offered a concise model of harmonic relationships possessing real tonal significance, a significance d'Alembert was not in a position to appreciate.

(3) The fundamental bass

The same rigid and reductionist character evident in d'Alembert's discussions of chordal generation and mode may be observed in his remarks concerning the fundamental bass. Like Rameau, d'Alembert wished to reduce all fundamental bass progressions to a perfect fifth whenever possible. To achieve this end, though, d'Alembert invoked the *double emploi* with far greater extravagance. Thus, as one example, the *cadence rompue* was analyzed by d'Alembert not as an ascending fundamental bass progression of the second, rather as a descending fifth.[69] As shown in Example 9.8, the A minor chord upon which the G dominant-seventh chord

---

67 D'Alembert, "Réflexions," *Oeuvres et correspondance inédites*, 153–54.
68 D'Alembert evidently retained a lingering doubt as to the validity of these solutions. He concluded with an invitation for "musical philosopher to enlighten us concerning these different questions." *Ibid.*, 154.
69 *Elémens* (1752), 82–83.

Example 9.8 D'Alembert's analysis of the "broken" cadence

resolves is only apparent. In reality, it is the chord of the added sixth with a fundamental of C. While Rameau did indeed suggest such an interpretation at points in the *Traité*, it was an interpretation he thereafter abandoned on account of its obvious musical deficiencies.[70] The chord could not represent an implied added-sixth chord without suggesting a modulation to F, since Rameau now argued that the chord of the added sixth *always* represents a subdominant. (In the *Code de musique pratique*, Rameau analyzes the *cadence rompue* as a *dominante-tonique* resolving to a consonant triad on the sixth scale degree that is *censée tonique*.[71]) This also means that the *cadence irrégulière* – another ambiguity in Rameau's earlier theory – now is interpreted as representing exclusively a move from subdominant to tonic.[72]

When discussing the *cadence interrompue* (interrupted cadence), d'Alembert makes further application of the *double emploi*. It will be recalled how Rameau defined the interrupted cadence as a dominant which descends a third to another dominant instead of resolving by the normal fifth motion.[73] D'Alembert suggests that, as with the *cadence rompue*, the last chord of this cadence is not really a dominant itself; by virtue of the *double emploi* it has the same fundamental as the first chord. D'Alembert's analysis here is problematic in several ways. For one thing, it suggests an improbable modulation: the first chord is a dominant in the key of C, while the second chord becomes a subdominant in the key of D.[74] For another, the main purpose of the *cadence interrompue* was to account for two dominant-seventh chords separated by a third. By suppressing the raised third in the second chord, d'Alembert obscures this critical feature (see Example 9.9).

As our final illustration of this topic consider Example 9.10. This is a fairly common chromatic sequence that might be found in any thorough-bass treatise of the eighteenth century. When Rameau cited the progression in his *Génération harmonique*, he indicated a fundamental bass that was musically plausible, although theoretically difficult to justify from strictly generative criteria.[75] The fundamental

---

70   See the discussion in Chapter 5, pp. 116–17.
71   *Code*, 61–62; 89.
72   *Ibid.*, 38.
73   See Chapter 7, p. 200.
74   *Elémens* (1752), 84.
75   *Génération harmonique*, Plate 25, transposed.

Example 9.9 D'Alembert's analysis of the interripted cadence

Example 9.10 Rameau's analysis of a descending chromatic sequence

bass skips two augmented fourths and one augmented fifth. None of Rameau's geometric progressions provides for this kind of motion. It is an "exception" granted to the diminished-seventh chord built upon a leading tone.[76]

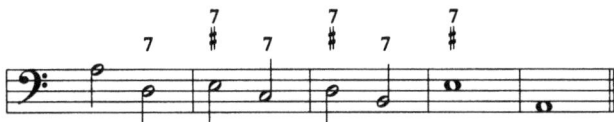

Example 9.11 D'Alembert's revised fundamental bass for Example 9.10

D'Alembert duly repeated Rameau's analysis of this harmonic sequence, but suggested that its real fundamental bass might be the one given in Example 9.11.[77] This solution, d'Alembert noted, follows all the rules of the fundamental bass when the two ascending seconds (D–E and C–D) are interpreted as broken cadences, and the two descending thirds (E–C and D–B) are interpreted as interrupted cadences.[78] This solution, additionally, had the advantage (he thought) of being more logical in terms of chordal generation. He could not see how either G♯ or F♯ could generate a diminished fifth. With E and D as the fundamentals, respectively, the chords are

---

[76] Ibid., 183. The same progression and fundamental bass analysis was repeated by Rameau in his *Code*, Plate 27 (reproduced as Example 9.12 on p. 289).
[77] *Elémens* (1752), Example 91.
[78] Ibid., 165.

easily accounted for. Unfortunately, this then created a problem with the soprano voice. If the true roots of the second and fourth chords were E and D, d'Alembert has no means of accounting for the ninths formed by the soprano line without contradicting the "boundary of the octave" by which no voice of a chord may exceed the fundamental by more than an octave.[79] By the theory of supposition, all ninth chords have roots a third above the "supposed" bass, in this case, the very fundamental bass suggested by Rameau: G♯ and F♯.

All these examples are telling evidence that, in comparison to d'Alembert, Rameau was becoming increasingly more flexible in his use of the fundamental bass, and less mechanistic in his notions of modulation. Whereas in the *Traité* he was acutely self-conscious about the chords that could not be directly generated by string divisions, or root progressions that defied the normative fifth motion, by the time of his latter writings few such qualms are detectable. Rameau felt confident enough to allow the fundamental bass to proceed with increasing flexibility. Certainly the extravagant recourse to modulation engendered by d'Alembert's literal reading of the fundamental bass was for Rameau a far greater sin. D'Alembert invoked the *double emploi* with such abandonment since the tonal significance of modulation meant so little to him. It was evidently more important that the fundamental bass be kept as consistent and static as possible, meaning that it was preferable to read a modulation in a progression by virtue of changing dissonances above the *same* fundamental bass than to displace that fundamental bass by a variety of intervals that proved less congruent with the ratios generated by the *corps sonore*.

(4) Rules of composition

As a final topic for comparison, let us look at d'Alembert's "rules of composition" and contrast them with Rameau's views on the same subject. D'Alembert's five rules can be summarized as follows.[80]

Given T as a *tonique*, DT as the *dominante-tonique*, DS as a *dominante simple*, and S as the *sous-dominante*, then:

1. Any T or DT must have at least one common tone with the preceding chord.
2. The seventh of any DS must be prepared as a consonance in the preceding chord.
3. Any S must have at least one of its consonances prepared in the preceding chord.

---

[79] In response to just this criticism from Bethizy and Roussier, d'Alembert requested his readers to change the suspended E in the soprano (on the first beat of the third measure) and replace it with an E♭ (*Journal Oeconomique* [January, 1753], 141; *CTW* VI, 277). Presumably this made the chord more suitable for d'Alembert's analysis, whereby E♭ could be interpreted as a root "borrowed" from the real fundamental bass of D. Whatever d'Alembert's intention was, he clearly was bothered by the problems this progression caused, and in his second edition of the *Elémens,* he restored without explanation the fundamental of the fifth chord to F♯ (*Elémens* [1762], 204).

[80] These are taken from Chapter 6, Book 2 of the *Elémens* (1752), 112–17.

4   The fundamentals of all dominants must descend a fifth at resolution.
    a DS may resolve to either another DS or to a DT.
    b DT may resolve to any chord type.
5   The fundamental of every S must ascend a fifth to a T, DT, or S.

D'Alembert considered these five rules to be "fundamental." He provided three additional rules as "consequences":

1   The fundamental of a T may ascend a third or a fifth to
    a DT, S, or another T, but not to a DS.
2   T may descend a third or a fifth to any chord type.
3   T may ascend a second to either DT or DS.

While d'Alembert's rules were never articulated by Rameau in such a systematic manner, they do draw together scattered recommendations and observations to be found in the *Génération harmonique,* particularly from Chapter 10 on the preparation of dissonance (*liaison*), and Chapter 18 on the motion of the fundamental bass. D'Alembert proceeded from this point to offer a number of observations concerning the relationship between the fundamental bass and the basso continuo (Book 2, Chapters 8 and 11), licenses occasioned by the broken and interrupted cadences, supposition, and the diminished-seventh chord (Chapter 9), guidelines for writing a melody (Chapters 7 and 10), and finding the fundamental bass of a given melody (Chapter 13). Again, almost everything d'Alembert says can be traced to sources in Rameau. The problem, of course, is that d'Alembert has distilled and synthesized too much. The wide variety of movements to be observed in practice of the fundamental bass or melody could not be accounted for by d'Alembert's guidelines. His enumeration of dissonant harmonies and their employment was woefully inadequate in the face of the rich palette of dissonant harmonies and progressions widely utilized by composers like Rameau.

D'Alembert was hardly oblivious to the inadequacies of his "composition" primer. A stinging critique of this section was voiced by the composer-theorist Jean-Laurent de Bethizy, who found his rules of composition "insufficient, obscure, and faulty."[81] D'Alembert admitted that they were indeed quite general, and that there were of course exceptions to his rules. But this was unavoidable given the pedagogical aim of his book:

In the rudiments of any art, one can scarcely give rules to beginners that are too rigorous or too general so as to accustom them to practice them exactly, and not to permit too lightly licenses that ought be guided only by taste and practice. . . In music, I have said, as in all the fine arts, it is up to the artist to lay down and follow the rules; it is up to the man of taste and genius to find the exceptions.[82]

For his part, Rameau was acutely conscious of the problems with his own chapter on composition in the *Génération harmonique*. It was one thing to lay out in an abstract

---

[81] *CTW* VI, 248.
[82] *CTW* VI, 251.

and deductive manner the musical vocabulary and basic grammatical rules of harmony. It was quite another thing to correlate these in any efficient manner with practical examples, let alone to teach students how to discriminate with sensitivity between the almost infinite variety of possible fundamental-bass progressions and melodies. While he was convinced that knowledge of the fundamental bass was the key to learning composition, Rameau was not so convinced that this could be done by reducing it to a handful of rules.

Rameau had already attempted to lay down the "principles of composition" in the third Book of his *Traité*. In this, the lengthiest Book of the whole treatise, he attempts to show how the fundamental bass will help the student learn to compose music rapidly and without fault, since in it lies the "essence" (*nœud*) of composition.[83] Rameau there begins by considering diatonic triads connected by consonant intervals in order to establish basic rules of voice leading (Chapters 2–5). He goes on to discuss "dominant" chords and the ways their dissonant sevenths may be prepared and resolved (Chapters 6–7). In rough succession Rameau then considers various cadence types (Chapters 13, 16, 25, 28), chords of supposition and suspension (Chapters 14–15, 29–33), inversions of chords in the basso continuo (Chapters 17–21), chromatics (Chapter 34), the behavior and "ornamentation" of a melody (Chapters 38–39), and the harmonization of a melody (Chapters 40–41). Now, all this constitutes material the reader would have encountered in Book 2 of the *Traité*, although without the theoretical explanations. Thus, the third Book can be seen as an elaboration and vindication of Rameau's claims on behalf of his fundamental bass.

Yet much remains in Rameau's composition instructions that harks back to older pedagogical traditions. (We recall from Chapter 3 above that the same was true for the fourth Book on Accompaniment.) For instance, the lengthy discussion of modulation using the *règle de l'octave* (Chapters 9–12) is quite conservative, and makes little real use of the fundamental bass. Likewise, his guidelines for composition in two voices and the fugue (Chapters 36–38, 44) depend much more upon seventeenth-century counterpoint theory than they do upon any ideas elaborated in the first half of the *Traité*. In any case, as the desultory chapter citations suggest, the organization and coherence of Rameau's "principles of composition" left much to be desired. He himself expressed dissatisfaction with them, going so far as disavowing the whole of the third Book in 1729![84]

RAMEAU'S METHODS OF COMPOSITION

Over the following decades, Rameau would periodically try his hand again at producing a more systematic primer of composition. The *Dissertation* of 1732, despite being a treatise for learning to accompany, can be seen as a kind of composition treatise in that the work contained extensive guidelines for employing harmonies,

[83] *Traité*, 185; Gossett, 206.
[84] *CTW* VI, 32.

voicings, modulations, and the like. Chapter 18 from the *Génération harmonique* was another attempt, although its abbreviated nature guaranteed its inadequacy as a really practical text. The lengthy manuscript "L'Art de la basse fondamentale" from the early 1740s represents still another try by Rameau. In detail that far surpasses any of his previous practical writings, including Book 3 of the *Traité*, Rameau lays out a comprehensive, if somewhat mechanical, program of composition pedagogy in three sections that is entirely built upon the fundamental bass, as its title would suggest. Rameau's approach there is purely practical, with no discussion whatsoever of any speculative-theoretical matters. Unfortunately, the manuscript we have of this text is a mess. It seems to be a first draft of a treatise, with many digressions, repetitions, and revisions. Worst of all, its musical illustrations are missing.[85]

Unable to put his ideas in order, Rameau evidently turned a draft of this manuscript over to d'Alembert, hoping that the scientist could summarize his rules of composition as succinctly as he had the theoretical arguments of the *Démonstration*. It is obvious why d'Alembert could make no use of it. It was far too detailed and musically acute for d'Alembert's needs – or comprehension. The manuscript was fortunately not thus condemned to oblivion. An otherwise obscure student of Rameau, the Italian violinist and composer Pietro Gianotti, revised the entire manuscript and published it under his own name in 1759 as the *Guide du compositeur*.[86] With Gianotti's *Guide*, it is now possible to infer from Rameau's tortuous prose his pedagogical intentions in "L'Art de la basse fondamentale," and reconstruct all of the lost musical examples.

Rameau begins Part 1 of the "Art," much as he did in the *Traité*, with consonant triads whose fundamental basses connect by diatonic steps. Using a highly simplified two-part framework, Rameau outlines the possible routes the fundamental bass may take in a diatonic context, the kinds of consonant triads that can be used in each case, and the possible notes that may be used in the "melody." Also considered are questions of modulation, "imitation" (i.e. melodic and harmonic sequences), the metric placement of chords, and the identification of key areas. (Example 7.3 cited in Chapter 7 from Part 1 of Gianotti's *Guide* is illustrative of this pedagogical approach.)

Part 2 of the "Art" is ostensibly devoted to problems of dissonance, although Rameau failed to follow this division consistently in his manuscript. He treats in succession various kinds of seventh chords, the added-sixth chord (by now, of course, a fundamental dissonance), chords of supposition, the suspension, possible chordal substitutions, the elaboration of a melodic line, and the various chromatic-enharmonic genres. Again, all of these topics are taught in relation to the fundamental bass. In fact, up to this point in his text, Rameau has not even broached the subject of chordal inversion or the basso continuo. The topic does not come up

---

85 A detailed history and analysis of Rameau's manuscript may be found in my article "Rameau's 'L'Art de la basse fondamentale,'" *Music Theory Spectrum* 9 (1987), 18–41.
86 Pietro Gianotti, *Le Guide du compositeur* (Paris, 1759). More information on Gianotti's text may be found in Appendix 2.

until Part 3 – the last and shortest section of the "Art." Quite clearly, the critical element Rameau wanted to concentrate upon was the fundamental bass. Evidently he believed that if the student understood how the fundamental bass behaved and the kinds of chords and melodies one can place above it, then the most important compositional questions are answered. This is why in Example 7.3 there is such evident disregard for the rules of counterpoint between the outer voices. Since the fundamental bass does not represent a true voice, prohibitions against parallel perfect consonances, unresolved dissonances, and the like, may be relaxed. Topics such as the contrapuntal relations between voices, the use of the basso continuo, and melodic elaborations were all secondary matters that were to be learned only after one has mastered the fundamental bass.[87]

From this perspective, "L'Art de la basse fondamentale" is an extraordinary work. For all its abstractions, disorganization, and limitations, it offers a completely new perspective from which to conceive, teach, and compose music. Its systematic attention to the fundamental bass arguably earns it the honor of being the first real harmony textbook in the modern sense. Until Gianotti published his version of Rameau's "Art" in 1759, no practical text of composition ever attempted to break so thoroughly with past conventions – not even the third Book of the *Traité* – nor offered such a radical and complete reconceptualization of music.

Still, Rameau was clearly dissatisfied with his first attempt at a self-sufficient composition treatise based upon the fundamental bass. His unwillingness to publish this bulky and disorganized treatise in the 1740s, and his efforts to secure the help of others in revising the work, betray deep-seated reservations. Rameau had by no means given up his plans for a composition manual, though. The *Code de musique pratique* was the culmination of Rameau's pedagogical ambitions.[88] In this important and fascinating document, Rameau incorporates most of the material contained in "L'Art de la basse fondamentale," although thankfully in a more efficient manner. As announced with some fanfare in a *Prospectus* that preceded its publication by three years, the *Code* contains "seven methods" for learning music.[89] Specifically, the seven methods cover (1) the rudiments of music ("even for the blind"); (2) the correct hand position for playing the harpsichord or organ; (3) vocal production; (4) playing the thorough bass; (5) composition; (6) accompanying without figures; and (7) improvising ("preluding"). Several of these topics were ones covered in previous writings of Rameau. The material on hand position and keyboard accompaniment (Chapters 2 and 5) essentially restate ideas first expressed in the Preface to his *Pièces de clavecin* of 1731 and the *Dissertation sur les différentes méthodes*

---

[87] Rameau initially was confused about the precise ordering of the "Art," as the several drafts of material show. For instance, he initially placed the discussion of supposition and the suspension in Part 1. Gianotti realized correctly that any discussion of these topics necessitated speaking of the basso continuo and chordal inversion; hence these sections were moved to Part 3 of the *Guide*, from which Example 5.10 is taken.

[88] Jacobi shows that this work, although ready by 1757, was actually not published until 1761 (although dated 1760) owing to delays involved with the completion of the *Nouvelles réflexions sur le principe sonore* appended to it (*CTW* IV, xxxiii).

[89] Transcribed in *CTW* IV, xx–xxvii.

d'accompagnement of 1732. The singing method (Chapter 3) is adumbrated in an article first published in the *Mercure* in 1752.[90] The lengthy method on composition (comprising Chapters 6 through 14) can be seen as a revision of "L'Art de la basse fondamentale."[91] Most of the topics contained in the "Art" are to be found in the *Code*, although Rameau does not attempt to replicate the former's pedagogical systematization, nor follow its order of presentation (e.g. dissonance and chordal inversions are introduced early on in the *Code*). Among the shared topics are the harmonization of melody (Chapter 8), the "rapport" of keys (Chapter 5, articles 10–14 and Chapter 12), composition in several voices (Chapter 13), elaborations of a melodic line (Chapter 12), the suspension and supposition (Chapter 5, articles 19–22), and imitation (Chapter 8, article 10).

But there was a new sense of confidence in the *Code* that animates his prose and unites the seven methods.[92] There was of course the unshakable conviction that knowledge of the fundamental bass was the key to mastering all of the skills outlined in his seven methods. Over the sixteen chapters of the *Code*, Rameau attempted to show how the fundamental bass helps the student learn everything from improvisation at the keyboard to singing chromatic intervals in tune. But there is also a conspicuous emphasis upon learning the fundamental bass not just intellectually, but kinaesthetically. His approach towards learning accompaniment, for instance, is remarkably tactile. The student is to "feel" the correct chords to be fingered at the keyboard before ever conceptualizing them. This advice stands in marked contrast to the mechanical rules of fingering offered in the *Dissertation* some thirty years earlier (described in Chapter 3), and reflects on an empirical level how deep-rooted was Rameau's sensationalist conversion. Everywhere the student is exhorted to use all his sensory instincts to learn and apply the fundamental bass. While we find the usual quantity of redundancy, awkward prose, and disorganization in the *Code* familiar from his other publications, there is now the unmistakable sign of a mature and self-confident theorist. (Not coincidentally, I think, we find the same sense of confidence and freedom in his last major composition: *Les Boréades*, finished in 1764.) The amply illustrated musical examples that accompany the *Code* far exceed in detail and musicality those found in any of his earlier treatises. The richness of his musical examples may be attributed, I think, less to any evolution of his compositional style that had transpired than to a greater suppleness that he brought to his theory. We encounter dozens of examples in the *Code* utilizing a far

---

[90] "Réflexions de Monsieur Rameau sur la manière de former la voix et d'apprendre la musique," *Mercure de France* (October, 1752), 87–100; reprinted in Marie-Germaine Moreau, "Jean-Philippe Rameau et la pédagogie," *La Revue Musicale* 260 (1964), 48–53.

[91] Although Chapter 5 is ostensibly a method on accompaniment, it contains much material that was considered to be germane to compositional skills. As we saw in Chapter 3, Rameau believed that the skills of composition and keyboard accompaniment were closely related.

[92] While working on the *Code*, Rameau apparently sought out literary advice in drafting his prose, just as he had with the *Génération harmonique* (Castel and Mairan), and the *Démonstration* (d'Alembert and Diderot). Rameau's assistant editor this time was the amateur musician and aspiring playwright Abbé François Arnaud. Several extant letters of Rameau dating from 1757 suggest that Arnaud helped not only to draft the *Prospectus* that preceded the *Code* but also to edit the manuscript of the *Code* itself (*CTW* VI, 335–36).

more ambitious harmonic palette and melodic freedom than seen in the "Art," including more striking dissonances, chromatic progressions, rhythmic variety, embellishments, figurations, and imitative textures. We also find Rameau assigning fundamental-bass lines that appear quite licentious in comparison to his earlier, more conservative analyses. On the one hand, Rameau showed few qualms in allowing the fundamental bass to proceed by most any interval in any direction. On the other hand, he was also more ready to describe many melodic tones and even entire chords as nonharmonic events ("notes de goût") unsupported by their own fundamental bass.

To see an illustration of the kinds of freedom I mean, let us look at a beautiful and expressive passage of chromatic music taken from Chapter 12 of the *Code* and transcribed in Example 9.12. The music ostensibly is meant to illustrate the principal subject of that chapter – the embellishment and elaboration of a melody ("Notes d'ornement ou de goût, où l'on traite encore de la modulation"). But we can use the example to infer much more about Rameau's evolving ideas concerning the fundamental bass and its practical interpretation by this time.

Rameau shows, among other things, how chromatics can be used to ornament harmony. The sharpened notes in the musical sequence of measures 1-3 do not represent "major dissonances" indicating leading tones; hence, they do not affect the fundamental bass. (It is revealing to compare these measures with Example 9.10 on p. 281.) The G♯ in measure 4, however, by virtue of its metrical placement on the downbeat of the measure and its supporting bass note in the basso continuo, does constitute a real leading tone.[93] Most of the eighth and sixteenth notes in the following measures, however, are embellishments of the main melodic tones that receive their own fundamental basses. Rameau suggests that in order to determine which notes of a melody are fundamental, one look at the strong beats of each measure, as in measures 5–6 and 9. When alternative fundamental basses are still available (as indicated by the cursors in mm. 10, 11, and 13), one makes a choice based upon the genre of the piece, its expressive nature, and one's taste. A special problem is seen with the diminished-third melodic progression caused by the Neapolitan sixth at the end of m. 12 (and called by Rameau "une pleureuse"). The *dominante-tonique* upon which the music ends is "broken" in the following measure by a *cadence rompue*, whereupon the resulting chromatic motion can be interpreted by a variety of fundamental basses. As Rameau notes it, the progression represents a chord of the *susdominant censée tonique*, followed by an applied diminished-seventh chord resolving to the dominant, again *censée tonique*. We can see from this single example – one far more musical than typically seen in such composition primers – that Rameau is much more tolerant of dissonant interval progressions in the fundamental bass. Also noteworthy is his liberal acceptance of accented appoggiaturas (mm. 11 and 13), "passing chords" (m. 13), suspensions in the fundamental bass (mm. 4 and 5), irregular voice-leadings (e.g. the parallel perfect consonances between the melody and basso continuo in m. 13),

---

[93] *Code*, 152.

Example 9.12 Analysis of chromatic music from the *Code*, Plate 27

syncopations in the fundamental bass (mm. 7 and 10), and irregularly resolved dissonances (mm. 1–3 and 11).

We must not conclude by this example that Rameau ended up eschewing all his previously-enunciated rules and desiderata. In one sense, Rameau very much wanted to reduce the rules of composition to a kind of mechanical system as had d'Alembert. The fundamental bass proved beyond doubt that principles of music did exist from which one could extract composition strictures. But at the same time, Rameau knew that any rules must be pliable enough to account for the diversity possible in music, whether it was the kinds of chords composers used, the way chord fundamentals linked up with one another, or the particular melodies and voice leadings by which these chord progressions were articulated. This is ultimately why d'Alembert's efforts were doomed to failure. D'Alembert had neither the means nor the will to master the "rules" of composition – knowledge, Rameau emphasizes, that comes only from experience, taste, and genius.[94] Rameau repeatedly warned his readers that the rules he offered were only a guide to musical composition – not a guarantee. All this freedom belies Jacobi's assertion that the *Code* represents some kind of definitive legislation of musical practice that Rameau dogmatically lays down "comparable to a Moses for music."[95] The title of his composition manuscript, after all, was the "*Art of the Fundamental Bass.*"

There remains an undeniable tension between Rameau's goals of pedagogical synthesis and compositional freedom. D'Alembert's second Book on composition does indeed reflect on one level Rameau's convictions that the art of composition was but a deductive consequence – if unrecognized by musicians – of the laws of the fundamental bass. Yet Rameau was never willing to draw the knot as tightly as d'Alembert did. But, then, perhaps he never felt he really had to. The fundamental bass, and beyond that, the *corps sonore* from which it was derived, assumed such an increasingly dominating role in Rameau's musical cosmology, that a literal mapping of composition rules to it was really beside the point. Almost in inverse proportion to the specificity of empirical diversity illustrated in the *Code,* Rameau generalized his principle of the *corps sonore* and extended its domain over every aspect of musical practice. Indeed, in his very last writings, Rameau abandoned whatever circumspection he had shown to this point and came out to assert in the most unambiguous terms the ontological primacy of the *corps sonore* as a fundamental principle of human knowledge.

[94] *Ibid.,* 133.
[95] *CTW* IV, xxix.

10

THE FINAL YEARS

By 1762 Rameau was a worn man. Now seventy-nine years old, he had spent the previous ten years in almost uninterrupted verbal combat with his critics. In numerous letters dating from this period, Rameau bemoans his loss of musical creativity, and how he must conserve carefully what remaining energy he has in order to work on his theoretical projects.[1] Chabanon described the poignant scene of the tired composer slowly wending his way alone through the Tuileries on his daily walk, sullen, sad, and lost in meditation upon his *corps sonore*. To be sure, such reports are somewhat dramaticized; Rameau had by no means withdrawn from the world nor lost his musical creativity. In his last years, he managed to compose two of his most splendid and original operas: *Les Paladins* in 1760, and *Les Boréades* in 1764. Rameau also found time to revise several older stage works, and even travel to the provinces in order to supervise new productions.[2] But it was music theory that continued most to preoccupy his mind. With almost frenetic intensity, Rameau poured out his thoughts on paper related to his beloved *corps sonore*. Diderot expressed in a particularly cutting passage from *Le Neveu de Rameau* the cynicism many of the philosophes must have felt towards the misanthropic Rameau's perceived *bavardage*:

The rest of the universe doesn't matter a tinker's damn to him. His wife, his daughter may die as soon as they please. Provided the parish bells that toll for them continue to sound the intervals of the twelfth and the seventeenth, all will be well.[3]

Diderot was not exaggerating by much. The *corps sonore* had by now become a fixation to Rameau. In his final treatise, the *Nouvelles réflexions sur le principe sonore* of 1760,[4] as well as his remaining essays – the "Origine des sciences" (1762), "Lettre aux philosophes" (1762), and the unpublished "Vérités interressantes" (1763–64) – Rameau sounds almost like a Rosicrucian when speaking of the *corps sonore*. It is the "key" that opens up the doors of all the sciences; it is sacred knowledge that can be

---

[1] See e.g. his letter to Casaubon dating from November, 1763, reprinted in *CTW* VI, xli–xlii.
[2] Lionel Sawkins, "Rameau's Last Years: Some Implications of Rediscovered Material at Bordeaux," *Proceedings of the Royal Musical Association* 111 (1984), 66–91.
[3] Denis Diderot, *Rameau's Nephew and Other Works*, trans. Jacques Barzun and Ralph H. Bowen (Indianapolis, 1964), 12.
[4] Although the *Nouvelles réflexions* was eventually published as a kind of appendix to the *Code de musique pratique*, it must really be seen as an independent treatise – the last Rameau would publish in his lifetime.

traced back thousands of years to a small cult of Egyptian priests, but has since been hidden to mankind until Rameau himself revealed its glorious truth. One is tempted when reading Rameau's last writings to concur with Diderot's scornful assessment (quoted in Chapter 1) that they comprise "so much visionary gibberish and apocalyptic truth" – the products of a mad composer who has lost whatever sense he might have once possessed. But having followed Rameau this far, I think we can afford to be a bit more charitable in our assessment. (We will also shortly see that Diderot, too, retained a good deal of charity in regard to Rameau's theory.) Audacious speculations and profound mysticism need not be incompatible with scientific discovery. For Arthur Koestler, elements of the mystical, irrational, and subliminal have led scientists to brilliant insight and revelation, as his case study of Kepler richly shows.[5] We could make much the same observation, I think, concerning Rameau's late writings. It was because of his almost evangelical convictions as to the veracity of his *corps sonore*, that by relentless contemplation, imagination, and sheer force of will Rameau was able to draw from this phenomenon a myriad of insightful theoretical ideas and sensitive tonal relationships.

Still, the *corps sonore* was more than a phantasm. There was empirical evidence for it – evidence that he constantly wished to remind his readers was furnished or confirmed by those who now criticized him. D'Alembert's attacks agitated Rameau so much more profoundly than anyone else's not because his criticisms were either more malevolent or comprehensive – there were numerous other critics of Rameau whose criticisms were far more scathing or encyclopedic, including Bemetzrieder, Serre, Ducharger, Mercardier, and, of course, Rousseau – but because these criticisms came from a scientist who Rameau believed should (and at one time did) recognize his theory's obvious scientific validity. Rameau was so keen that the *corps sonore* be accepted as a *scientific* truth that when he realized d'Alembert was deserting his camp, he undertook strenuous efforts to secure approval from other scientific quarters.

Rameau initiated contact with the Italian Accademia delle Scienze dell'Istituto di Bologna in 1759, sending to this organization a preliminary draft of his *Nouvelles réflexions sur le principe sonore*. In a series of letters addressed to two members, the scientist Jacopo Bartolomeo Beccari and the music historian Padre Martini, Rameau implored them with increasing impatience to review his manuscript and pronounce their judgment on behalf of the Accademia.[6] He was clearly hoping to receive some kind of official approbation in order to counter the criticisms of d'Alembert, which threatened to undermine the entire scientific basis of his theory. Unfortunately for Rameau, no such approbation was forthcoming. Padre Martini took his time in reviewing the manuscript, even going so far as commissioning Italian translations of the majority of Rameau's other published treatises. When Martini finally did get around to writing an evaluation of Rameau's ideas,

---

[5] Arthur Koestler, *The Sleep Walkers: A History of Man's Changing Vision of the Universe* (New York, 1959).
[6] The principal documents are recorded and analyzed by Erwin Jacobi in "Rameau and Padre Martini: New Letters and Documents," *Musical Quarterly* 50 (1964), 452–75.

Plate 10.1 Frontispiece to the *Code de Musique* (1760). The three muses rendered in this engraving are an allegory of Rameau's theory of the *corps sonore*. In the center, the muse Euterpe plucks a lyre string and listens to its overtones (the *corps sonore*). The muse to her right putting down notes on paper symbolizes the musician applying the proportions of these overtones to composition. To her left another muse is measuring the proportions of these overtones on a monochord; she symbolizes the reliance of all the sciences upon proportions and hence upon the *corps sonore*.

he expressed cautious agreement with parts of the fundamental bass, but skepticism in regard to his acoustical and metaphysical ideas concerning the *corpo sonoro*.[7] But this evaluation came too late for Rameau.

While Rameau was waiting for a response from the Academia throughout 1759, he continued to work on his *Nouvelles réflexions sur le principe sonore*. The draft of the text received by Padre Martini contained a number of Rameau's new ideas involving historical issues related to the *corps sonore*. Before the final publication of this treatise in 1760, though, Rameau had edited out or substantially altered many of the most speculative passages.[8] Yet he by no means abandoned these ideas for they will all make an appearance in his remaining essays. And what historical questions absorbed Rameau's attention at this time? They concerned nothing less than the origins of music itself.

THE ORIGINS OF MUSIC

Throughout the 1750s, Rameau began collecting scattered historical evidence that he could interpret in favor of his theory. As the decade progressed, we find Rameau spending ever more effort to ground his theory historically. Thus, reports of Chinese musical practice, ancient biblical instruments, Greek music theory, Egyptian science, and Medieval modal theory all became mixed together in Rameau's mind as evidence that the *corps sonore* was the universal principle of music at all times and in all places, even if many musicians had lost sight of this truth along the way. More audaciously, he saw in this historical evidence further confirmation of his growing conviction that the *corps sonore* was the principal progenitor of all the sciences.

In the "Origine des sciences" – a short essay he published in the *Mercure* in 1762 – Rameau presented some of this new historical "evidence." It seems he had recently come across a history of mathematics written by Jean-Etienne Montucla, in which Montucla argued that the geometrical and mathematical sciences originated in ancient Egypt.[9] Rameau inferred from this information that a cabal of Egyptian priests must have been in possession of the knowledge of the *corps sonore*, and from this were inspired to develop the sciences of geometry and algebra. As one example: it must have been by listening to the *corps sonore* that the Egyptian priests first discovered the Pythagorean theorem, to wit, the square of the hypotenuse of a right-angled triangle is equal to the sum of the squares of its two sides.[10] How could this be? Rameau thought that in perceiving the arithmetic series 3 : 4 : 5 in the *corps sonore*, as well as their squares in the geometric progression, the Egyptians were led to investigate these relations, and thereby to the discovery that the sum of the squares of the third and fourth partials (9 + 16) was equal to the square of the

---

[7] The complete report of Martini may be found in *CTW* VI, 387–407.
[8] The excised material is transcribed by Jacobi in *CTW* VI, 353–72.
[9] The work is Jean-Etienne Montucla, *Histoire des Mathématiques dans laquelle on rend compte de leurs progrès depuis leur origine jusqu'à nos jours* (Paris, 1758).
[10] *CTW* IV, 289.

fifth partial (25). But unfortunately these priests failed to share their knowledge of the *corps sonore* with others. Thus the true origins of geometry and algebra were soon forgotten except by a small and secretive sect of Pythagoreans.[11]

Rameau also drew inspiration for his theory from reports concerning Chinese music sent by the Jesuit missionary Joseph Marie Amiot.[12] In a widely circulated manuscript that arrived in Paris in 1754, Amiot described the theory and practice of Chinese music to his curious countrymen.[13] (It was on Amiot's report that Diderot based the *Encyclopédie* articles on Chinese music and instruments.) Rameau read Amiot's report with keen interest, and seized upon a few remarks therein as evidence that the Chinese pentatonic scale was generated by the triple geometric progression (e.g. the scale G A C D E could be generated by the geometric terms 3, 1, 3, 9, 3). Rameau concluded from this marvelous fact that both Chinese and Greek music must have evolved from the same source. (Rameau had earlier concluded, it will be recalled, that the Greek tetrachord must have been generated by the triple geometric progression.) How did the triple geometric progression come to be known by both the Chinese and the Egyptians? Rameau speculated that it was because Noah carried with him on the ark the knowledge of the geometric triple progression (perhaps by virtue of having a lyre tuned to perfect fifths). After the deluge, the sons of Noah were dispersed to the various corners of the world, and carried with them this knowledge.[14]

It probably need not be stressed that the historical evidence for Rameau's arguments was shaky, to say the least. Even those sympathetic with Rameau's theory, such as the Abbé Roussier, evinced little sympathy for his historical speculations.[15] Obviously Rameau could only make sense of the Chinese musical system by filtering it through the fundamental bass, much as he had earlier done with Zarlino's contrapuntal practice.[16] Yet however clumsy or culturally myopic Rameau's attempt

11   Montucla, it should be pointed out, mentions Rameau's theory in several places in his work, and offers up the usual pieties about Rameau having revealed (along with Pythagoras) the principles of music (*Histoire des Mathématiques*, 14, 122–36). While Montucla does argue that the geometric sciences were first cultivated by a small group of Egyptian priests, nowhere does he suggest that these priests got their first notions of geometry from the *corps sonore*. He hypothesizes, rather, that economic, environmental, and engineering demands motivated the development of geometry (e.g. the need to resurvey land holdings when the waters of the Nile receded after their annual floodings). *Ibid.*, 93–95.

12   *Nouvelles réflexions sur le principe sonore*, 189, note a. For information on Amiot and his role in disseminating knowledge of Chinese music theory in France, see Jim Levy, "Joseph Amiot and Enlightenment Speculations on the Origin of Pythagorean Tuning in China," *Theoria* 4 (1989), 63–88.

13   It should be noted that there was something of a vogue among intellectuals in the 1750s for Chinese culture – Frederick's Chinese tea house at Sans-Souci being only one of the more famous examples.

14   *Nouvelles réflexions sur le principle sonore*, 225–27.

15   Roussier's critique of Rameau's historical arguments may be found in his *Mémoire sur la musique des anciens, où l'on expose le principe des proportions authentiques* (Paris, 1770). Diderot, who studied Roussier's work with interest, reported his own views in the "Mémoire sur le fondement des systèmes de musique des anciens peuples grecs, chinois et égyptiens par M. l'abbé Roussier," contained in *Oeuvres complètes* (Paris, 1975–), XIX, 35–43.

16   Rameau was not the only one who had difficulties understanding a different culture's musical practice, though. It seems that while in residence in Peking, Amiot played for the Emperor some harpsichord pieces of Rameau; the ruler was evidently baffled by the experience. (Reported in Béatrice Didier, *La Musique des Lumières: Diderot – L'Encyclopédie – Rousseau* [Paris, 1985], 74.)

at ethnomusicology was, it was not necessarily more unreasonable or biased than the historical or ethnographic evidence employed by many of the other philosophes for their own hobby-horses; it was a popular ploy among all the philosophes to cite exotic non-European customs or historical conventions in their critique of contemporary French *mœurs*. Bayle, Montesquieu, Voltaire, Diderot, and Rousseau all employed this strategy liberally in their writings.[17] As information concerning non-European musical practice was just beginning to be circulated in France during the mid eighteenth century through emissaries such as Amiot, and scholars such as Bonnet and du Halde, it is not surprising that Rameau's understanding of Chinese music was spotted.[18]

In any case, historical evidence of non-Western musical practices was only one more source Rameau could draw upon to buttress his thesis that the *corps sonore* was the principle of musical harmony. In his last writings he continued to stress how both musical practice and objective observation of nature prove the existence of the *corps sonore*. No one phenomenon is more ubiquitous in nature, he claimed, nor more deeply inculcated in the human mind. It is the "sonorous root" (*racine sonore*) of a tree whose trunks and limbs are the proportions and progressions that it engenders, and whose branches, twigs, leaves, and fruits are the applications of these proportions and progressions to the various arts and sciences.[19] Repeating over and over how the *corps sonore* is a sensory phenomenon apparent to three of our senses (although naturally the ear is the most sensitive of the senses), Rameau expresses amazement that someone like d'Alembert should fail to acknowledge this fact, let alone not recognize this as the primeval source from which mankind attained its knowledge – and sense – of proportions. For ultimately, what gives the *corps sonore* its metaphysical potency in Rameau's theory is that it is not an abstract, quantitative postulate but rather an acoustical *experience* that transcends and precedes any analytic description.

It is said that numerical ratios represent truths that can be confirmed by means of the senses. Ah ha! By what sense other than the ear can one obtain this favor? As soon as the singular sensations that the soul receives make us aware of the ratios that we distinguish in the third, fourth, fifth and so on, we are able to communicate this sense of numerical ratio to that of

---

[17] Which is not to say that the philosophes approached history blindly. Peter Gay has persuasively rehabilitated the philosophes as historians and anthropologists by showing how they were far more careful and sensitive in their research than traditionally acknowledged: *The Enlightenment: An Interpretation*, 2 vols. (New York, 1966–69), II, 368ff.

[18] It should be noted that Rousseau's ethnographic evidence to support his musical ideas was no more historically grounded than was Rameau's. In the *Encyclopédie* article "musique," for example, Rousseau speculated that "it was in Egypt that music began to be reestablished after the deluge. The first notions of sound may have come about from blowing through the tubes of reeds that grew along the edge of the Nile." Naturally, Rousseau inferred from this that melody was the first music to be sounded. Rameau may have felt compelled to counter Rousseau's argument by showing how harmony – in the guise of the *corps sonore* – was the true original guide for Egyptian musicians. For further information on the dissemination and impact of non-European musical practice in France during the eighteenth century, see Didier, *La Musique des Lumières*, 61–72.

[19] "Lettre de M. XXX à M.D. XXXX, sur un Ouvrage intitulé l'origine des sciences," *Mercure de France* (April, 1762), 103–19; CTW VI, 441–46.

sight by means of an instrument by which reason may judge the perfection of the different objects it measures. But what certitude is there in any measurement unless it is confirmed by a perfection that is already indubitably understood? Can one find such indubitable perfection in any object that our senses can perceive other than that of the *corps sonore*, in which all the greatest principles of mathematics resonate together, even if one believes himself to be hearing only a single sound? . . . Is it not a monumental error to attribute to numbers a virtue that one knows is born of sensible ratios, and of which those numbers are only signs? The error is nonetheless a commonplace one which all writers have accepted on faith.[20]

This is precisely why Rameau expressed such hostility, in his last writings, to the Pythagoreans.[21] It was not any attribute of numbers by which the ratios of music enjoy their ontological status. Rather, it is that these ratios originate as a fundamental *sensory* experience of a natural phenomenon; they can be described by numbers, certainly, but cannot be ascribed to them.[22]

Rameau's language in his last writings takes on a pantheistic air when he speaks of the *corps sonore*. It is a phenomenon that seems to be ubiquitous. Much like Leibniz's monods and Spinoza's God, the *corps sonore* permeates nature; the world surrounding us is full of continually vibrating, pulsating matter resonating the proportions of the *corps sonore*. In his last manuscript, "Vérités également ignorées et interressantes tirées du sein de la nature," the *corps sonore* assumes almost divine powers:

It seems to me possible to see in the *corps sonore* (if one will pardon me this suspicion in favor of the most striking image of a Creator, as one will see) a sun suspended above our heads in order to enlighten us.[23]

From the *corps sonore* and its divisions into a seemingly endless series of aliquot divisions and aliquant multiples, we receive the idea of infinity.[24] It is the "first cause" of the other arts and sciences in exactly the same way God is the first cause of the universe:

---

20 "Vérités interressantes," 13.
21 Rameau cites in particular a writer of the seventeenth century, Johannes Meursius, who wrote a neo-Pythagorean treatise on numbers: *Denarius Pythagoricus* (Leyden, 1631). Rameau's criticisms of Meursius may be found in the *Nouvelles réflexions*, 228–37, and the "Vérités interressantes," 13, 62. As early as 1726, though, Rameau was already condemning Pythagorean ideas (*Nouveau système*, 9).
22 Many historians to this day misunderstand Rameau's arguments in this regard, and wrongly describe his ideas as neo-Pythagorean (e.g. Charles Paul, "Rameau's Musical Theories and the Age of Reason" [Ph.D. dissertation, University of California, Berkeley, 1966], 105). Herbert Schneider is one of the few to have correctly recognized that the opposite is really closer to the truth in his article "Rameau's musiktheoretisches Vermächtnis," *Musiktheorie* 1/2 (1986), especially 154–55.
23 There exist two versions of this manuscript. A short version now in the Bibliothèque Nationale was transcribed by Jacobi in *CTW* VI, 516–33. More recently, Herbert Schneider discovered a much longer version in Stockholm that he showed to be a later draft. Schneider has transcribed and annotated both versions with his customary thoroughness in his book *Jean-Philippe Rameaus letzter Musiktraktat* (Wiesbaden, 1986). The present citation is found on p. 14 of this edition.
24 *Ibid.*, 54. Of course this then suggests that the *corps sonore* generates partials and multiples that exceed the confines of the quintuple geometric progression – a problem Rameau seems not to notice!

In order to see in all these models [of proportions and progressions] the most perfect geometry offered by the *corps sonore* . . . in order to see the striking images of an antecedent Creator (*Antécédent Créateur*) and its secondary causes – images of our phenomenon that reason directs us to learn from – what are we to think of the goodness of the Creator? (I do not say nature any more, although they are the same thing for me.) Having wished to communicate these images to us by all the means most appropriate so that the cause does not escape us, He offers more still: in order to supplement our fallible reason, He has endowed us with an instinct by means of which, if He has taken great care and attention, we have finally obtained the treasure in which all is contained.[25]

Extravagant as Rameau's rhetoric might be to us, the various sentiments he expresses in these writings were not so dissimilar to other writings of his day. Pantheistic and pseudoanimistic ideas were far from uncommon in the Enlightenment.[26] As for his references to the *corps sonore* and God as "antecedent Creator," Rameau is not attempting to equate – as a number of critics and historians to this day continue to maintain – the resonating partials of the *corps sonore* with the holy Trinity.[27] His idea was much more subtle than that. He is making an unambiguous reference to another doctrine that had wide currency in the eighteenth century: occasionalist philosophy.

OCCASIONALISM

Occasionalism was a neo-scholastic doctrine articulated in the seventeenth century by the academician Arnold Geulinex and elaborated most fully by the philosopher and scientist Nicholas Malebranche (1638–1715). Malebranche's goal, simply put, was to find a place for God in Descartes's mechanistic universe of extended matter and motion. While all motion we see in the universe may appear to be caused only by matter impacting upon matter, Malebranche argued this constitutes only a "secondary" or "occasional" cause ordained by God who is the true prime mover. By this reasoning, Malebranche believed he could also explain the paradox of Cartesian mind–body dualism; God was the agent by which non-material thoughts can be transferred into actions.

In much this manner, Rameau thought the *corps sonore* could be the primary "cause" of music and the other arts and sciences dependent upon proportions.[28]

---

[25] *Ibid.*, 64. I have liberally translated this passage, which in the original French is quite obscure.

[26] For a number of illuminating illustrations, see Margaret Jacob, *The Radical Enlightenment: Pantheists, Freemasons and Republicans* (London, 1981), 215–49.

[27] e.g., Doolittle, "A Would-Be Philosophe, Jean-Philippe Rameau," *Publication of the Modern Language Association* 74 (1950), 248. Doolittle, I should warn the reader, is unflagging in his ridicule of Rameau's late writings, seeing them as little more than the ravings of a deluded crackpot. But Doolittle arrives at his conclusion only by imposing the most arrogantly Whiggish interpretation upon Rameau's debate with the Encyclopedists, and disregarding entirely the musical questions with which Rameau was wrestling. It is a pity that this one-sided article continues to be cited so frequently in the secondary literature, prejudicing untold numbers of readers who accept its faulty conclusions on faith.

[28] Charles Paul is the first I am aware of to have identified the occasionalist roots of many of Rameau's last writings: Charles Paul, "Jean-Philippe Rameau (1683–1764), The Musician as *Philosophe*," *Proceedings of the American Philosophical Society* 114/2 (April, 1970), 147; and "Rameau's Musical Theories," 83–91.

The various numbers and proportions that Pythagorean philosophers had previously believed to be the principles behind all arts and sciences are really only secondary causes occasioned by the *corps sonore* that is their true cause. But if Rameau believed the *corps sonore* shared the attributes of the divinity, he by no means thought it to be an icon of the Trinity. While he credited the *corps sonore* with some extraordinary attributes, he always considered it to be a mechanistic phenomenon of nature.

Rameau appropriated occasionalist ideas not only to make abstract philosophical arguments. He was able to use Malebranche's theology to solve some very concrete musical problems in his theory. As the "first cause" in music, the proportions of the *corps sonore* enjoy the power of "occasioning" secondary proportions. In other words, the ratio of the perfect fifth generated as the first harmonic proportion of the *corps sonore* can "occasion" other proportions and progressions that otherwise might seem unrelated to this source.

> Everything that constitutes a harmonic proportion enjoys the right of establishing such correspondences as it can. If the fifth establishes what is the most perfect, its geometric [expansion] leads us to the primitive order [of the fundamental bass], allowing the thirds that are dependent upon it to imitate its functions in the less perfect and less frequent instances . . . thus everything in music is accounted for by just these proportions; the immense variety to which music is susceptible is based entirely upon these proportions, all because of the fifth chosen by the antecedent as its first means of variety. . .[29]

Let us consider how Rameau applies this new reasoning to a number of well-rehearsed problems in his theory.

First, Rameau was able to offer a new – or more accurately, a revived – argument to explain the derivation of the minor triad. The *corps sonore*, as we know by now, generates directly only the major triad through the harmonic series. But as the principal *ordonnateur* of mode, the perfect fifth and major third enjoy the right of rearranging themselves in an arithmetic proportion – in essence, reversing their order. This can be modeled by the progression 1/8–1/10–1/12–1/15. The first three terms form the harmonic proportion given by nature and from which is derived the major triad. By adding a fourth term to this progression, or more correctly, by occasioning a new fifth (1/10–1/15), the major third now has the privilege of occupying a new position within the fifth above the minor third.[30] The argument here has nothing to do with Rameau reaching into higher partials, as several historians have claimed.[31] The terms that exceeded the sixth partial – the term Rameau unwaveringly held as the audible limit of the *corps sonore* – were not acoustically perceptible partials but rather derivative terms *occasioned* by the *corps sonore*.

---

29 Schneider, *Rameaus letzter Musiktraktat*, 35.
30 *Ibid.*, 32–33. This argument naturally suggests the theory of "triadic parallelism" enunciated in the *Traité*. (See Chapter 4, p. 96.) But there is a critical difference in that in the first work, Rameau categorically rejected the arithmetic proportion as the cause of the minor triad, whereas here he attributes the minor triad to the arithmetic proportion – the latter proportion itself "occasioned" by the harmonic proportion.
31 e.g., Joan Ferris, "The Evolution of Rameau's Harmonic Theories," *Journal of Music Theory* 3/1 (1959), 232; Matthew Shirlaw, *The Theory of Harmony* (London, 1917), 266.

Secondly, similar arguments were included by Rameau in the "Vérités interressantes" to explain dissonance. Since the two divisions of the perfect fifth (harmonic and arithmetic) were the most direct products of the *corps sonore*, one only needed to interlock these in order to derive dissonant sevenths (see Figure 10.1).[32] An interlocking harmonic and arithmetic proportion produces the "augmented" (major) seventh, while the inverse relationship creates a "natural" (minor) seventh. Once again, variety in music is shown to arise from that "first cause": the simple proportions generated by the *corps sonore*.

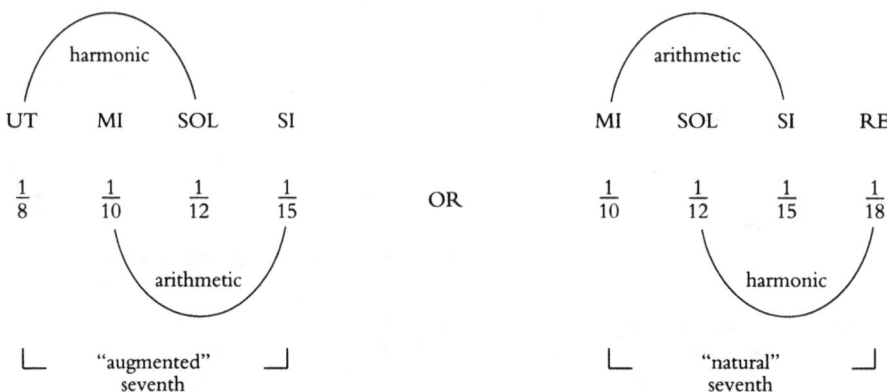

10.1 The derivation of sevenths by interlocking harmonic and arithmetic proportions

Finally, Rameau was able to employ occasionalist arguments to solve a problem that had hitherto proved intractable in his theory: how to reconcile his functional definition of mode (which was symmetrical) with his generative derivation of mode through the geometric triple progression (which was one-directional). His solution lay in a reconceptualization of the three terms of the geometric triple progression (1, 3, 9), or as he called them in the "Vérités interressantes," the "three keys." The fundamental generative unity (1) of the triple geometric progression was the "first cause" of mode (i.e. the source of the subsequent terms of the progression, 3 and 9). At the same time, as the principal *ordonnateur*, this unity could cede to the "middle term" (*terme moyen*) of the geometric triple progression the role of tonic. In the *Nouvelles réflexions sur le principe sonore*, Rameau explained himself as follows:

> As soon as the geometric proportion is generated, it is no longer the *principe* that governs [the whole]; rather, the *terme moyen* (½) of this proportion is. This *terme moyen* is thus placed in the centre of the proportion, occasioned by the liberty [the *principe*] enjoys to direct its route from one side to the other ... I give this *terme moyen* (½) the title of *ordonnateur* – a title that characterizes its function and at the same time distinguishes it from its generator, with which it is easily confounded, since the *ordonnateur* represents the generator with which it is consubstantial.[33]

[32] Schneider, *Rameaus letzter Musiktraktat*, 46.
[33] *Nouvelles réflexions sur le principe sonore*, 195–96.

With the middle term now functioning as tonic, the first term becomes an *antécédent*, and assumes a subsidiary role as subdominant, while a third term – the *conséquent* – assumes the role of dominant.[34] By this sleight of hand, Rameau believes he has remained consistent with his principle of generating the mode through the geometric triple progression, while at the same time retaining the integrity of the tonic as the primary function of a mode. Admittedly Rameau's logic was tenuous here at best. But the point is that the solution afforded by Malebranche's theology, however far removed it may have been from music theory, offered an irresistible way out for Rameau.

The exact sources for Rameau's knowledge of Malebranche cannot be identified with any certainty. Given the lack of any direct citations of Malebranche, the hesitancy of his occasionalist digressions, and knowing what we already do about Rameau's informal "scholarship," there is little to suggest that he personally engaged at any time in any extensive study of Malebranche's writings. A more likely scenario would be that Rameau gathered ideas relating to occasionalism from several second-hand sources, which he then appropriated – as he did throughout his life when similar ideas were presented to him – for his own music-theoretical arguments. Herbert Schneider has identified a number of possible sources for Rameau's occasionalist ideas, including several articles in the *Encyclopédie* by Jean-Henri Samuel Formey, as well as ideas drawn from Salomon de Priézac and Pierre-Louis Maupertuis. The influence Schneider places most emphasis upon, though, is the arch-rationalist German philosopher Christian Wolff (1679–1754).[35]

Rameau cites Wolff's *Cosmologia Generalis* (Frankfurt, 1737) at several points in the "Vérités interressantes"; according to Schneider, many of his arguments are closer to Wolff than to Malebranche. Buttressing Schneider's opinion is a recently discovered letter of Wolff written to Rameau in 1751, in which he thanks the composer for having sent him a copy of the *Démonstration*. Wolff tells his "dear friend" Rameau that he had read the work "with relish," and proceeds to praise the author for his "extraordinary discoveries" and having found the "true explanation of harmony."[36] Schneider cites in particular Rameau's pantheistic equation of God with nature as an example of Wolffian influence. But I remain unconvinced that Wolff's ideas alone played such a significant role in Rameau's own intellectual development – no more, anyway, than did the numerous other authors whose ideas Rameau would periodically cite. Rameau's "philosophy" was always a syncretic one. As we have amply seen throughout this study, Rameau would borrow ideas freely and frequently, often without regard to the overall coherence of his theory.

---

34 "Vérités interressantes," 17–27
35 Schneider, *Rameaus letzter Musiktraktat*, 78–80.
36 The letter, written in Latin, is transcribed and translated into French in Jacques Chouillet's article "Présupposés, contours, et prolongements de la polémique autour des écrits théoriques de Jean-Philippe Rameau," *Rameau Colloque International*, 442–43. Wolff evidently was included among the scientists and celebrities to whom Rameau sent copies of his *Démonstration*. See Chapter 1, pp. 11.

One therefore ought not to read too much into his Wolffian citations in the "Vérités interressantes."[37]

When Rameau passed away on September 12, 1764, the French public's interest in both his music and his theoretical writings was on the decline. While some of his stage works remained in the repertoire of the Opéra over the next decade, it was clear that the Bouffon quarrel had sounded the death knell for the *Tragédie en musique*. Rameau's operas epitomized an art form and aesthetic falling increasingly into disfavor and soon displaced by Italian-influenced conventions. Likewise, for all that the fundamental bass remained a useful pedagogical device, few theorists bothered with the metaphysical implications Rameau attributed to the *corps sonore*. The rhetoric Rameau employed in his late speculative writings explaining the powers of the *corps sonore* failed, so to speak, to resonate among his readers. For the latter half of the eighteenth century, French theory became largely practical and non-speculative in tone, culminating in the decision of the post-Revolutionary *Conservatoire* to adopt Catel's distinctly utilitarian "theory" as its official textbook.[38]

THE RHETORIC OF THEORY

What, then, remains of Rameau's effort to forge a science of music theory? What of the evidently insurmountable obstacles he faced in building a complete system of harmony founded upon the natural principle of the *corps sonore*? D'Alembert was neither the first nor the last to point out empirical deficiencies and logical contradictions in Rameau's project. Yet despite these problems, we have seen how Rameau succeeded in convincing a great many of his contemporaries of the truth of his theory. How could this be? The answer, as I have suggested at several points in the course of this study, is that the criteria for evaluating the efficacy of a scientific theory – and particularly one in the eighteenth century – cannot be established by any single litmus test of empirical sufficiency or logical coherence.

Diderot understood this well enough. In the *Leçons de clavecin* he "ghost-penned" for Bemetzrieder in 1771, Diderot reviewed many of the by now familiar difficulties Rameau faced in finding a consistent generative principle for all chords. Speaking in the voice of the hidebound schoolmaster, Diderot asks,

What does a sensible scientist do when he encounters a phenomenon that contradicts his hypothesis? Why, he renounces it. But what does a systematizer do?[39] He twists and turns the facts until they fit his ideas willy-nilly. And this is what Rameau did . . .[40]

---

37 I therefore cannot agree with Schneider when he concludes that this new evidence confirms that Rameau was surprisingly well read (*Rameaus letzter Musiktraktat*, 101–02). While Rameau clearly was more familiar with contemporaneous intellectual ideas than has been previously thought, this does not make him the diligent scholar Schneider suggests.

38 For a fine history of this development, see Cynthia Gessele, "The Institutionalization of Music Theory in France: 1764–1802" (Ph. D. Dissertation, Princeton University, 1989).

39 Diderot is here referring to the kind of abstract, non-empirical philosophizing characteristic of the "esprit de système."

40 Diderot, *Oeuvres complètes*, XIX, 378.

The philosophe, who in Diderot's dialogue assumes the reflective voice of mediation between the master and pupil, listens quietly to the schoolmaster's reproach. After a considerable pause in which the philosophe ponders the words of the schoolmaster, he finally speaks up: "And what would you have me say? I have long been aware of the defects in Rameau's system – I and many others." Warming up to his subject, the philosophe continues: "But how can one dispute a great authority who penned such magnificent works [of music]?" More importantly, he wonders, how could one not be persuaded by "a doctrine supported by a natural phenomenon that offered a solid base for an art that until then had as a guide only routine and genius? Any method that shortened one's time and study I would defend against the most minor objection."

Here was the crux for the philosophe, and I believe for Diderot, too. Rameau's fundamental bass may have had its contradictions, and his principle of the *corps sonore* may have been unwisely over-extended. (The skeptical author of *Le Rêve de d'Alembert* needed no convincing by this time that the search for universal metaphysical principles in either science or the arts was a vain one.) Yet Diderot also recognized a deeper value to Rameau's fundamental bass in the efficiency by which it could clarify and simplify musical practice, and this virtue outweighed any systematic or metaphysical blemishes. (We might recall from Chapter 2 that both Condillac and d'Alembert came at one point to somewhat similar conclusions.)

What ultimately sealed the success of Rameau's theory was that it offered solutions to a number of critical problems deemed important to its readers. The fundamental bass first of all solved a pressing practical problem facing musicians of the early eighteenth century who wished to learn to compose and play the thorough bass: how are chords put together, and how do they normally succeed one another? As the philosophe in Diderot's *Leçons* noted, whether the fundamental bass can account systematically for *every* chord or chord progression matters less than the fact that *most* chords and chord progressions could indeed be explained successfully by the fundamental bass. In a similar way, Rameau's discovery and demonstration of a principle of music in the *corps sonore* answered what was perceived by many observers in the eighteenth century to be the most important question of all: what is the natural principle underlying each particular art and science? Yet even the criteria of efficiency and topicality cannot explain the extraordinary acclaim Rameau's theory achieved, since there were numerous other rival harmonic theories, pedagogical methods, and acoustical principles that ostensibly aimed to answer the same practical and philosophical questions, and did so quite adequately (e.g. *partimenti* traditions and Tartini's combination tones). What ultimately set Rameau's theory apart from the others is that it offered a solution to these questions using language that enjoyed high prestige. Put another way, its *rhetoric* was persuasive.

Throughout this study, I have tried to show how Rameau was a more sophisticated intellectual figure than has traditionally been portrayed by music historians. We have seen how he tested a variety of philosophical methods and scientific languages, which, while individually insufficient in accommodating the richness and vicissitudes of his thoughts, together help to define the complex enterprise that was his system of harmony: neoplatonism, Cartesian mechanism, Newtonian experimental science, sensationalist psychology, neoclassical aesthetics, and occasionalism. His writings, as I have argued, traverse a surprisingly large amount of the variegated intellectual terrain that was the eighteenth-century French Enlightenment.

Beginning with the *Traité* in 1722, Rameau employed a self-conscious Cartesian rhetoric of mechanistic causation superimposed upon remnants of neoplatonic thinking. Each of these qualities was calculated to appeal to members of Rameau's projected audience. When in the 1730s Rameau's rhetoric became more "Newtonian," and then more "Lockean" in the 1750s, it was in order to persuade different readers of the value of the *corps sonore*; his differing philosophical postures (the experimental evidence he cited in the *Génération harmonique* on behalf of his *corps sonore*, or the reconstruction of the sensationalist process by which he first "experienced" the *corps sonore*) were not so much depictions of the actual way he arrived at his principle of harmony as rhetorical strategies for securing the widest possible acceptance for that principle.

The influence Rameau's theory enjoyed during his lifetime must be attributed, I think, in no small part to the fact that he was able to tap so successfully into culturally resonant rhetorics. He showed an uncanny genius for casting his theory in a rich assortment of intellectual metaphors and models that enjoyed high prestige among his readers. Of course he was not uniformly successful in this regard. Not all of Rameau's models could be so easily reconciled with one another. Nor were they all equally convincing. It was largely because his later occasionalist arguments on behalf of the *corps sonore*, with its aura of a cosmic *musica mundana*, were so anachronistic in the context of a prevailing materialist metaphysics that this aspect of his theory failed so conspicuously to take hold among his readers. We should not conclude from this, though, that the answer is to strip away Rameau's rhetoric in order to expose some underlying and uncontaminated empirical core (the practical solutions he offered to pressing pedagogical questions described above). Rhetoric is not simply an embellishment of some underlying idea, or worse, an obfuscation of that idea. Already in the eighteenth century, writers from Vico to Burke recognized how rhetoric is an integral and even inseparable part of a thought's articulation.[41] We have seen how so many of the most significant tenets of Rameau's theory, from his definitions of dissonance and mode, to his conception of the fundamental bass, were not merely cast into the language of extra-musical ideologies (neoplatonism, Newton's theory of gravity, and Cartesian mechanism), but indeed motivated by them.[42] And

---

41 For a fascinating collection of case studies addressing the critical role of rhetoric in the formulation and acceptance of scientific theories, see *Persuading Science: The Art of Scientific Rhetoric*, ed. Marcello Pera and William R. Shea (Canton, Mass., 1991). A different collection of essays addressing a similar theme within the chronological domain of the present study is *The Figural and the Literal: Problems of Language in the History of Science and Philosophy, 1630–1800*, ed. Andrew E. Benjamin, Geoffrey N. Cantor, and John R. R. Christie (Manchester, 1987).

42 We should also not be so naive as to think that we have somehow escaped ideology in our own theories. The "rhetoric" of contemporary music theory is just as heavily laden with cultural ideology and prejudice as was Rameau's, however value-free we may pretend it is. One need only consider the ideological roots of

we saw the folly of trying to disentangle Rameau's theory from the language with which it is expressed in the case of d'Alembert, who threw out what he perceived to be bogus scientific and metaphysical trappings of Rameau's theory, and not only produced an emaciated picture of this "theory," but thereby exposed his own unmistakable – if unarticulated – biases.

There can never be a completely objective or value-free theoretical observation or analytic statement, since any such statement or observation is prejudiced by one's specific biographical situation or cultural location.[43] The individual notes and rhythms of some musical practice will never present themselves to any observer, no matter how unbiased or perspicacious, as a complete theory of music. Rameau was not a great theorist because he could look more objectively or synoptically at musical practice. If anything, we might say that one of Rameau's talents lay in knowing what empirical evidence to ignore or defer lest it deter him from developing his more global ideas. A music theory, like any kind of theory, is a construction, not an induction. It represents an interpretive grid superimposed upon musical material that determines the analytic questions to be posed, and the language and arguments deemed sufficient to answer them. And this interpretive grid is necessarily one built from plans and material indigenous to its author's historical-cultural location. This is not to say that a theory and its answers are already predetermined by its culture. It is to say, though, that the construction of such a theory is necessarily circumscribed by the culture within which it is articulated and received.

The dependence of music theory – or really any kind of theory – upon political and rhetorical factors may strike some readers as a baleful situation, one the theorist ought to strive to mitigate as much as possible. I would argue, on the contrary, that such a dependence can be a virtue. Only to the degree that music theory responds to questions of pressing import of its time in a culturally-resonant language does it accrue vitality. Music theory for someone like Rameau was not a discipline standing outside his culture, but one intrinsically a part of it.[44] Of course, a theory has the possibility of not just responding to cultural forces, but also of redirecting them.

Schenkerian theory – probably the most culturally saturated and politically motivated perspective on music to be enunciated in the twentieth century.

[43] Many readers will recognize that my comments here intersect with much post-positivist criticism that has achieved widespread currency in fields ranging from the history of science to literary theory. While I cannot possibly do justice to this idea by any further elaboration within this footnote, I shall let suffice a single striking example from a book I happened to have been reading while writing this chapter: Stephen Jay Gould, *Time's Arrow, Time's Cycle* (Cambridge, Mass., 1987). In tracing the discovery of "deep time" in the annals of geology, Gould looked at the theories of three chronologically distinct British geologists: Thomas Burnet (seventeenth century), James Hutton (eighteenth century), and Charles Lyell (nineteenth century). Gould shows how all three men embraced differing theological and philosophical world views that both motivated and delimited their research, and consequently the kinds of conclusions they could draw from their field investigations. Their respective theories of geological time, Gould concludes, came about not by "superior knowledge of rocks in the field." Rather, "their visions stood prior – logically, psychologically, and in the ontogeny of their thoughts – to their attempts at empirical support" (pp. 9–10).

[44] I have developed this hermeneutic thesis in some detail in my article "Music Theory and its Histories," *Music Theory and the Exploration of the Past*, ed. David Bernstein and Christopher Hatch (Chicago, 1993), 23–51.

The truly revolutionary accomplishment of Rameau, I think, consisted in the overall reconceptualization of music and the music-theoretical enterprise he envisioned. Almost single-handedly, he redirected the focus of music theory to questions involving chordal generation, harmonic coherence, and tonal identity, questions that still resonate today. Moreover, he offered a convincing analytic method and vocabulary informed by contemporaneous science by which these questions could be answered. Yet for all the solutions Rameau's theory offered, there still remained nagging empirical discrepancies. Far from falsifying his theory, though, these discrepancies offered an agenda of puzzles to be solved by the immediate generation of theorists following Rameau (Marpurg, Roussier, etc.). Each of these theorists attempted to revise or extend the fundamental bass to solve particular empirical discrepancies or systematic deficiencies. Nonetheless, they all remained within the general epistemological framework laid down by Rameau.[45] To this day, much of the discourse related to tonal harmony is still carried out in the scientific terms and perspectives first articulated by Rameau, however much our own cultural rhetoric has transformed them. Never was a music theory so pliable in the face of such an extraordinary evolution of musical style, or so tenacious and resilient in the face of such conflicting exegetes. And in spite of the bewildering diversity and pluralism that so characterizes our own musical and intellectual climate, no music theorist continues to exert such a profound presence.

[45] The qualities I have assigned Rameau's theory here deliberately resemble Thomas Kuhn's description of a scientific research "paradigm" as articulated in his famous study, *The Structure of Scientific Revolutions*, 2nd edition (Chicago, 1970). I would not want to push the analogy between Rameau's music theory and Kuhn's paradigm too far, though, as there exist a number of obvious differences between the two, not the least being the quite differing ontological objects of musical analysis and natural science. There also need not be an incommensurability between rival theories in music as Kuhn claims exists in science. Nonetheless, to the degree that Rameau's theory has provided a heuristic "exemplar" of a successful music theory, I do find many of Kuhn's ideas highly suggestive in respect of the historical reception of Rameau's theory.

Appendix 1

A NOTE ON HARMONIC AND ARITHMETIC PROPORTIONS

Because the harmonic and arithmetic proportions are critical to canonist theory – and especially Rameau's – it is important that the reader understand their respective mathematical operations if confusion is to be avoided.

The primary function of the monochord is to offer an efficient means of measuring and sounding intervals with meaningful musical applications. This is accomplished by "dividing" the monochord following some prescribed formula. Greek mathematics offers two such ways in the harmonic and arithmetic proportions. (A third proportion – the geometric – has a somewhat different application that will not be considered here.)

The arithmetic and harmonic proportions are two complementary techniques for finding a mean between any two numerical terms. Put simply, the arithmetic mean B lies an equal distance between the extremes A and C. Thus, $A - B = B - C$.

Solving for B, the arithmetic mean will be: $B = \dfrac{A+C}{2}$

The harmonic mean B exceeds and is exceeded by equal parts of the extremes. Thus, $\dfrac{A-B}{B-C} = \dfrac{A}{C}$

Solving for B, the harmonic mean will be: $B = \dfrac{2AC}{A+C}$

To put this now into musical terms, let us take two strings tuned to an octave. The ratio of their lengths will be 2 : 1, or to avoid fractions, the ratio 12 : 6. The number 12 designates the longer string and represents the lower note of the interval, while 6 (being half the length of 12) the note lying an octave higher. In the arithmetic division, 9 is the mean, since 9 is an equal distance from 12 and 6 (12 − 9 = 9 − 6). In the harmonic division, however, 8 is the mean, since 8 is one third greater than 6, and one third less than 12 ($\frac{12-8}{8-6} = \frac{12}{6}$). Musically, then, the arithmetic division of an octave results in a perfect fourth on the bottom and a perfect fifth on top (12 : 9 and 9 : 6 = 4 : 3 and 3 : 2), while the harmonic division results in a reversed ordering (12 : 8 and 8 : 6 = 3 : 2 and 4 : 3).

We can likewise divide the perfect fifth (3 : 2) using arithmetic and harmonic proportions. This results in divisions of the minor and major thirds (6 : 5 and 5 : 4), and major and minor thirds (5 : 4 and 6 : 5), respectively. We can begin to see by these results (and it is easy to prove) that the arithmetic and harmonic proportions are inversionally related to one another. If we concatenate each of these proportions in a series, we would produce starting from 1 an arithmetic series: 1, 2, 3, 4, 5, 6, etc.; and a harmonic series: 1, ½, ⅓, ¼, ⅕, ⅙, etc.

While the mathematics involved in both these operations is relatively straightforward, confusion often arises when theorists change the terms by which they define their intervals. In the seventeenth century, for example, there were two common ways of marking monochord divisions: as string parts or string multiples. By the former method, the string divisions represent fractional *parts* of the whole string. The octave ratio is thus represented by 1 : ½ (or 12 : 6 as we just saw). In the latter method, the string divisions represent *multiples* of the string. Now the octave ratio is inverted and becomes 1 : 2. (Such inverted designations make sense when interval ratios are understood as representing frequencies.) This renumbering has the effect of once again inverting the two processes, so a harmonic division by string parts become an arithmetic division by string multiples, and vice versa. The results are summarized below.

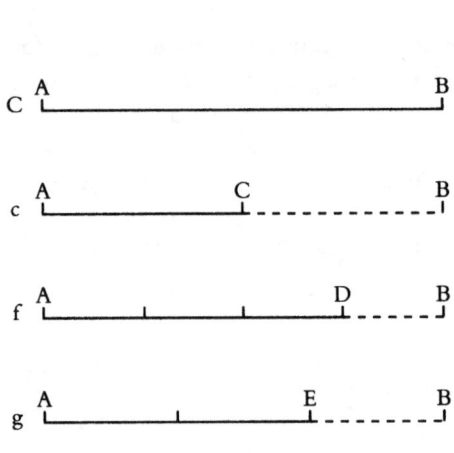

	String "Parts"	String "Multiples"
	AB = 1	AB = 1
	AC = $\frac{1}{2}$	AC = 2
	Arithmetic Mean	
	AD = $\frac{3}{4}(1:\frac{3}{4}:\frac{1}{2})$	AE = $\frac{3}{2}(1:\frac{3}{2}:2)$
	Harmonic Mean	
	AE = $\frac{2}{3}(1:\frac{2}{3}:\frac{1}{2})$	AD = $\frac{4}{3}(1:\frac{4}{3}:2)$

Appendix 2

"L'ART DE LA BASSE FONDAMENTALE" AND GIANOTTI'S *LE GUIDE DU COMPOSITEUR*

Among the papers of d'Alembert now housed in the archives of the Institut de France, there is a lengthy bound manuscript entitled "L'Art de la basse fondamentale" (*F-Pi* Ms 2474). While no author is indicated on the title page, a reading of the opening paragraph suggests that it is none other than Rameau:

> After having declared my discoveries concerning the principle of harmony and of all our faculties of music contained in a single sound, after having cleared the way for what I have called the fundamental bass, and after having revealed [its] relationship through an infinity of experiments [in the] *traité de l'harmonie, nouveau sisteme*, and *generation harmonique*, 172[2], [17]2[6], and [17]3[7], I have finally undertaken to bring forth a method for composition and accompaniment entitled "The Art of the Fundamental Bass."

Based upon both internal and external evidence, there can be little doubt that the manuscript is indeed an authentic work of Rameau's. As I have analyzed the history and content of this manuscript in some detail elsewhere, I shall here only repeat the main evidence and conclusions of this study.[1]

Shortly after Rameau had published his *Génération harmonique* in 1737, he sought to capitalize on his fame as composer by soliciting composition students. To be sure, Rameau already must have had a good deal of experience teaching composition in Clermont-Ferrand, as both Suaudeau's study and the third book of the *Traité* testify. In his polemic with Montéclair, we have further evidence that pedagogical issues continued to interest Rameau after his arrival in Paris. But it is not hard to imagine that he found it easier to attract composition students after his triumphant operatic debut in 1733. Thus it is that we find the following announcement printed in several of the Parisian periodicals towards the end of 1737:

> Monsieur Rameau wishes to inform all amateurs that he proposes to establish a school of composition meeting three times a week from three until five o'clock. The class will be limited to only 12 students and cost 20 francs a month. If the need arises, extra classes will be added, and a limited number of additional students may thereby be accommodated. It is guaranteed that 6 months shall be sufficient for the student to master the science of harmony and its practice, for whatever application, even for those who can scarcely read music, but all the more for those more advanced. It is to satisfy the repeated entreatment of

---

[1] The reader interested in a more detailed analysis of this treatise with a table of its complete contents is referred to my article "Rameau's 'L'Art de la basse fondamentale,'" *Music Theory Spectrum* 9 (1987), 18–41.

certain individuals who are already students of M. Rameau that he has agreed to open his class to the public, hoping by this means that their number may be augmented.[2]

We do not know very much about Rameau's composition school, although according to Rousseau – admittedly not a very objective source – the number of his students multiplied with astonishing rapidity.[3] It seems probable that the "Art of the Fundamental Bass" was written during this period to serve as a kind of composition textbook. We may deduce from the opening paragraph of the text which I quoted that it was written after the publication of the *Génération harmonique* (1737) but before the appearance of the *Démonstration* (1750). We can further narrow the dates from a remark in the *Démonstration* – one of the few by Rameau concerning this manuscript – wherein he complains, "Some years ago . . . I was forced to abandon a method of composition which was already quite advanced. But I entrusted it to a person who is very capable of making both himself and the public profit from it."[4] This would move back the date of the manuscript probably before 1744, the year in which Rameau resumed extensive opera composing after a five-year respite. To whom did Rameau entrust his manuscript? Two individuals are possible candidates. The first is d'Alembert, and the second the Italian violinist-composer Pietro Gianotti.

In Chapter 8 we saw how d'Alembert had become so enamored of Rameau's theory upon first acquaintance in 1749, that he undertook to write his own extensive popularization of it. The result, as we know, was the *Elémens de musique théorique*. Now, the first half of d'Alembert's text was essentially theoretical in nature (being, as we saw in Chapter 9, a revision of the *Démonstration*). The second half of the *Elémens*, however, was to be practical in nature and contain the "rules of composition." While we know that d'Alembert ended up relying upon Chapter 18 of the *Génération harmonique* in writing the section on composition, he evidently also had in his possession manuscript material related to a method of composition. In speaking of his *Elémens*, he expressed the hope that

> I could produce from this treatise one day, if no one prevents me, a work like the one I made for the *Génération harmonique*, and give a complete method of composition of which my elements would be only the base and summary. But it appears that I will not find the three or four years of leisure necessary for such a work. . . But aided by the excellent printed material and manuscripts which I have in my hands, I believe I should be able to succeed . . . in making my treatise clear, precise, and useful.[5]

It would seem probable from this evidence that the manuscript to which d'Alembert refers is none other than the manuscript now among his papers at the Bibliothèque de l'Institut de France: "L'Art de la basse fondamentale." Yet matters are slightly complicated by the existence of a book published in 1759 by Pietro Gianotti.

---

2 *Mercure de France* (December, 1737), 1,648-49; *Le Pour et contre* 13 (1738), 336.
3 Jean-Jacques Rousseau, "Lettre à M. Grimm au sujet des remarques ajoutées à sa lettre sur Omphale," (1752), 22.
4 *Démonstration*, xxiii.
5 *Journal Oeconomique* (December, 1751), 89; *CTW* VI, 264.

The book in question is a composition treatise written by Pietro Gianotti under the title *Le Guide du compositeur* (Paris, 1759). A comparison of Gianotti's treatise with the manuscript "L'Art de la basse fondamentale" reveals that it is based entirely upon the latter manuscript. With the exception of Rameau's preface, every section of the "Art of the Fundamental Bass" is to be found in Gianotti's *Guide*. Gianotti, however, has significantly revised Rameau's turgid and repetitious prose, condensing it into about half its original length, and reorganized the material into a coherent, readable, and even lucid text. Most happily, the musical examples that are missing from Rameau's manuscript are found in Gianotti's book. For all practical purposes, then, Gianotti's *Le Guide du compositeur* can be taken as the published version of "L'Art de la basse fondamentale."[6]

Needless to say, the existence of Gianotti's treatise poses a number of new questions. If Rameau wrote this treatise, how did it end up in published form in 1759 under Gianotti's name? Moreover, if d'Alembert received possession of the text in the early 1750s (and apparently retained possession, considering that the manuscript has remained with his other papers), how could Gianotti have had access to the work? A clue is found in the preface of Gianotti's text: "If I appear to have acquired any knowledge, it is due to M. Rameau," he tells us. Gianotti then imparts this telling information: "The work which I am offering today is the result of lessons I took under his [Rameau's] eyes. His concern has deigned to guide me" (p. vi). This statement, plus what little biographical information we have about Gianotti (from nineteenth-century lexicographers such as Gerber and Fétis), helps the pieces of the puzzle fall into place.

Pietro Gianotti was one of the many Italian émigrés who worked as musicians in Paris in the eighteenth century. Exactly when he moved to Paris from his native Italy is not certain. (We do not even know the year of his birth.) Our first documented record of Gianotti is from 1728, the year in which there appeared in Paris a collection of violin sonatas published under his name. In 1739, we find Gianotti playing double bass in the Paris Opéra orchestra, a position he retained until 1758 when he was pensioned. He died in 1765 – one year after Rameau, and probably not much younger, either.

As an orchestra member of the Paris Opéra active in the 1740s and 50s, Gianotti would have had numerous occasions to meet Rameau. It is clear that he had great respect for Rameau the music theorist. And despite his being an already established – if not particularly distinguished – composer and performer, he evidently sought out Rameau for tutelage in music theory. It may well be that he was one of the "pupils" Rameau taught in his "composition school." The question still remains, though, as to the origins of Gianotti's *Guide*. If the "Art of the Fundamental Bass" indeed represents an authentic work by Rameau reflecting his compositional atelier of the 1740s, how was it that a revised version of it was published in 1759 under Gianotti's name?

---

6 At the time I published the article cited in footnote 1 above, I had not yet discovered the connection between Rameau's manuscript and Gianotti's *Guide*. I first reported this connection in a "Communication to the Editor," *Music Theory Spectrum* 12/2 (1990), 276–77.

Here is what I suspect happened. Recognizing the obvious problems of organization and style in his original text, Rameau turned, as he so often did in his life, to others for help in redacting his ideas for publication. As one of Rameau's most musically experienced "pupils," Gianotti may have been an ideal candidate for the task after d'Alembert declined to undertake the job. (It may even be that the scribe of the manuscript was Gianotti himself, but I have been unable to find an authenticated autograph of his in order to verify this hypothesis.) That Gianotti published his revision of the "Art of the Fundamental Bass" under his own name rather than Rameau's is not at all improbable.

First of all, Gianotti so thoroughly revised the prose of Rameau's manuscript – if leaving untouched the theoretical content – that in a real sense, the text could legitimately be said to be his own. Perhaps Rameau was so grateful to find someone who would spend the time and energy in revising his own prose (and still give due credit to him) that he did not object to it being published under the redactor's name (much as was the case with d'Alembert's *précis*, the *Elémens de musique theorique et pratique suivant les principes de M. Rameau*). Certainly if Rameau thought his ideas were being plagiarized or misrepresented, we have ample evidence to suggest that the irascible and jealous composer would have come out in the open and said so loudly and clearly. (It may be meaningful in this regard that the publisher of Gianotti's *Guide* – Durand – was the same one Rameau used for the publication of his *Démonstration du principe de l'harmonie* of 1750 and the *Nouvelles réflexions* of 1752.)

Secondly, by the time Gianotti published his *Guide*, Rameau was already finished with his own composition treatise, the *Code de musique pratique*. I suspect that Rameau felt his ideas had matured sufficiently so he saw no conflict in having his earlier ideas appear under the name of Gianotti alongside his own publication. The *Code* is a much richer work than is the "Art of the Fundamental Bass," offering far more supple musical illustrations and new material on learning to accompany, sing, and improvise. As to whether the manuscript now in the d'Alembert archive was the same one Gianotti used, we do not know. There could well have been several copies or drafts of this manuscript in circulation. In any case, it was Gianotti, not d'Alembert, who undertook the unenviable task of revising Rameau's original text. Thanks to his efforts, we now have a comprehensive document of inestimable value recording Rameau's practical ideas related to composition pedagogy written during his most productive and prolific years as a composer.

SELECT BIBLIOGRAPHY

Major theoretical publications of Rameau in chronological order

Traité de l'harmonie réduite à ses principes naturels. Paris: Ballard, 1722.
Nouveau système de musique théorique et pratique. Paris: Ballard, 1726.
Dissertation sur les différentes métodes d'accompagnement pour le clavecin ou pour l'orgue. Paris: Boivin, Le Clair, 1732.
Génération harmonique ou traité de musique théorique et pratique. Paris: Prault fils, 1737.
Démonstration du principe de l'harmonie servant de base à tout l'art musical théorique et pratique. Paris: Durand, 1750.
Nouvelles réflexions de M. Rameau sur sa démonstration du principe de l'harmonie. Paris: Durand, 1752.
Extrait d'une réponse de M. Rameau à M. Euler sur l'identité des octaves. Paris: Durand, 1753.
Observations sur notre instinct pour la musique et sur son principe. Paris: Prault fils, 1754.
Erreurs sur la musique dans l'Encyclopédie. Paris: Sébastien Jorry, 1755.
Suite des erreurs sur la musique dans l'Encyclopédie. Paris: Sébastien Jorry, 1756.
Réponse de M. Rameau à MM. les éditeurs de l'Encyclopédie sur leur dernier avertissement. Paris: Sébastien Jorry, 1757.
Code de musique pratique ou méthodes pour apprendre la musique . . . avec de nouvelles réflexions sur le principe sonore. Paris: Imprimerie royale, 1760.
Lettre à M. d'Alembert sur ses opinions en musique insérées dans les articles "Fondamental" et "Gamme" de l'Encyclopédie. Paris, 1760.

Primary sources published before 1800 (includes modern editions and translations)

Alembert, Jean Le Rond d'. *Elémens de musique théorique et pratique suivant les principes de M. Rameau*. Paris, 1752. 2nd edition, Lyons, 1762.
 Oeuvres philosophiques, historiques, et littéraires. 5 vols. Paris, 1821–22.
 Preliminary Discourse to the Encyclopedia of Diderot. Trans. Richard N. Schwab. Indianapolis, 1963.
 Traité de dynamique. Paris, 1743.
 "Recherches sur les vibrations des cordes sonores." *Opuscules Mathematiques*, vol. VI. Paris, 1761.
Batteux, Charles. *Les Beaux-arts réduits à un même principe*. Paris, 1746.
Berardi, Angelo. *Documenti armonici*. Bologna, 1687.
Bernoulli, Daniel. "Réflexions et éclaircissemens sur les nouvelles vibrations des cordes exposées dans les mémoires de 1747 & 1748." *Histoire de l'Académie royale des sciences et belles lettres* 9 (Berlin, 1753): 148–72.
 "Sur le mélange de plusieurs especes de vibrations simples isochrones, qui peuvent coexister dans un même système de corps." *Histoire de l'Académie royale des sciences et belles lettres* 9 (Berlin, 1753): 173–95.

Bethizy, Jean-Laurent de. *Exposition de la théorie et de la pratique de la musique.* Paris, 1764.
Blainville, Charles-Henri. *Harmonie théorico-pratique.* Paris, 1746.
   Historie générale critique et philologique de la musique. Paris, 1767.
Briseux, Charles Etienne. *Traité du Beau essentiel dans les Arts.* 2 vols. Paris, 1752.
Brossard, Abbé Sébastien de. *Dictionaire de musique.* Paris, 1703.
Campion, François. *Traité d'accompagnement et de composition selon la règle des octaves de musique.* Paris, 1716.
Castel, Louis-Bertrand. *L'Optique des couleurs.* Paris, 1740.
   Le Vrai Système de physique générale de M. Isaac Newton exposé et analysé en paralléle avec celui de Descartes. Paris, 1743.
Chabanon, Michel-Paul-Guy de. *Eloge de M. Rameau.* Paris, 1764.
   Observations sur la musique et principalement sur la metaphysique de l'art. Paris, 1779.
Condillac, Étienne Bonnot de. *Oeuvres.* 16 vols. Paris 1778.
Dandrieu, Jean-François. *Principes de l'accompagnement du clavecin.* Paris, 1719.
Delair, Denis. *Traité d'accompagnement.* Paris, 1690.
Descartes, René. *The Philosophical Works of Descartes.* Trans. E. Haldane and G. Ross. 2 vols. New York, 1955.
   Compendium of Music. Trans. Walter Roberts. American Institute of Musicology, 1961.
Diderot, Denis. *Correspondance,* ed. G. Roth. 16 vols. Paris, 1955–70.
   Oeuvres complètes. Paris, 1975–.
   Rameau's Nephew and Other Works. Trans. Jacques Barzun and Ralph H. Bowen. Indianapolis, 1964.
Diderot, Denis, et al. *Encyclopédie, ou Dictionnaire raisonné des sciences des arts et des métiers.* 17 vols. Paris, 1751–65.
Dubos, Abbé Jean-Baptiste. *Réflexions critiques sur la poesie et sur la peinture.* Paris, 1719.
Ducharger. *Réflexions sur divers ouvrages de M. Rameau.* Rennes, 1761.
Estève, Pierre. *Nouvelle découverte du principe de l'harmonie.* Paris, 1751.
Euler, Leonhard. *Opera Omnia.* 4 Series. Various editors and publishers. Leipzig, etc., 1912–.
Fontenelle, Bernard Le Bovier de. "Sur l'application des sons harmoniques aux jeux d'orgues." *Histoire de l'Académie royale des sciences* 1702 (Paris, 1704): 90–93.
   "Sur un nouveau systême de musique." *Histoire de l'Académie royale des sciences* 1701 (Paris, 1704): 123–39.
   Conversations on the Plurality of Worlds. Trans. H. A. Hargreaves. Cambridge, 1990.
Fouchy, Jean-Paul Grandjean de. *Histoire de l'Académie royale des sciences: Centiéme ou dernier Volume de la premiére centurie.* Amsterdam, 1760.
Frere, Alexandre. *Transpositions de musique réduite au naturel par le secours de la modulation.* Paris, 1706.
Gasparini, Francesco. *L'armonico pratico al cimbalo.* Venice, 1708.
Gervais, Laurent. *Méthode pour l'accompagnement du clavecin.* Paris, 1733.
Gianotti, Pietro. *Le Guide du compositeur.* Paris, 1759.
Grimm, Friedrich Melchior von, Diderot, etc. *Correspondance littéraire, philosophique, et critique,* ed. Maurice Tourneux. 16 vols. Paris, 1877–82.
Hawkins, John. *A General History of the Science and Practice of Music.* 5 vols. London, 1776.
Hotteterre, Jacques. *Principes de la flute traversière.* Paris, 1707.
Laborde, Jean Benjamin de. *Essai sur la musique ancienne et moderne.* 4 vols. Paris, 1780.
Lagrange, Joseph-Louis. *Oeuvres,* ed. M. Serret and L. Lalanne. 14 vols. Paris, 1867–92.
Levens, Charles. *Abrégé des regles de l'harmonie pour apprendre la composition.* Bordeaux, 1743.
Loulié, Etienne. *Eléments ou Principes de musique.* Paris, 1698.
Mairan, Jean-Jacques Dortous de. "Discours sur la propagation du son dans les différens tons qui le modifient." *Mémoires de l'Académie royale des sciences* 1737 (Amsterdam, 1737): 1–87.

Maret, Hugues. *Eloge historique de Mr. Rameau*. Dijon, 1766.
Marpurg, Friedrich Wilhelm. *Systematische Einleitung in die Musicalische Setzkunst nach den Lehrsätzen des Herrn Rameau*. Leipzig, 1757.
Masson, Charles. *Nouveau Traité des règles pour la composition de la musique*. Paris, 1699.
Mersenne, Marin. *Harmonie universelle contenant la théorie et la pratique de la musique*. Paris, 1636. Reprint edition. Paris, 1963.
  Correspondance du P. Marin Mersenne, ed. Cornelis de Waard. 16 vols. Paris, 1932–86.
Mignot, La Voye. *Traité de musique pour bien et facilement apprendre à chanter et composer*. Paris, 1656.
Montucla, Jean-Etienne. *Histoire des mathématiques dans laquelle on rend compte de leurs progrès depuis leur origine jusqu'à nos jours*. Paris, 1758.
Newton, Sir Isaac. *Opticks*. 4th edition. London, 1730. Reprint edition, New York, 1952.
Nivers, Guillaume Gabriel. *Traité de la composition de musique*. Paris, 1667.
Nollet, Jean-Antoine. *Leçons de physique expérimentale*. 6 vols. Paris, 1743–48.
Ouvrard, René. *Architecture harmonique ou application de la doctrine des proportions de la musique à l'architecture*. Paris, 1679.
Pluche, Abbé. *Le Spectacle de la nature*. 8 vols. Paris, 1732.
Poliniére, Pierre. *Expériences de physique*. Paris, 1709.
Rousseau, Jean-Jacques. *Correspondance complète*, ed. R. A. Leigh. 36 vols. Geneva, 1965–.
  Oeuvres complètes. 12 vols. Paris, 1872.
  Confessions. London, 1925.
Sauveur, Joseph. *Collected Writings on Musical Acoustics (Paris 1700–1713)*, ed. Rudolf Rasch. Utrecht, 1984.
Serre, Jean-Adam. *Essais sur les principes de l'harmonie*. Paris, 1753.
  Observations sur les principes de l'harmonie. Geneva, 1763.
Taylor, Brook. "De Motu Nervi Tensi." *Philosophical Transactions* 28 (1713): 26–32.
Voltaire. *Eléments de la philosophie de Neuton, mis à la portée de tout le monde*. Amsterdam, 1738.
  Œuvres complètes, ed. Louis Moland. 52 vols. Paris, 1877–85
Wallis, John. "A Letter to the Publisher Concerning a New Musical Discovery." *Philosophical Transactions* 12 (April, 1677): 839–42.
Werckmeister, Andreas. *Musicae mathematicae hodegus curiosus*. Frankfurt, 1687.
Zarlino, Gioseffo. *Le istitutioni harmoniche* (Venice, 1558). English trans. of Book 3 as *The Art of Counterpoint*. Trans. Guy A. Marco and Claude Palisca. New Haven, 1968. English trans. of Book 4 as *On the Modes*. Trans. Vered Cohen. New Haven, 1983.

Secondary bibliography published after 1800

Adkins, Cecil C. "The Technique of the Monochord." *Acta Musicologica* 39 (1967): 34–41.
Anderson, Gene Henry. "Musical Terminology in J. P. Rameau's *Traité de l'harmonie*; a Study and Glossary Based on an Index." Ph.D. dissertation, The University of Iowa, 1981.
Arnold, Franck T. *The Art of Accompaniment from a Thorough Bass*. Oxford, 1931.
Auger, Léon. "Les apports de J. Sauveur (1653–1716) à la création de l'acoustique." *Revue d'histoire des sciences* 1 (1947–48): 323–36.
Baumeister, Xenia. *Diderots Ästhetik der Rapports*. Frankfurt, 1985.
Beaussant, Philippe, ed. *Rameau de A à Z*. Paris, 1983.
Becker, Carl. *The Heavenly City of the Eighteenth-Century Philosophers*. New Haven, 1935.
Bernard, Jonathan. "The Principle and the Elements: Rameau's Controversy with d'Alembert." *Journal of Music Theory* 24/1 (1980): 37–62.
Berthier, Paul. *Réflexions sur l'art et la vie de Jean-Philippe Rameau*. Paris, 1957.
Brenet, Michel. *La Jeunesse de Rameau*. Turin, 1902.

Brunet, Pierre. *L'Introduction des théories de Newton en France au XVIIIe siècle*. Paris, 1931.
Burtt, E. A. *The Metaphysical Foundations of Modern Science*. Revised edition. Garden City, N.Y., 1954.
Busch, Hermann R. *Leonhard Eulers Beitrag zur Musiktheorie*. Regensburg, 1970.
Cannon, John, and Sigalia Dostrovsky. *The Evolution of Dynamics: Vibration Theory from 1687 to 1742*. New York, 1981.
Cassirer, Ernst. *The Philosophy of the Enlightenment*. Trans. Fritz C. A. Koelln and James P. Pettegrove. Boston, 1955.
Chailley, Jacques. "Rameau et la théorie musicale." *La Revue Musicale* 260 (1964): 65–95.
Christensen, Thomas. "Eighteenth-Century Science and the *corps sonore*: the Scientific Background to Rameau's Principle of Harmony." *Journal of Music Theory* 31/1 (1987): 23–50.
   "Music Theory as Scientific Propaganda: The Case of D'Alembert's *Elémens de musique*." *Journal of the History of Ideas* 50 (1989): 409–27.
   "Rameau's 'L'Art de la basse fondamentale.'" *Music Theory Spectrum* 9 (1987): 18–41.
   "The *Règle de l'octave* in Thorough-Bass Theory and Practice." *Acta Musicologica* 64/2 (1992): 91–117.
   "The Spanish Baroque Guitar and Seventeenth-Century Triadic Theory." *Journal of Music Theory* 36/1 (1992): 1–42.
   "Science and Music Theory in the Enlightenment: D'Alembert's Critique of Rameau." Ph.D. dissertation, Yale University, 1985.
Cohen, Albert. "*La Supposition* or the Changing Concepts of Dissonance in Baroque Theory." *Journal of the American Musicological Society* 24 (1971): 63–85.
   "17th Century Music Theory: France." *Journal of Music Theory* 16/1–2 (1972): 16–35.
   Music in the French Royal Academy of Sciences: A Study in the Evolution of Musical Thought. Princeton, 1981.
Cohen, Albert, and Leta E. Miller. *Music in the Paris Academy of Sciences 1666–1793. A Source Archive in Photocopy at Stanford University: An Index*. Detroit Studies in Music Bibliography No. 43. Detroit, 1979.
Cohen, H. F. *Quantifying Music: The Science of Music at the First Stage of the Scientific Revolution 1580–1650*. Dordrecht, 1984.
Cohen, I. Bernard. *The Newtonian Revolution, with Illustrations of the Transformation of Scientific Ideas*. Cambridge, 1980.
Cranston, Maurice. *Jean-Jacques: The Early Life and Work of Jean-Jacques Rousseau 1712–1754*. London, 1983.
Crocker, Lester. "The Enlightenment: What and Who?" *Studies in Eighteenth-Century Culture* 17 (1987): 335–47.
Dahlhaus, Carl. *Studies on the Origin of Harmonic Tonality*. Trans. Robert O. Gjerdingen. Princeton, 1990.
   "Ist Rameau's *Traité de l'harmonie* eine Harmonielehre?" *Musiktheorie* 1/2 (1986): 123–27.
Dear, Peter. *Mersenne and the Learning of the Schools*. Ithaca, 1988.
Demidov, S. S. "Création et développement de la théorie des équations différentielles aux dérivées partielles dans les travaux de J. d'Alembert." *Revue d'histoire des sciences* 35/1 (1982): 3–42.
Didier, Béatrice. *La Musique des lumières: Diderot – L'Encyclopédie – Rousseau*. Paris, 1985.
Dinter, Annegret. *Der Pygmalion-Stoff in der europäischen Literatur*. Heidelberg, 1979.
Doolittle, James. "A Would-be Philosophe, Jean-Philippe Rameau." *Publication of the Modern Language Association* 74 (1959): 233–48.
Dostrovsky, Sigalia. "Early Vibrational Theory: Physics and Music in the Seventeenth Century." *Archive for History of Exact Sciences* 14 (1975): 169–218.

"The Origins of Vibrational Theory: The Scientific Revolution and the Nature of Music." Ph.D. dissertation, Princeton University, 1969.

Duchez, Marie-Elisabeth. "D'Alembert diffuseur de la théorie harmonique de Rameau: déduction scientifique et simplification musicale." *Jean d'Alembert savant et philosophe: Portrait à plusieurs voix.* Ed. Monique Emery and Pierre Monzani. Paris, 1989, 475–99.

"Valeur épistémologique de la théorie de la basse fondamentale de Jean-Philippe Rameau: connaissance scientifique et représentation de la musique." *Studies on Voltaire and the Eighteenth Century* 254 (1986): 91–130.

Durand-Sendrail, Béatrice. "Diderot et Rameau: Archéologie d'une polémique." *Diderot Studies* 24 (1991): 85–104.

Engelsman, Steven B. "D'Alembert et les équations aux dérivées partielles." *Dix-Huitième Siècle* 16 (1984): 27–37.

Escal, François. "D'Alembert et la théorie harmonique de Rameau." *Dix-Huitième Siècle* 16 (1984): 151–62.

"Musique et Science: d'Alembert contre Rameau." *International Review of the Aesthetics and Sociology of Music* 14/2 (1983): 167–89.

Essar, Dennis. "The Language Theory, Epistemology and Aesthetics of Jean Le Rond d'Alembert." *Studies on Voltaire and the Eighteenth Century* 159 (1976).

Farrar, Lloyd P. "The Concept of Overtones in Scientific and Musical Thought (Descartes to Rameau)." Master's thesis, University of Illinois, Urbana, 1956.

Fauvel, John, editor. *Let Newton Be! A New Perspective on his Life and Works.* Oxford, 1988.

Ferris, Joan. "The Evolution of Rameau's Harmonic Theories." *Journal of Music Theory* 3/1 (1959): 231–55.

Fétis, François-Joseph. *Biographie universelle des musiciens.* 2nd edition. 8 vols. Paris: 1873–75.

Fuss, P. *Correspondance mathématique et physique de quelques célèbres géomètres du XVIIIème siècle.* 2 vols. St. Petersburg, 1843.

Gay, Peter. *The Enlightenment: An Interpretation.* 2 vols. New York, 1966–69.

The Party of Humanity: Essays on the French Enlightenment. Princeton, 1959.

Gessele, Cynthia. "The Institutionalization of Music Theory in France: 1764–1802." Ph.D. dissertation, Princeton University, 1989.

Gillispie, Charles C. *The Edge of Objectivity: An Essay in the History of Scientific Ideas.* Princeton, 1960.

Girdlestone, Cuthbert M. *Jean-Philippe Rameau: His Life and Work.* 2nd edition. New York, 1969.

Gorce, Jérome de la, editor. *Jean-Philippe Rameau: Colloque international organisé par La Société Rameau.* Paris, 1987.

Grant, Cecil Powell. "The Real Relationship Between Kirnberger's and Rameau's Concept of the Fundamental Bass." *Journal of Music Theory* 21/2 (Fall, 1977): 324–38.

Green, Burdette. "The Harmonic Series from Mersenne to Rameau: An Historical Study of Circumstances Leading to its Recognition and Application to Music." Ph.D. dissertation, The Ohio State University, 1969.

Grimsley, Ronald. *Jean d'Alembert.* Oxford, 1970.

Grossman, Lionel. "Time and History in Rousseau." *Studies on Voltaire and the Eighteenth Century* 30 (1964).

Groth, Renate. "Italienische Musiktheorie im 17. Jahrhundert." *Geschichte der Musiktheorie*, vol. 7. Darmstadt, 1989, 307–90.

Guerlac, Henry. *Newton on the Continent.* Ithaca, 1981.

Hankins, Thomas L. *Jean d'Alembert, Science and the Enlightenment.* Oxford, 1970.

Science and the Enlightenment. Cambridge, 1985.

Hayes, Deborah. "Rameau's 'Nouvelle Méthode.'" *Journal of the American Musicological Society* 27/1 (1974): 65–74.

Hazard, Paul. *European Thought in the Eighteenth Century*. New Haven, 1954.
Helmholtz, Hermann. *On the Sensations of Tone*. Trans. Alexander Ellis. New York, 1954.
Hine, Ellen McNiven. *A Critical Study of Condillac's "Traité des systèmes."* The Hague, 1979.
Hunt, Frederick V. *Origins in Acoustics*. New Haven, 1978.
Hunt, Thomas W. "The *Dictionnaire de musique* of Jean-Jacques Rousseau." Ph.D. dissertation, North Texas State University, 1967.
Hyde, Frederick. "The Position of Marin Mersenne in the History of Music." Ph.D. dissertation, Yale University, 1954.
Isherwood, Robert. *Music in the Service of the King: France in the Seventeenth Century*. Ithaca, 1973.
Jacob, Margaret C. *The Radical Enlightenment: Pantheists, Freemasons and Republicans*. London, 1981.
Jacobi, Erwin, editor. *Jean-Philippe Rameau: Complete Theoretical Writings*. 6 vols. Rome, 1967–72.
  "Vérités intérressantes: Le Dernier Manuscrit de Rameau." *Revue de Musicologie* 50 (1964): 76–109.
  "Rameau and Padre Martini: New Letters and Documents." *The Musical Quarterly* 50 (1964): 452–75.
Jam, Jean-Louis, ed. *Rameau en Auvergne MCMLXXXIII*. Clermont-Ferrand, 1986.
Keiler, Allan R. "Music as Metalanguage: Rameau's Fundamental Bass." *Music Theory Special Topics*, ed. Richmond Browne. New York, 1981, 83–100.
Kiernan, Colm. "The Enlightenment and Science in Eighteenth-Century France." *Studies on Voltaire and the Eighteenth Century* 59 (1973).
Kintzler, Catherine. *Jean-Philippe Rameau: Splendeur et naufrage de l'esthétique du plaisir à l'age classique*. Paris, 1983.
  "Rameau et Voltaire: les enjeux théoriques d'une collaboration orageuse." *Revue de Musicologie* 67 (1981): 139–68.
Kleinbaum, Abby R. "Jean Jacques Dortous de Mairan (1687–1771): A Study of an Enlightenment Scientist." Ph.D. dissertation, Columbia University, 1970.
Knight, Isabel. *The Geometric Spirit: The Abbé de Condillac and the French Enlightenment*. New Haven, 1968.
Koyré, Alexander. *From the Closed World to the Infinite Universe*. Baltimore, 1957.
Kuhn, Thomas. *The Essential Tension: Selected Studies in Scientific Traditions and Change*. Chicago, 1977.
  The Structure of Scientific Revolutions. 2nd edition, Chicago, 1970.
Lalo, Charles. *Eléments d'une esthétique musicale scientifique*. Paris, 1939.
Lang, Paul Henry. "Diderot as Musician." *Diderot Studies* 10 (1969): 95–107.
Launay, Denise, ed. *Querelle des Bouffons*. 3 vols. Geneva, 1973.
Lester, Joel. *Between Modes and Keys: German Theory 1592–1802*. Stuyvesant, N.Y., 1989.
  Compositional Theory in the Eighteenth Century. Cambridge, Mass., 1992.
Lewin, David. "Two Interesting Passages in Rameau's *Traité de l'harmonie*." *In Theory Only* 4/3 (1978): 3–11.
Lovejoy, Arthur. *The Great Chain of Being: A Study of the History of an Idea*. Cambridge, 1936.
Ludwig, Hellmut. *Marin Mersenne und seine Musiklehre*. Halle, 1935.
Malignon, Jean. *Rameau*. Paris, 1960.
Masson, Paul-Marie. *L'Opéra de Rameau*. Paris, 1930.
Maxham, Robert E. "The Contributions of Joseph Sauveur (1653–1716) to Acoustics." Ph.D. dissertation, University of Rochester, 1976.
May, Henry. *The Enlightenment in America*. New York, 1976.
Miller, Leta E. "Rameau and the Royal Society of London: New Letters and Documents." *Music and Letters* 66/1 (January, 1985): 19–33.

Morche, Gunther. "Règle de l'Octave und Basse Fondamentale." *International Musicology Society; Report of the 11th Congress*. Copenhagen, 1972. (Kassel, 1974): 556–61.
Oliver, Alfred R. *The Encyclopedists as Critics of Music*. New York, 1947.
Palisca, Claude. "Scientific Empiricism in Musical Thought." *Seventeenth Century Science in the Arts*, ed. Hedley Howell Rhys. Princeton, 1961, 91–137.
Pappas, John. "Berthier's *Journal de Trévoux* and the Philosophes." *Studies on Voltaire and the Eighteenth Century* 3 (1957).
Paul, Charles. "Rameau's Musical Theories and the Age of Reason." Ph.D. dissertation, University of California, Berkeley, 1966.
  "Jean-Philippe Rameau (1683–1764), The Musician as *Philosophe*." *Proceedings of the American Philosophical Society* 114/2 (April, 1970): 140–54.
Pirro, André. *Descartes et la musique*. Paris, 1907.
Pischner, Hans. *Die Harmonielehre Jean-Philippe Rameaus*. Leipzig, 1963.
Porter, Roy. *The Enlightenment*. Atlantic Highlands, N.J., 1990.
Ravetz, Jerome R. "Vibrating Strings and Arbitrary Functions." *The Logic of Personal Knowledge: Essays Presented to Michael Polanyi on his Seventieth Birthday*. London, 1961, 71–88.
Richbourg, Louisette. *Contribution à l'histoire de la querelle des Bouffons*. Paris, 1937.
Riemann, Hugo. *Geschichte der Musiktheorie*. 2nd edition. Leipzig, 1920.
Robrieux, Jean-Jacques. "Jean-Philippe Rameau et l'Opinion philosophique en France au dix-huitième siècle." *Studies on Voltaire and the Eighteenth Century* 238 (1985): 269–395.
Rousseau, G. S., and Roy Porter, eds. *The Fermentation of Knowledge: Studies in the Historiography of Eighteenth-Century Science*. London, 1980.
Sabra, A. I. *Theories of Light from Descartes to Newton*. Cambridge, 1981.
Sawkins, Lionel. "Rameau's Last Years: Some Implications of Rediscovered Material at Bordeaux." *Proceedings of the Royal Musical Association* 111 (1984): 66–91.
Schenker, Heinrich. "Rameau oder Beethoven? Erstarrung oder geistiges Leben in der Musik?" *Das Meisterwerk in der Musik* 3 (1930): 11–24.
Schier, Donald S. *Louis-Bertrand Castel, Anti-Newtonian Scientist*. Cedar Rapids, Iowa, 1941.
Schneider, Herbert. *Die französische Kompositionslehre in der ersten Hälfte des 17. Jahrhunderts*. Tutzing, 1972.
  "Charles Masson und sein *Nouveau Traité*." *Archiv für Musikwissenschaft* 30/4 (1973): 245–74.
  "Rameau's Musiktheoretisches Vermächtnis." *Musiktheorie* 1/2 (1986): 153–61.
  Jean-Philippe Rameaus letzter Musiktraktat. Wiesbaden, 1986.
Seidel, Wilhelm. "Französische Musiktheorie im 16. und 17. Jahrhundert." *Geschichte der Musiktheorie*. Vol. 9. Darmstadt, 1986, 1–140.
Semmens, Richard. "Etienne Loulié and the New Harmonic Counterpoint." *Journal of Music Theory* 27/2 (1984): 73–88.
Shirlaw, Matthew. *The Theory of Harmony*. London, 1917.
Suaudeau, René. *Introduction à l'harmonie de Rameau*. Clermont-Ferrand, 1960.
Tiersot, J. *Leçons de Musique de Jean-Jacques Rousseau*. Paris, 1912–13.
Truesdell, Clifford. "A Program Toward Rediscovering the Rational Mechanics of the Age of Reason." *Archive for History of Exact Sciences* 1/1 (1960): 1–36.
  "The Rational Mechanics of Flexible or Elastic Bodies, 1638–1788." *Euleri Opera Omnia*. Leipzig, etc., 1912–. Series 2, vol. XI/2.
  "The Theory of Aerial Sound 1687–1788." *Euleri Opera Omnia*. Leipzig, etc., 1912–. Series 2, vol. XIII, xix–lxxii.
Vartanian, Aram. *Diderot and Descartes: A Study of Scientific Naturalism in the Enlightenment*. Princeton, 1953.
Verba, Cynthia. "The Development of Rameau's Thoughts on Modulation and Chromaticism." *Journal of the American Musicological Society* 26/1 (1973): 69–97.

"Rameau's Views on Modulation and Their Background in French Theory." *Journal of the American Musicological Society* 31/3 (1978): 467–79.

Music and the French Enlightenment: Reconstruction of a Dialogue. New York, 1992.

Vyveberg, Henry. *Historical Pessimism in the French Enlightenment.* Cambridge, Mass., 1958.

Wade, Ira. *The Structure and Form of the French Enlightenment.* 2 vols. Princeton, 1977.

Wilson, Arthur. *Diderot: The Testing Years.* New York, 1957.

Wolf, Johannes. *Handbuch der Notationskunde.* 2 vols. Leipzig, 1913–19.

INDEX OF SUBJECTS

Académie Royale des Sciences, 8, 11, 12, 137, 159, 160–63, 166, 214–15, 242, 243
affections, *see* passions
architecture, and music, 232–35

Bouffon Quarrel, 209–11, 248

cadence
    broken (*rompue*), 116, *117*, 122, 200, *280*, 288
    evaded, 122, *123*
    interrupted (*interrompue*), 200, 280–81
    irregular (imperfect), 117, *118*, 184, 280
    perfect, 115, *116*
    seventeenth-century theories of, 113–14
Cartesianism, *see* mechanistic philosophy
chords
    added-sixth, *see* subdominant
    augmented-sixth, *53*, 273
    diminished-seventh, *53*, 54 (*see also* genre, enharmonic); with borrowed root, *100*; as composite of dominant and subdominant functions, *203*
    dominant-seventh (*dominante-tonique*), *53*, 54, 98–99, 116, 180, 182, 195
    fundamentals of, 84–87, 90–98; *see also* fundamental bass
    inversional theories of, 25, 52, 67–70, 88–89, 93–95, 97–98
    major (*accord parfait*), 25, 44–45, 94–95, 97; acoustical generation of, 138–41; derived by monochord divisions, 90–95; see also *corps sonore, senario*
    minor: as arithmetic proportion, 96–97, 148; co-generative theory of, 166–68, 271–72, 273; modified resonance theory of, 162–65; as relative to major triad, 198–99, 272, 299; sympathetic resonance theory of, 148–49; explained through "triadic parallelism," 96–97; explained through "numerical generation," 95–96
    ninth and eleventh, *99*, *100*, 123–29; *see also* supposition
    seventh (*dominant*), 11–13, 98–99, 272–75, 300
    seventeenth-century theories of, 44–46, 67–70, 88–89
chromatic, *see* genre
clausula, *see* cadence
color and music, 109, 142–45, 191, 242

consonance
    "coincidence" theory of, 80–84, 244–46
    derivation on the monochord, 72–80
    equated with equilibrium, 107, 115–16, 129
corps sonore, 5, 133, 228–31, 232–33, 235–38, 240–41, 250, 261, 296–98, 299–302
    compared to three primary colors, 145, 191
    experimental establishment of, 141–42
    inharmonic partials, 136, *151*, 154–55
    as metaphysical principle, 232, 235, 241, 290, 291–94, 297–98
    as principle in Rameau's theory, 39, 141–42, 148–49, 155, 167–68, 231–32
    Rameau's discovery of, 133, 138–39
    scientific explanations of, 139–41, 154–59, 244, 270–75
    sensationalist confirmation of, 217–18, 234–35, 241
    seventeenth-century study of, 135–38
    theoretical derivations summarized, 207–08
    "undertones," 148–49
    upper partials, 136, 137, 138, 159, 246, 297

dissonance
    added-sixth, 119–20, 192
    generation of, 98–100, 272–75, 300
    imputed, 129–31
    as mechanistic agent, 107–09, 185–86, 189, 191–93
    seventh as fundamental dissonance, 111–13
    seventeenth-century views of, 63–67
    see also chords, *double emploi*, *and* supposition
dominant-seventh chords, *see* chords, dominant-seventh
double emploi, 184, 193, *194*, 195–99, 278, 280, 282

eleventh chords, *see* chords *and* supposition
Encyclopédie, 6–7, 11–12, 14, 15–16, 210–12, 247–51
enharmonic, *see* genre
Enlightenment
    eclectic character of, 16–19
    problems of defining, 15–16
    Rameau's theory as emblematic of, 15, 18–20
    science in, 15–18
experimental science, 187, 202
    Newton's *Opticks* as model of, 142–46
    Rameau's imitation of, 141–42, 147–49

321

figured bass, *see* thorough bass
fugue, 63
fundamental bass, 5, 24–26, 28–29, 31, 33–35, 51–61, 70, 90, 91–93, 129–32
    as mechanistic model, 105–09, 122–23
    difficulties in systematizing, 243
    interpolations of, 171–72
    origins in thorough bass practice, 51, 61
    rules governing, 120
    seventeenth-century precedents of, 43–46, 67–70, 84–87, 87–89, 113–15
    success in eighteenth century, 6–11, 209–10

genre
    chromatic, 199–200
    chromatic-enharmonic, 205–07
    enharmonic, 200–205
geometric progressions, 138, 178–85, 193, 199–201, 276–79, 295, 300–01; *see also* mode
gravity
    influence of concept in the Enlightenment, 185–89
    tonal attraction explained by, 189–90
guitar, 47–49

harmonia, 26, 29, 106–07
harmonia perfetta, *see* chord, major, *and senario*

imitation, 130, 236–38
inversion, *see* chords, inversional theory of

liaison, 182, 189, 217

materialism, *see* mechanistic philosophy
mechanistic philosophy, 103–08, 191–92
melody, origins of, 248–50
mode, 170–73, 180–81, 193–96, 242–43, 276, 300–01
    minor, 196–99, 277–79
    see also modulation *and* geometric progressions
modulation, 120–21, 169–78, 189, 195–98; *see also règle de l'octave*
monochord, 28, 30
    as allegory of cosmic generation, 71–72, *73*
    arithmetic and harmonic divisions explained, 307–08
    Descartes's use of, 77–80
    Rameau's use of, 90–96
    traditional applications of, 72, 74–76
music theory
    musica pratica, 29–31, 39–41
    musica theorica, 29–31, 41–42, 87, 89, 102
    rhetorical elements of, 302–06

neoplatonism, 71–77, 84–87
ninth chords, *see* chords *and* supposition

occasionalism, 298–302
octave, 75–77, 93–95, 245–47
    as boundary of intervals, 99, 124
    Euler's views on, 245–47
    as generator of intervals, *75*, 76
    theory of octave identity, 85–86, 244, 245–47
    see also chords, inversional theories of
overtones, *see corps sonore*

passions, 236–38
Pythagoreanism, 71–73, 297

Quarrel of the Bouffons (Querelle des Bouffons), *see* Bouffon quarrel

rapport, 207, 232–35, 236–41, 276
règle de l'octave, 48, *49*, 50, 56–57, 170–71, *172*, 179, 195, 198, 277–79, 284

senario, 44, 74–75, 82, 106, 132
sensationalist psychology, 215–18
seventh, *see* chords *and* dissonance
subdominant, 25, 28, 54, 58, 118–19, 138, 171, 179–85, 192, 193–99; *see also double emploi*
supposition, 25, 52, 54, 64–66, 99–100, 123, *124*, 125–29, 192, 273
suspension, *see* supposition
syncopation, 107

temperament, 200–03, 243
thorough bass
    French reception of, 46–47
    eighteenth-century pedagogy of, 50–51
    as origin of the fundamental bass, 51, 61
    seventeenth-century pedagogy of, 44–46
    Rameau's pedagogy of, 51–61
tonic, 180, 185, 288–89
    as gravitational center, 189–90
    occasionalist explanation of, 300–01
    tonique principale, 175
    tonique censée, 175–77, 195
    tonique étrangère, 175–77
transposition, 170, 173

unison, 84–87

vibrating string, 135, 150–59; *see also corps sonore*
vortices (*tourbillons*), 186

INDEX OF PROPER NAMES

Adams, D. J., 216
Adkins, Cecil, 72
Alembert, Jean Le Rond d', 2, 4, 10, 11, 14, 17–18,
    40–42, 134, 162, 163, 166, 168, 184, 198,
    210, 211–12, 213, 214, 236, 251, 254, 303,
    305, 310–12
  deductivist epistemology, 157–58, 257, 264–66,
    268–69
  interpretation of the *corps sonore*, 152–53, 156–59,
    262, 270–76, 304
  rules of composition, 256–57, 282–84
  relation to Rameau, 259–64
  restrictions on the fundamental bass, 280–82
  views on mode, 276–79
  Elémens de musique théorique, 253, 255–57, 252,
    258, 259, 263–64, 266–69, 277
  Encyclopédie articles, 6–7, 12, 14, 154, 157,
    253–55, 262, 274
  Preliminary Discourse to the *Encyclopédie*, 6–7, 12,
    264–66, 272,
  Traité de dynamique, 265
Amiot, Joseph Marie, 295, 296
Ammann, Peter, J., 72
André, Yves M., 238
Anglebert, Jean Henry d', 48
Antoniotto, Giorgio, 129
Aristotle, 103, 136
Arnaud, Abbé François, 287
Arnold, Franck T., 49, 51
Augst, Bertrand, 77

Bacon, Francis, 105, 135, 146
Barbour, J. Murray, 201
Baridon, Michel, 238
Batteux, Charles, 236, 238
Baumeister, Xenia, 239
Bayle, Pierre, 296
Bayne, Alexander, 179
Beccari, Jacopo Bartolemeo, 292
Becker, Carl, 17
Beeckman, Isaac, 80–81, 135, 136, 140
Bemetzrieder, Anton, 213, 292, 302–03
Benedetti, Giovanni Battista, 80, 135
Benjamin, Andrew, E., 35
Berardi, Angelo, 7
Berger, Christian, 231
Bernard, Jonathan, 262
Bernhard, Christian, 63

Bernoulli, Daniel, 134, 150, *151*, 152–55, 158–59
Bernoulli, Johann, 245
Berthier, Guillaume-François, 257, 261, 262
Bertocci, Peter, A., 85
Bethizy, Jean-Laurent de, 177, 257, 282, 283
Blainville, Charles-Henri, 242–43
Blondel, François, 233
Boileau, Nicolas, 34
Boisgelou, François-Paul, 160
Bollioud-Mermet, Louis, 202, 242
Bonnet, Jacques, 296
Boureau, André François, 219
Boureau-Deslandes, André-François, 146
Brisieux, Charles Etienne, 232–33, *234*, 235, 238
Brossard, Sébastien de, 7, 23, 30, 45, 65, 87, 107
Buffon, Georges-Louis Leclerc, 144
Burette, Jean-Pierre, 181
Burke, Edmund, 304
Burmeister, Joachim, 44
Burtt, E. A., 103
Busch, Hermann, 245
Buttstett, Johann Heinrich, 89

Campion, François, 48–49, 57, 196
Campion, Thomas, 69
Cantor, Geoffrey, 148
Carr, J. L., 219
Casaubon, 291
Cassirer, Ernst, 17, 19, 238
Castel, Louis-Bertrand, 10, 43, 52, 138, 197, 212,
    242, 257, 261, 266
  conveyed scientific ideas to Rameau, 110, 133, 178
  critique of Rameau's theory, 191–93
  early support of Rameau, 109–11
  optical theories, 109, 145, 191
Catel, Charles Simon, 302
Caus, Salomon de, 30, 92
Chabanon, Michel-Paul-Guy de, 21, 241, 291
Chailley, Jacques, 25–26
Charpentier, Marc Antoine, 31, 64, *65*
Chaumont, Lambert, 47
Chouillet, Jacques, 239, 301
Chouillet-Roche, Anne-Marie, 145
Cicero, 33, 232
Clairaut, Alexis-Claude, 262
Clarke, Desmond, 35
Clérambault, Louis Nicolas, 115, 196
Cohen, Albert, 45, 46, 65, 137, 159–61

Index of proper names

Cohen, H. F., 80, 81, 134
Cohen, I. Bernard, 38, 146
Condillac, Abbé de, 6, 16, 35–37, 39, 85, 144, 213, 219, 239, 257, 276, 303
Condorcet, Antoine-Nicolas, 266
Cooper, Barry, 69
Corbetta, Francesco, *48*
Corelli, Arcangelo, 59–60, *130*
Cousu, Antoine de, 30, 31, 45, 69
Cramer, Gabriel, 14
Cranston, Maurice, 247
Crocker, Lester, 16, 239
Crousaz, J. P., 238

Dahlhaus, Carl, 26, 48, 89, 105, 106, 122, 131
Dandrieu, Jean-François, 180
Darnton, Robert, 20
Dear, Peter, 84, 85, 86
Delair, Denis, 51, *66*, 112, 119
Demidov, S. S., 152
Descartes, René, 23, 30, 35, 82–84, 90–92, 103–06, 135, 136, 186, 245, 298
    Compendium musicae, 77, *78*, *79*, 80,
    Discours de la méthode, 11–12, 36
Desmoulins, M., 278–79
Diderot, Denis, 16, 17, 144, 210–11, 218, 228, 257, 266, 291–92, 296
    aesthetic views, 239–41, 276
    collaboration with Rameau, 214–15
    Lockean epistemology, 215–17
    views on Rameau's theory, 213, 302–03
    Encyclopédie editing, 212–13; article "Beau," 239–40
    Leçons de clavecin, 213, 302–03
    Les Bijoux indiscrets, 15, 211
    Lettre sur les aveugles, 215–16
    Lettre sur les sourds, 216–17
    Mémoires . . . de mathématiques, 212–13, 214
    Le Neveu de Rameau, 15, 291
Didier, Béatrice, 145, 210, 295, 296
Dinter, Annegret, 219
Doolittle, James, 15, 210, 262, 298
Du Bos, Jean-Baptiste, 240
Ducharger, 278, 292
Duchez, Elisabeth, 34–35, 132, 237, 262, 269
Dugré, Jean-Baptiste, 43
Du Halde, 296
Du Mont, Henry, 46
Durand, Laurent, 215
Durand-Sendrail, Béatrice, 212
Dylsedime, Piero, 153

Engelsman, Steven B., 152
Erhard, Jean, 111
Escal, Françoise, 262
Estève, Pierre, 165, 244
Euler, Leonhard, 134, 149, 151–56, 245–47, 262, 266

Fajon, Robert, 56
Farrar, Lloyd, 138
Federhofer, Hellmut, 132
Ferris, Joan, 3, 99, 299
Fétis, François-Joseph, 3

Fludd, Robert, 72, *73*
Fontenelle, Bernard le Bovier de, 104, 186, 137–38
Formey, Jean-Henri, 301
Fouchy, Jean-Paul Grandjean de, 8
Fourier, Jean Baptiste Joseph, 154
Frere, Alexandre, 170, 173
Fréron, Elie-Catherine, 257, 261, 262

Galilei, Galileo, 7, 80–81, 103, 105, 135
Galilei, Vincenzo, 81, 135
Gamaches, Abbé Etienne-Simon de, 141
Gasparini, Francesco, 171
Gassendi, Pierre, 140
Gaukroger, Stephan, 76
Gay, Peter, 15, 16, 18, 19, 296
Gervais, Laurent, 6
Gessele, Cynthia, 302
Geulinex, Arnold, 298
Gianotti, Pietro, 125–26, *127*, 128, 175, *176*, 285–86, 309–12
Girdlestone, Cuthbert, 1, 21, 34, 56, 69, 139, 193
Goethe, Johann Wolfgang von, 144
Golinski, J. V., 18
Gossett, Philip, 8, 50, 91
Gouk, Penelope, 143
Gould, Stephen Jay, 305
'sGravesande, James, 149
Green, Burdette, 136
Grimm, Baron von, 211, 228, 250, 257
Grimsley, Ronald, 157, 255, 262
Groth, Renate, 30, 31
Gruber, Albion, 84
Guerlac, Henry, 38, 139, 146

Hankins, Thomas, 18, 152, 266
Harnisch, Otto Siegfried, 44
Harré, Rom, 18
Hawkins, John, 8
Hayes, Deborah, 60
Heinichen, Johann, 70, 89, 180
Helmholtz, Hermann, 165, 244, 273
Henry, John, 187
Hiller, Johann, 241
Hine, Ellen McNiven, 36
Hooke, Robert, 135, 139, 142
Hotteterre, Jacques, 69, *70*, 114
Hume, David, 238
Hunt, Frederick, V., 105
Hunt, Thomas W., 248
Hutcheson, Francis, 238
Huygens, Christian, 135

Isherwood, Robert, 45, 259

Jacob, Margaret, 16, 298
Jacobi, Erwin, 160, 162, 166, 262, 286, 292
Jamard, T., 112

Kaufmann, Emil, 233
Keiler, Allan, 131
Keller, Gottfried, 51
Kepler, Johann, 72, 292

Index of proper names

Kiernan, Colm, 18
Kintzler, Catherine, 32
Kircher, Athanasius, 23, 43, 72, 191, 192, 193
Kleinbaum, Abby R., 14
Koestler, Arthur, 292
Koyré, Alexander, 104
Krebs, Harald, 44
Kuhn, Thomas, 3, 35, 38, 306

L'Affilard, Michel, 31
Laborde, Jean Benjamin de, 7, 18, 160
Lagrange, Joseph, 134, 153, 155–56, 266
La Hire, Philippe de, 140
Laisement, de, 112
Lalo, Charles, 32, 235
La Mettrie, Julien Offroy, 16, 215
La Motte, Houdar de, 34, 219
Lang, Paul Henry, 212
Laplace, Pierre, 153
La Pouplinière, Alexandra-Jean-Joseph le Riche de, 188, 219
La Salle, Demoz de, 60
Laudon, Larry, 157
Laugier, Marc-Antoine, 233
La Voye Mignot, 31, 61, 114, 116
Lenoble, Robert, 84
Lescot, Philippe, 264
Lester, Joel, 44, 62, 68, 99, 130, 170
Levens, Charles, 112
Levy, Jim, 295
Lewin, David, 96, 98, 106
Lippius, Johann, 44, 45, 68, 70, 87
Lippman, Edward, 85
Locke, John, 12–13, 16, 215, 218
Loulié, Etienne, 31, *62*
Ludwig, Hellmut, 84, 112
Lully, Jean-Baptiste
  Armide, 120, *121*, 122, 174, 248–49

Mace, Dean, 84
Maillert, Pierre, 30
Mairan, Jean-Jacques Dortous de, 11, 14, 81, 134, 139–41, 144, 148, 162–63, 188, 192, 212, 244, 266
Malebranche, Nicholas, 298–99, 301
Mann, Alfred, 63
Marchand, Louis, 22, 69
Maret, Hugues, 21, 22
Marmontel, Jean-François, 8
Marpurg, Friedrich Wilhelm, 30, 99, 253, 306
Martini, Padre, 292–94
Masson, Charles, 23, 31, 61–64, *65*, 69, 114, 115, 119, 170
Masson, Paul-Marie, 231
Mattheson, Johann, 113, 180
Maupertuis, Pierre-Louis, 301
Maxham, Robert, 137
May, Henry, 19
Mayer, Jean, 212
Mercardier, Jean-Baptiste de Belesta, 292
Mersenne, Marin, 23, 30, 31, 72, 80, 84–87, 88, 92, 93, 100, 103, 112, 133, 135, 136, 137, 245

Meursius, Johannes, 297
Miller, Leta, 11, 150
Mitchell, William, 173
Mizler, Lorenz, 89
Molyneux, William, 219
Montéclair, Michel Pignolet de, 43, 56–58, 60–61, 125, 128, 130, 198, 242
Montesquieu, Charles, 16, 296
Montucla, Jean-Etienne, 294–95
Moreau, Marie-Germaine, 23, 287

Newton, Isaac, 16–17, 37–38, 185–93
  Opticks, 37, 139, 142–46, 187–88
  Principia Mathematica, 7, 186
Nichomachus, 76, 77
Nicolson, Marjorie Hope, 146
Nivers, Guillaume-Gabriel, 31, 65, 114
Noble, William, 136
Nollet, Abbé, 146, *147*
North, Nigel, 68
North, Roger, 69

Oettingen, Arthur von, 165
Oliver, Alfred Richard, 210, 211, 262
Onslow, George, 24
Ouvrard, René, 65, 235

Palisca, Claude, 80, 82, 134, 136
Pappas, John, 257
Pardies, Ignace-Gaston, 107–08, 110
Parran, Antoine, 45, 61
Patrides, C. A., 71
Paul, Charles, 35, 297–98
Perol, Lucette, 212
Perrault, Claude, 233–33
Pigot, Thomas, 136
Pirro, André, 77, 83
Pischner, Hans, 108
Plato, 71; see also neoplatonism
Pluche, Abbé, 143, 146
Polinière, Pierre, 146
Pompadour, Madame, 209
Poncelet, Polycarpe, 144
Porter, Roy, 15
Priézac, Salomon de, 301

Rameau, Claude, 243
Rameau, Jean-Philippe
  aesthetic views, 236–41
  anti-Pythagorean views, 297
  Cartesian sympathies, 11–13, 32–33, 35, 109–10, 267
  contact with scientists, 10–11, 134, 267, 292–94; see also d'Alembert, Bernoulli, Castel, Euler, Mairan
  difficulties in assessing, 1–3, 302–04
  early training in music, 21–23
  eclecticism of his theories, 3–4, 13, 303–04
  empiricist views, 24–26, 33–35, 141–42, 215–18, 232, 246, 287–90, 303
  battle with the Encyclopedists, 209–10, 147–51
  legacy, 305–06
  mechanistic views, 105–09, 131–32, 189–90

on method, 39–42, 160–61, 217–18
monochord technique, 90–95, 102
Newtonian influences, 7–11, 35–37, 39–41, 141–42, 145, 187–93
occasionalist views, 298–302
on the origins of music, 181–82, 218, 294–98
on the priority of harmony, 237–38, 249–50
pedagogy of composition, 24–26, 284–90
pedagogy of the thorough bass, 51–61
philosophes' admiration of, 6–9, 209–12, 247–48, 302–03,
quarrel with d'Alembert, 251, 259–64
sensationalist conversion, 215–18, 219, 228, 231
see also *corps sonore*, fundamental bass, *and* chords
"L'Art de la basse fondamentale," 41, 51, 125–28, 175, 252, 285–86, 287, 290, 309–12
"Carte générale de la basse fondamentale," 52, *53*
"Clermont notes," 23–26, 29, 39, 118
Code de musique pratique, 41, 51, 52, 60–61, 117, 120, 126, 129, 182, 184, 199, 200, 216, 237, 252, 263, 271, 280, 281, 286–88, *289*, 290, *293*, 312
"Conference," 52–53, 56–58
Démonstration du principe de l'harmonie, 11, 12, 22, 41, 159–62, 164–67, 180, 195, *196*, 197–99, *204*, *205*, 207, 214–15, 218, 235, 242, 243, 248, 252, 255, 256, 260, 271, 276–77, 285, 301, 310, 312
Dissertation sur les différentes métodes d'accompagnement, 41, 51, 58, *59*, 60–61, 105, 162, 284, 286–87
"L'Enharmonique," 203, *204-05*
Erreurs sur la musique dans l'Encyclopédie, 231, 249–51
Extrait d'une réponse . . . à M. Euler, 245–46
Génération harmonique, 11, 23, 41, 117, 119, 131, 141–42, 145, 147–49, 155, 160, 164, 167, 173, 175, 178,179, 180, *181*, *182*, *183*, 185, 188, 196, *197*, *198*, *199*, *200*, 202–03, 207, 235, 237, 242, 244, 248, 252, 256–57, 280, 283, 285, 304, 309–10
Hippolyte et Aricie, 21, 56, 205, *206*
"Lettre à M. D'Alembert," 262–63, 273
"Mémoire," 160–62, 163–64, 166, 203, 214–15, 217–18, 240, 253, 260, 266
Nouveau système, 10, 51, 120, *130*, 138, 145, 150, 174, 178, 181, 182, 184, 201, 248, 250, 256
Nouvelles réflexions sur le principe sonore, 199, 231–32, 235, 263, 291, 294–95, 300
Nouvelles réflexions . . . sur sa démonstration, 33, 168, 231–32, 241–44, 245, 261, 312
Observations sur notre instinct pour la musique, 120, 200, 237, 240, 249
"Origine des sciences," 294–95
Pygmalion, 218–19, *220-27*, 228, *229-30*, 231, 238
Réponse de M. Rameau à MM. les éditeurs, 261
Traité de l'harmonie, 5, 8, 10, 11, 12, 21, 23, 26, 27, 28–29, 32, 41, 54, *55*, 56, 63, 72, 76, 91, *92*, 93–96, *97*, 98, *99*, *100*, *101*, 102, 105–07, *108*, 109, 112–20, 123–24, 129, 131–33, 138, 170, *172*, 173, *174*, 175, 180, 183, 185, 190, 199, 201, 217, 235, 247, 276, 280, 282, 284, 286, 299, 304
"Vérités interressantes," 291, 297–302
Ravetz, Jerome R., 153
Raynal, Guillaume-Thomas-François, 214
Richbourg, Louisette, 211
Riemann, Hugo, 3, 44, 98
Rivera, Benito, V., 44
Robrieux, Jean-Jacques, 210
Rousseau, Jean-Jacques, 2, 14, 22, 42, 60, 144, 145, 164, 175, 210, 219, 261–62, 292, 296, 310
articles for the *Encyclopédie*, 247–48, 253–55, 258, 260
quarrel with Rameau, 248–51, 259–60
views on melody, 236–37, 248–51
Dictionnaire de musique, 248
Lettre sur la musique française, 211–12, 236–37, 248, 259
Roussier, Pierre-Joseph, 282, 295, 306
Rudio, Ferdinand, 245

Sabra, A. I., 139
Sadler, Graham, 188
Saint-Amand, 239
Saint-Lambert, Michel de, 23, 50–51, 52
Salinas, Francisco, 30, 86
Sauveur, Joseph, 137–38, 150
Sawkins, Lionel, 291
Schenker, Heinrich, 44, 132, 173, 177, 197, 305
Schier, Donald S., 109, 145, 191
Schmalzriedt, Siegfried, 113
Schneider, Herbert, 30, 31, 45, 61, 63, 64, 67, 69, 297, 299, 301–02
Seidel, Wilhelm, 30, 31, 64, 66, 180
Semmens, Richard, 62
Serre, Jean-Adam, 167, 274, 292
Shaftesbury, Anthony Ashley Cooper, 238
Shakespeare, 228
Shea, William, R., 35
Shirlaw, Matthew, 2, 51, 96, 122, 124, 132, 165, 166, 184, 197, 299
Simpson, Christopher, 69
Sovot, Ballot de, 219
Spiess, Meinrad, 89
Strong, E. W., 38
Suaudeau, René, 24–26, 39, 309

Tartini, Giuseppe, 275
Taylor, Brook, 135, 137, 150, 153
Terrasson, Abbé Jean, 5
Tiersot, Julien, 247
Topper, David, 143
Tournadre, Géraud, 35
Trouflaut, Gilbert, 43
Truesdell, Clifford, 18, 153, 134, 157, 163

Vartanian, Aram, 17, 215
Verba, Cynthia, 120, 130, 173, 177, 210, 248, 262
Vico, Giambattista, 304
Villiers, Christophe de, 136
Vitruvius, 232–33

Index of proper names

Vivian, Percival, 69
Vogel, Martin, 112
Voltaire, 16, *144*, 187, 188, 193, 268, 296
Vyveberg, Henry, 16

Waard, Cornelis de, 82
Wade, Ira, 18–19, 146
Wallis, John, 136, 137
Walters, R. L., 187
Werckmeister, Andreas, 68, 70, 87, *88*, *89*, 95,

Westfall, Richard S., 104
Wilson, Arthur, 213
Wokler, Robert, 237
Wolff, Christian, 301–02

Zarlino, Gioseffo, 10, 23, 26, 30, 31, 44, 67–71, 74, *75*, 76–78, 90, 92, 106, 111, 165, 180, 191, 295; see also *senario*
Zaslaw, Neal, 21–22
Zuckerkandl, Victor, 196